STOP!

This is the back of the book.
You wouldn't want to spoil a great ending!

This book is printed "manga-style," in the authentic Japanese right-to-left format. Since none of the artwork has been flipped or altered, readers get to experience the story just as the creator intended. You've been asking for it, so TOKYOPOP® delivered: authentic, hot-off-the-press, and far more fun!

DIRECTIONS

If this is your first time reading manga-style, here's a quick guide to help you understand how it works.

It's easy... just start in the top right panel and follow the numbers. Have fun, and look for more 100% authentic manga from TOKYOPOP®!

ALSO AVAILABLE FROM ◎TOKYOPOP®

For more information visit www.TOKYOPOP.com

12.20.03T

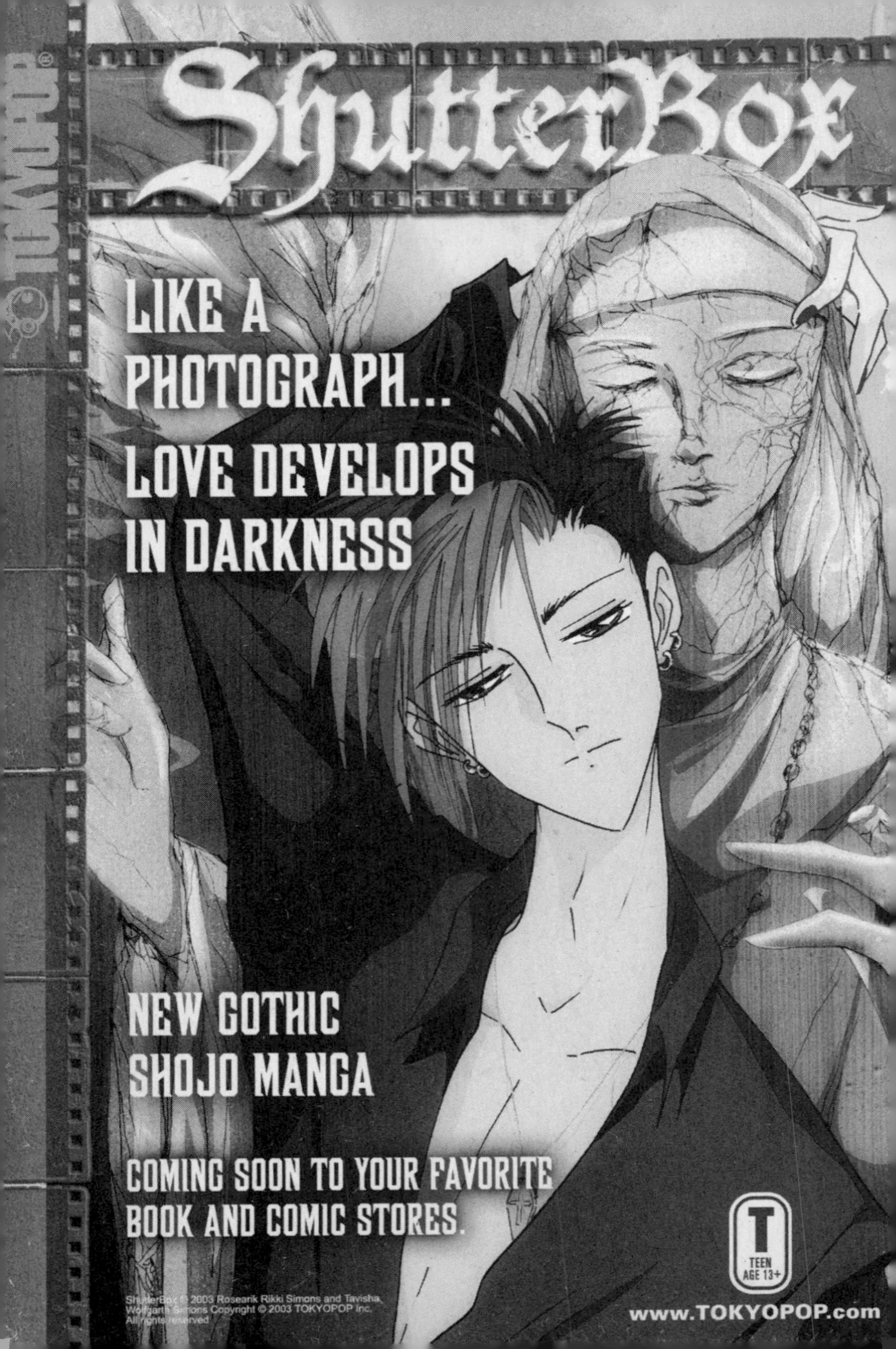
TOKYOPOP®
ShutterBox
LIKE A PHOTOGRAPH...
LOVE DEVELOPS IN DARKNESS
NEW GOTHIC SHOJO MANGA
COMING SOON TO YOUR FAVORITE BOOK AND COMIC STORES.
T TEEN AGE 13+
ShutterBox © 2003 Rosearik Rikki Simons and Tavisha Wolfgarth Simons Copyright © 2003 TOKYOPOP Inc. All rights reserved
www.TOKYOPOP.com

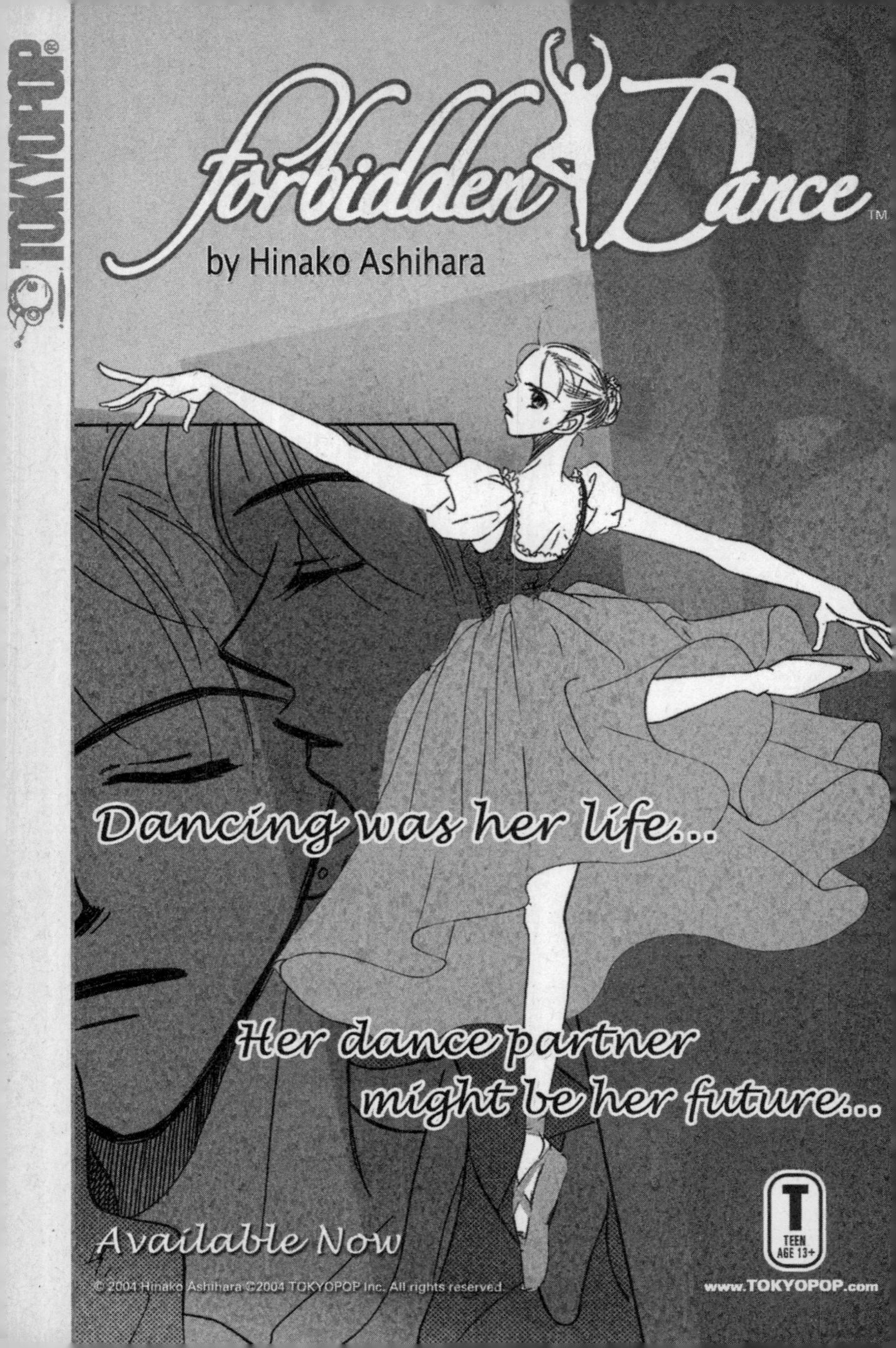
TOKYOPOP®
Forbidden Dance™
by Hinako Ashihara
Dancing was her life...
Her dance partner
might be her future...
Available Now
T
TEEN
AGE 13+
© 2004 Hinako Ashihara ©2004 TOKYOPOP Inc. All rights reserved.
www.TOKYOPOP.com

MARS

Volume 1
By Fuyumi Soryo

LOS ANGELES • TOKYO • LONDON

Translator - Shirley Kubo
Retouch Artist - Roselyn Santos
Graphic Designer - Thea Willis
Production Specialist - Dolly Chan
Editors - Stephanie Donnelly and Robert Coyner
Associate Editors - Trisha Kunimot, Eric Althoff and Paul Morrissey
Reprint Editor - Mark Paniccia

Senior Editor - Jake Forbes
Managing Editor - Jill Freshney
Production Coordinator - Antonio DePietro
Production Manager - Jennifer Miller
Art Director - Matt Alford
Editorial Director - Jeremy Ross
VP of Production - Ron Klamert
President & C.O.O. - John Parker
Publisher & C.E.O. - Stuart Levy

Email: editor@TOKYOPOP.com
Come visit us online at www.TOKYOPOP.com

A  Manga

TOKYOPOP Inc.
5900 Wilshire Blvd. Suite 2000
Los Angeles, CA 90036

ISBN: 1-931514-58-5

First TOKYOPOP® printing: March 2002

18 17 16 15 14 13 12 11 10 9

Printed in the USA

MARS

1

THIS IS THE FIRST PORTRAIT I DREW.
THE MODEL WAS A 17-YEAR-OLD BOY.
I TITLED IT "MARS."

MARS SIGNIFIES TWO THINGS-
ONE IS THE PLANET,
THE OTHER IS A SOLDIER-
THE GOD OF WAR.

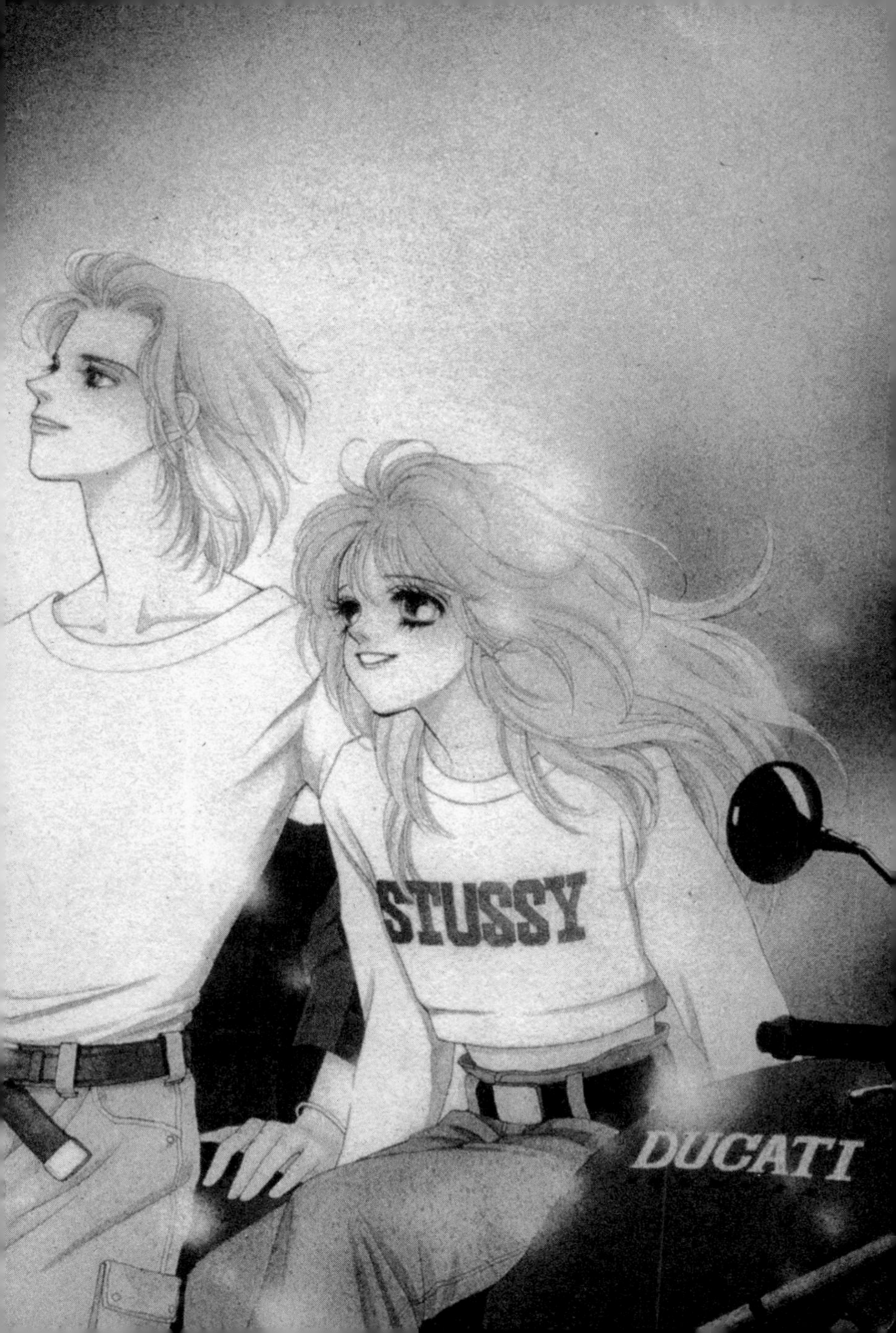
STUSSY
DUCATI

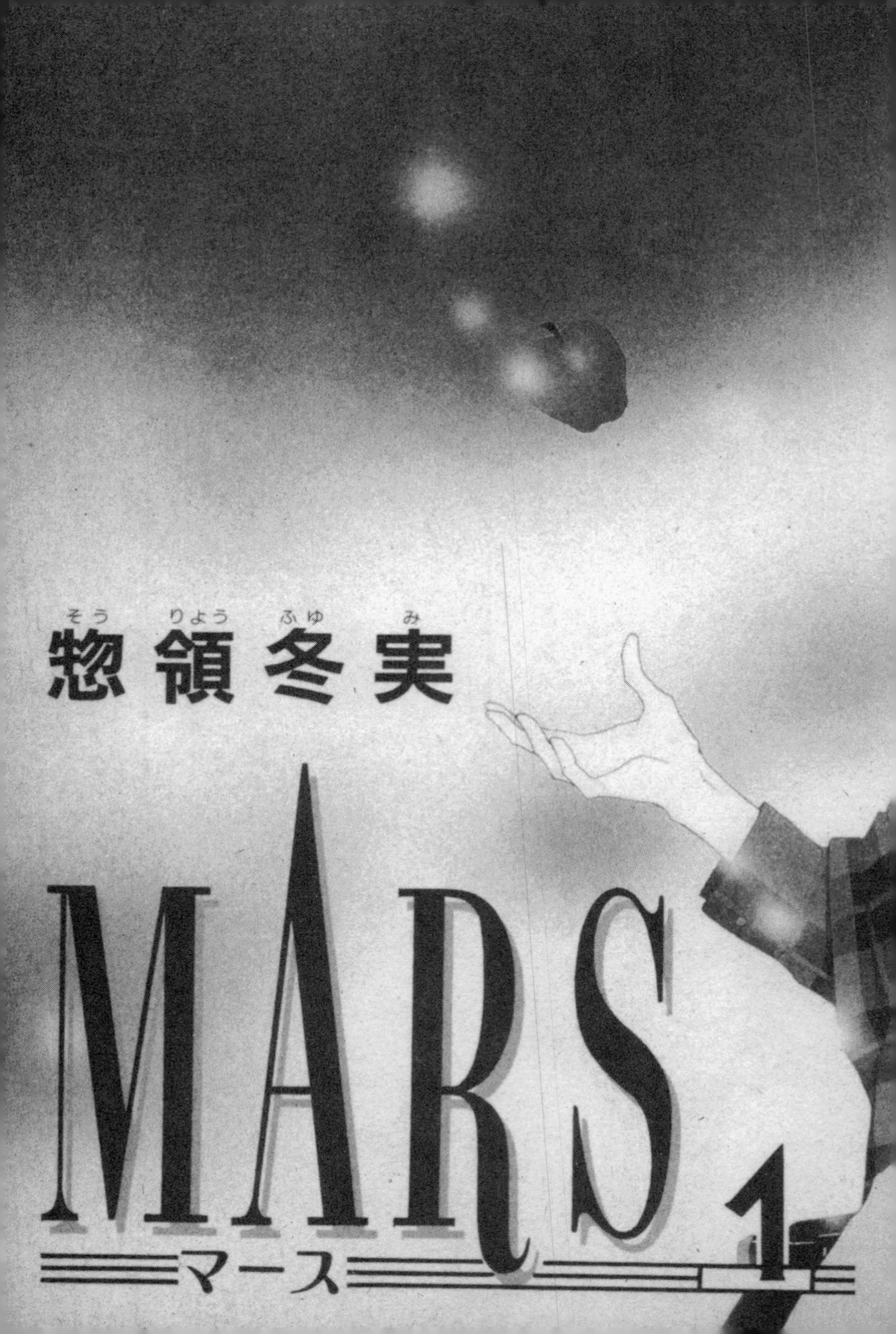

惣領冬実
そうりょうふゆみ
MARS
マース
1

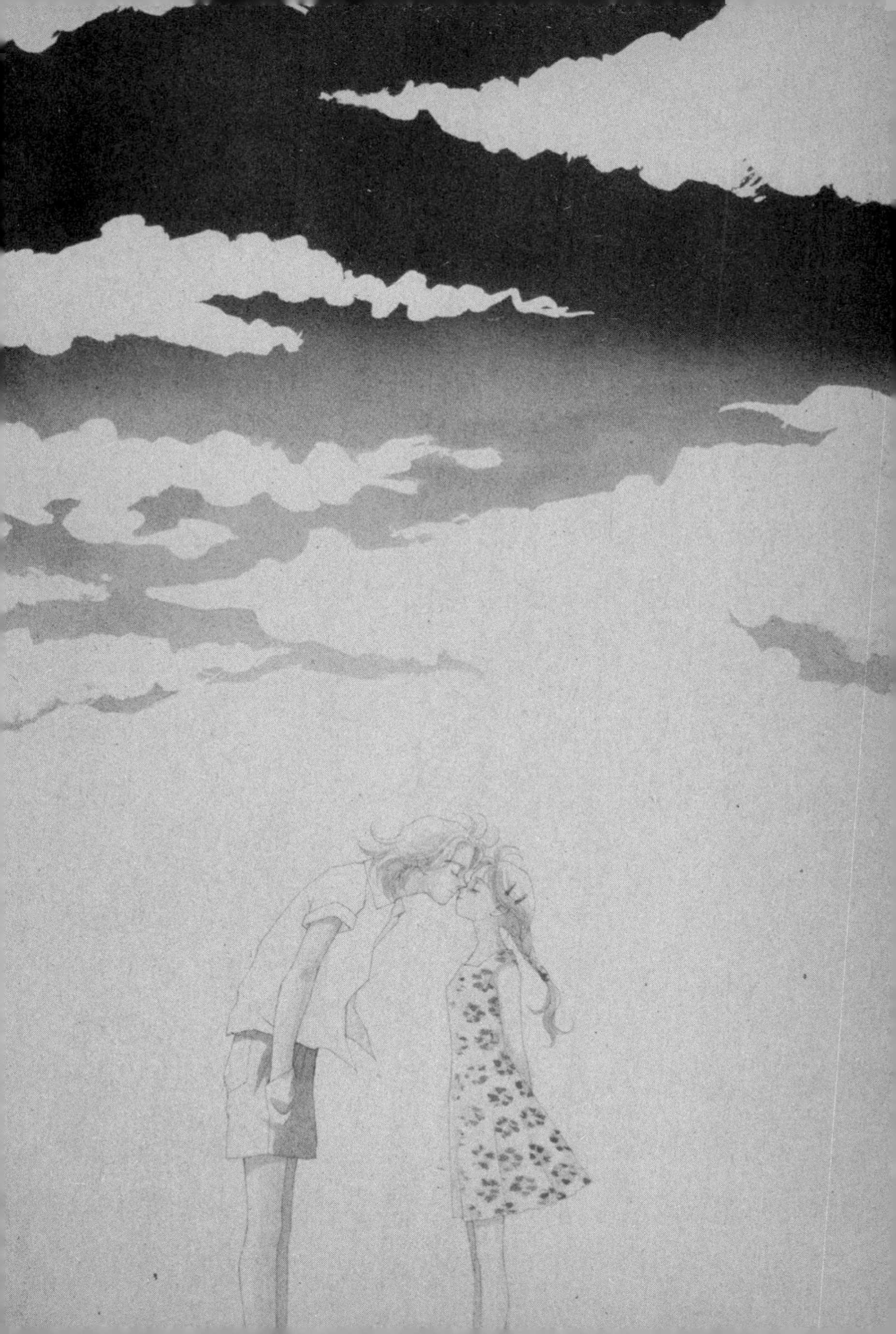

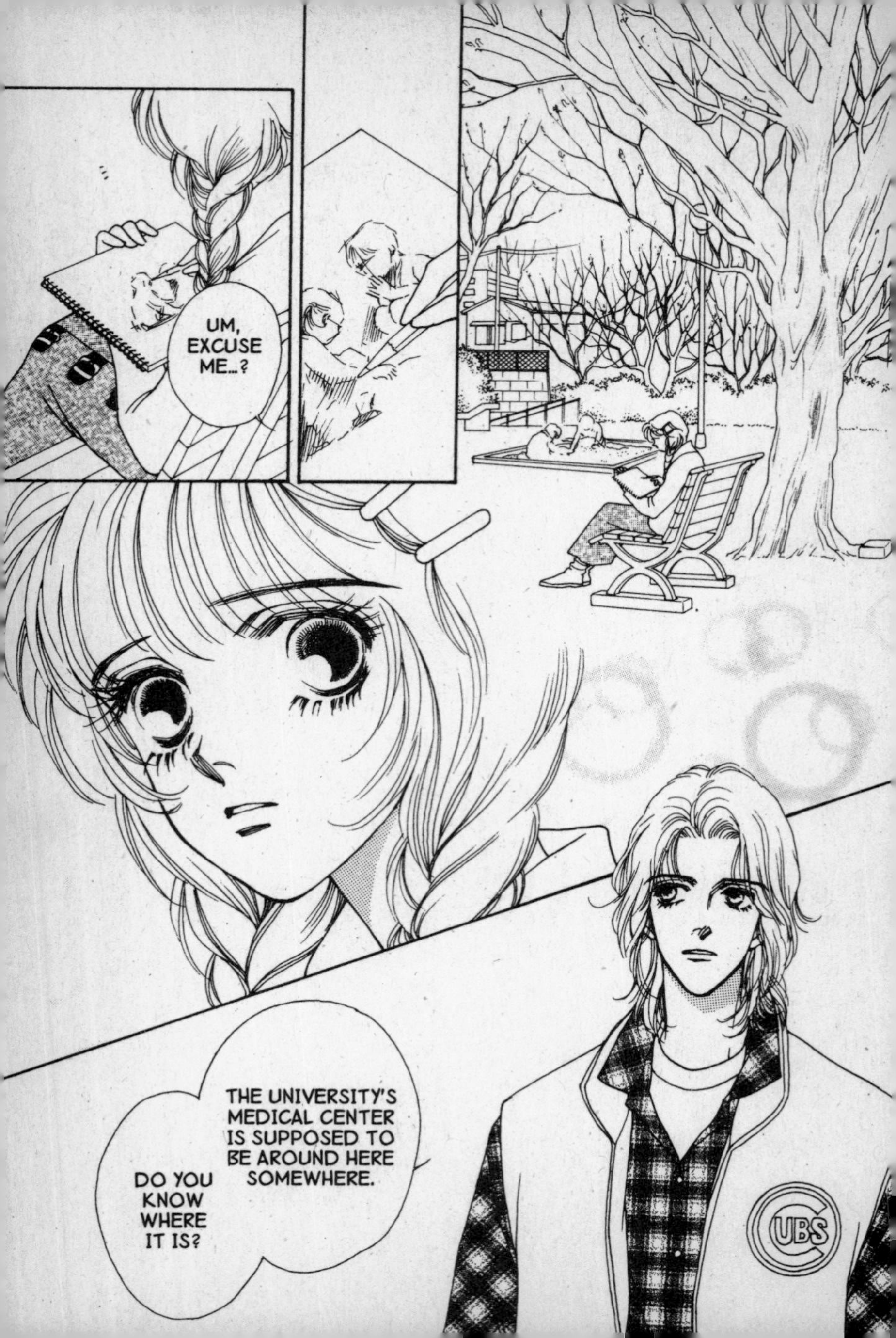
UM, EXCUSE ME...?
THE UNIVERSITY'S MEDICAL CENTER IS SUPPOSED TO BE AROUND HERE SOMEWHERE.
DO YOU KNOW WHERE IT IS?
CUBS

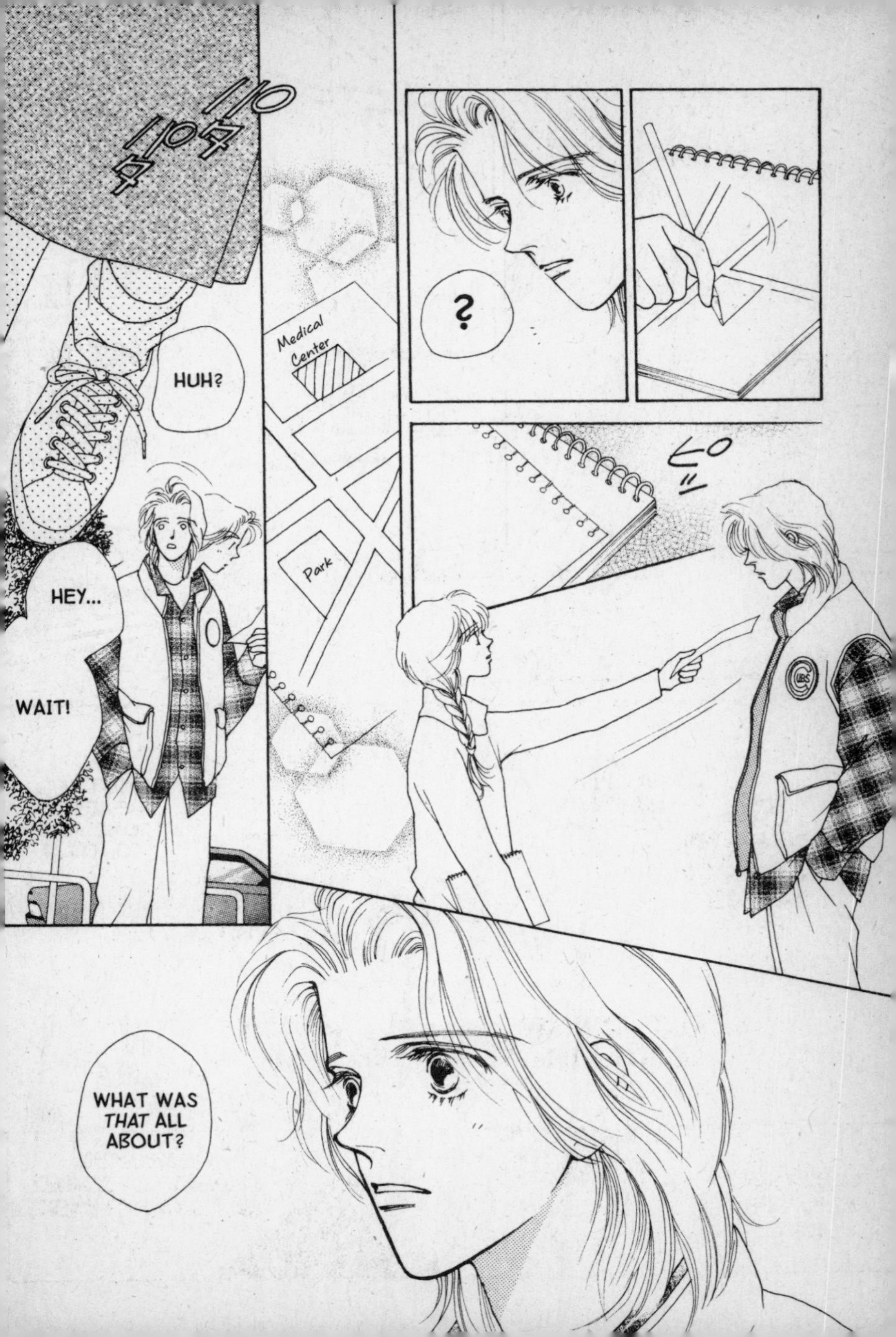
?
Medical Center
Park
HUH?
HEY...
WAIT!
WHAT WAS *THAT* ALL ABOUT?

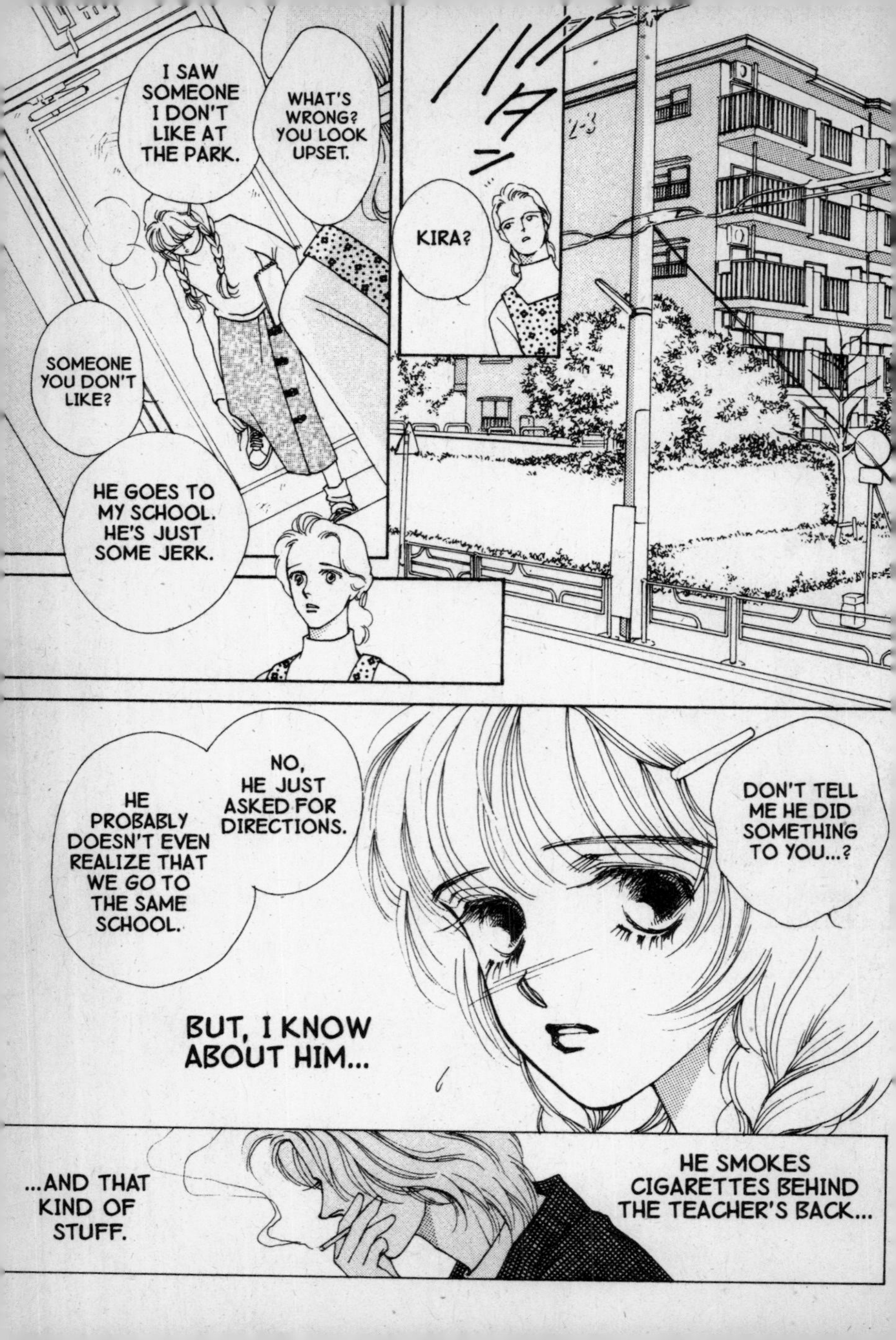
バタン
KIRA?
WHAT'S WRONG? YOU LOOK UPSET.
I SAW SOMEONE I DON'T LIKE AT THE PARK.
SOMEONE YOU DON'T LIKE?
HE GOES TO MY SCHOOL. HE'S JUST SOME JERK.
DON'T TELL ME HE DID SOMETHING TO YOU...?
NO, HE JUST ASKED FOR DIRECTIONS.
HE PROBABLY DOESN'T EVEN REALIZE THAT WE GO TO THE SAME SCHOOL.
BUT, I KNOW ABOUT HIM...
HE SMOKES CIGARETTES BEHIND THE TEACHER'S BACK...
...AND THAT KIND OF STUFF.

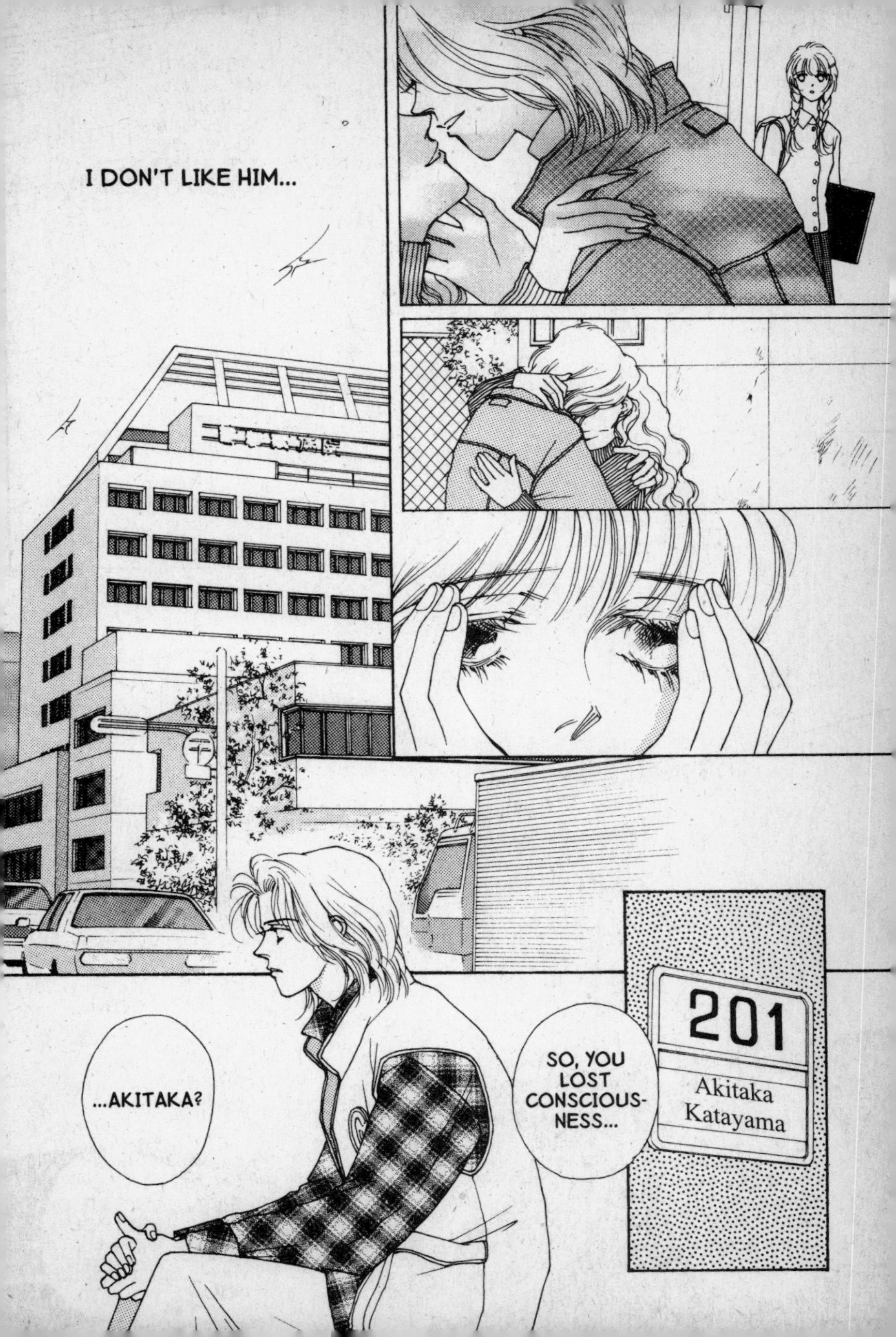
I DON'T LIKE HIM...
201
Akitaka Katayama
SO, YOU LOST CONSCIOUS-NESS...
...AKITAKA?

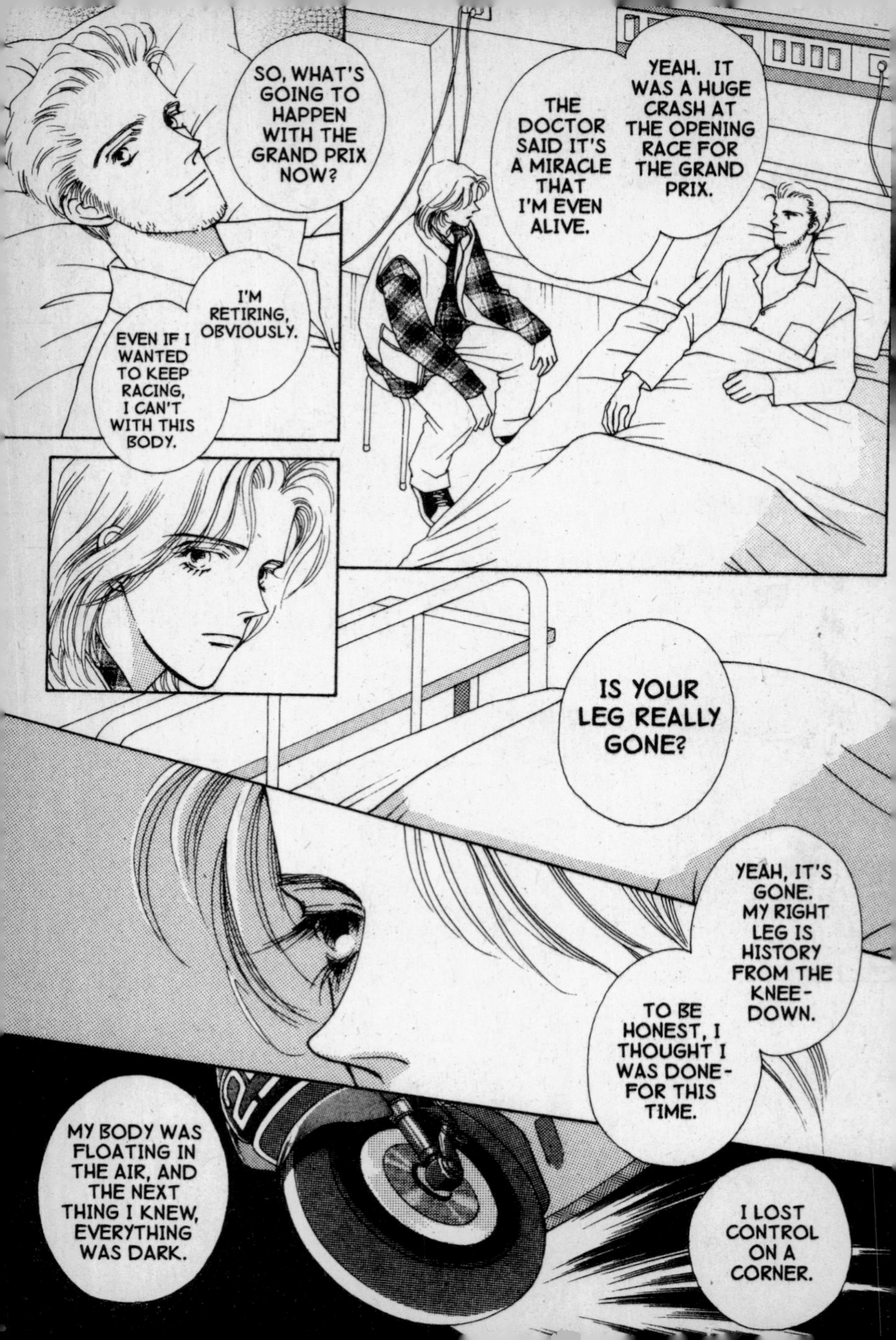
YEAH. IT WAS A HUGE CRASH AT THE OPENING RACE FOR THE GRAND PRIX.
THE DOCTOR SAID IT'S A MIRACLE THAT I'M EVEN ALIVE.
SO, WHAT'S GOING TO HAPPEN WITH THE GRAND PRIX NOW?
I'M RETIRING, OBVIOUSLY.
EVEN IF I WANTED TO KEEP RACING, I CAN'T WITH THIS BODY.
IS YOUR LEG REALLY GONE?
YEAH, IT'S GONE. MY RIGHT LEG IS HISTORY FROM THE KNEE-DOWN.
TO BE HONEST, I THOUGHT I WAS DONE-FOR THIS TIME.
I LOST CONTROL ON A CORNER.
MY BODY WAS FLOATING IN THE AIR, AND THE NEXT THING I KNEW, EVERYTHING WAS DARK.

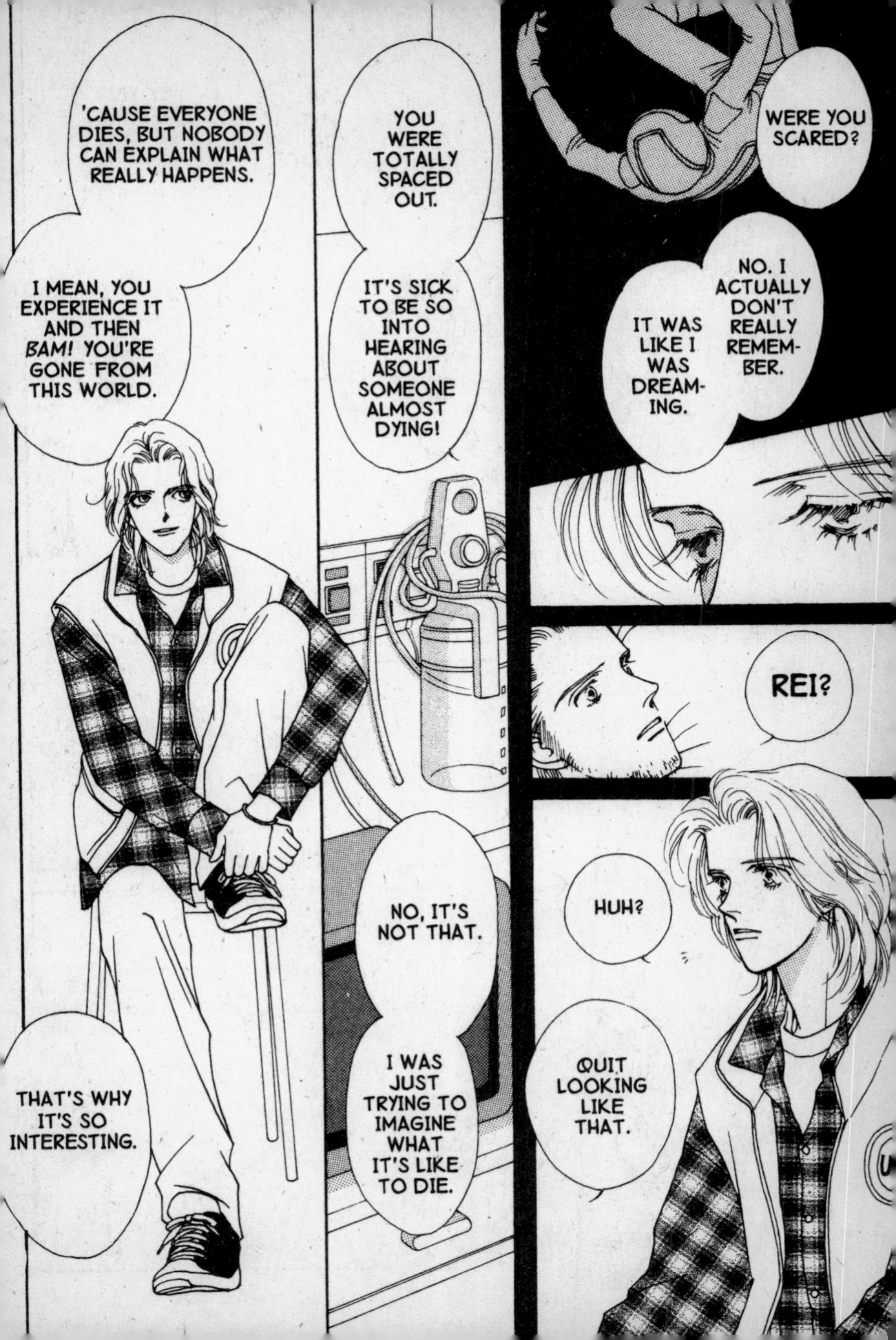
WERE YOU SCARED?
NO. I ACTUALLY DON'T REALLY REMEM-BER.
IT WAS LIKE I WAS DREAM-ING.
REI?
HUH?
QUIT LOOKING LIKE THAT.
YOU WERE TOTALLY SPACED OUT.
IT'S SICK TO BE SO INTO HEARING ABOUT SOMEONE ALMOST DYING!
NO, IT'S NOT THAT.
I WAS JUST TRYING TO IMAGINE WHAT IT'S LIKE TO DIE.
'CAUSE EVERYONE DIES, BUT NOBODY CAN EXPLAIN WHAT REALLY HAPPENS.
I MEAN, YOU EXPERIENCE IT AND THEN *BAM!* YOU'RE GONE FROM THIS WORLD.
THAT'S WHY IT'S SO INTERESTING.

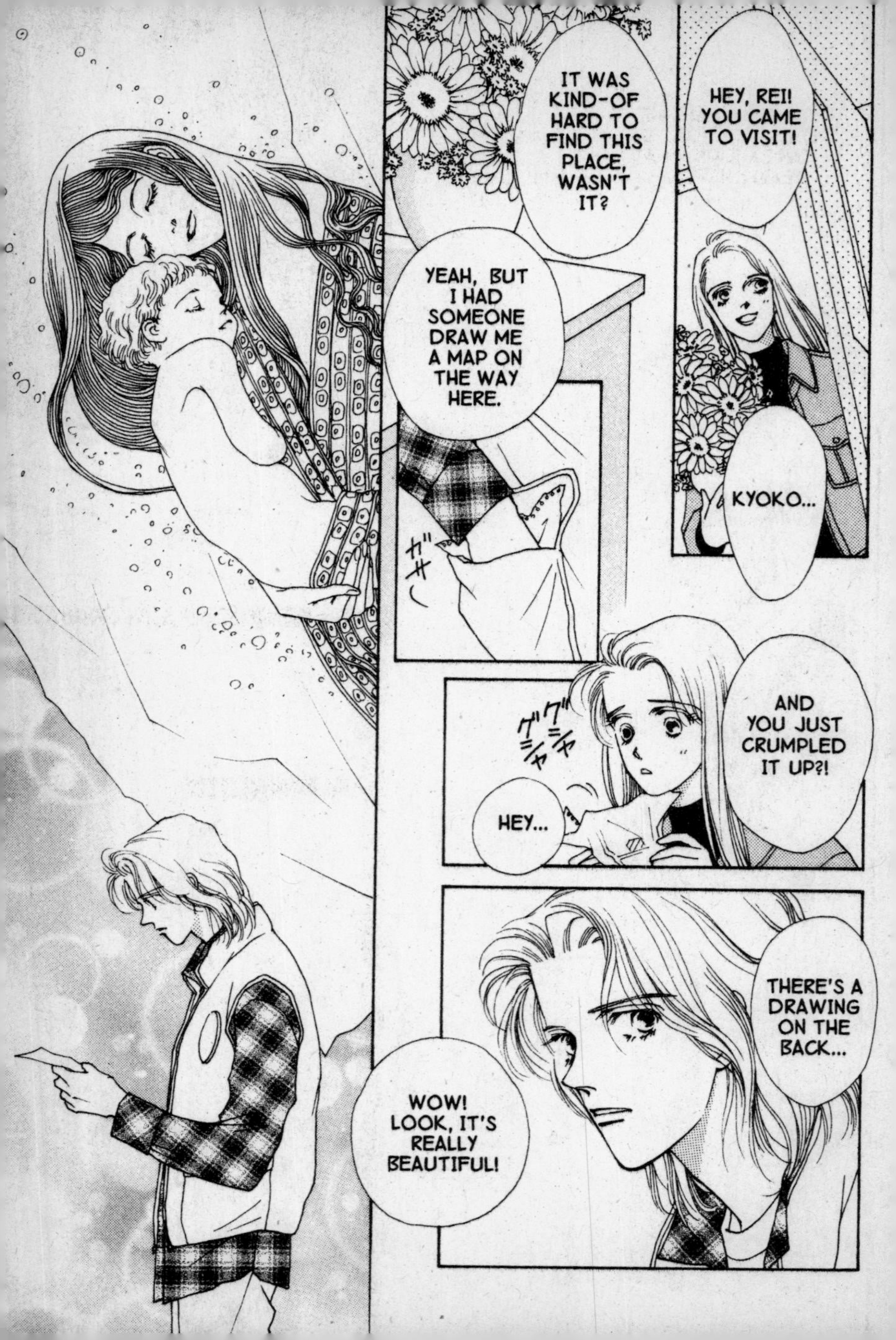
HEY, REI! YOU CAME TO VISIT!
KYOKO...
IT WAS KIND-OF HARD TO FIND THIS PLACE, WASN'T IT?
YEAH, BUT I HAD SOMEONE DRAW ME A MAP ON THE WAY HERE.
AND YOU JUST CRUMPLED IT UP?!
グシャグシャ
HEY...
THERE'S A DRAWING ON THE BACK...
WOW! LOOK, IT'S REALLY BEAUTIFUL!

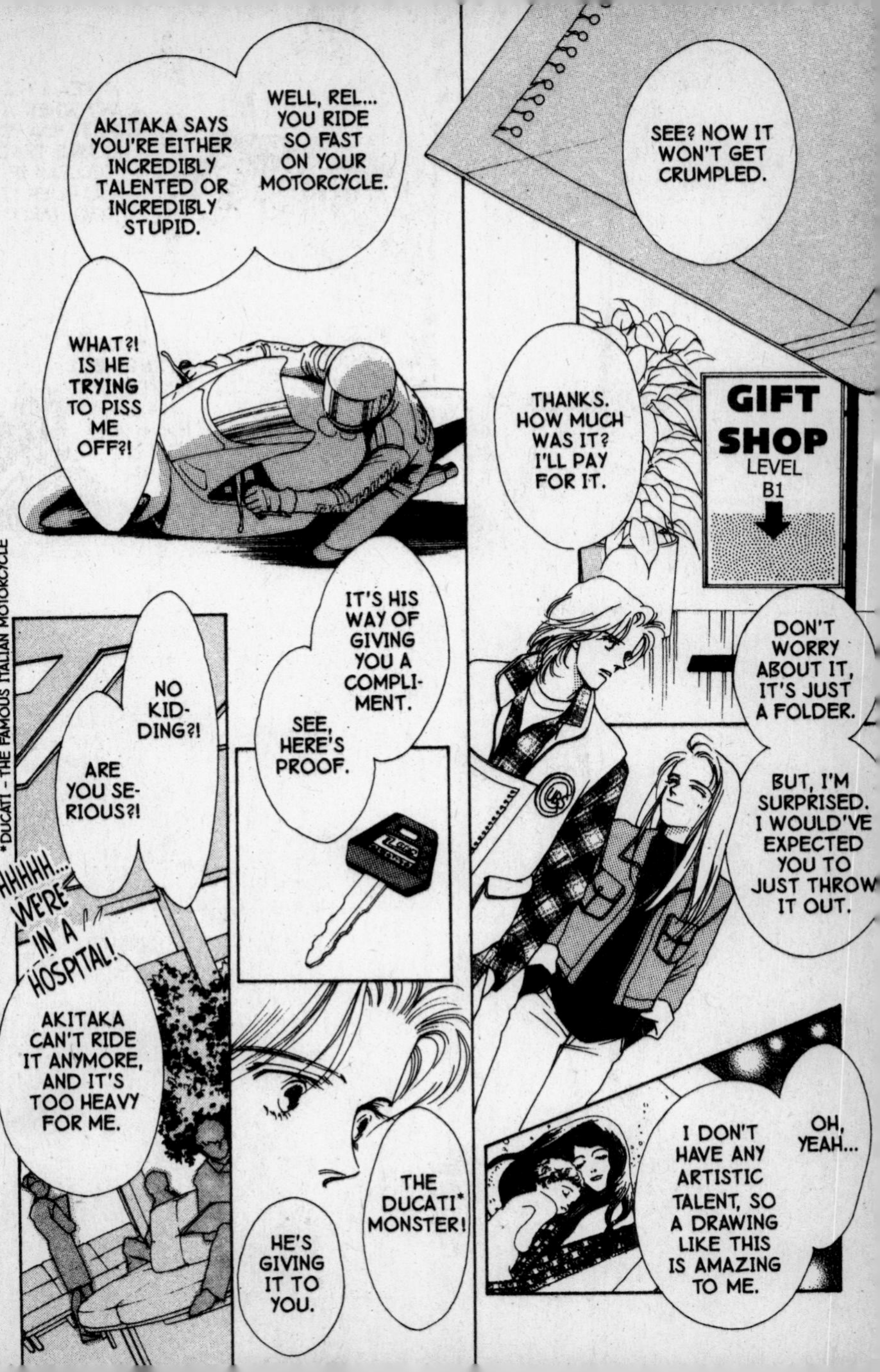
SEE? NOW IT WON'T GET CRUMPLED.
THANKS. HOW MUCH WAS IT? I'LL PAY FOR IT.
GIFT SHOP LEVEL B1
DON'T WORRY ABOUT IT, IT'S JUST A FOLDER.
BUT, I'M SURPRISED. I WOULD'VE EXPECTED YOU TO JUST THROW IT OUT.
OH, YEAH...
I DON'T HAVE ANY ARTISTIC TALENT, SO A DRAWING LIKE THIS IS AMAZING TO ME.
WELL, REL... YOU RIDE SO FAST ON YOUR MOTORCYCLE.
AKITAKA SAYS YOU'RE EITHER INCREDIBLY TALENTED OR INCREDIBLY STUPID.
WHAT?! IS HE TRYING TO PISS ME OFF?!
IT'S HIS WAY OF GIVING YOU A COMPLIMENT.
SEE, HERE'S PROOF.
THE DUCATI* MONSTER!
HE'S GIVING IT TO YOU.
NO KIDDING?!
ARE YOU SERIOUS?!
SHHHHH... WE'RE IN A HOSPITAL!
AKITAKA CAN'T RIDE IT ANYMORE, AND IT'S TOO HEAVY FOR ME.

*DUCATI - THE FAMOUS ITALIAN MOTORCYCLE

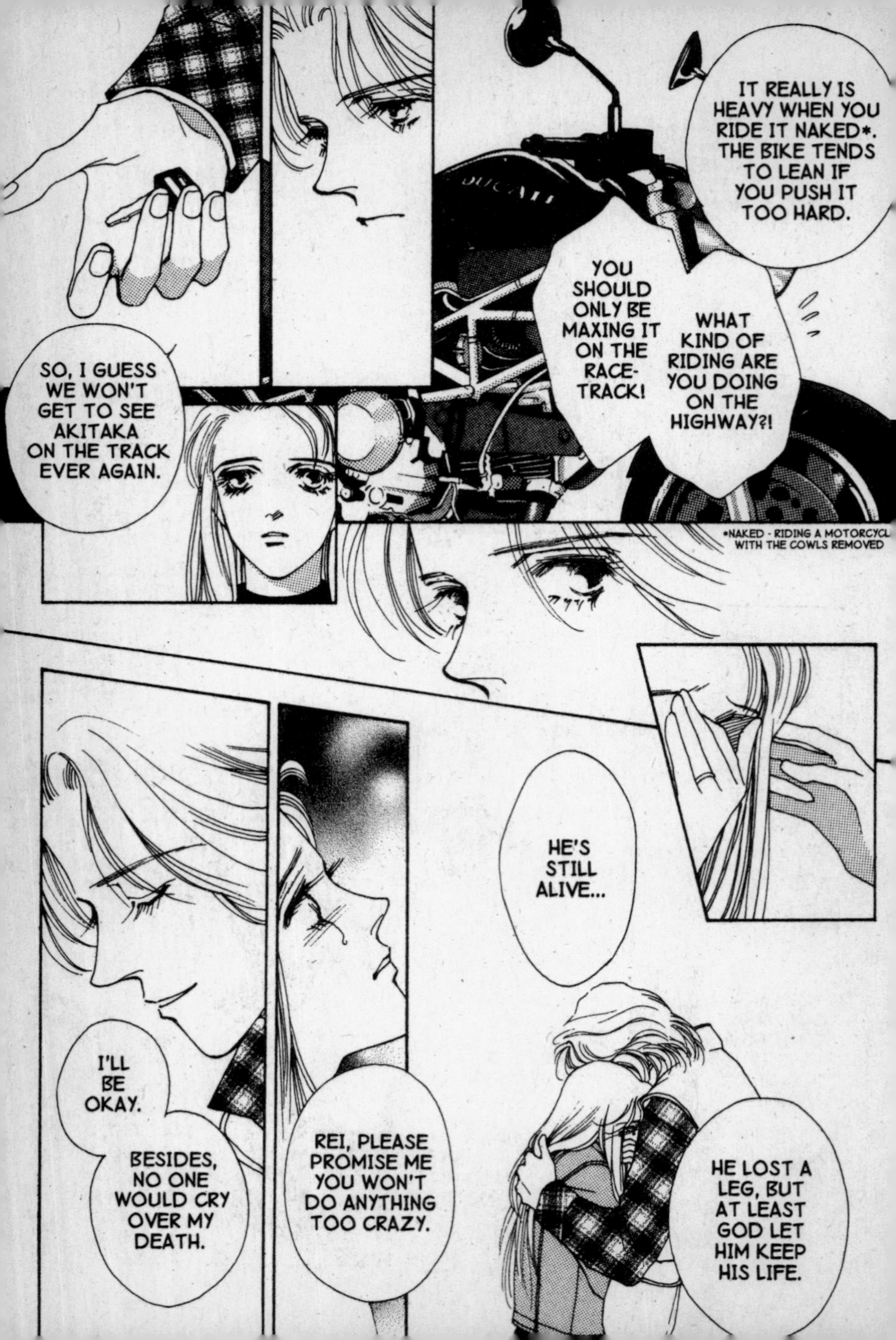
IT REALLY IS HEAVY WHEN YOU RIDE IT NAKED*. THE BIKE TENDS TO LEAN IF YOU PUSH IT TOO HARD.
WHAT KIND OF RIDING ARE YOU DOING ON THE HIGHWAY?!
YOU SHOULD ONLY BE MAXING IT ON THE RACE-TRACK!
SO, I GUESS WE WON'T GET TO SEE AKITAKA ON THE TRACK EVER AGAIN.
HE'S STILL ALIVE...
HE LOST A LEG, BUT AT LEAST GOD LET HIM KEEP HIS LIFE.
REI, PLEASE PROMISE ME YOU WON'T DO ANYTHING TOO CRAZY.
I'LL BE OKAY.
BESIDES, NO ONE WOULD CRY OVER MY DEATH.

*NAKED - RIDING A MOTORCYCL WITH THE COWLS REMOVED

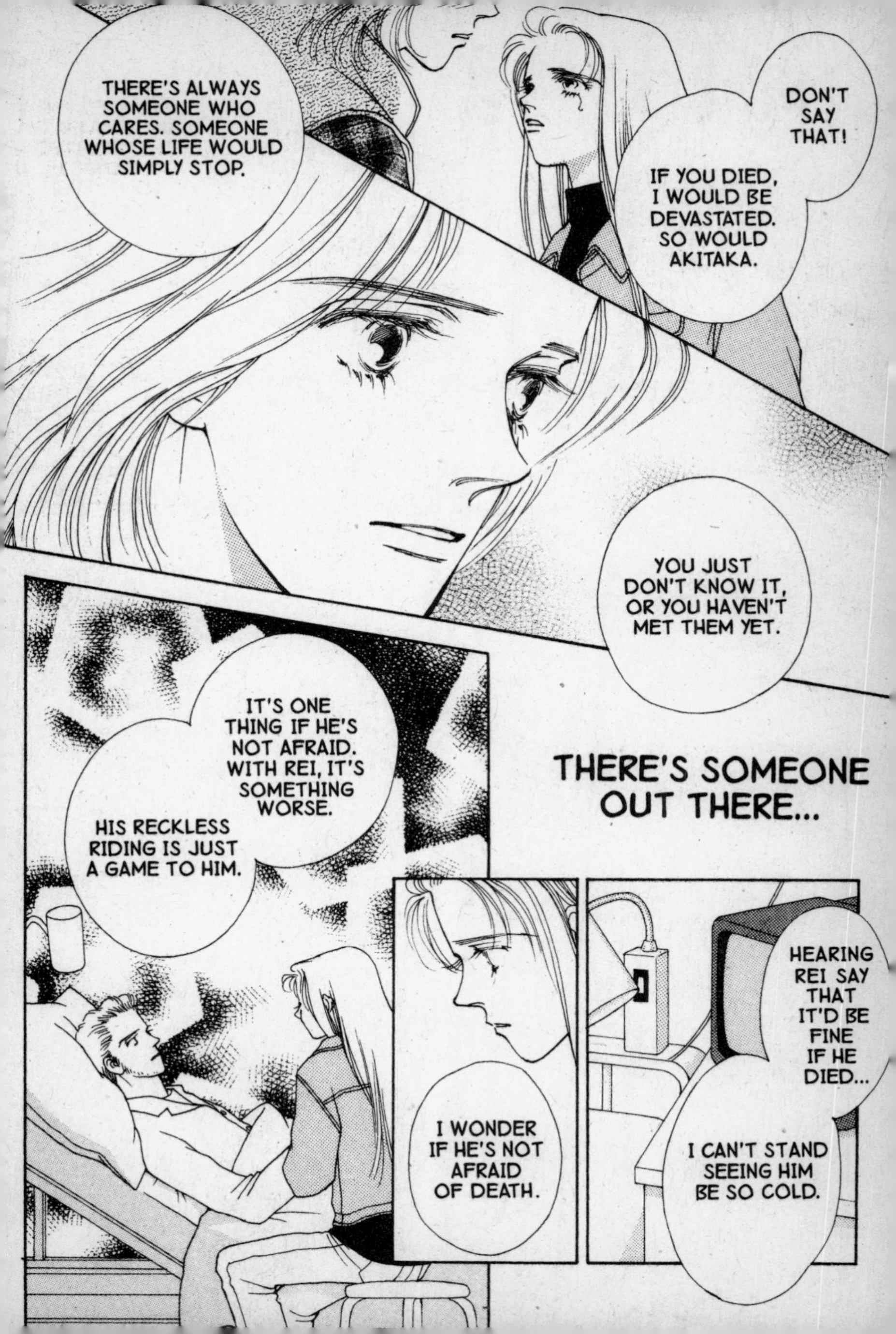
DON'T SAY THAT!
IF YOU DIED, I WOULD BE DEVASTATED. SO WOULD AKITAKA.
THERE'S ALWAYS SOMEONE WHO CARES. SOMEONE WHOSE LIFE WOULD SIMPLY STOP.
YOU JUST DON'T KNOW IT, OR YOU HAVEN'T MET THEM YET.
THERE'S SOMEONE OUT THERE...
HEARING REI SAY THAT IT'D BE FINE IF HE DIED...
I CAN'T STAND SEEING HIM BE SO COLD.
I WONDER IF HE'S NOT AFRAID OF DEATH.
IT'S ONE THING IF HE'S NOT AFRAID. WITH REI, IT'S SOMETHING WORSE.
HIS RECKLESS RIDING IS JUST A GAME TO HIM.

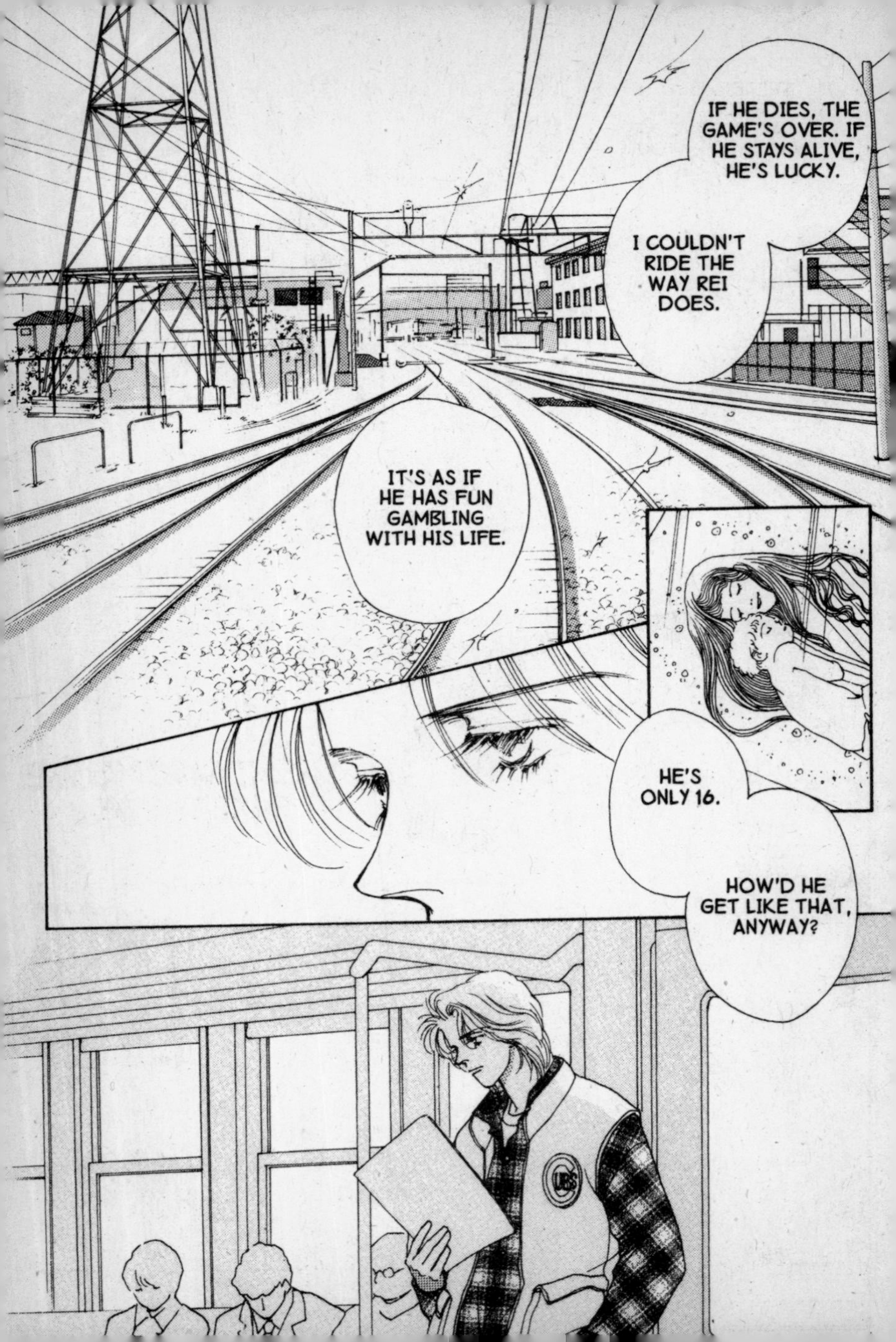
IF HE DIES, THE GAME'S OVER. IF HE STAYS ALIVE, HE'S LUCKY.
I COULDN'T RIDE THE WAY REI DOES.
IT'S AS IF HE HAS FUN GAMBLING WITH HIS LIFE.
HE'S ONLY 16.
HOW'D HE GET LIKE THAT, ANYWAY?

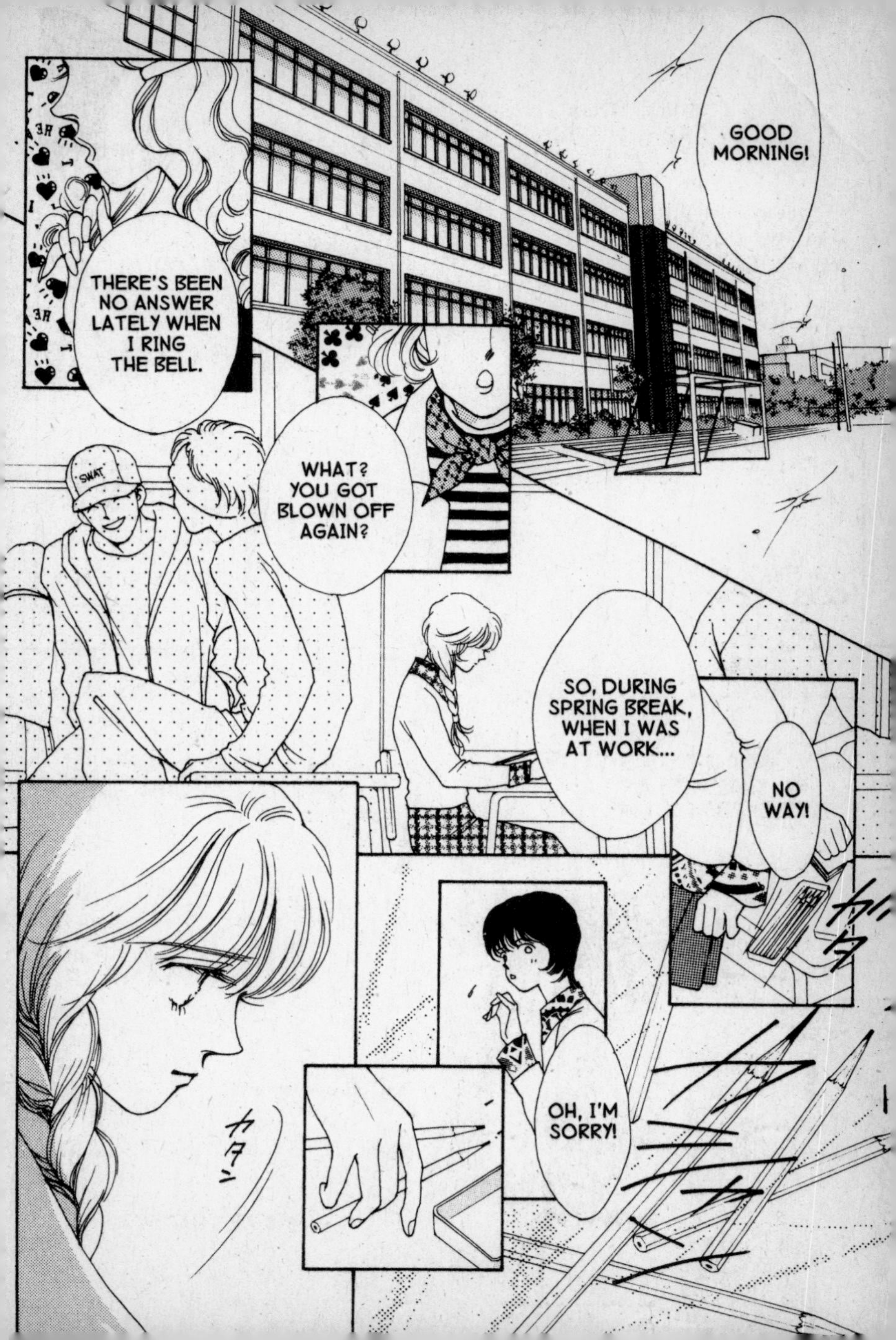
GOOD MORNING!
THERE'S BEEN NO ANSWER LATELY WHEN I RING THE BELL.
WHAT? YOU GOT BLOWN OFF AGAIN?
SO, DURING SPRING BREAK, WHEN I WAS AT WORK...
NO WAY!
ガタ
OH, I'M SORRY!
カタン

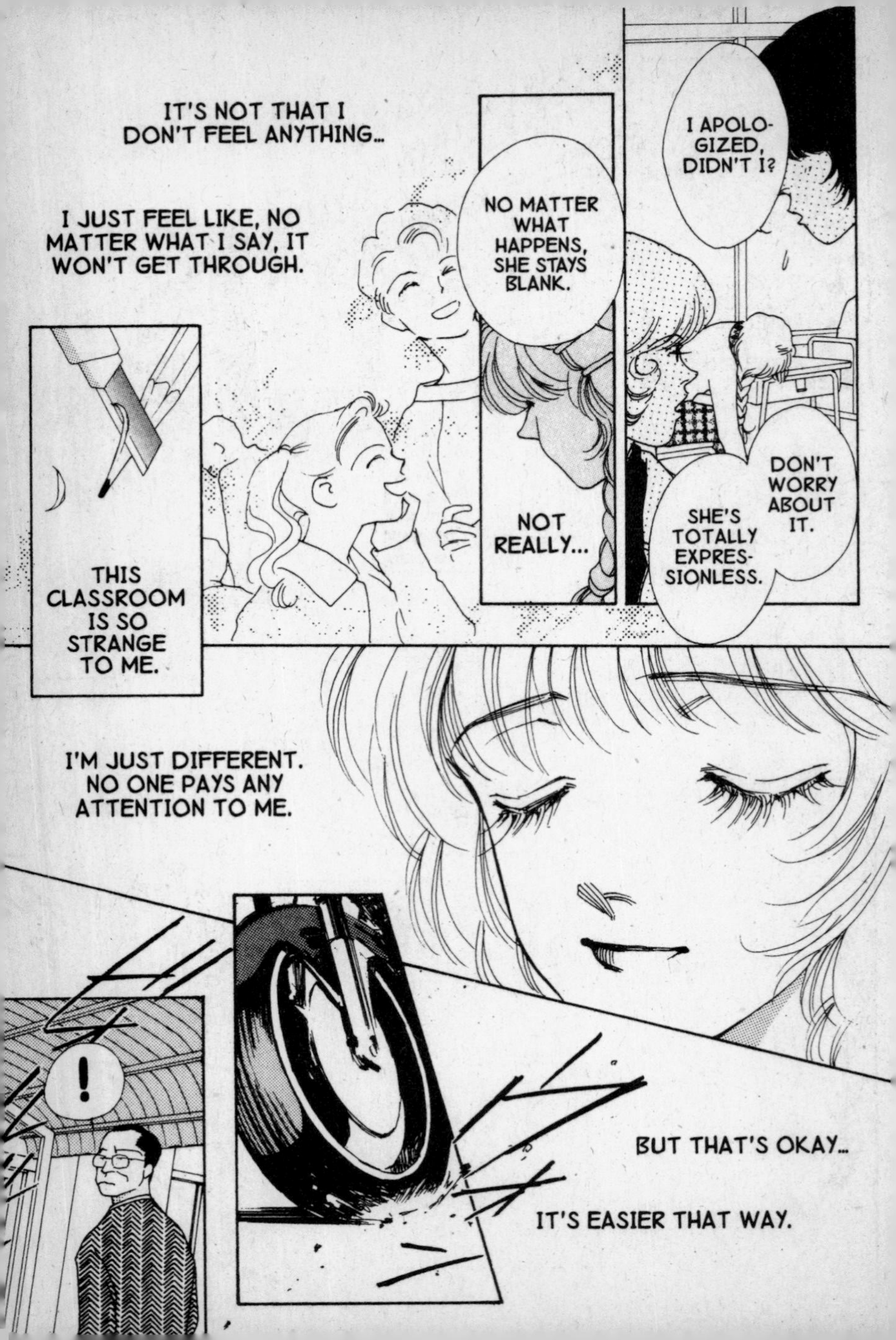
I APOLOGIZED, DIDN'T I?
DON'T WORRY ABOUT IT.
SHE'S TOTALLY EXPRESSIONLESS.
NO MATTER WHAT HAPPENS, SHE STAYS BLANK.
NOT REALLY...
IT'S NOT THAT I DON'T FEEL ANYTHING...
I JUST FEEL LIKE, NO MATTER WHAT I SAY, IT WON'T GET THROUGH.
THIS CLASSROOM IS SO STRANGE TO ME.
I'M JUST DIFFERENT. NO ONE PAYS ANY ATTENTION TO ME.
BUT THAT'S OKAY...
IT'S EASIER THAT WAY.
!

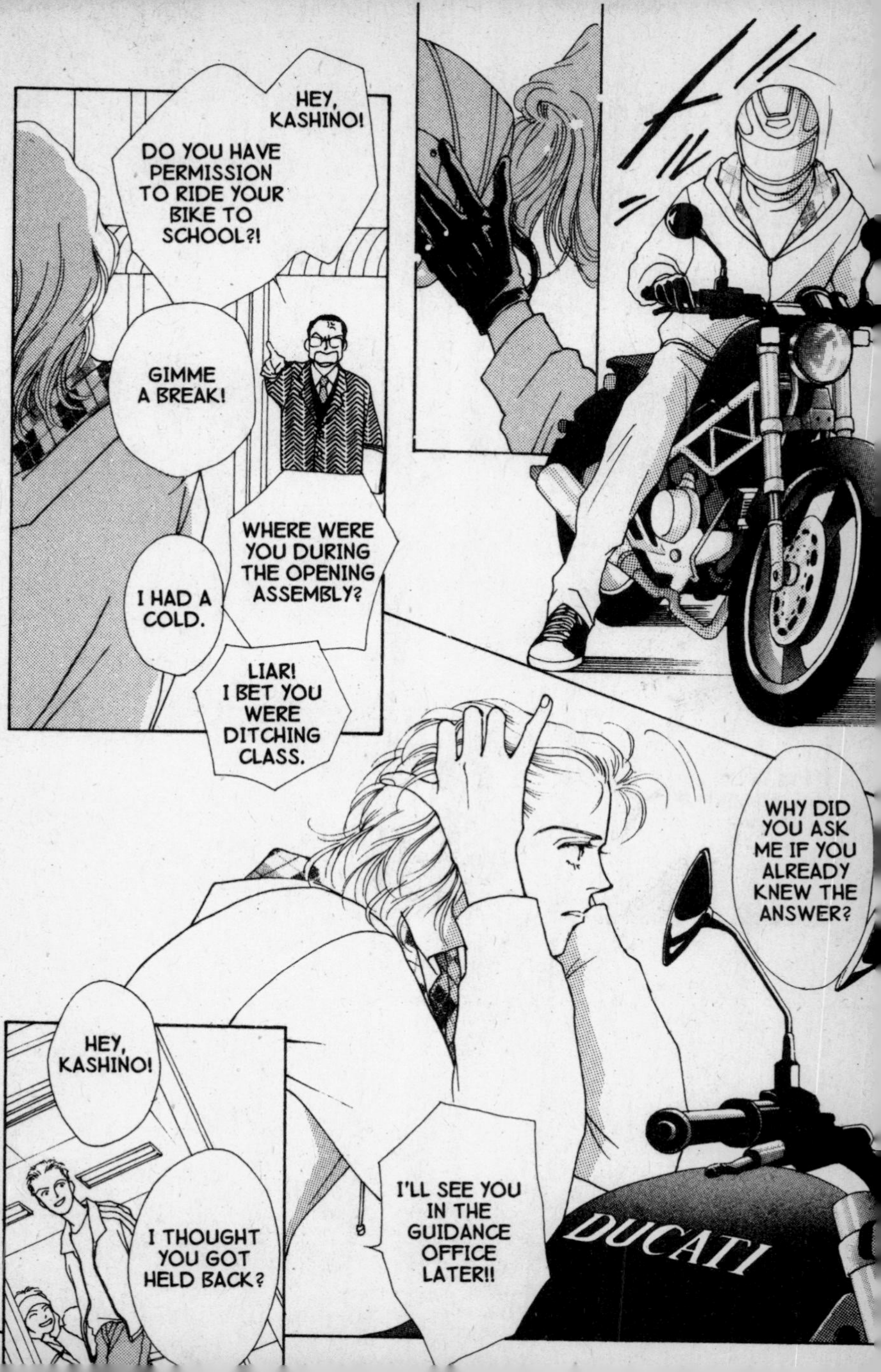
HEY, KASHINO!
DO YOU HAVE PERMISSION TO RIDE YOUR BIKE TO SCHOOL?!
GIMME A BREAK!
WHERE WERE YOU DURING THE OPENING ASSEMBLY?
I HAD A COLD.
LIAR! I BET YOU WERE DITCHING CLASS.
WHY DID YOU ASK ME IF YOU ALREADY KNEW THE ANSWER?
I'LL SEE YOU IN THE GUIDANCE OFFICE LATER!!
DUCATI
HEY, KASHINO!
I THOUGHT YOU GOT HELD BACK?

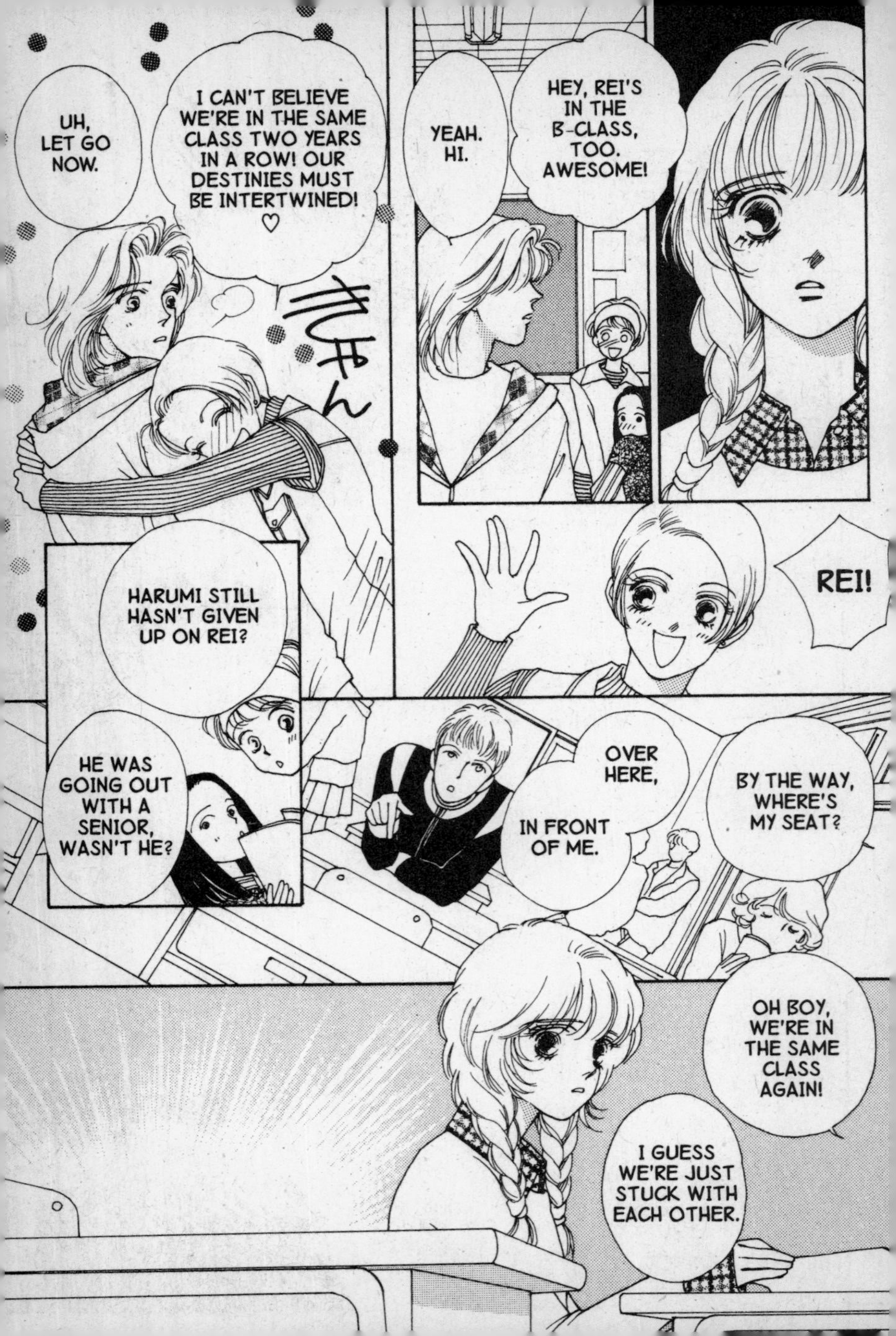
HEY, REI'S IN THE B-CLASS, TOO. AWESOME!
YEAH. HI.
REI!
I CAN'T BELIEVE WE'RE IN THE SAME CLASS TWO YEARS IN A ROW! OUR DESTINIES MUST BE INTERTWINED! ♡
UH, LET GO NOW.
きゃん
BY THE WAY, WHERE'S MY SEAT?
OVER HERE,
IN FRONT OF ME.
HARUMI STILL HASN'T GIVEN UP ON REI?
HE WAS GOING OUT WITH A SENIOR, WASN'T HE?
OH BOY, WE'RE IN THE SAME CLASS AGAIN!
I GUESS WE'RE JUST STUCK WITH EACH OTHER.

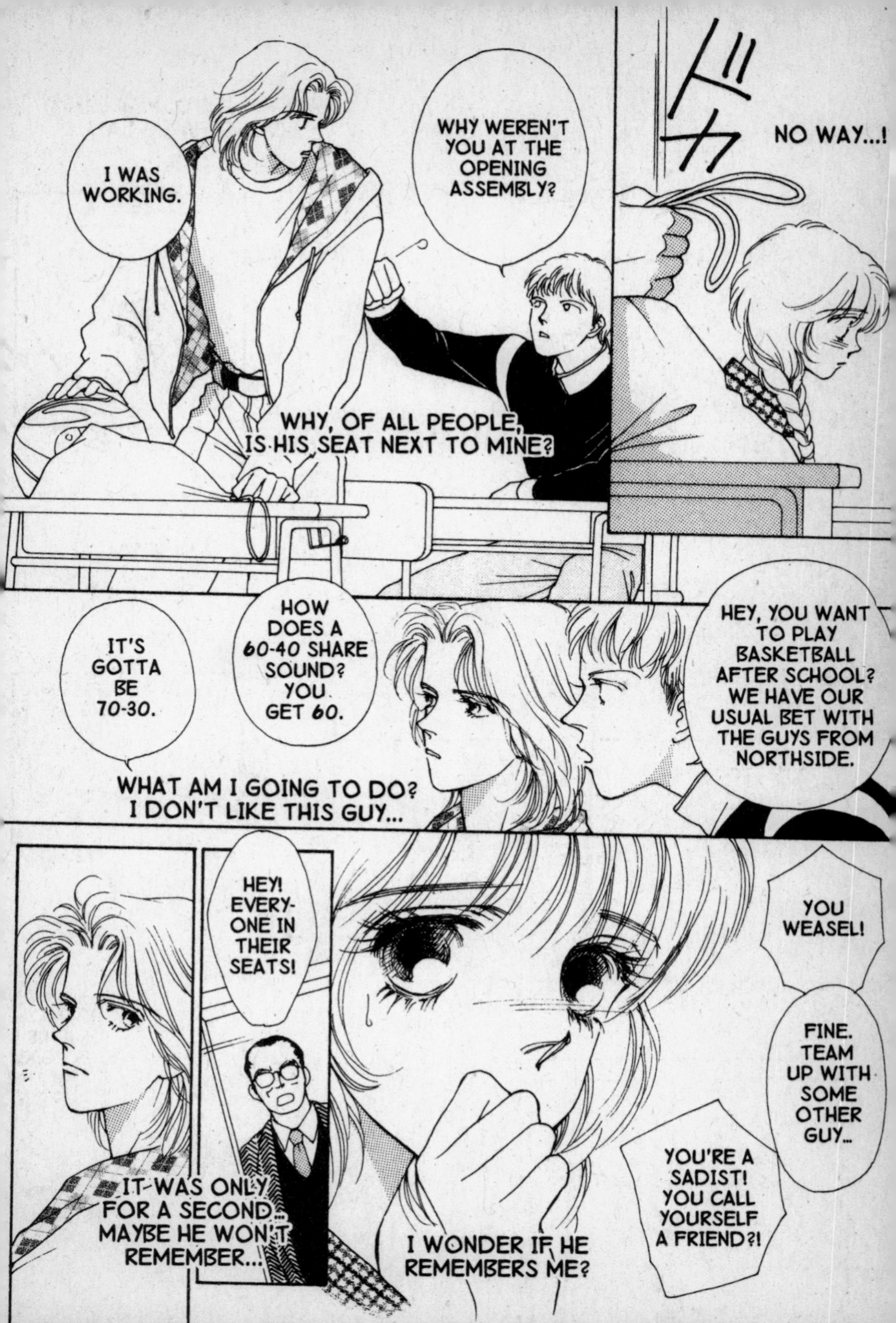
ドカ
NO WAY...!
WHY WEREN'T YOU AT THE OPENING ASSEMBLY?
I WAS WORKING.
WHY, OF ALL PEOPLE, IS HIS SEAT NEXT TO MINE?
HEY, YOU WANT TO PLAY BASKETBALL AFTER SCHOOL? WE HAVE OUR USUAL BET WITH THE GUYS FROM NORTHSIDE.
HOW DOES A 60-40 SHARE SOUND? YOU GET 60.
IT'S GOTTA BE 70-30.
WHAT AM I GOING TO DO? I DON'T LIKE THIS GUY...
YOU WEASEL!
FINE. TEAM UP WITH SOME OTHER GUY...
YOU'RE A SADIST! YOU CALL YOURSELF A FRIEND?!
I WONDER IF HE REMEMBERS ME?
HEY! EVERYONE IN THEIR SEATS!
IT WAS ONLY FOR A SECOND... MAYBE HE WON'T REMEMBER...

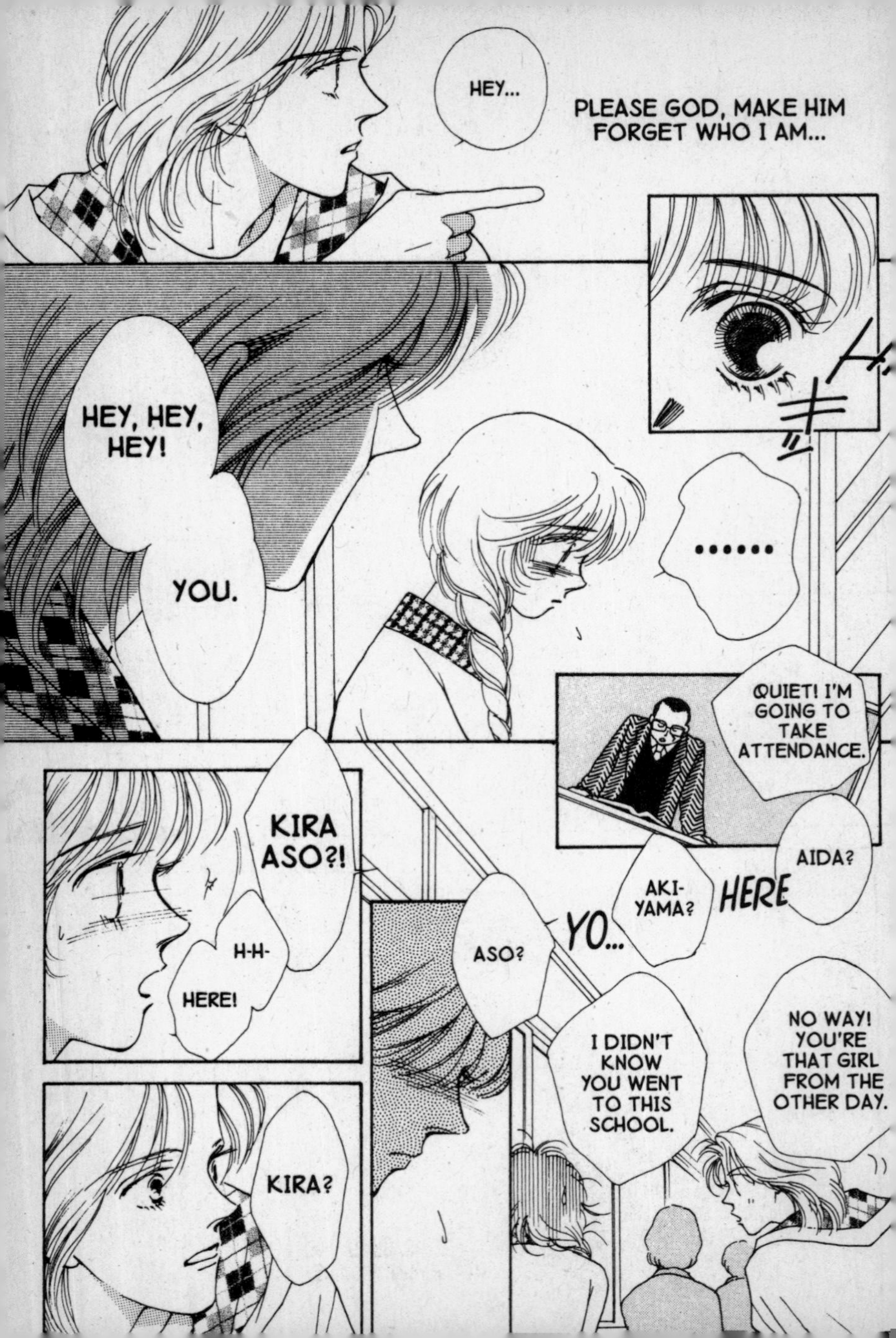
PLEASE GOD, MAKE HIM FORGET WHO I AM...
HEY...
......
HEY, HEY, HEY!
YOU.
QUIET! I'M GOING TO TAKE ATTENDANCE.
AIDA?
HERE
AKI-YAMA?
YO...
ASO?
NO WAY! YOU'RE THAT GIRL FROM THE OTHER DAY.
I DIDN'T KNOW YOU WENT TO THIS SCHOOL.
KIRA ASO?!
H-H-
HERE!
KIRA?

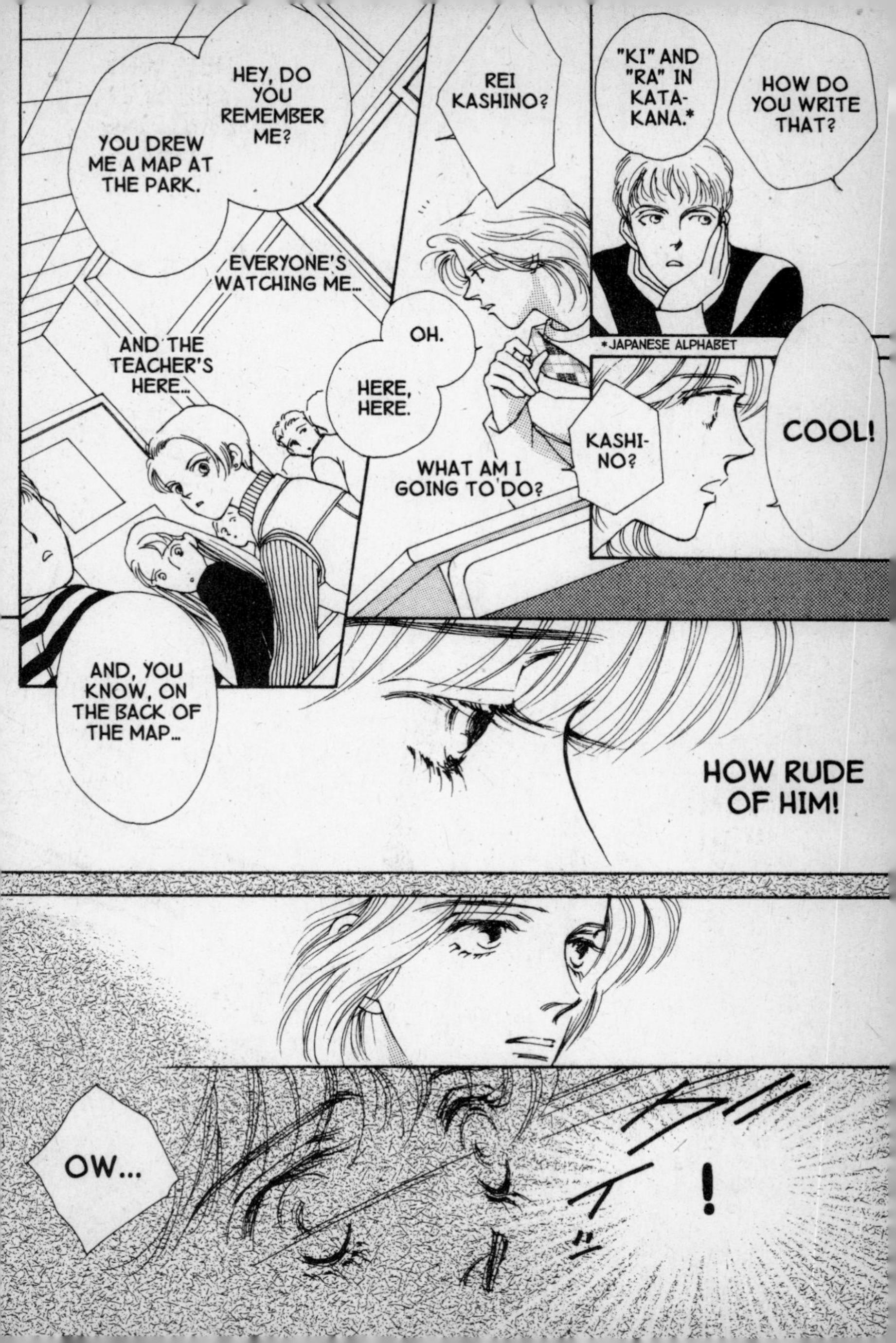
HOW DO YOU WRITE THAT?
"KI" AND "RA" IN KATA-KANA.*
*JAPANESE ALPHABET
COOL!
KASHI-NO?
REI KASHINO?
OH.
HERE, HERE.
WHAT AM I GOING TO DO?
HEY, DO YOU REMEMBER ME?
YOU DREW ME A MAP AT THE PARK.
EVERYONE'S WATCHING ME...
AND THE TEACHER'S HERE...
HOW RUDE OF HIM!
AND, YOU KNOW, ON THE BACK OF THE MAP...
!
OW...

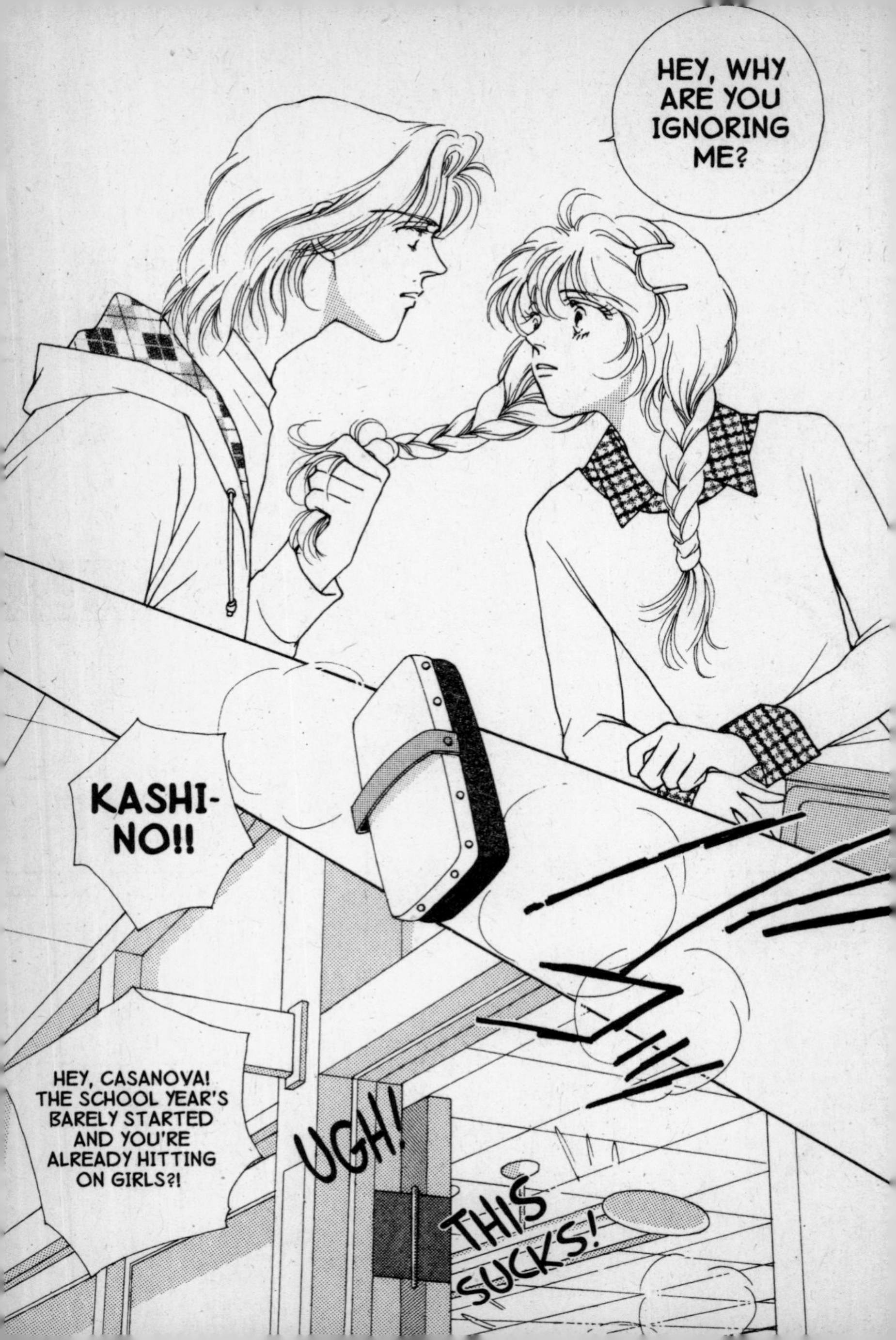
HEY, WHY ARE YOU IGNORING ME?
KASHI-NO!!
THIS SUCKS!
UGH!
HEY, CASANOVA! THE SCHOOL YEAR'S BARELY STARTED AND YOU'RE ALREADY HITTING ON GIRLS?!

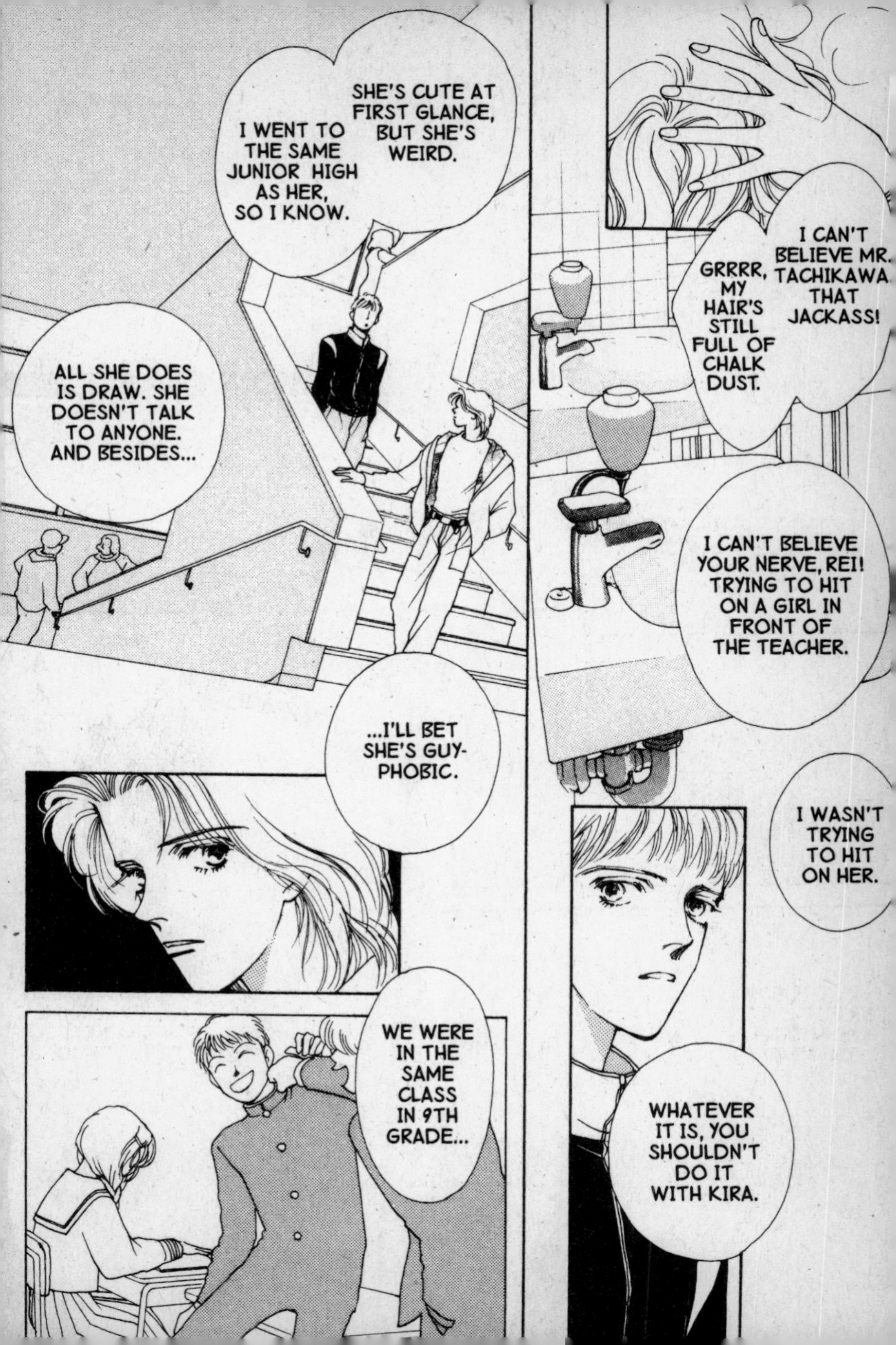
I CAN'T BELIEVE MR. TACHIKAWA THAT JACKASS!
GRRRR, MY HAIR'S STILL FULL OF CHALK DUST.
I CAN'T BELIEVE YOUR NERVE, REI! TRYING TO HIT ON A GIRL IN FRONT OF THE TEACHER.
I WASN'T TRYING TO HIT ON HER.
WHATEVER IT IS, YOU SHOULDN'T DO IT WITH KIRA.
SHE'S CUTE AT FIRST GLANCE, BUT SHE'S WEIRD.
I WENT TO THE SAME JUNIOR HIGH AS HER, SO I KNOW.
ALL SHE DOES IS DRAW. SHE DOESN'T TALK TO ANYONE. AND BESIDES...
...I'LL BET SHE'S GUY-PHOBIC.
WE WERE IN THE SAME CLASS IN 9TH GRADE...

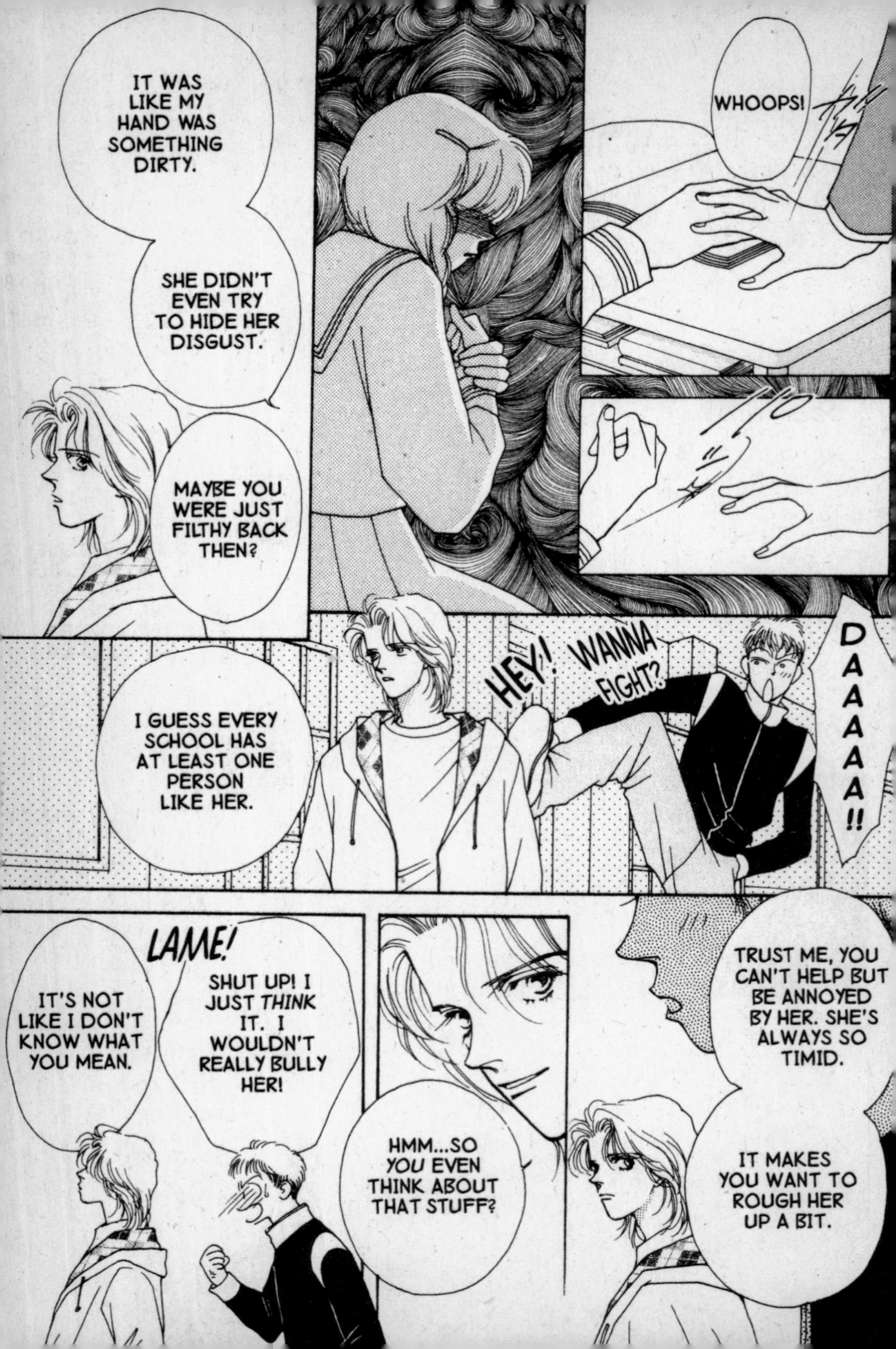
WHOOPS!
IT WAS LIKE MY HAND WAS SOMETHING DIRTY.
SHE DIDN'T EVEN TRY TO HIDE HER DISGUST.
MAYBE YOU WERE JUST FILTHY BACK THEN?
DAAAAAA!!
HEY! WANNA FIGHT?
I GUESS EVERY SCHOOL HAS AT LEAST ONE PERSON LIKE HER.
TRUST ME, YOU CAN'T HELP BUT BE ANNOYED BY HER. SHE'S ALWAYS SO TIMID.
IT MAKES YOU WANT TO ROUGH HER UP A BIT.
HMM...SO *YOU* EVEN THINK ABOUT THAT STUFF?
SHUT UP! I JUST *THINK* IT. I WOULDN'T REALLY BULLY HER!
LAME!
IT'S NOT LIKE I DON'T KNOW WHAT YOU MEAN.

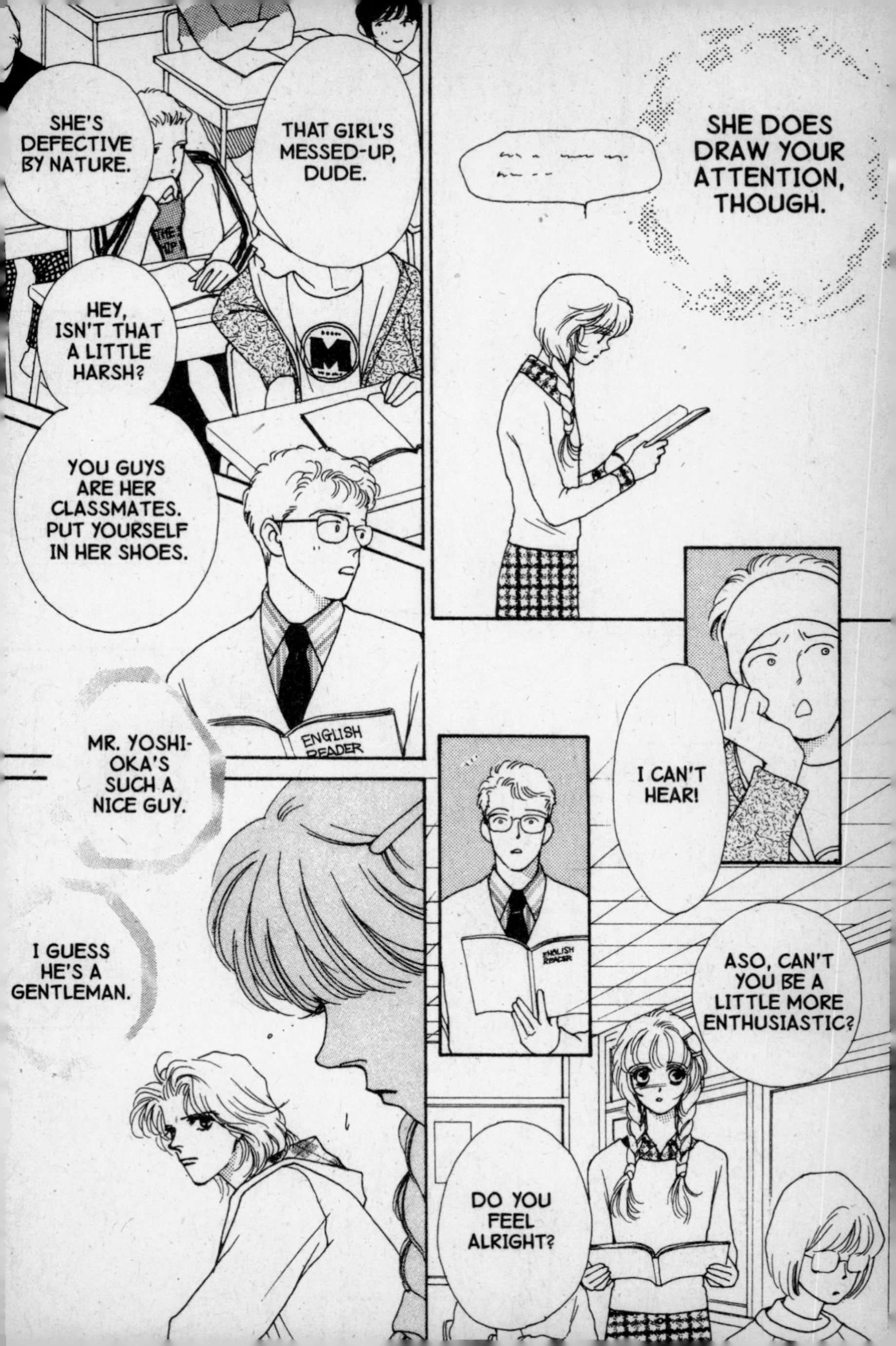
SHE DOES DRAW YOUR ATTENTION, THOUGH.
THAT GIRL'S MESSED-UP, DUDE.
SHE'S DEFECTIVE BY NATURE.
HEY, ISN'T THAT A LITTLE HARSH?
YOU GUYS ARE HER CLASSMATES. PUT YOURSELF IN HER SHOES.
ENGLISH READER
I CAN'T HEAR!
ENGLISH READER
ASO, CAN'T YOU BE A LITTLE MORE ENTHUSIASTIC?
DO YOU FEEL ALRIGHT?
MR. YOSHI-OKA'S SUCH A NICE GUY.
I GUESS HE'S A GENTLEMAN.

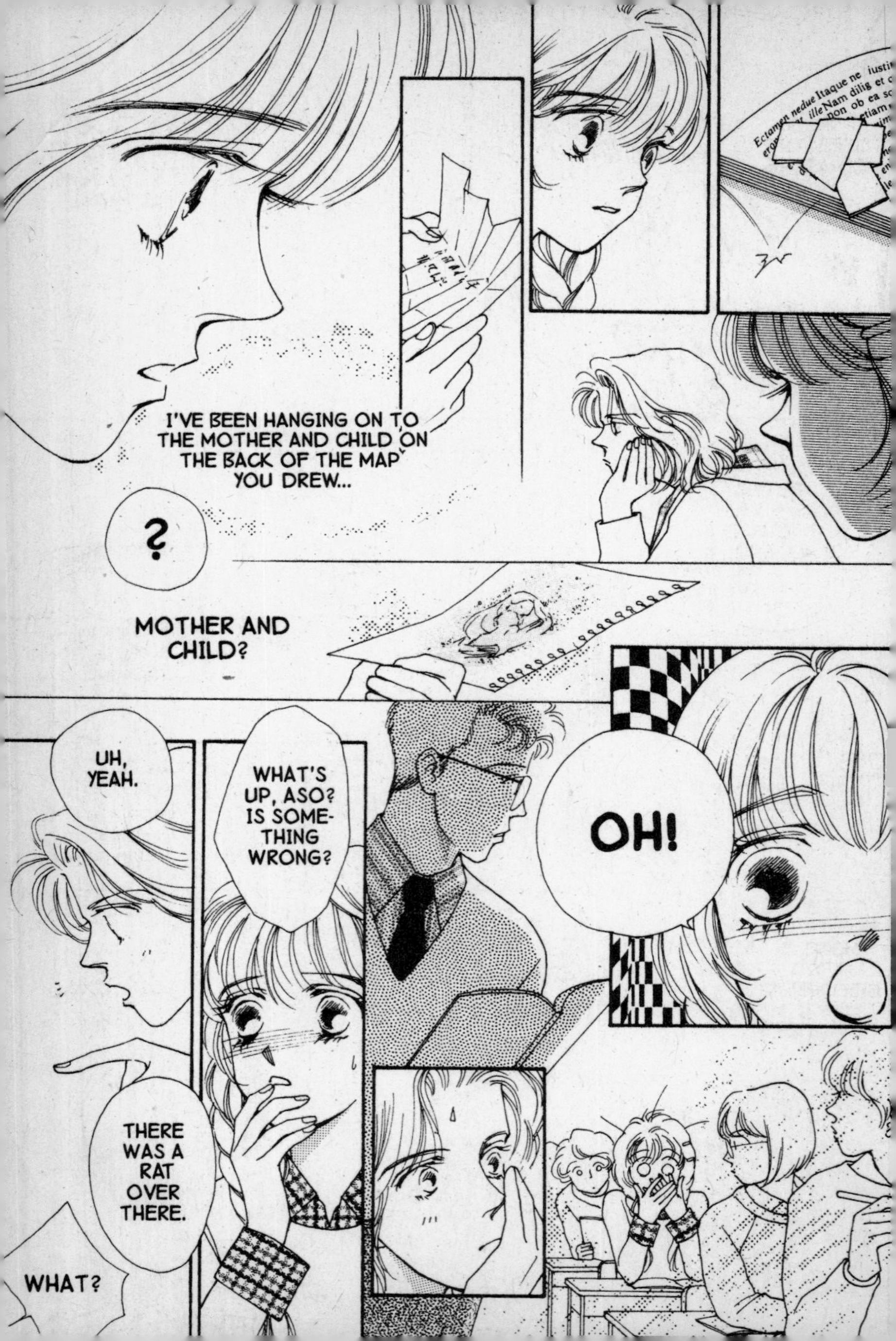
I'VE BEEN HANGING ON TO THE MOTHER AND CHILD ON THE BACK OF THE MAP YOU DREW...
?
MOTHER AND CHILD?
OH!
WHAT'S UP, ASO? IS SOME-THING WRONG?
UH, YEAH.
THERE WAS A RAT OVER THERE.
WHAT?

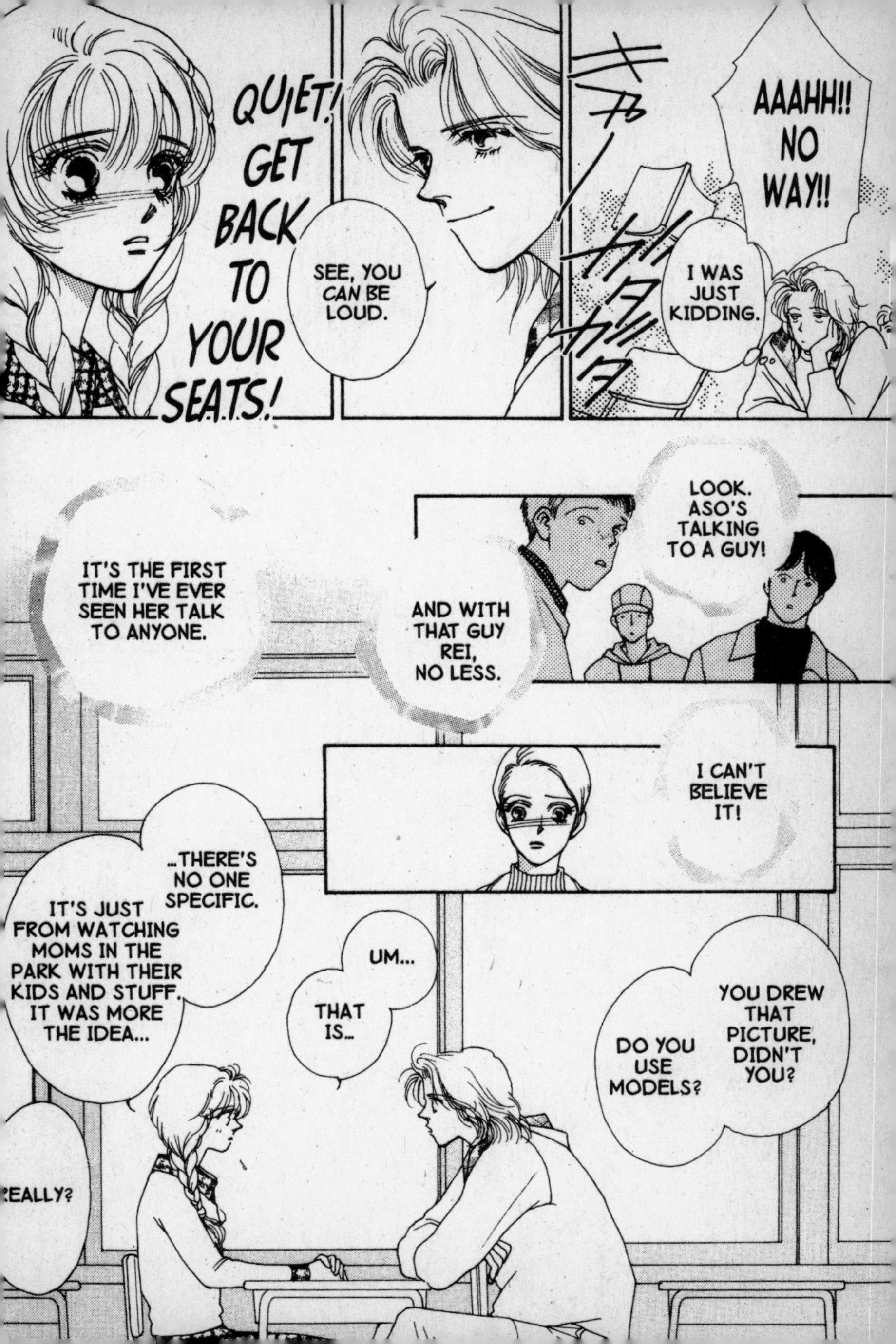
AAAHH!! NO WAY!!
I WAS JUST KIDDING.
SEE, YOU CAN BE LOUD.
QUIET! GET BACK TO YOUR SEATS!
LOOK. ASO'S TALKING TO A GUY!
AND WITH THAT GUY REI, NO LESS.
IT'S THE FIRST TIME I'VE EVER SEEN HER TALK TO ANYONE.
I CAN'T BELIEVE IT!
YOU DREW THAT PICTURE, DIDN'T YOU?
DO YOU USE MODELS?
UM...
THAT IS...
...THERE'S NO ONE SPECIFIC.
IT'S JUST FROM WATCHING MOMS IN THE PARK WITH THEIR KIDS AND STUFF. IT WAS MORE THE IDEA...
EALLY?

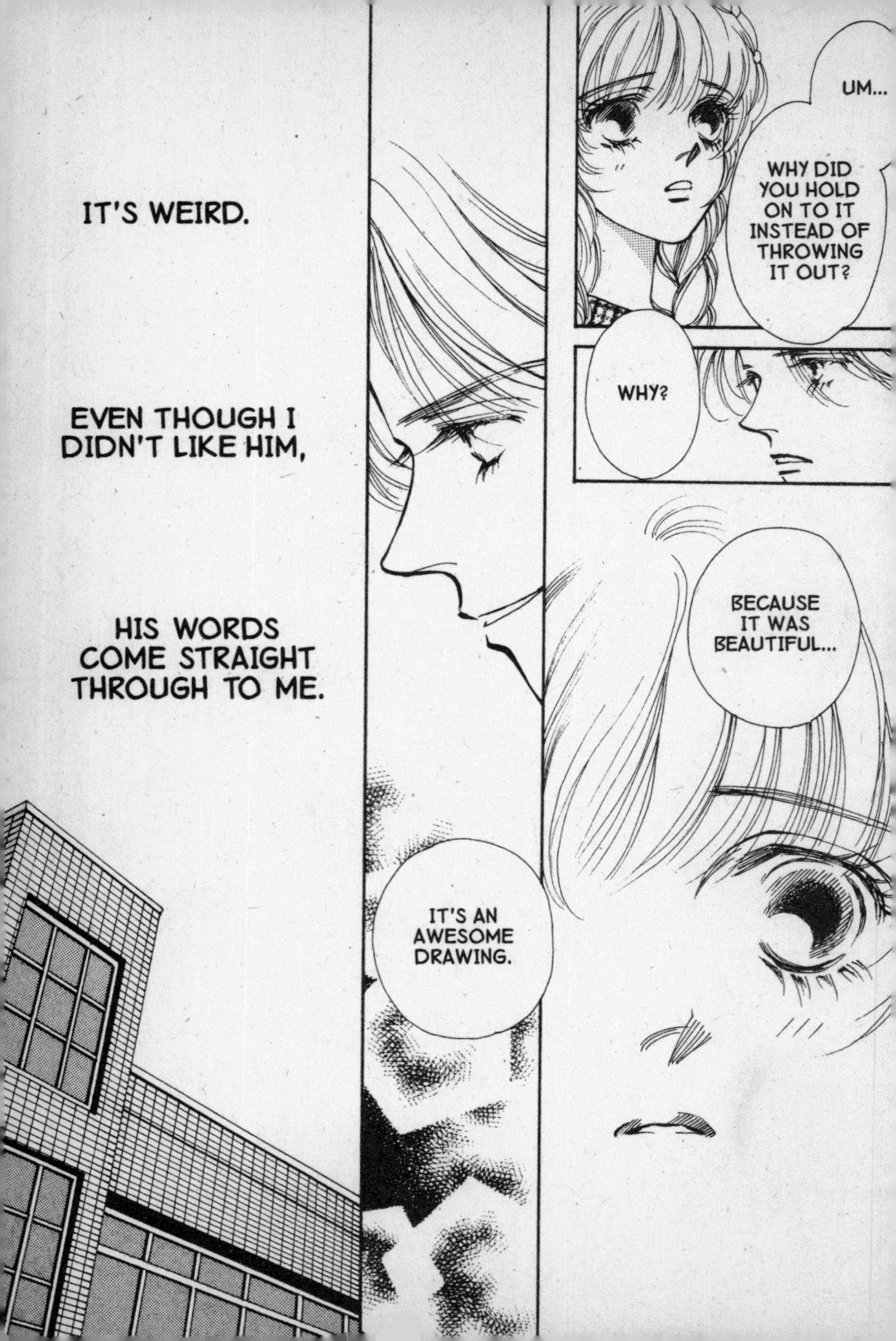
UM...
WHY DID YOU HOLD ON TO IT INSTEAD OF THROWING IT OUT?
WHY?
BECAUSE IT WAS BEAUTIFUL...
IT'S AN AWESOME DRAWING.
IT'S WEIRD.
EVEN THOUGH I DIDN'T LIKE HIM,
HIS WORDS COME STRAIGHT THROUGH TO ME.

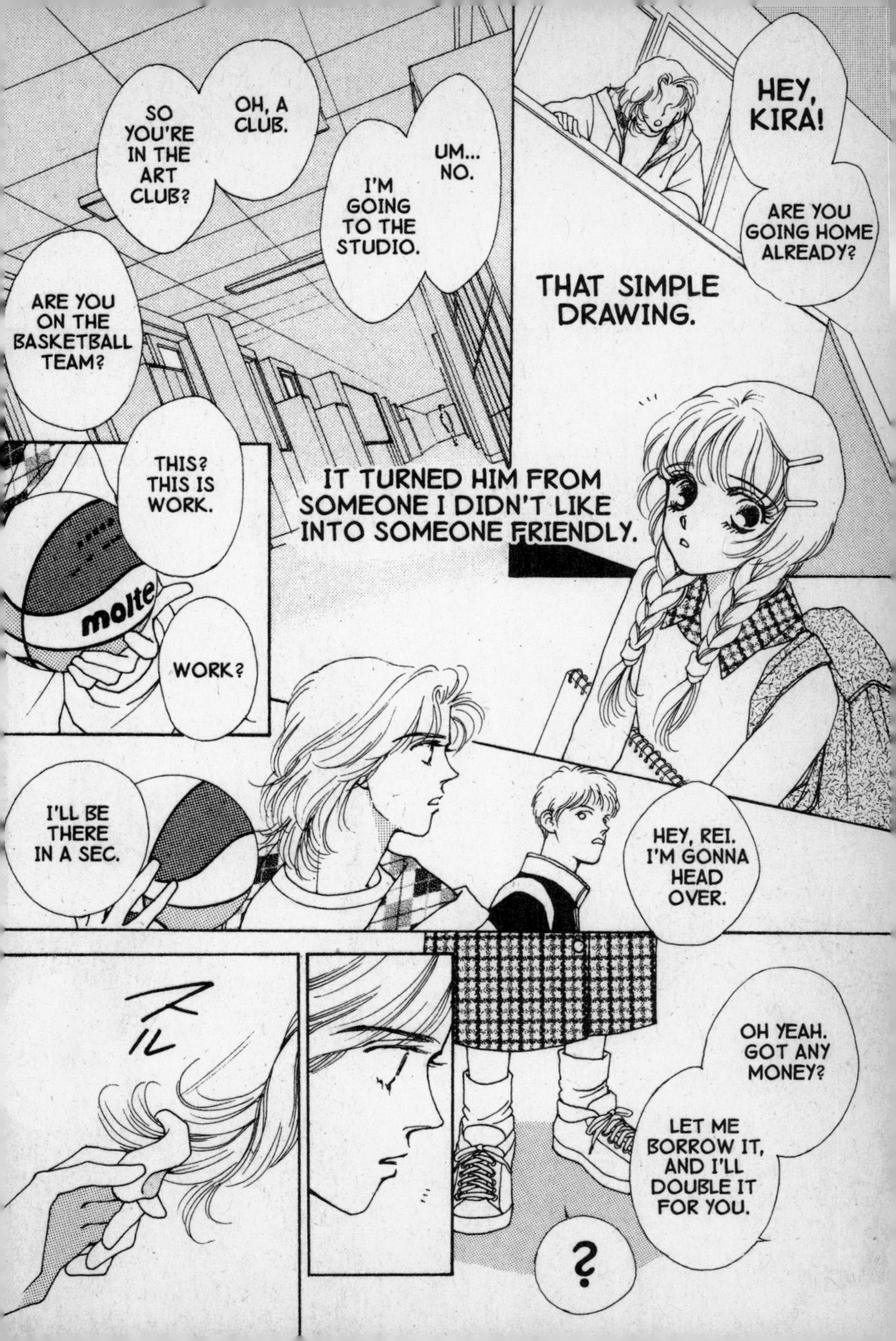
HEY, KIRA!
ARE YOU GOING HOME ALREADY?
UM... NO.
I'M GOING TO THE STUDIO.
OH, A CLUB.
SO YOU'RE IN THE ART CLUB?
ARE YOU ON THE BASKETBALL TEAM?
THAT SIMPLE DRAWING.
IT TURNED HIM FROM SOMEONE I DIDN'T LIKE INTO SOMEONE FRIENDLY.
THIS? THIS IS WORK.
molte
WORK?
HEY, REI. I'M GONNA HEAD OVER.
I'LL BE THERE IN A SEC.
OH YEAH. GOT ANY MONEY?
LET ME BORROW IT, AND I'LL DOUBLE IT FOR YOU.
?
スル

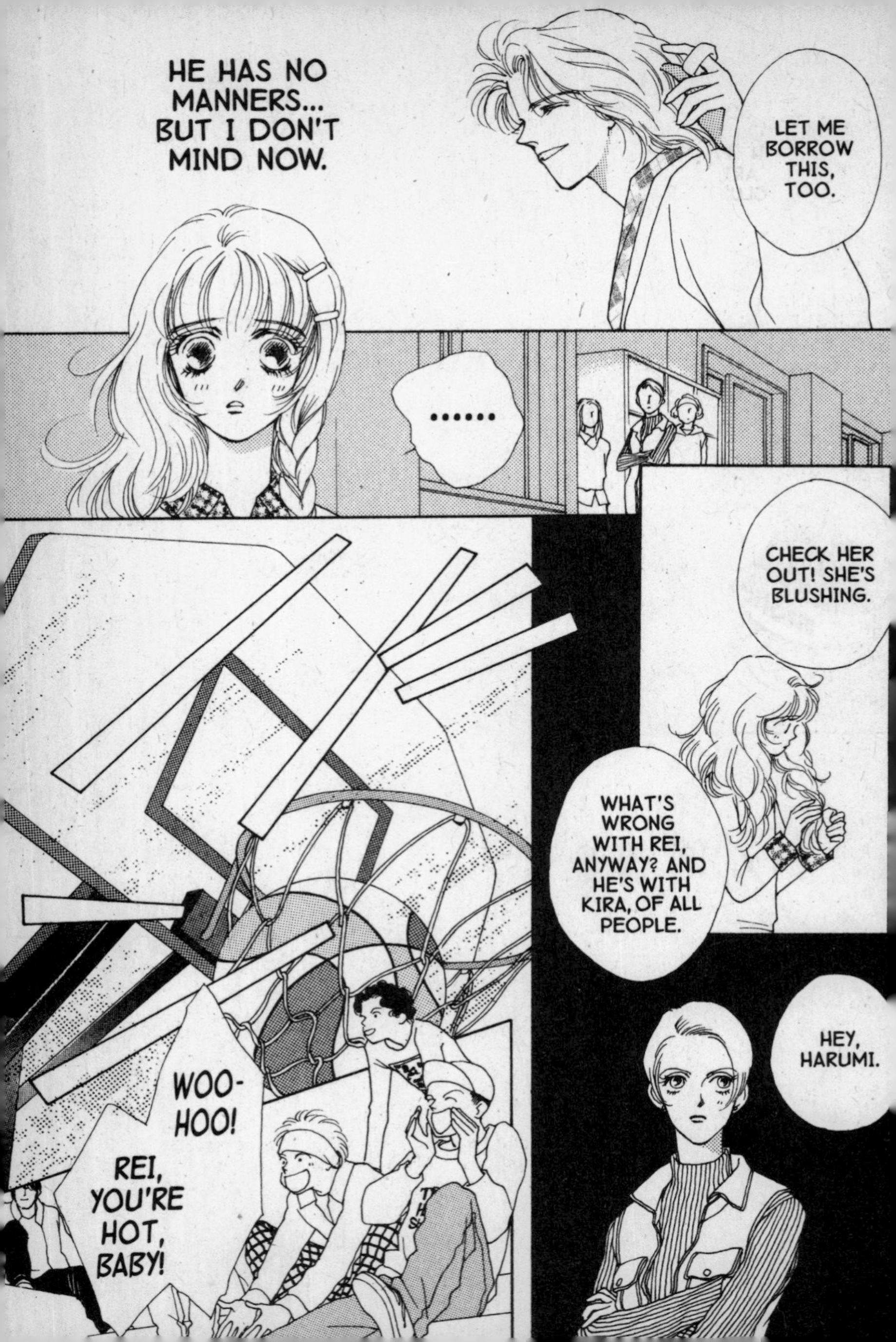
LET ME BORROW THIS, TOO.
HE HAS NO MANNERS... BUT I DON'T MIND NOW.
......
CHECK HER OUT! SHE'S BLUSHING.
WHAT'S WRONG WITH REI, ANYWAY? AND HE'S WITH KIRA, OF ALL PEOPLE.
HEY, HARUMI.
WOO-HOO!
REI, YOU'RE HOT, BABY!

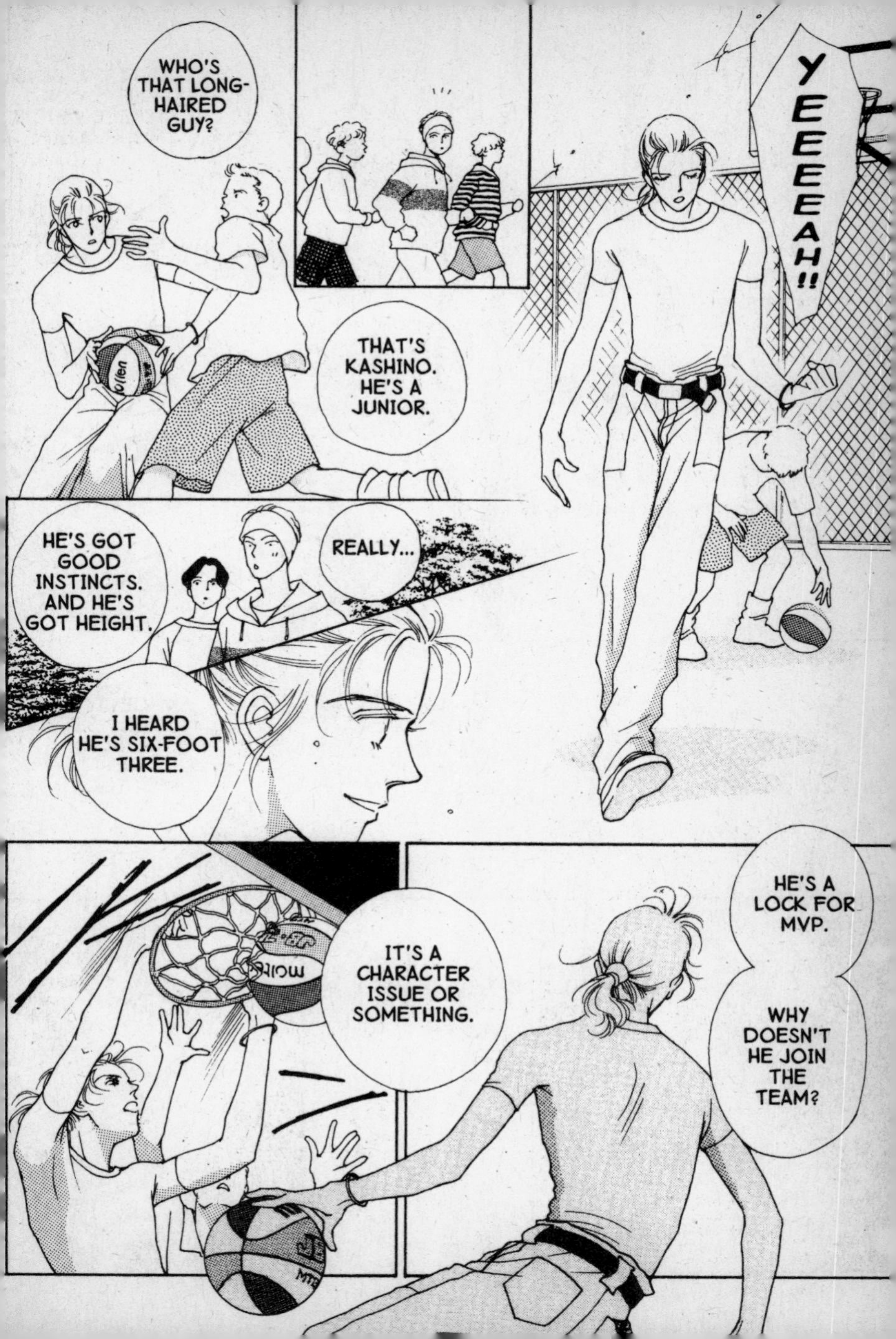

YEEEEAH!!
WHO'S THAT LONG-HAIRED GUY?
THAT'S KASHINO. HE'S A JUNIOR.
HE'S GOT GOOD INSTINCTS. AND HE'S GOT HEIGHT.
REALLY...
I HEARD HE'S SIX-FOOT THREE.
HE'S A LOCK FOR MVP.
WHY DOESN'T HE JOIN THE TEAM?
IT'S A CHARACTER ISSUE OR SOMETHING.

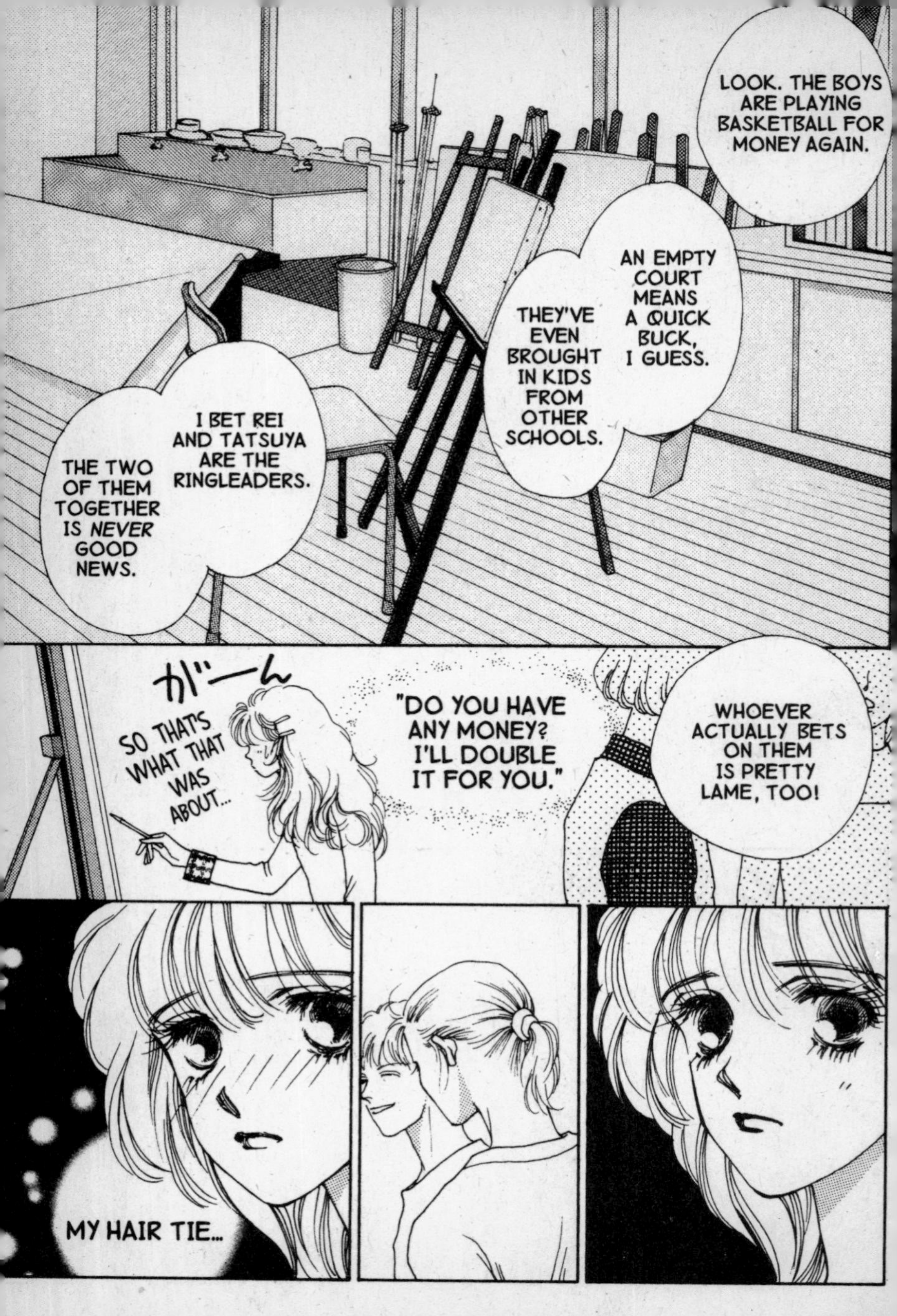
LOOK. THE BOYS ARE PLAYING BASKETBALL FOR MONEY AGAIN.
AN EMPTY COURT MEANS A QUICK BUCK, I GUESS.
THEY'VE EVEN BROUGHT IN KIDS FROM OTHER SCHOOLS.
I BET REI AND TATSUYA ARE THE RINGLEADERS.
THE TWO OF THEM TOGETHER IS *NEVER* GOOD NEWS.
WHOEVER ACTUALLY BETS ON THEM IS PRETTY LAME, TOO!
"DO YOU HAVE ANY MONEY? I'LL DOUBLE IT FOR YOU."
がーん
SO THAT'S WHAT THAT WAS ABOUT...
MY HAIR TIE...

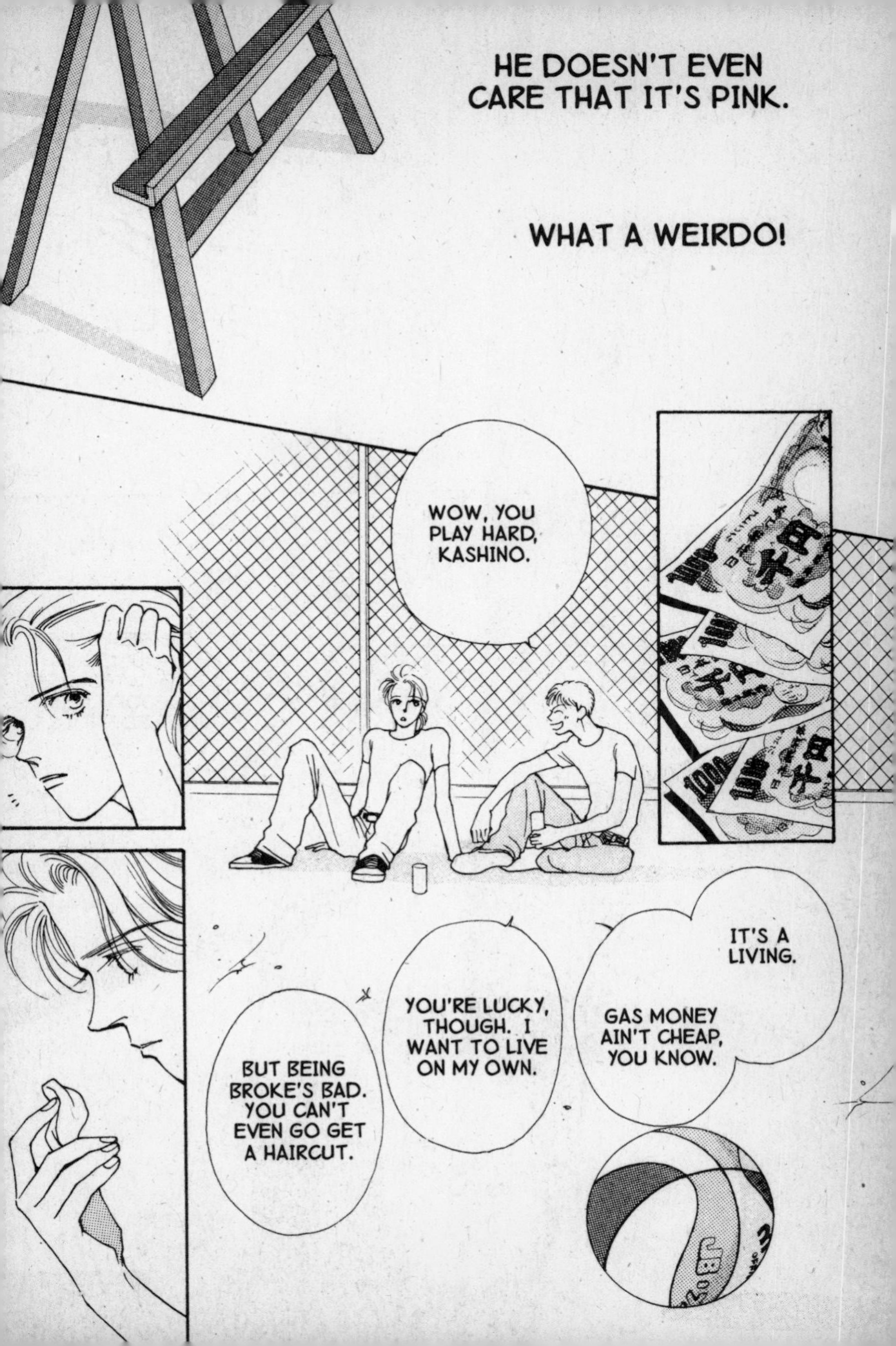
HE DOESN'T EVEN CARE THAT IT'S PINK.
WHAT A WEIRDO!
WOW, YOU PLAY HARD, KASHINO.
IT'S A LIVING.
GAS MONEY AIN'T CHEAP, YOU KNOW.
YOU'RE LUCKY, THOUGH. I WANT TO LIVE ON MY OWN.
BUT BEING BROKE'S BAD. YOU CAN'T EVEN GO GET A HAIRCUT.

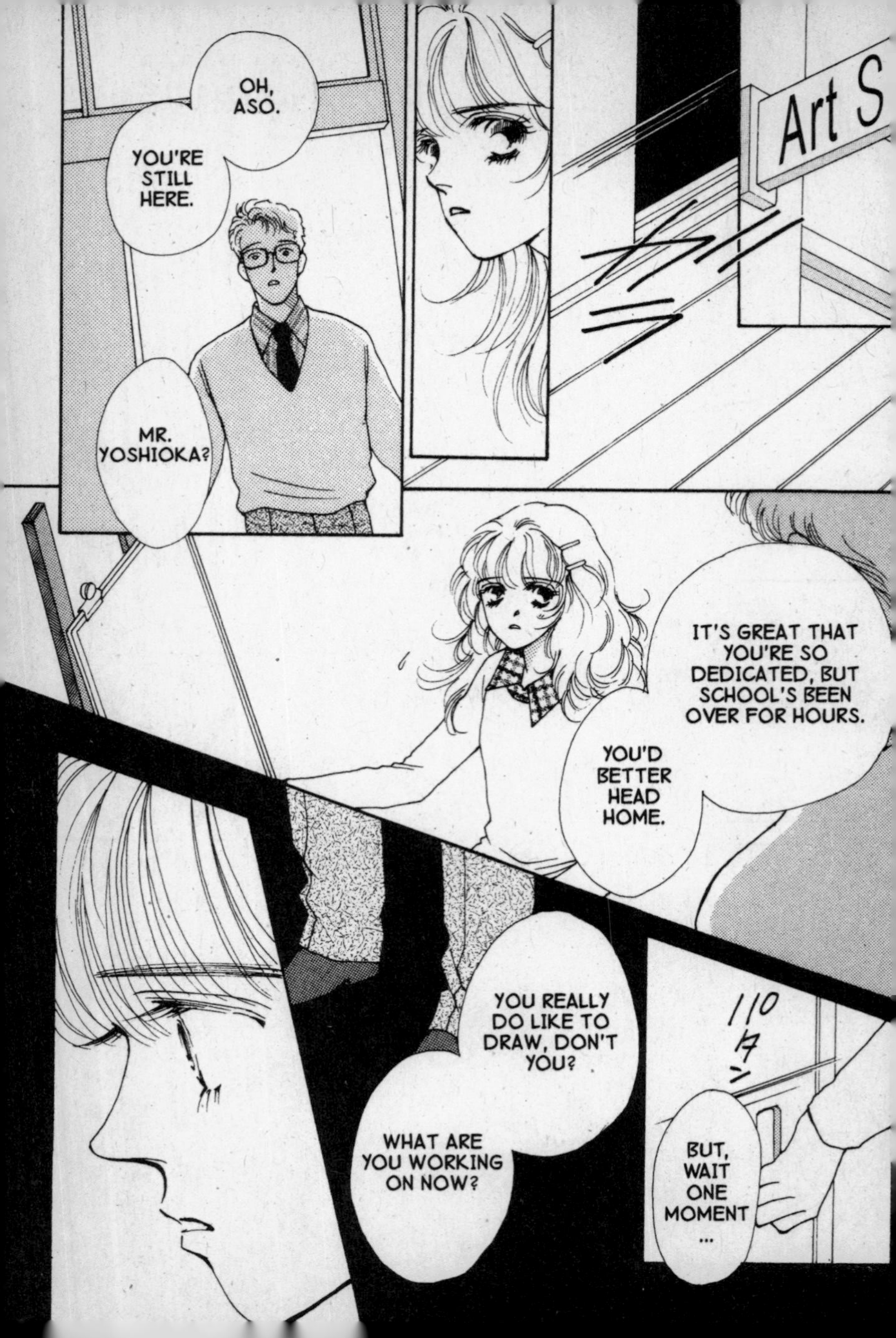
Art S
MR. YOSHIOKA?
OH, ASO.
YOU'RE STILL HERE.
IT'S GREAT THAT YOU'RE SO DEDICATED, BUT SCHOOL'S BEEN OVER FOR HOURS.
YOU'D BETTER HEAD HOME.
BUT, WAIT ONE MOMENT ...
YOU REALLY DO LIKE TO DRAW, DON'T YOU?
WHAT ARE YOU WORKING ON NOW?

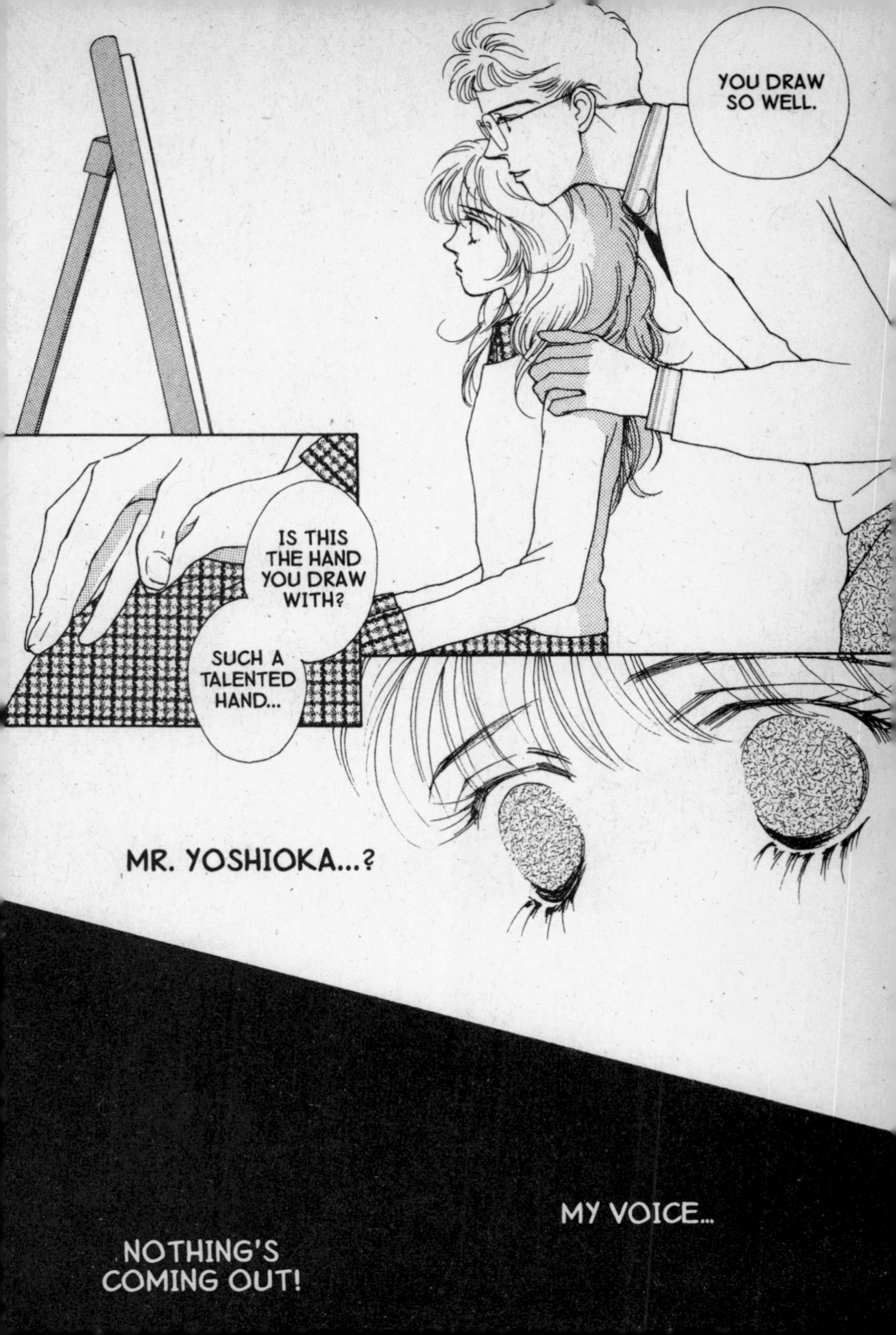
YOU DRAW SO WELL.
IS THIS THE HAND YOU DRAW WITH?
SUCH A TALENTED HAND...
MR. YOSHIOKA...?
MY VOICE...
NOTHING'S COMING OUT!

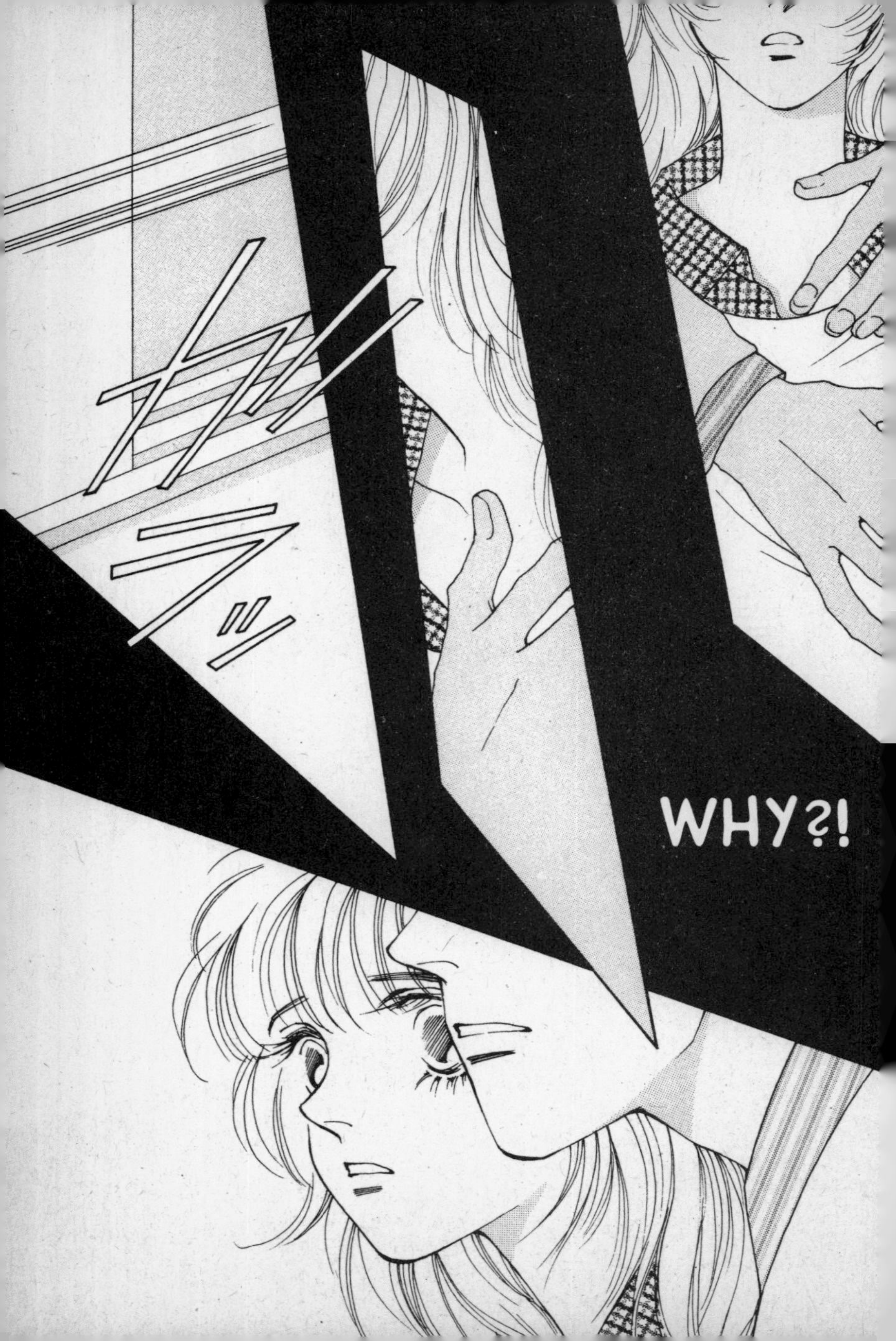
WHY?!

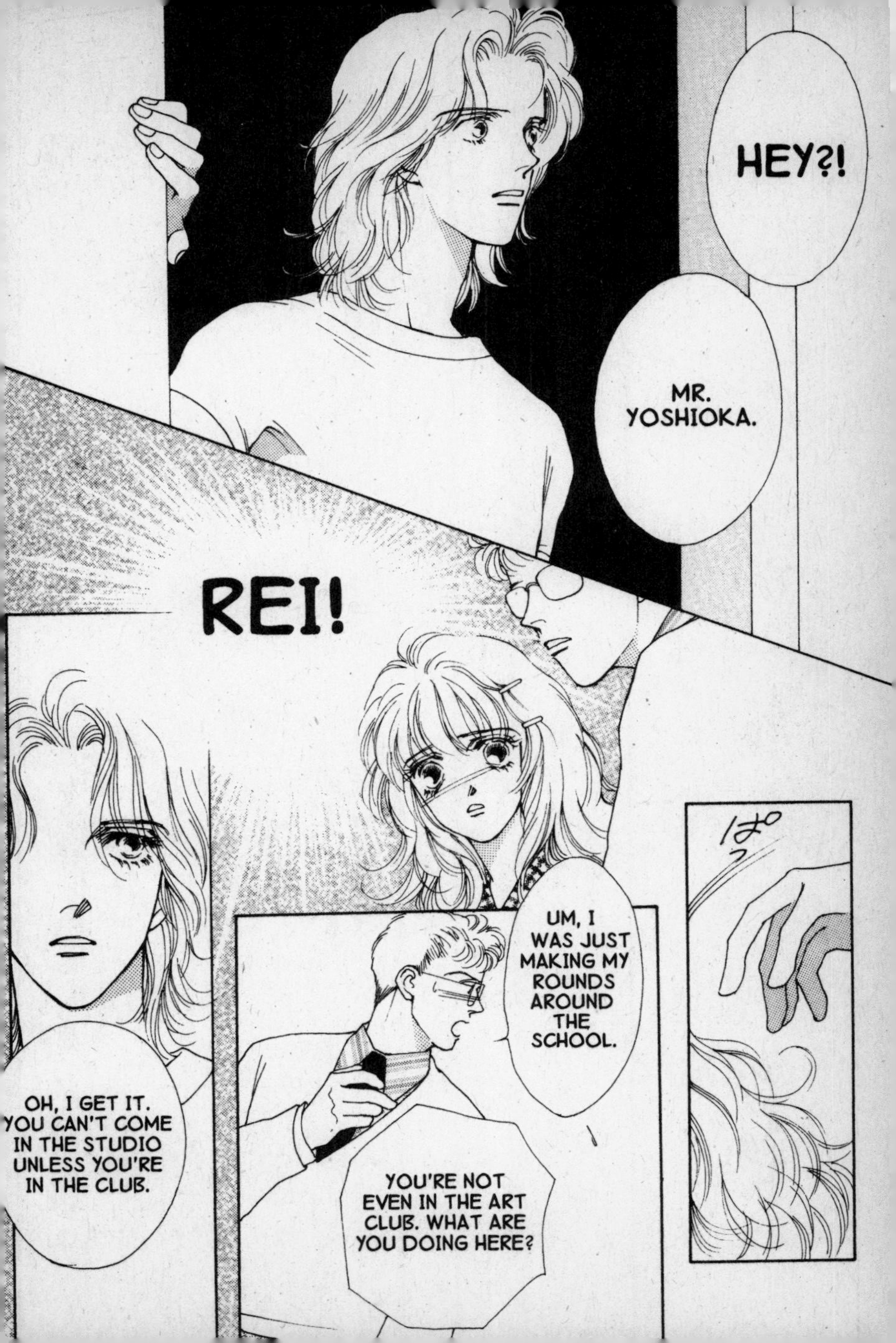
HEY?!
MR. YOSHIOKA.
REI!
ぱっ
UM, I WAS JUST MAKING MY ROUNDS AROUND THE SCHOOL.
YOU'RE NOT EVEN IN THE ART CLUB. WHAT ARE YOU DOING HERE?
OH, I GET IT. YOU CAN'T COME IN THE STUDIO UNLESS YOU'RE IN THE CLUB.

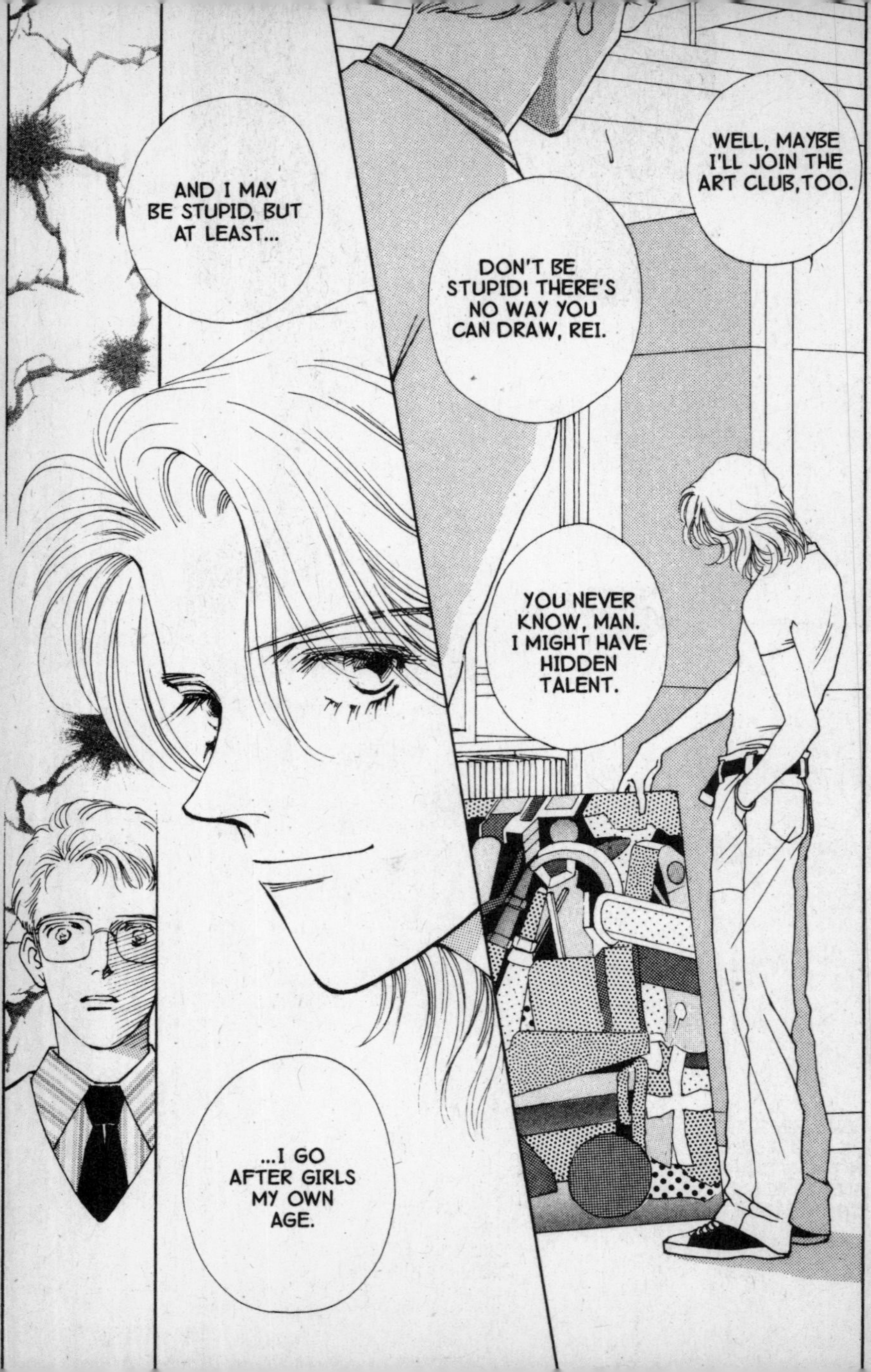
WELL, MAYBE I'LL JOIN THE ART CLUB, TOO.
DON'T BE STUPID! THERE'S NO WAY YOU CAN DRAW, REI.
YOU NEVER KNOW, MAN. I MIGHT HAVE HIDDEN TALENT.
AND I MAY BE STUPID, BUT AT LEAST...
...I GO AFTER GIRLS MY OWN AGE.

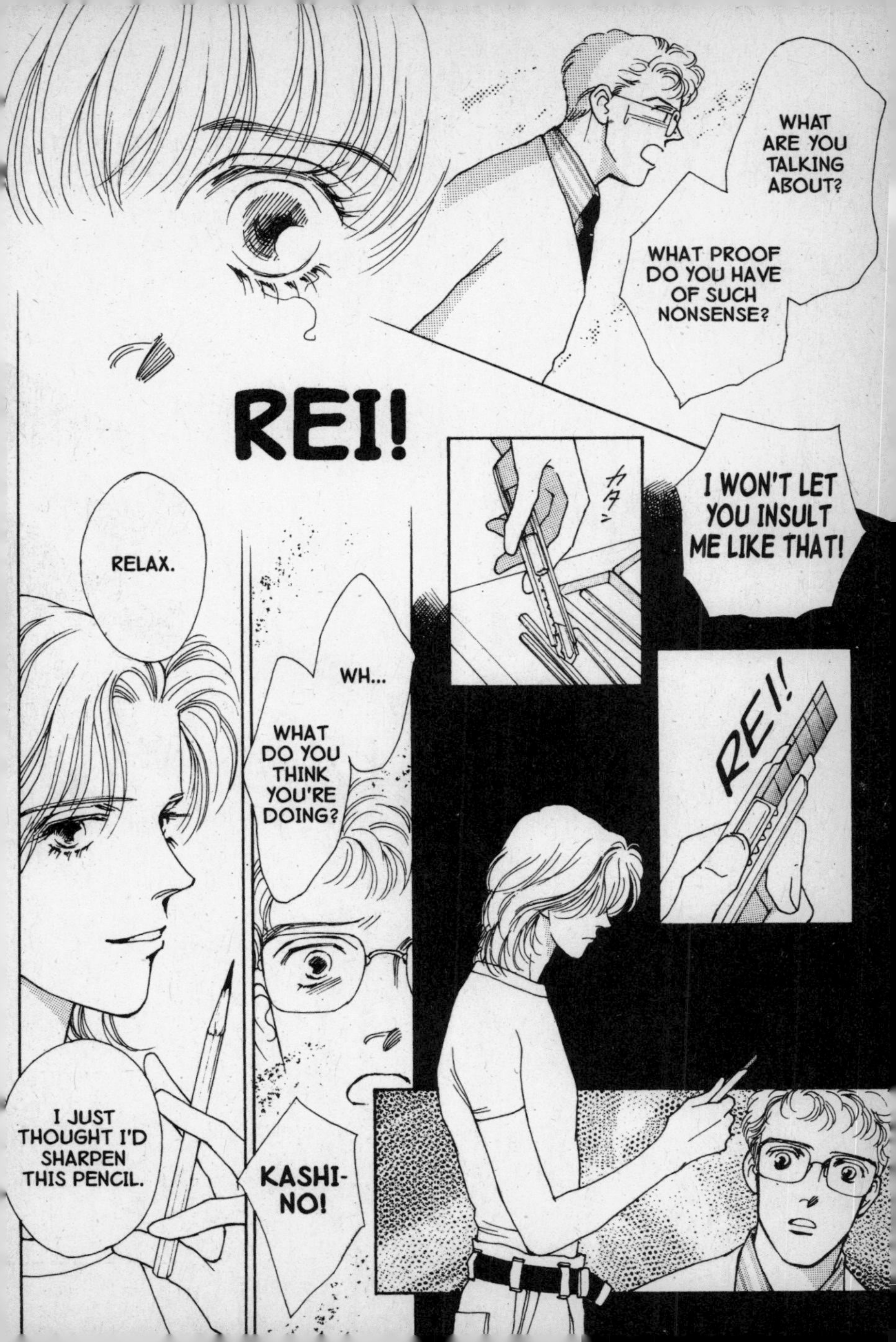
WHAT ARE YOU TALKING ABOUT?
WHAT PROOF DO YOU HAVE OF SUCH NONSENSE?
REI!
I WON'T LET YOU INSULT ME LIKE THAT!
カタン
REI!
WH...
WHAT DO YOU THINK YOU'RE DOING?
KASHI-NO!
RELAX.
I JUST THOUGHT I'D SHARPEN THIS PENCIL.

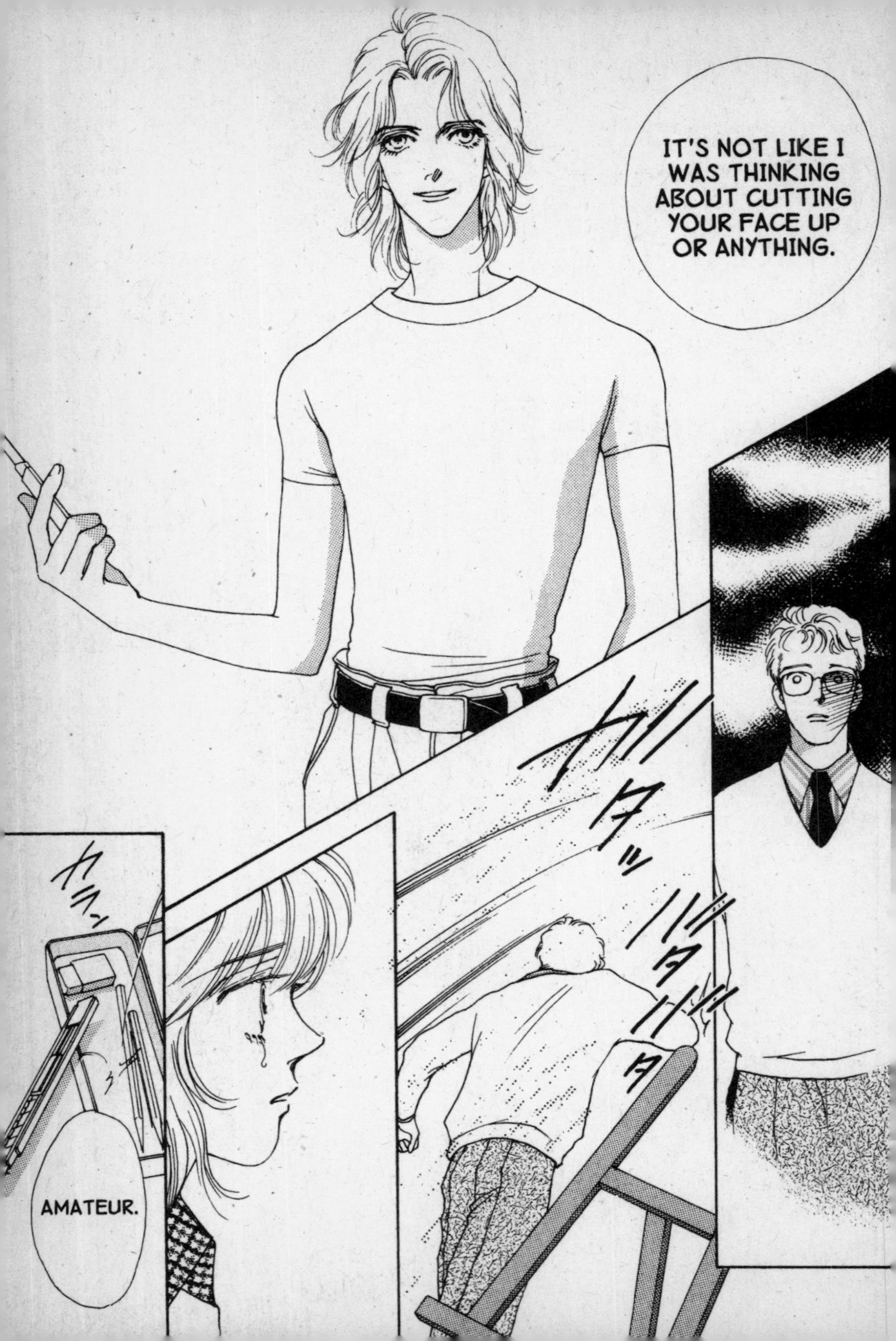
IT'S NOT LIKE I WAS THINKING ABOUT CUTTING YOUR FACE UP OR ANYTHING.
ガタッ
バタバタ
カラン
AMATEUR.

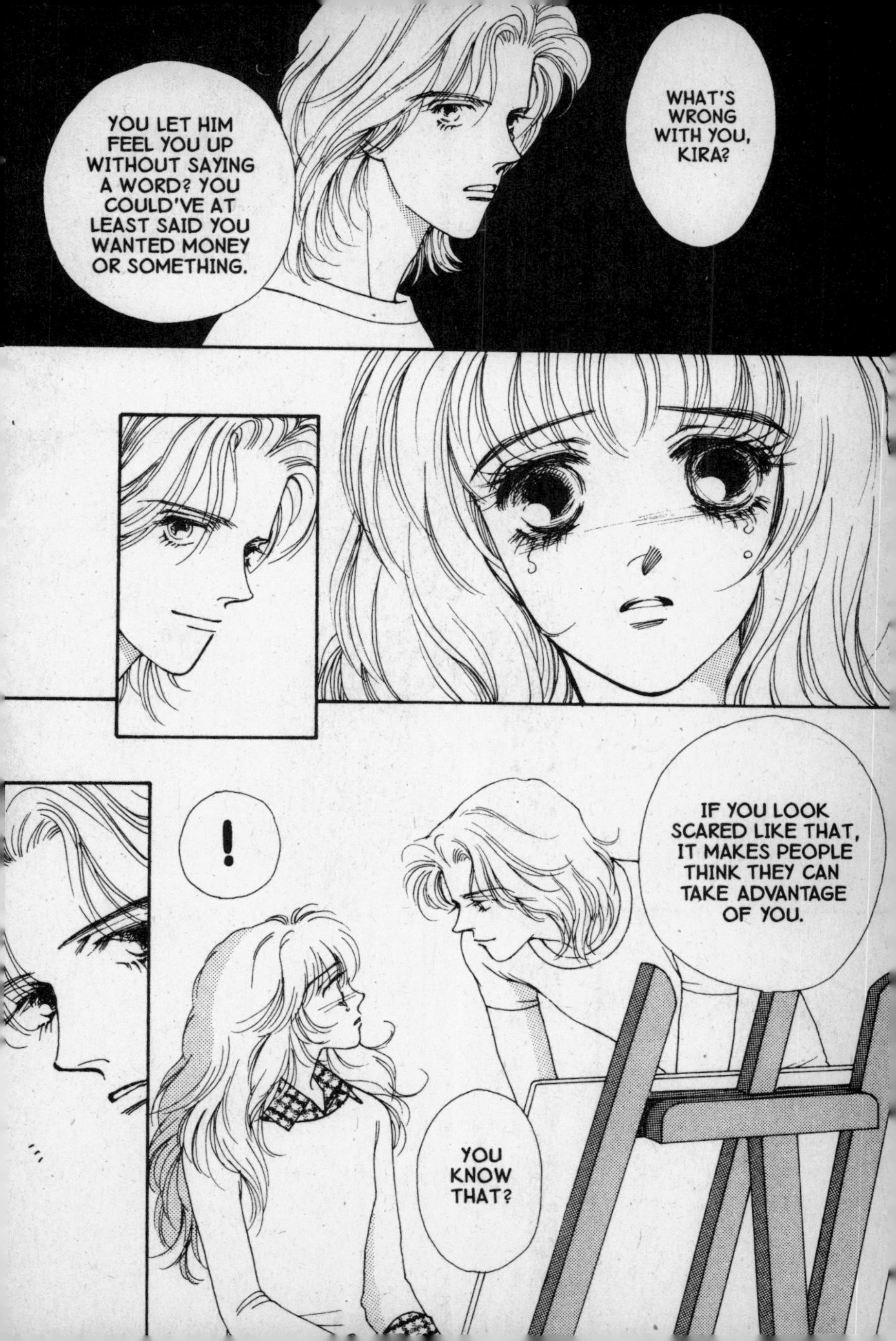
WHAT'S WRONG WITH YOU, KIRA?
YOU LET HIM FEEL YOU UP WITHOUT SAYING A WORD? YOU COULD'VE AT LEAST SAID YOU WANTED MONEY OR SOMETHING.
IF YOU LOOK SCARED LIKE THAT, IT MAKES PEOPLE THINK THEY CAN TAKE ADVANTAGE OF YOU.
YOU KNOW THAT?
!
...

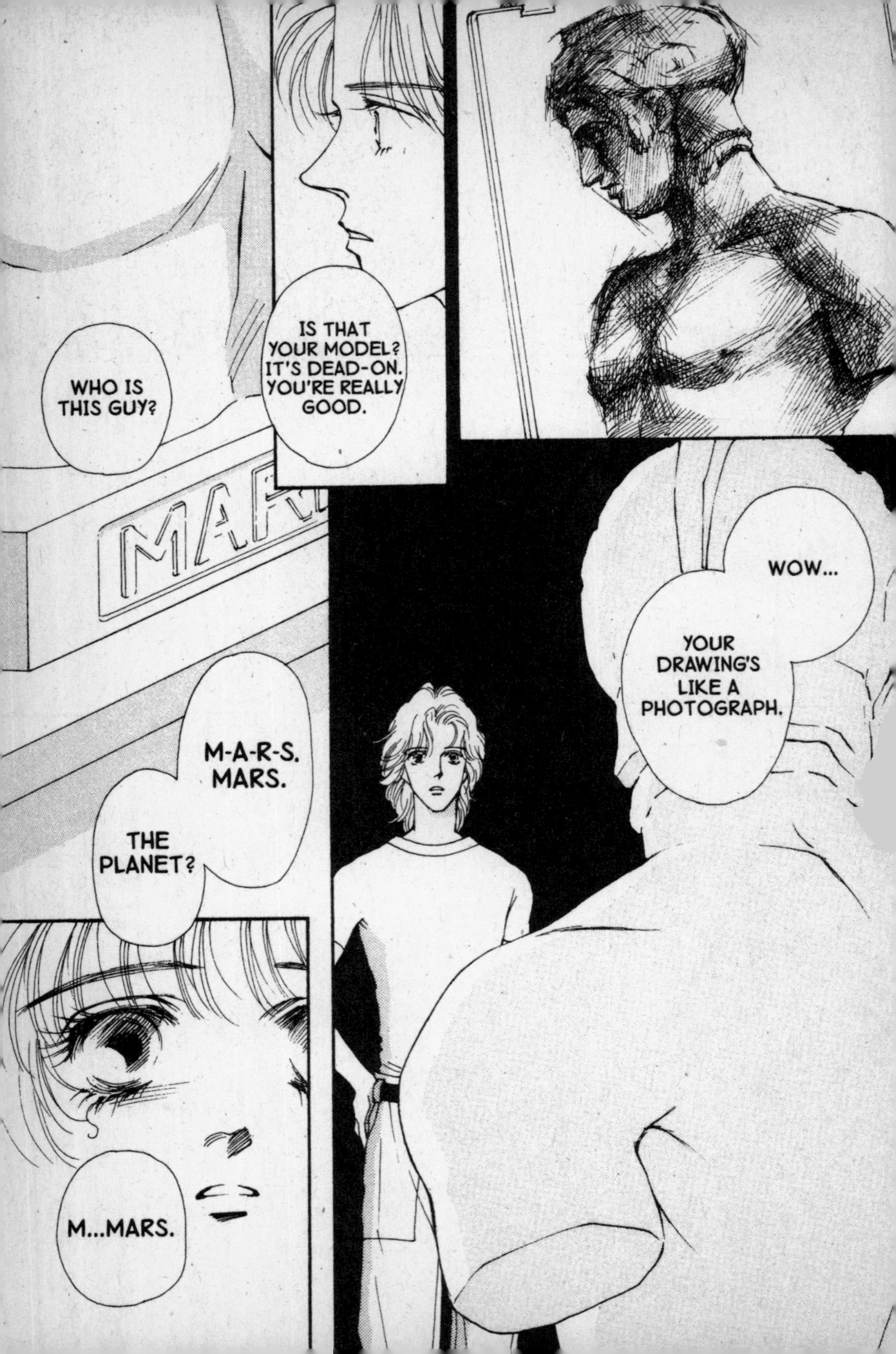
IS THAT YOUR MODEL? IT'S DEAD-ON. YOU'RE REALLY GOOD.
WHO IS THIS GUY?
WOW...
YOUR DRAWING'S LIKE A PHOTOGRAPH.
MAR
M-A-R-S. MARS.
THE PLANET?
M...MARS.

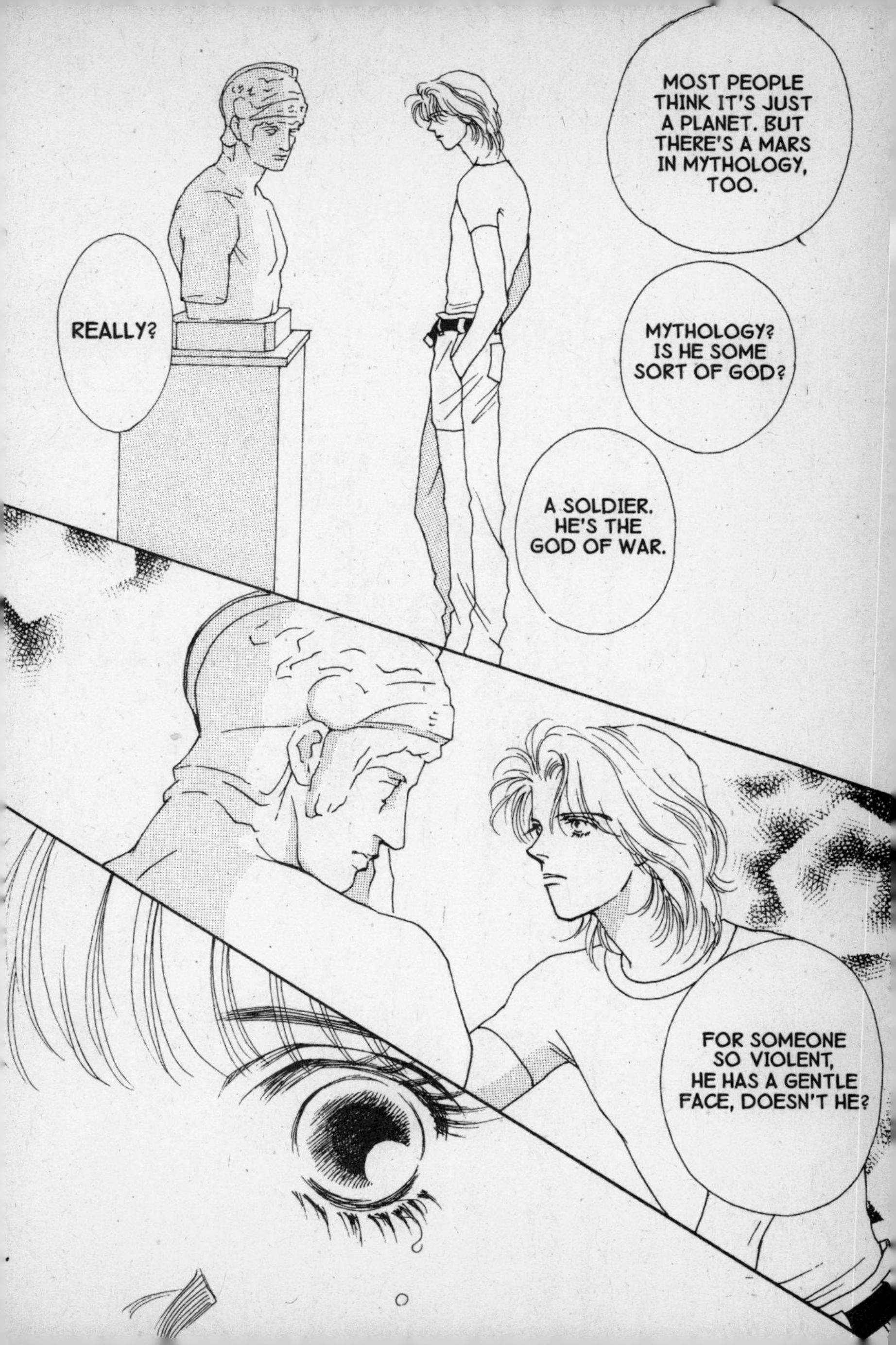
MOST PEOPLE THINK IT'S JUST A PLANET. BUT THERE'S A MARS IN MYTHOLOGY, TOO.
REALLY?
MYTHOLOGY? IS HE SOME SORT OF GOD?
A SOLDIER. HE'S THE GOD OF WAR.
FOR SOMEONE SO VIOLENT, HE HAS A GENTLE FACE, DOESN'T HE?

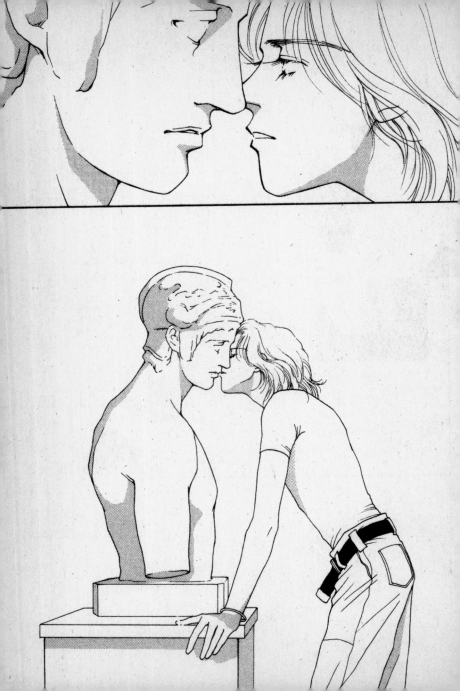

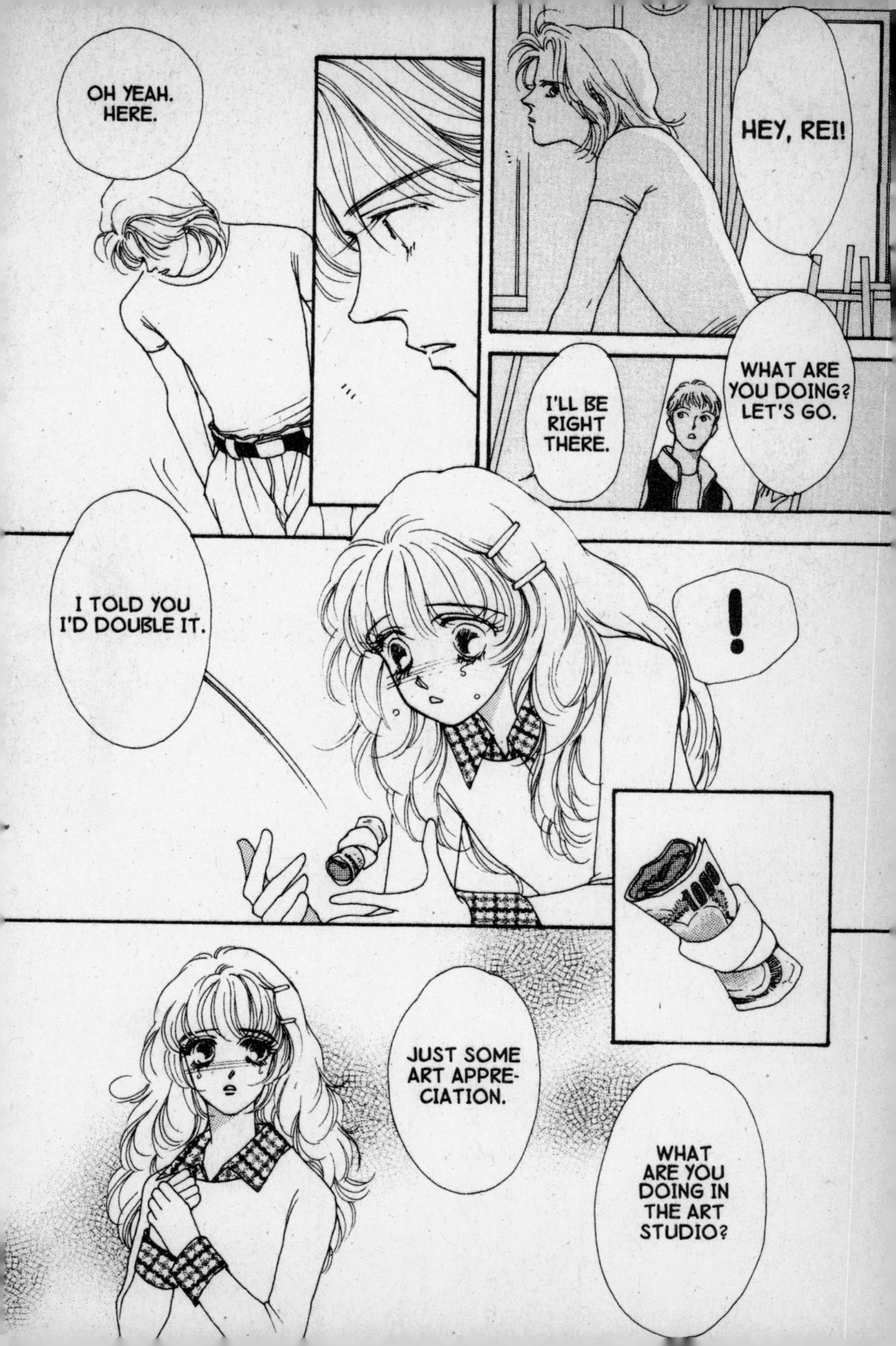
HEY, REI!
WHAT ARE YOU DOING? LET'S GO.
I'LL BE RIGHT THERE.
OH YEAH. HERE.
!
I TOLD YOU I'D DOUBLE IT.
WHAT ARE YOU DOING IN THE ART STUDIO?
JUST SOME ART APPRECIATION.

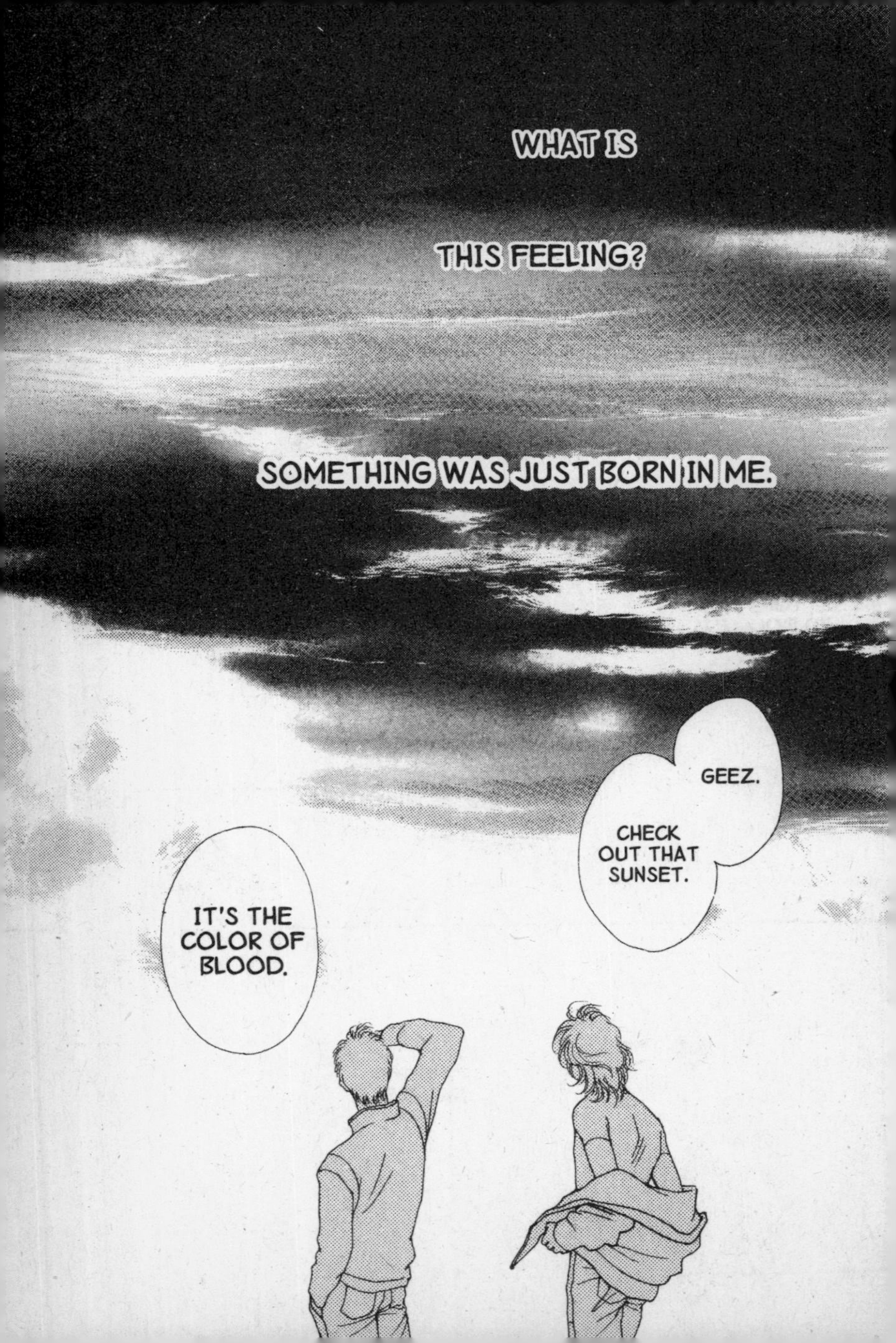
WHAT IS
THIS FEELING?
SOMETHING WAS JUST BORN IN ME.
GEEZ. CHECK OUT THAT SUNSET.
IT'S THE COLOR OF BLOOD.

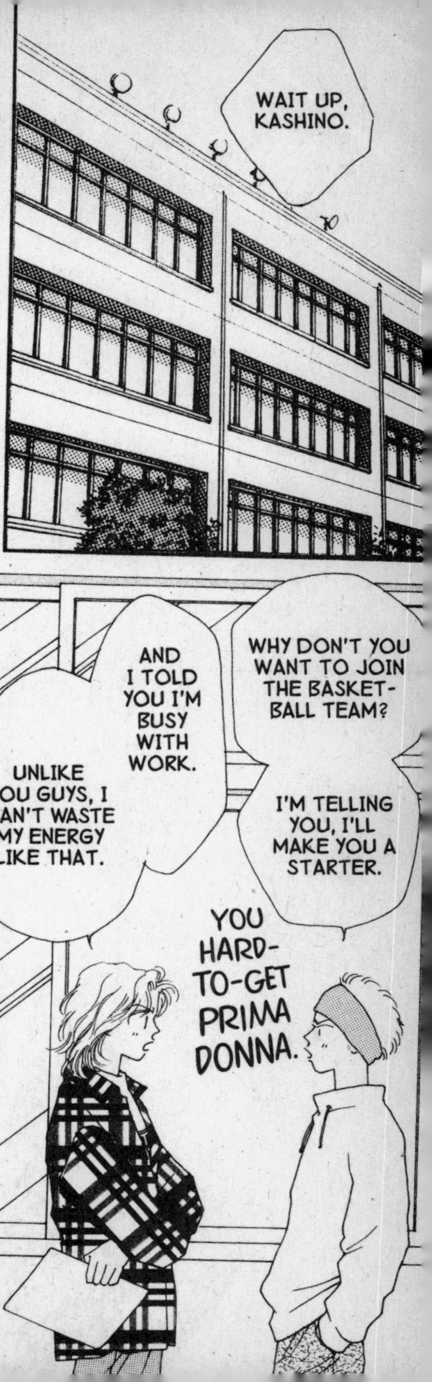
WAIT UP, KASHINO.
WHY DON'T YOU WANT TO JOIN THE BASKET-BALL TEAM?
I'M TELLING YOU, I'LL MAKE YOU A STARTER.
AND I TOLD YOU I'M BUSY WITH WORK.
UNLIKE YOU GUYS, I CAN'T WASTE MY ENERGY LIKE THAT.
YOU HARD-TO-GET PRIMA DONNA.
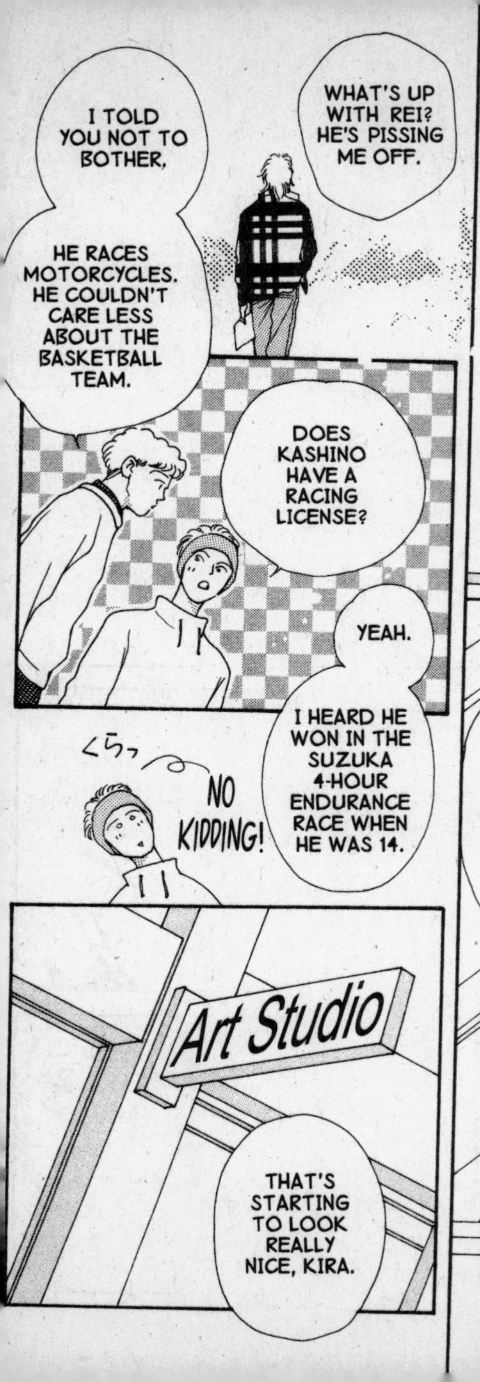
WHAT'S UP WITH REI? HE'S PISSING ME OFF.
I TOLD YOU NOT TO BOTHER.
HE RACES MOTORCYCLES. HE COULDN'T CARE LESS ABOUT THE BASKETBALL TEAM.
DOES KASHINO HAVE A RACING LICENSE?
YEAH.
I HEARD HE WON IN THE SUZUKA 4-HOUR ENDURANCE RACE WHEN HE WAS 14.
くらっ
NO KIDDING!
Art Studio
THAT'S STARTING TO LOOK REALLY NICE, KIRA.

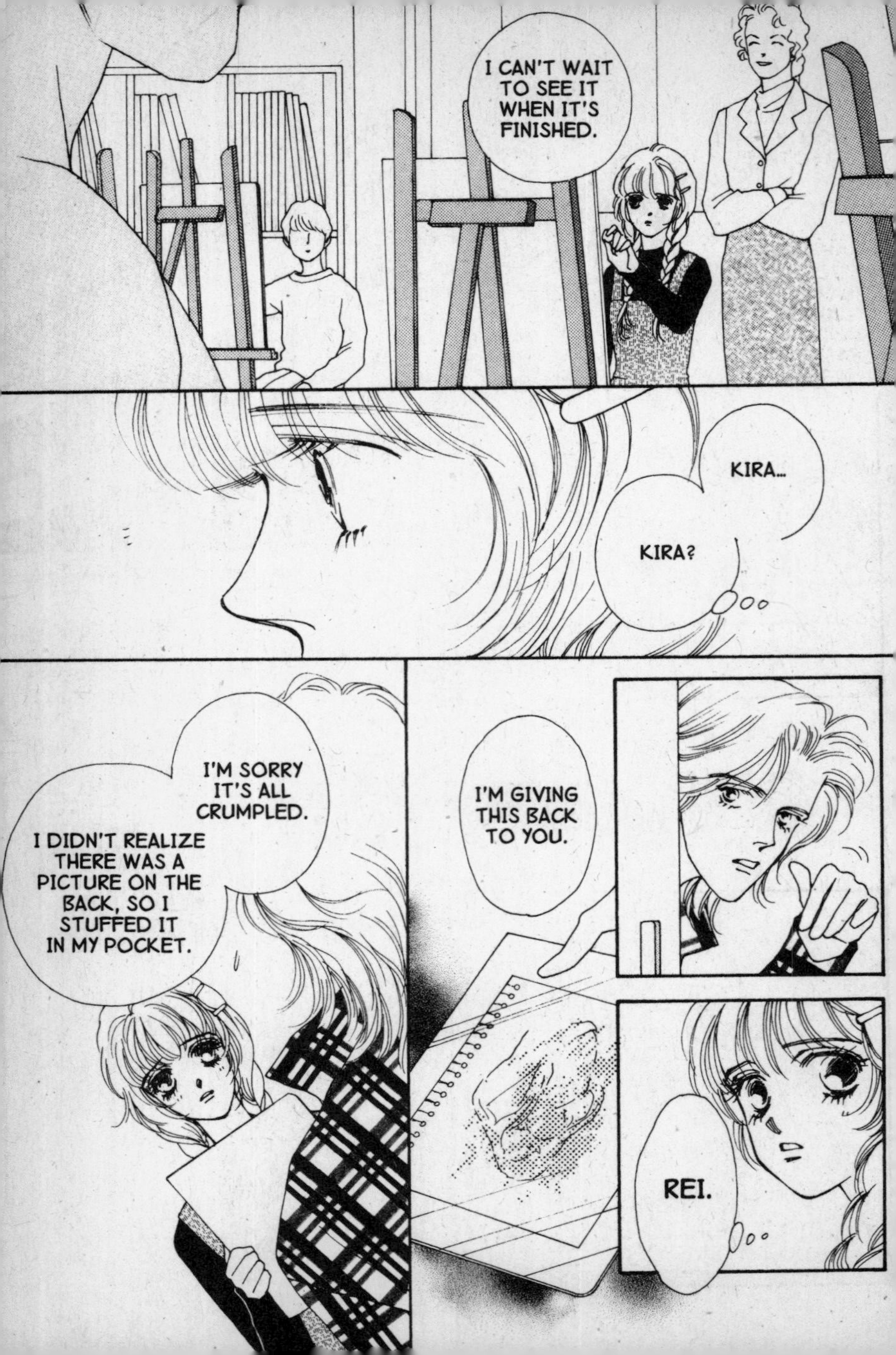
I CAN'T WAIT TO SEE IT WHEN IT'S FINISHED.
KIRA...
KIRA?
REI.
I'M GIVING THIS BACK TO YOU.
I'M SORRY IT'S ALL CRUMPLED.
I DIDN'T REALIZE THERE WAS A PICTURE ON THE BACK, SO I STUFFED IT IN MY POCKET.

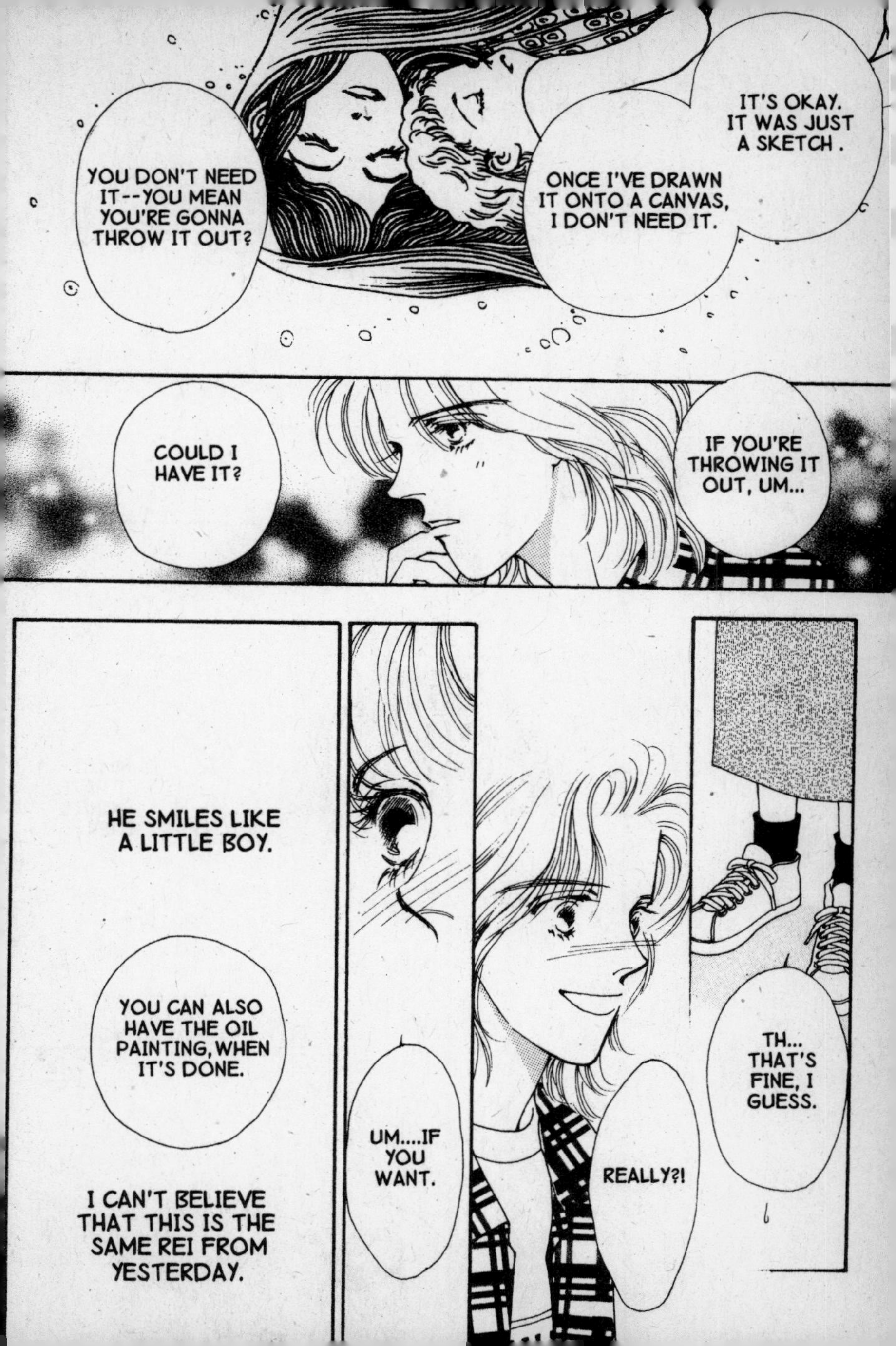
IT'S OKAY. IT WAS JUST A SKETCH .
ONCE I'VE DRAWN IT ONTO A CANVAS, I DON'T NEED IT.
YOU DON'T NEED IT--YOU MEAN YOU'RE GONNA THROW IT OUT?
IF YOU'RE THROWING IT OUT, UM...
COULD I HAVE IT?
TH... THAT'S FINE, I GUESS.
REALLY?!
UM....IF YOU WANT.
HE SMILES LIKE A LITTLE BOY.
YOU CAN ALSO HAVE THE OIL PAINTING, WHEN IT'S DONE.
I CAN'T BELIEVE THAT THIS IS THE SAME REI FROM YESTERDAY.

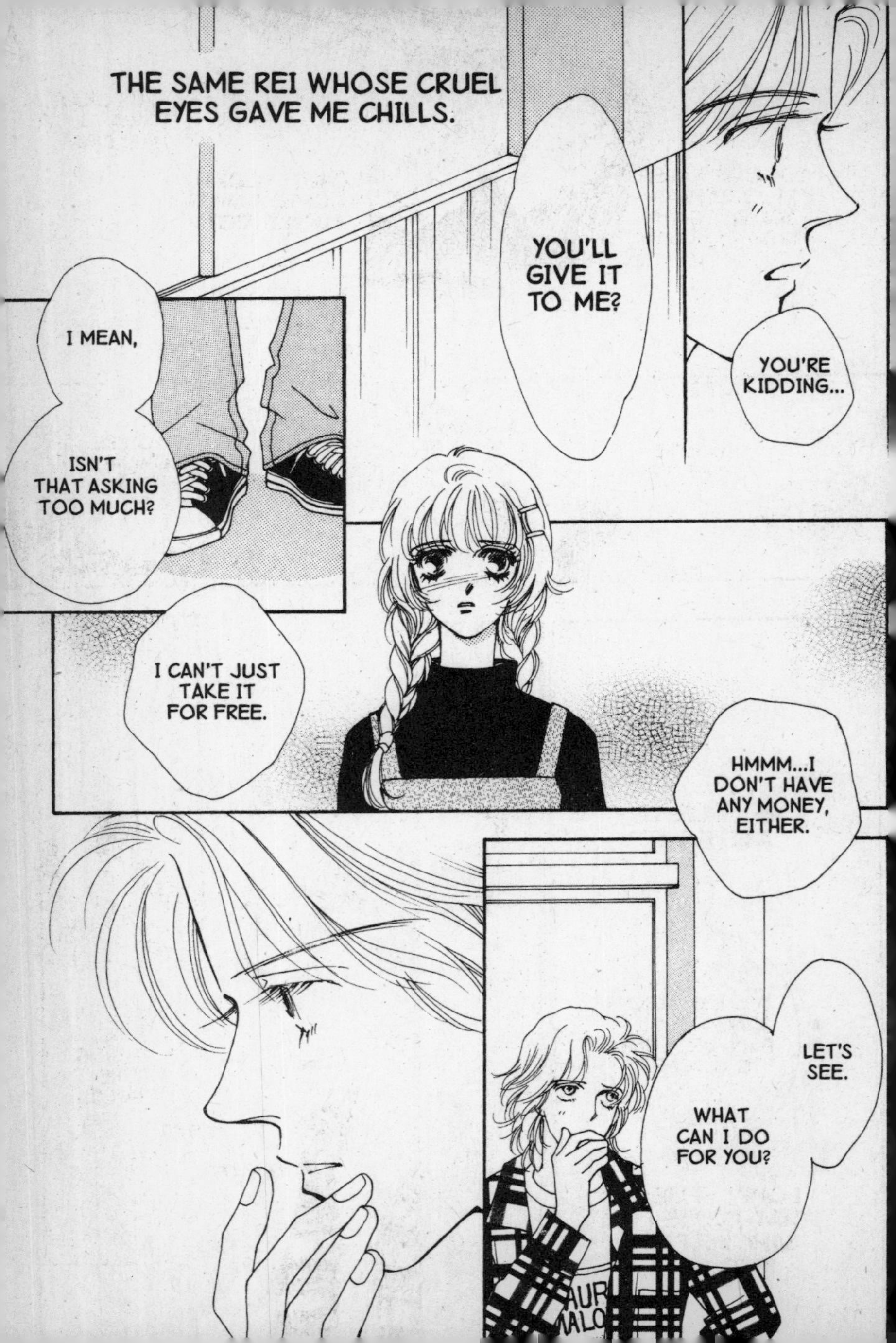
THE SAME REI WHOSE CRUEL EYES GAVE ME CHILLS.
YOU'RE KIDDING...
YOU'LL GIVE IT TO ME?
I MEAN,
ISN'T THAT ASKING TOO MUCH?
I CAN'T JUST TAKE IT FOR FREE.
HMMM...I DON'T HAVE ANY MONEY, EITHER.
LET'S SEE.
WHAT CAN I DO FOR YOU?

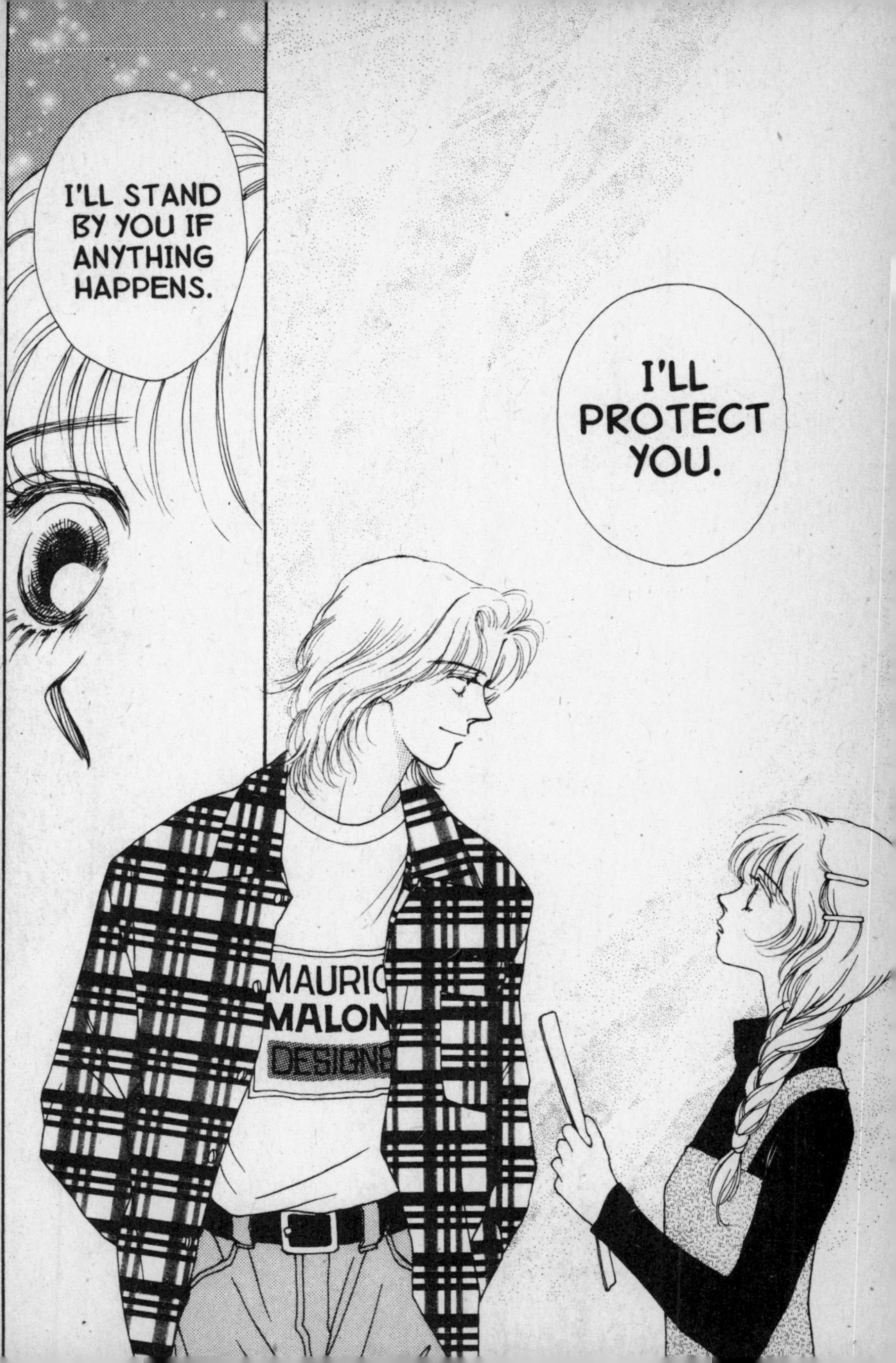
I'LL PROTECT YOU.
MAURIC
MALON
DESIGN
I'LL STAND BY YOU IF ANYTHING HAPPENS.

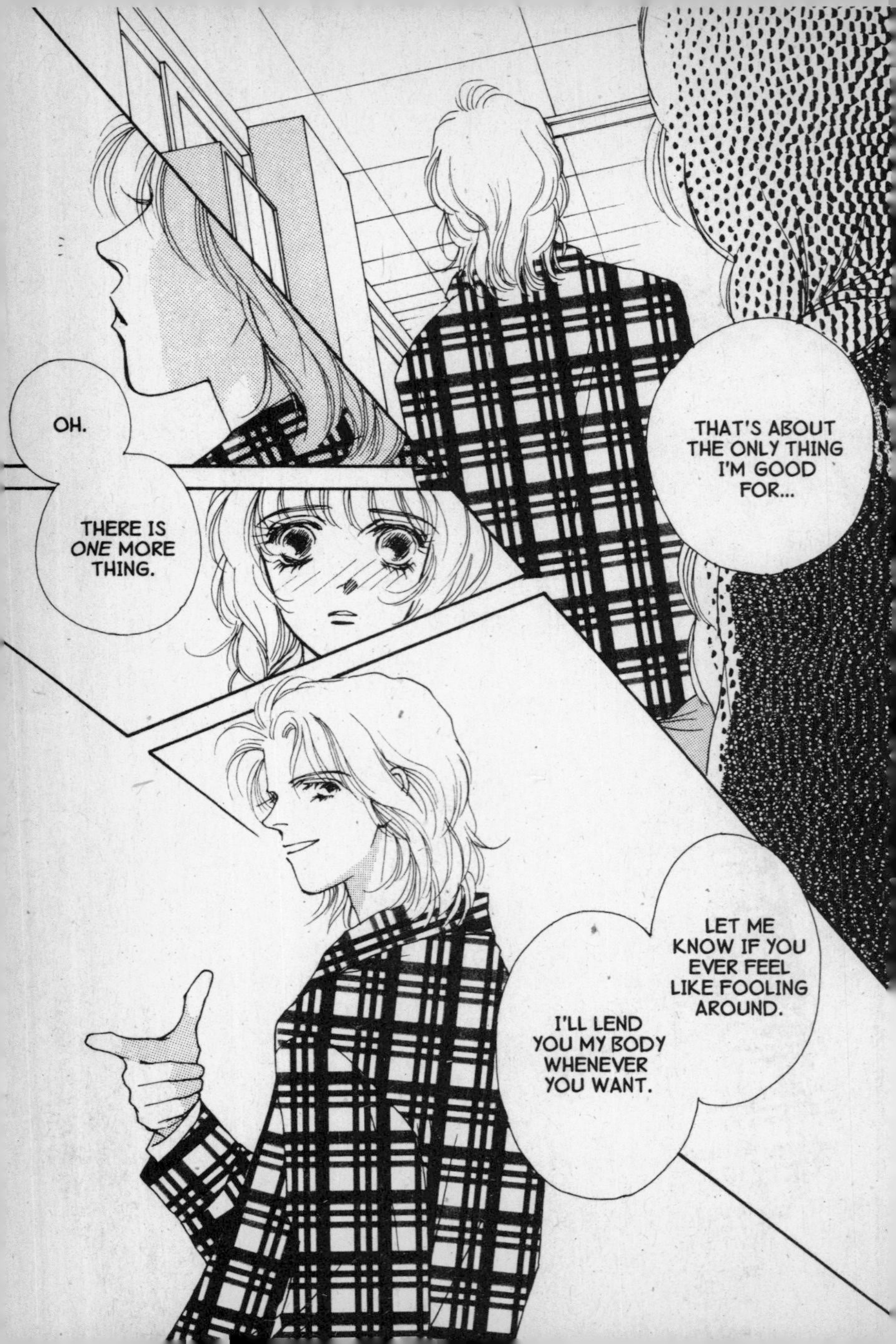
THAT'S ABOUT THE ONLY THING I'M GOOD FOR...
OH.
THERE IS *ONE* MORE THING.
LET ME KNOW IF YOU EVER FEEL LIKE FOOLING AROUND.
I'LL LEND YOU MY BODY WHENEVER YOU WANT.

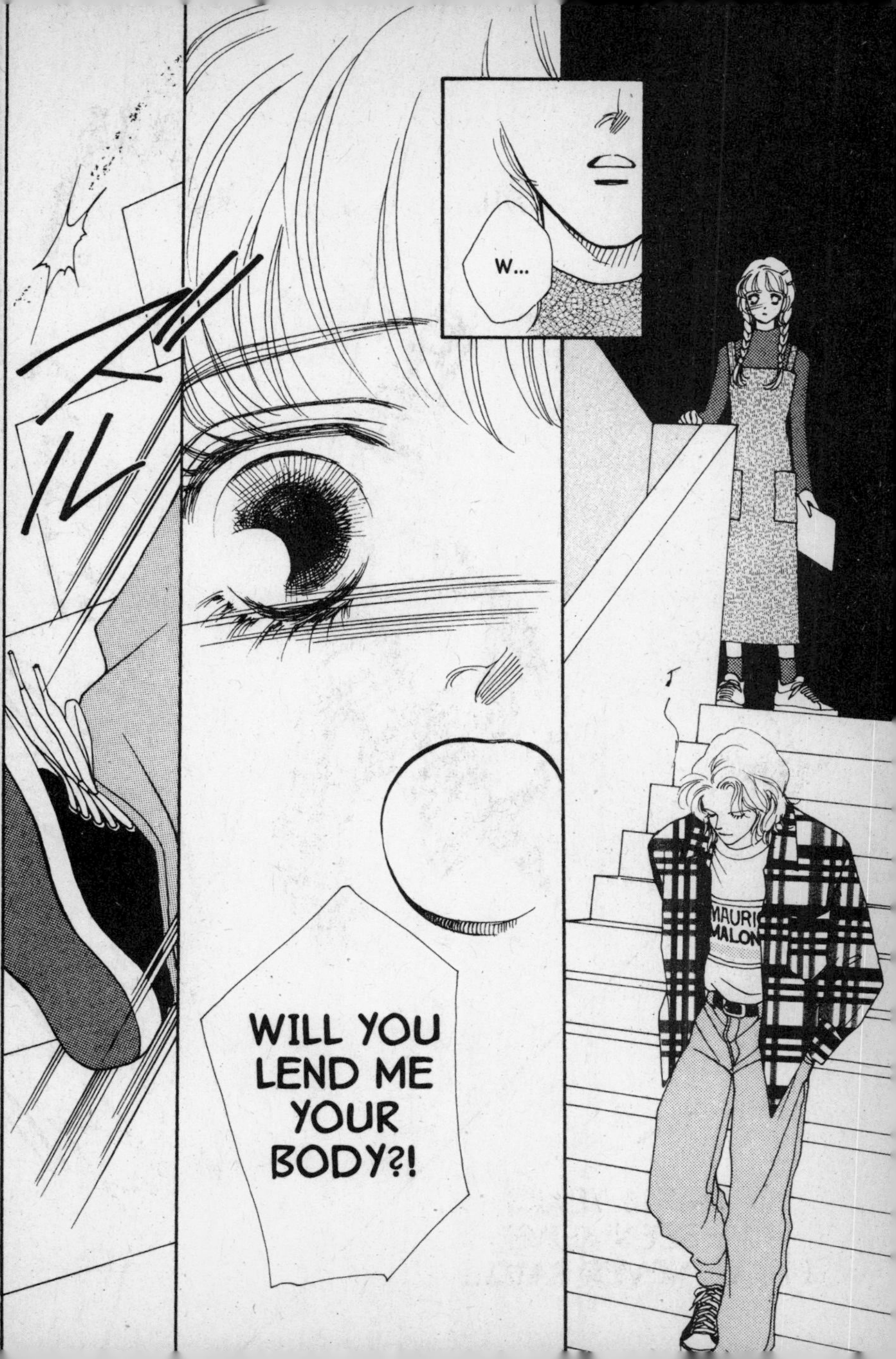
W...
WILL YOU LEND ME YOUR BODY?!

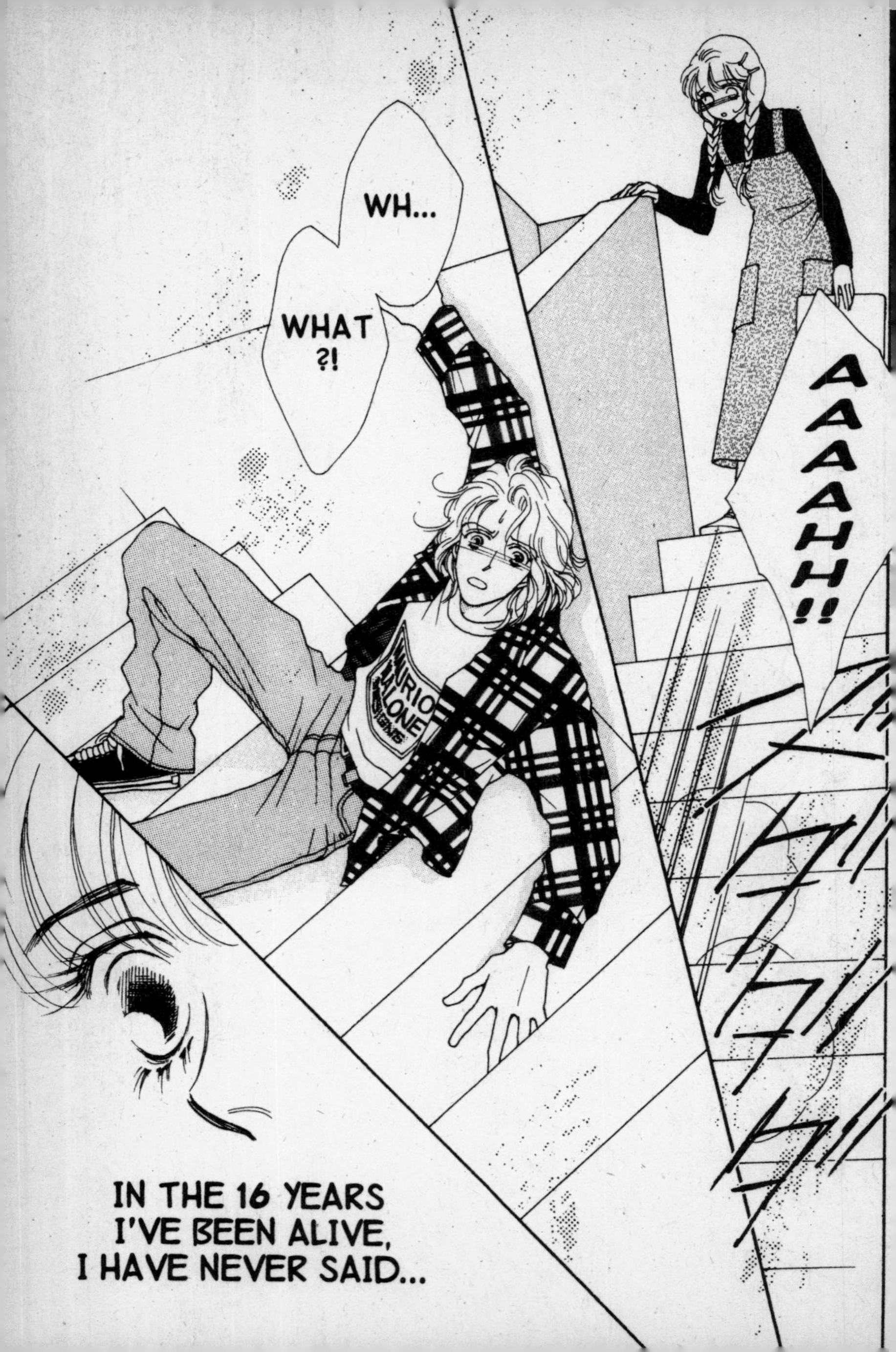
AAAAHH!!
WH...
WHAT?!
IN THE 16 YEARS I'VE BEEN ALIVE, I HAVE NEVER SAID...

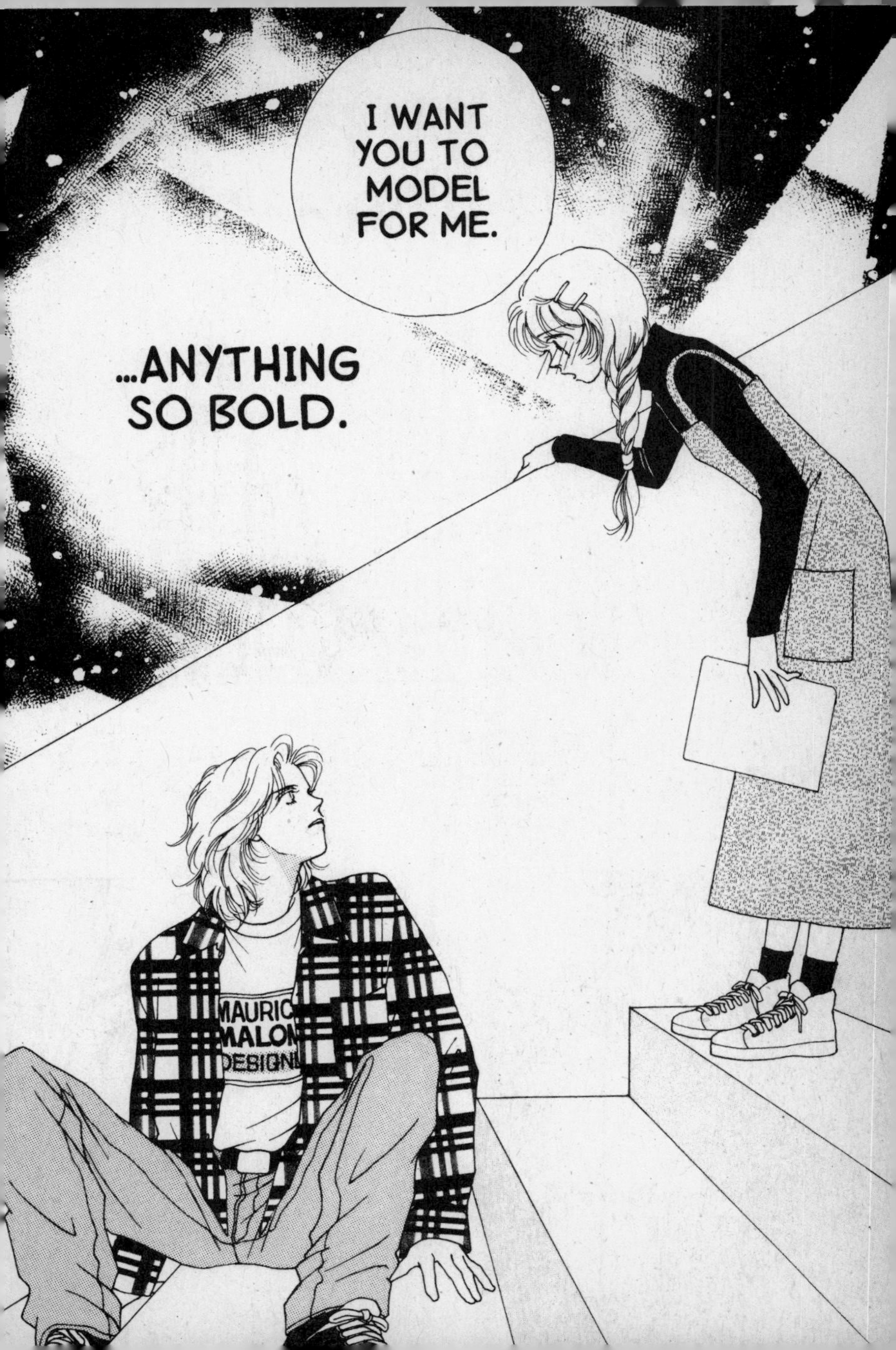
I WANT YOU TO MODEL FOR ME.
...ANYTHING SO BOLD.
MAURIC
MALON
DESIGN

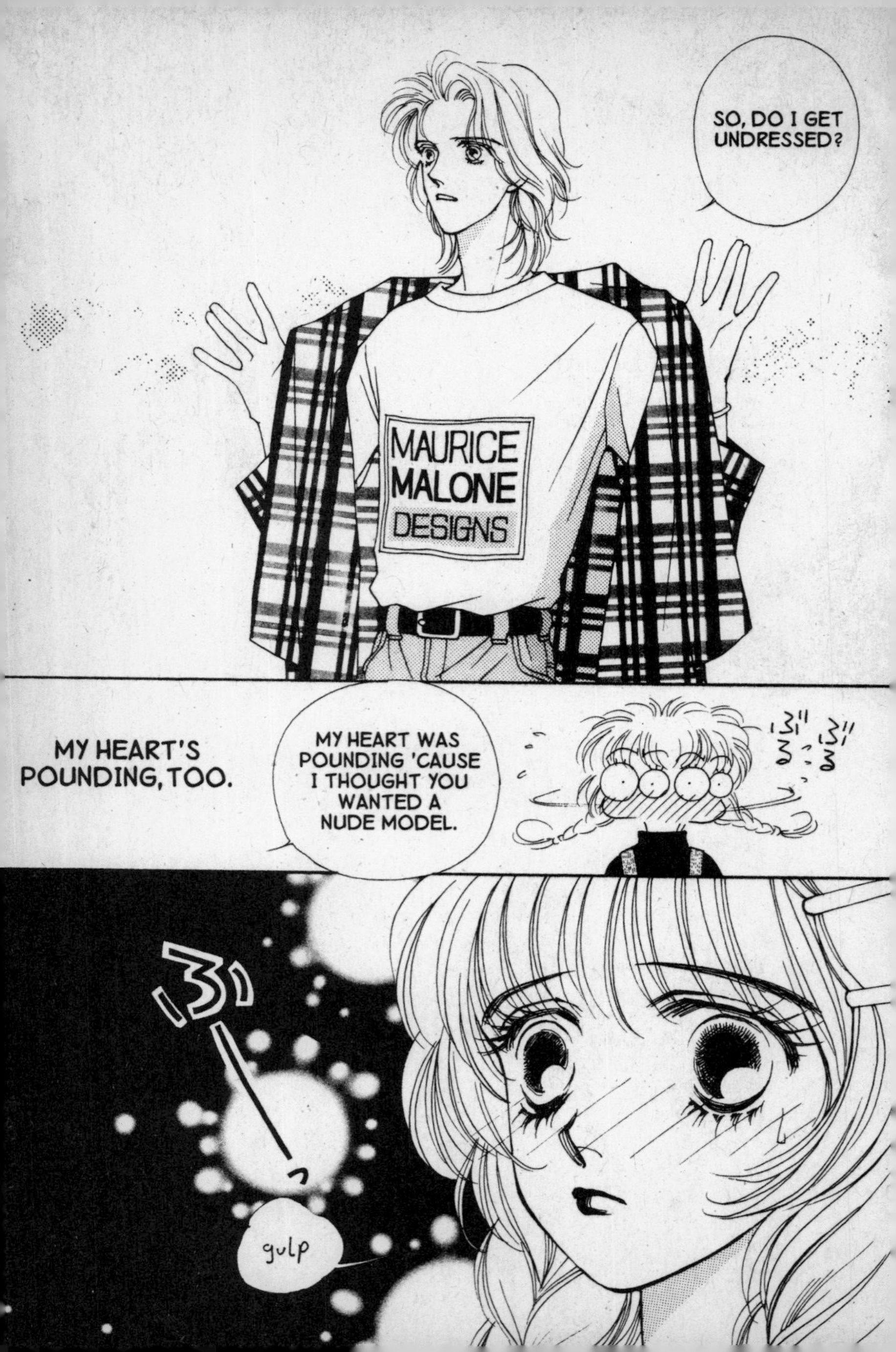
SO, DO I GET UNDRESSED?
MAURICE MALONE DESIGNS
MY HEART WAS POUNDING 'CAUSE I THOUGHT YOU WANTED A NUDE MODEL.
MY HEART'S POUNDING, TOO.
gulp

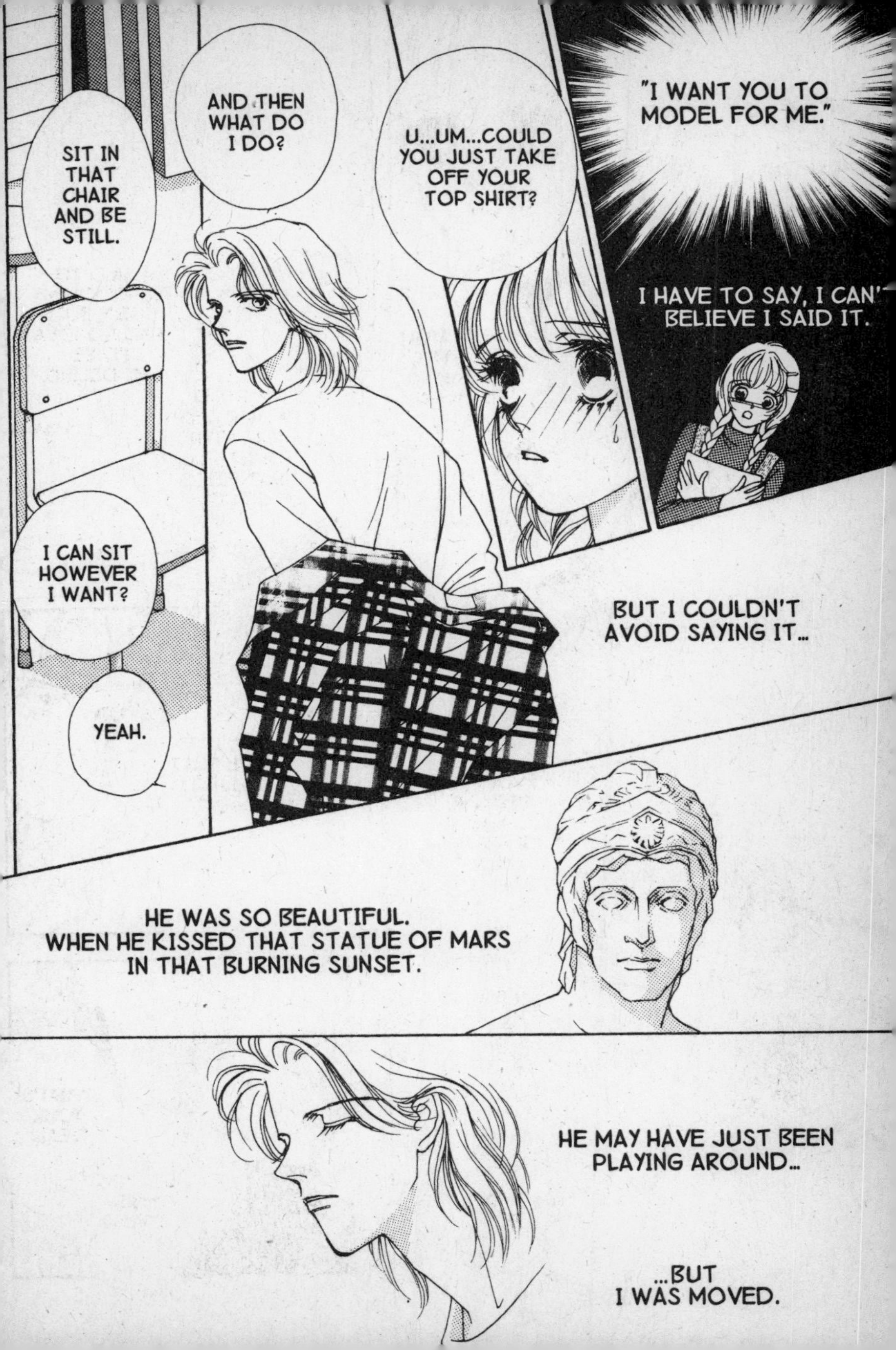
"I WANT YOU TO MODEL FOR ME."
I HAVE TO SAY, I CAN'T BELIEVE I SAID IT.
BUT I COULDN'T AVOID SAYING IT...
U...UM...COULD YOU JUST TAKE OFF YOUR TOP SHIRT?
AND THEN WHAT DO I DO?
SIT IN THAT CHAIR AND BE STILL.
I CAN SIT HOWEVER I WANT?
YEAH.
HE WAS SO BEAUTIFUL. WHEN HE KISSED THAT STATUE OF MARS IN THAT BURNING SUNSET.
HE MAY HAVE JUST BEEN PLAYING AROUND...
...BUT I WAS MOVED.

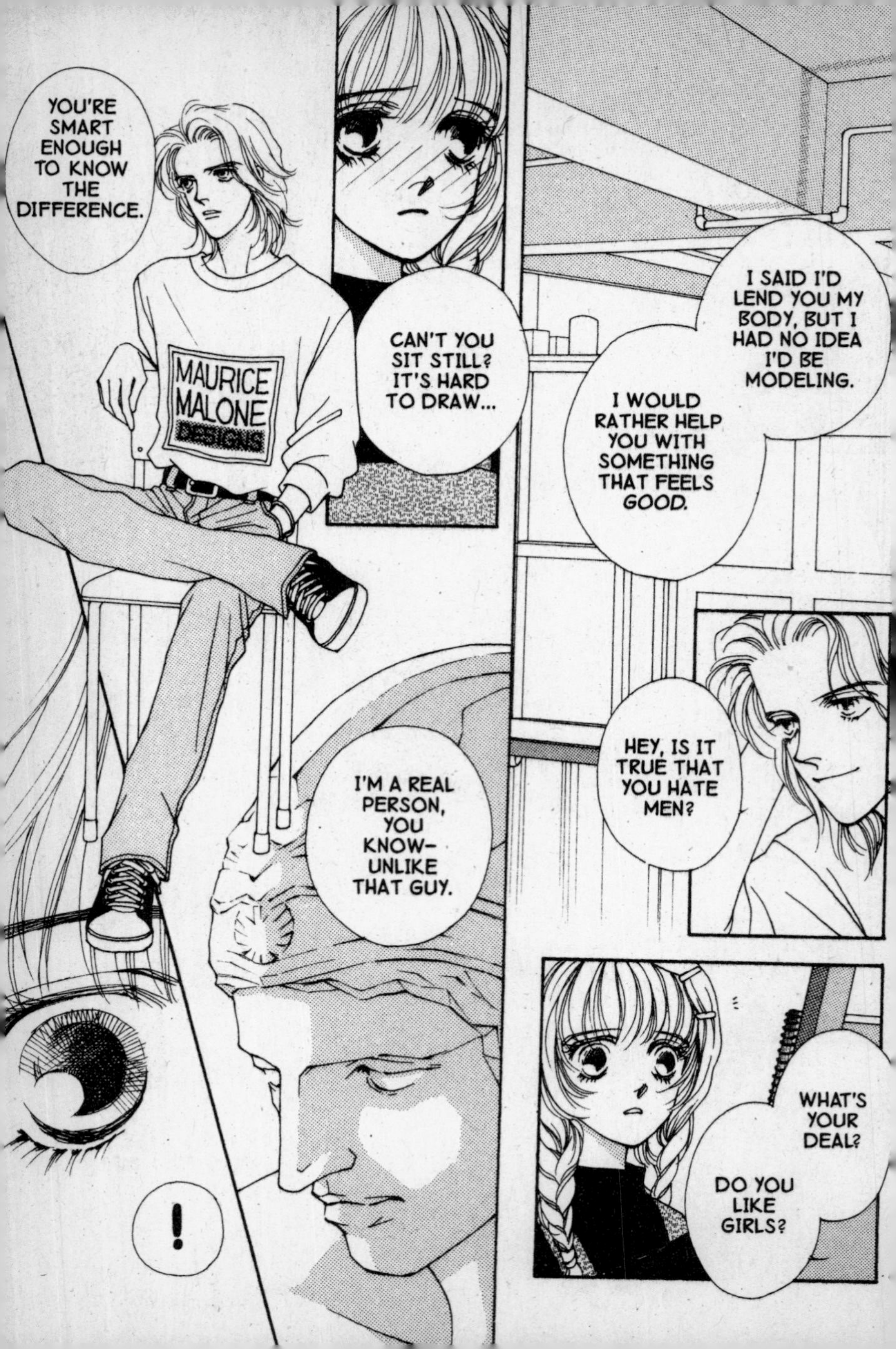
I SAID I'D LEND YOU MY BODY, BUT I HAD NO IDEA I'D BE MODELING.
I WOULD RATHER HELP YOU WITH SOMETHING THAT FEELS *GOOD.*
HEY, IS IT TRUE THAT YOU HATE MEN?
WHAT'S YOUR DEAL?
DO YOU LIKE GIRLS?
CAN'T YOU SIT STILL? IT'S HARD TO DRAW...
YOU'RE SMART ENOUGH TO KNOW THE DIFFERENCE.
MAURICE MALONE DESIGNS
I'M A REAL PERSON, YOU KNOW— UNLIKE THAT GUY.
!

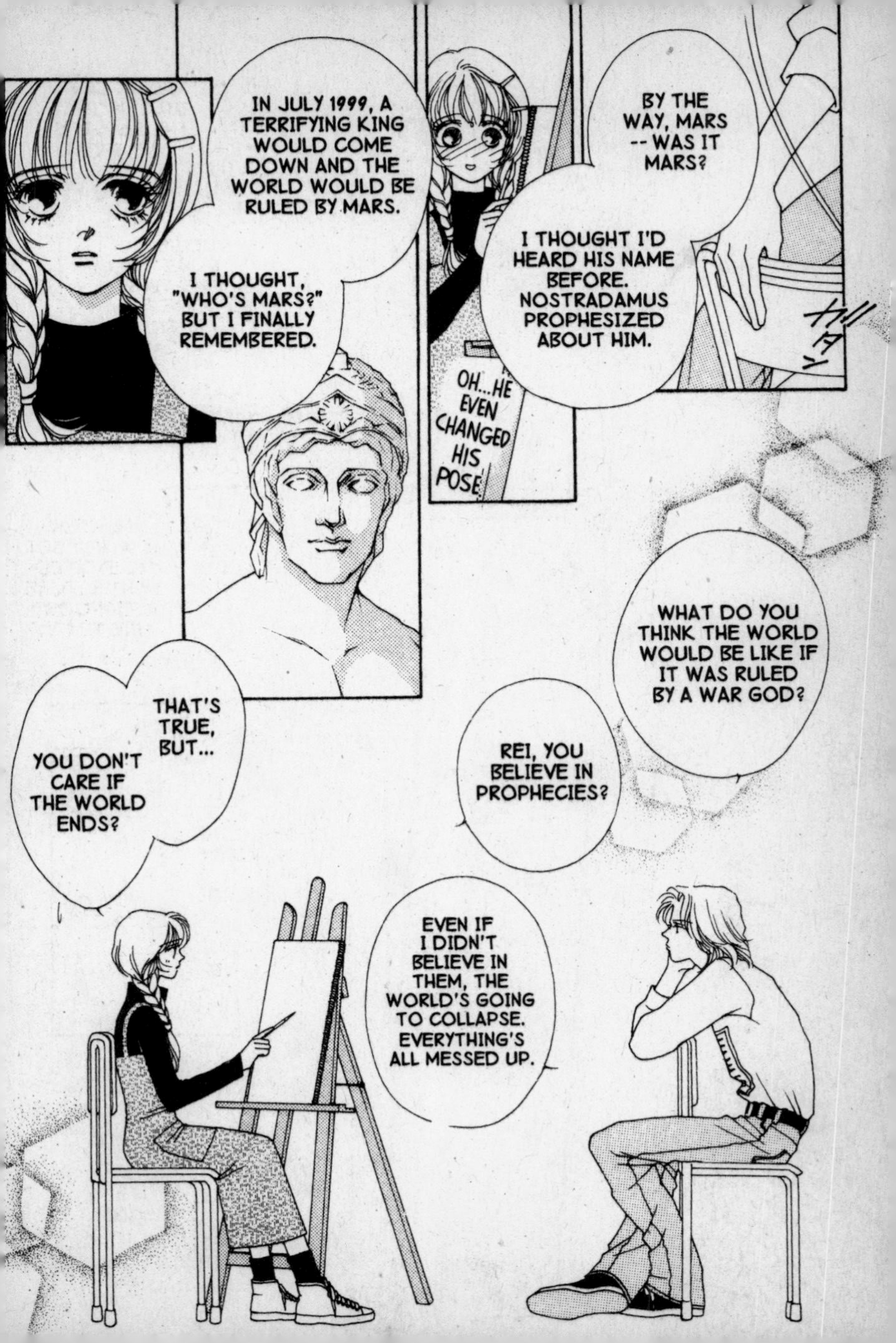
BY THE WAY, MARS -- WAS IT MARS?
I THOUGHT I'D HEARD HIS NAME BEFORE. NOSTRADAMUS PROPHESIZED ABOUT HIM.
OH...HE EVEN CHANGED HIS POSE
IN JULY 1999, A TERRIFYING KING WOULD COME DOWN AND THE WORLD WOULD BE RULED BY MARS.
I THOUGHT, "WHO'S MARS?" BUT I FINALLY REMEMBERED.
WHAT DO YOU THINK THE WORLD WOULD BE LIKE IF IT WAS RULED BY A WAR GOD?
REI, YOU BELIEVE IN PROPHECIES?
EVEN IF I DIDN'T BELIEVE IN THEM, THE WORLD'S GOING TO COLLAPSE. EVERYTHING'S ALL MESSED UP.
THAT'S TRUE, BUT...
YOU DON'T CARE IF THE WORLD ENDS?

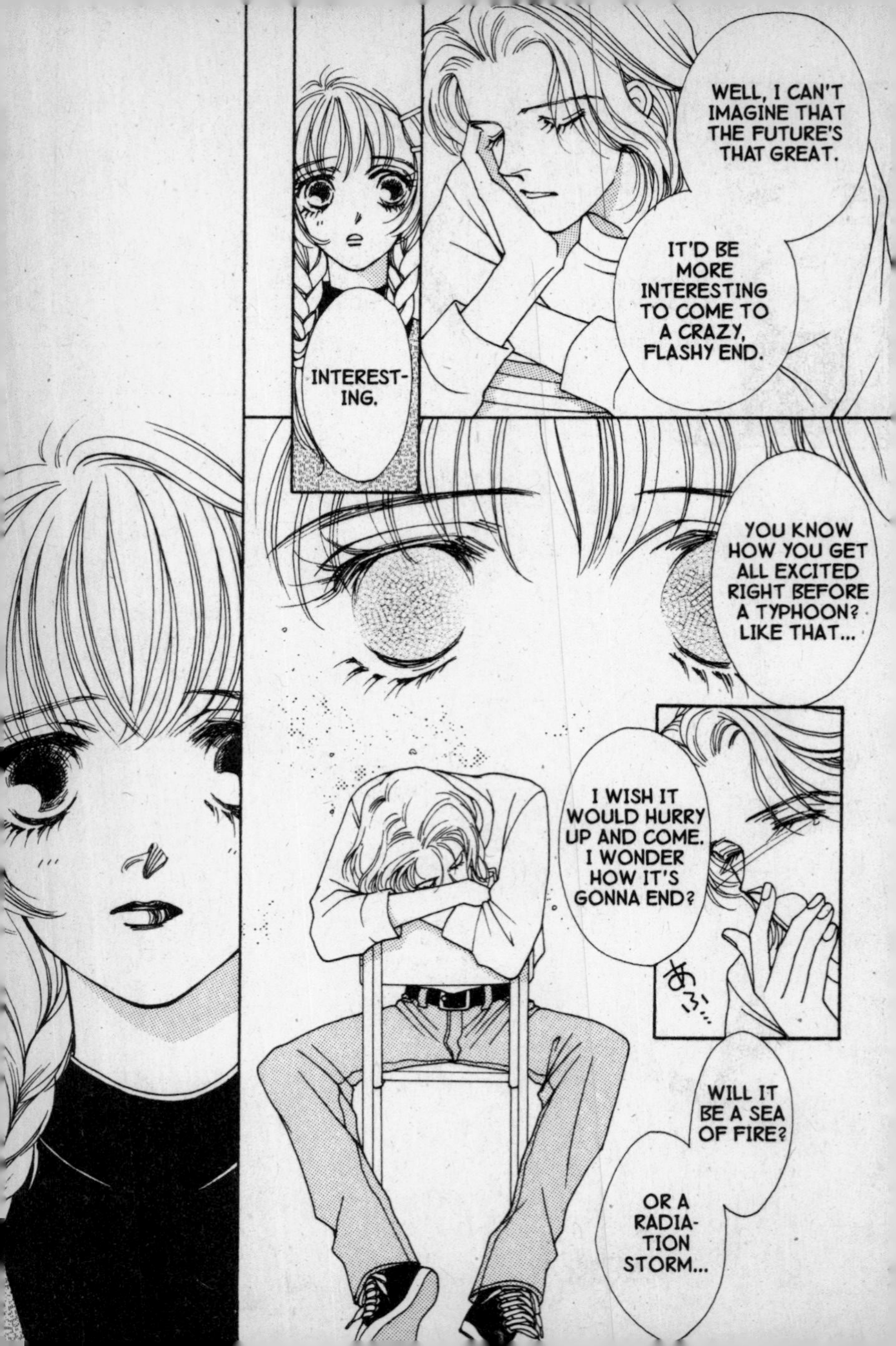
WELL, I CAN'T IMAGINE THAT THE FUTURE'S THAT GREAT.
IT'D BE MORE INTERESTING TO COME TO A CRAZY, FLASHY END.
INTEREST-ING.
YOU KNOW HOW YOU GET ALL EXCITED RIGHT BEFORE A TYPHOON? LIKE THAT...
I WISH IT WOULD HURRY UP AND COME. I WONDER HOW IT'S GONNA END?
あふ…
WILL IT BE A SEA OF FIRE?
OR A RADIATION STORM...

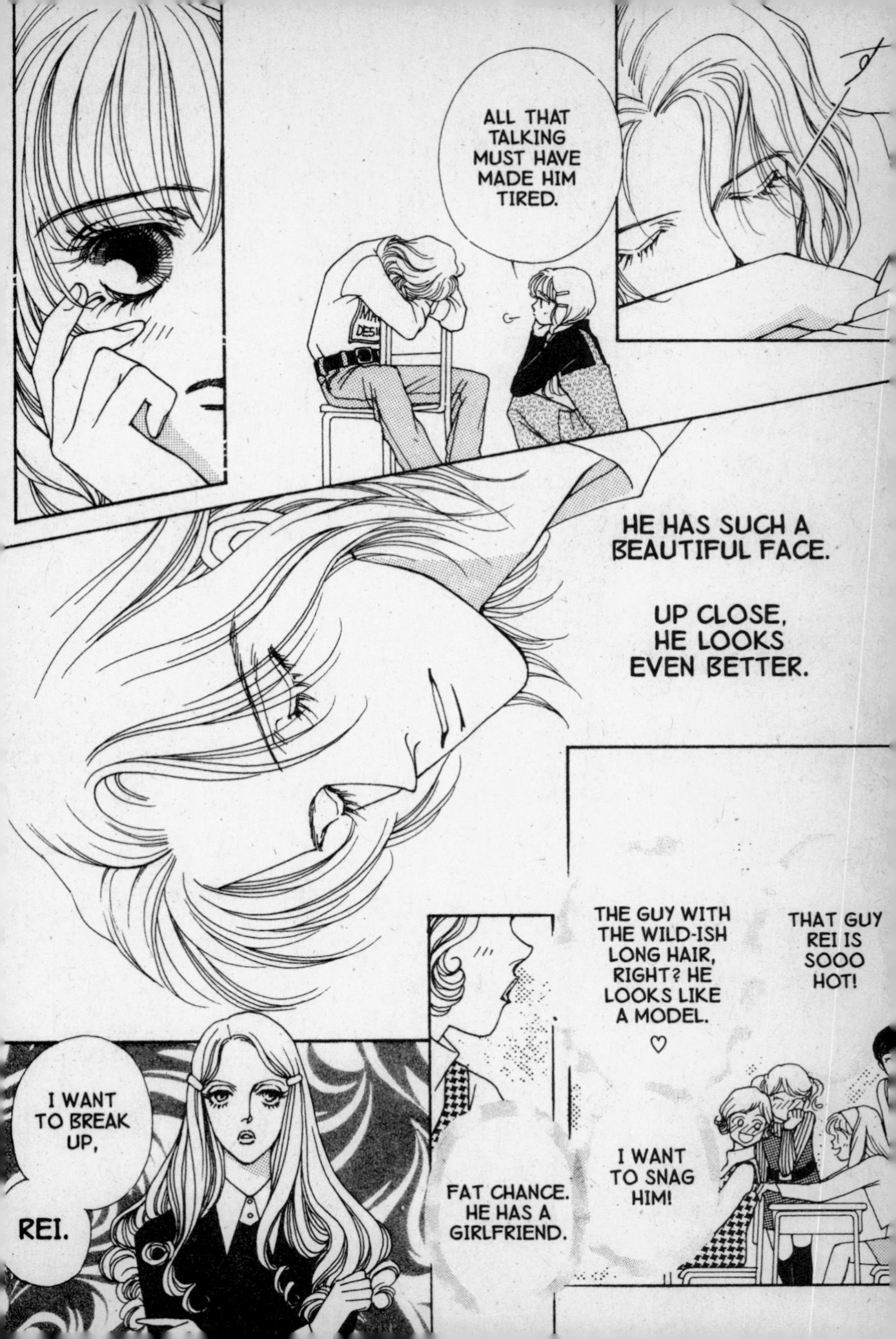
ALL THAT TALKING MUST HAVE MADE HIM TIRED.
HE HAS SUCH A BEAUTIFUL FACE.
UP CLOSE, HE LOOKS EVEN BETTER.
THAT GUY REI IS SOOO HOT!
THE GUY WITH THE WILD-ISH LONG HAIR, RIGHT? HE LOOKS LIKE A MODEL. ♡
I WANT TO SNAG HIM!
FAT CHANCE. HE HAS A GIRLFRIEND.
I WANT TO BREAK UP,
REI.

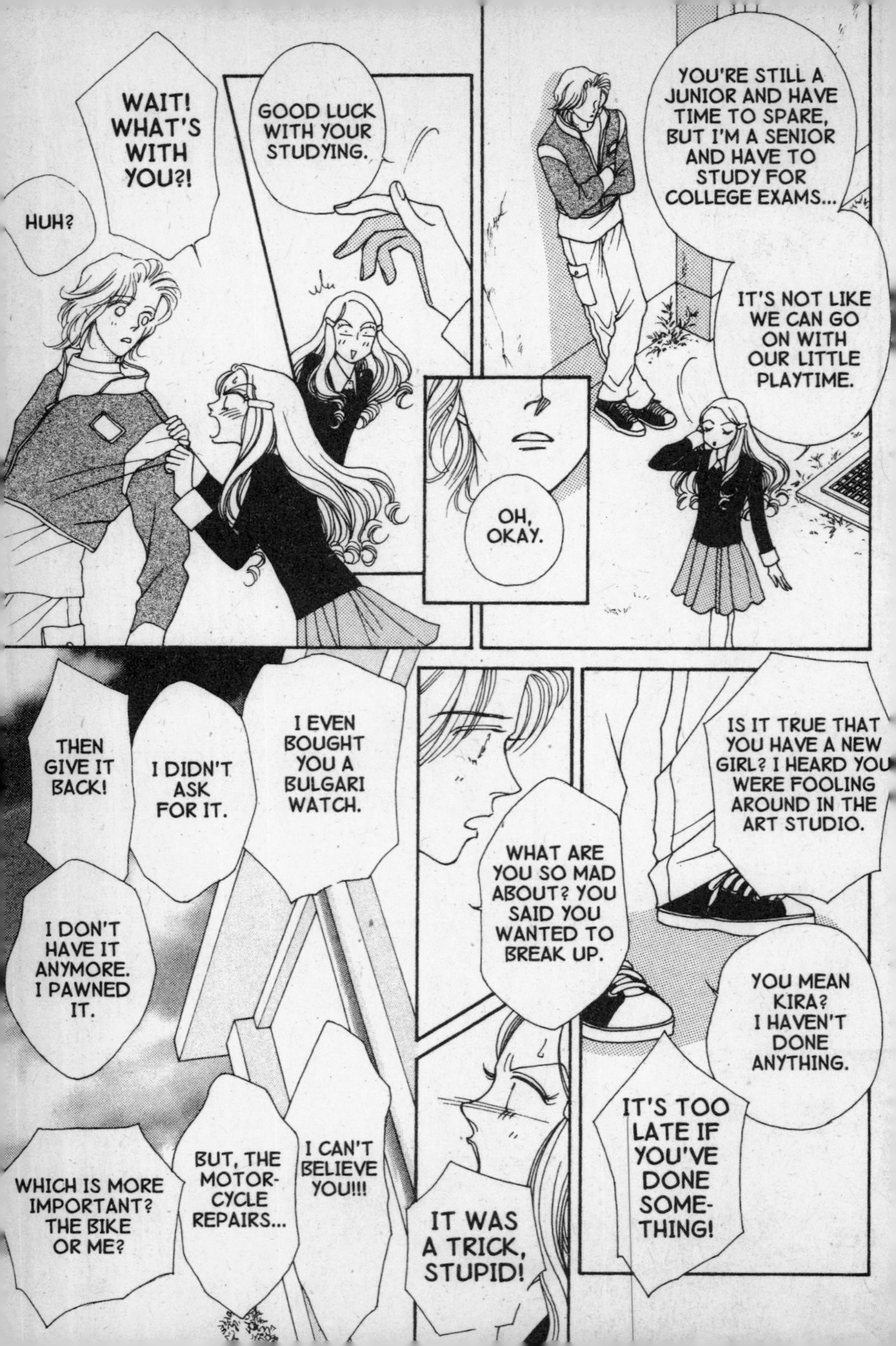
YOU'RE STILL A JUNIOR AND HAVE TIME TO SPARE, BUT I'M A SENIOR AND HAVE TO STUDY FOR COLLEGE EXAMS...
IT'S NOT LIKE WE CAN GO ON WITH OUR LITTLE PLAYTIME.
OH, OKAY.
GOOD LUCK WITH YOUR STUDYING.
WAIT! WHAT'S WITH YOU?!
HUH?
IS IT TRUE THAT YOU HAVE A NEW GIRL? I HEARD YOU WERE FOOLING AROUND IN THE ART STUDIO.
YOU MEAN KIRA? I HAVEN'T DONE ANYTHING.
IT'S TOO LATE IF YOU'VE DONE SOME-THING!
WHAT ARE YOU SO MAD ABOUT? YOU SAID YOU WANTED TO BREAK UP.
IT WAS A TRICK, STUPID!
I EVEN BOUGHT YOU A BULGARI WATCH.
I DIDN'T ASK FOR IT.
THEN GIVE IT BACK!
I DON'T HAVE IT ANYMORE. I PAWNED IT.
I CAN'T BELIEVE YOU!!!
BUT, THE MOTOR-CYCLE REPAIRS...
WHICH IS MORE IMPORTANT? THE BIKE OR ME?

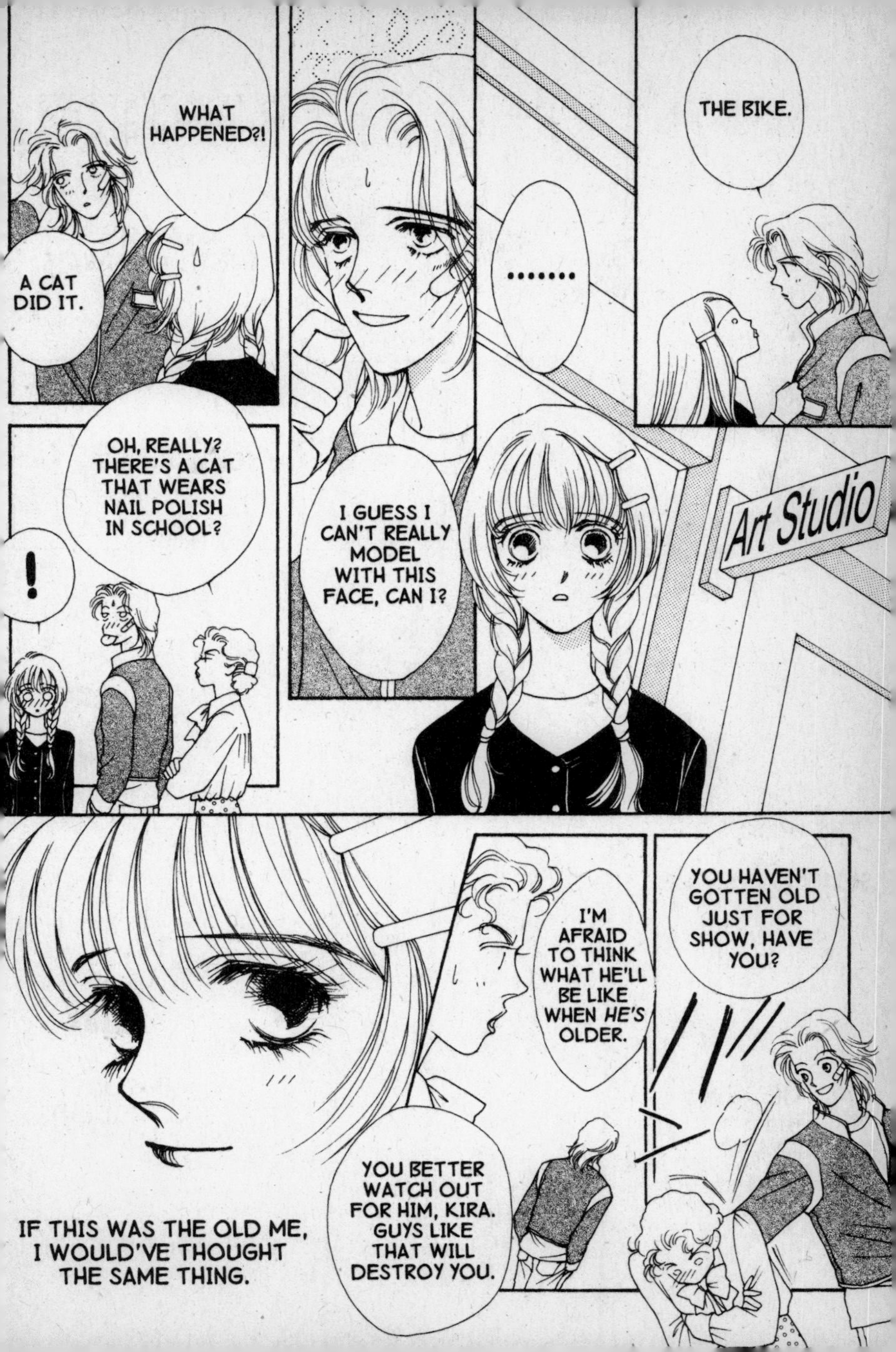

THE BIKE.
....
Art Studio
I GUESS I CAN'T REALLY MODEL WITH THIS FACE, CAN I?
WHAT HAPPENED?!
A CAT DID IT.
OH, REALLY? THERE'S A CAT THAT WEARS NAIL POLISH IN SCHOOL?
!
YOU HAVEN'T GOTTEN OLD JUST FOR SHOW, HAVE YOU?
I'M AFRAID TO THINK WHAT HE'LL BE LIKE WHEN *HE'S* OLDER.
YOU BETTER WATCH OUT FOR HIM, KIRA. GUYS LIKE THAT WILL DESTROY YOU.
IF THIS WAS THE OLD ME, I WOULD'VE THOUGHT THE SAME THING.

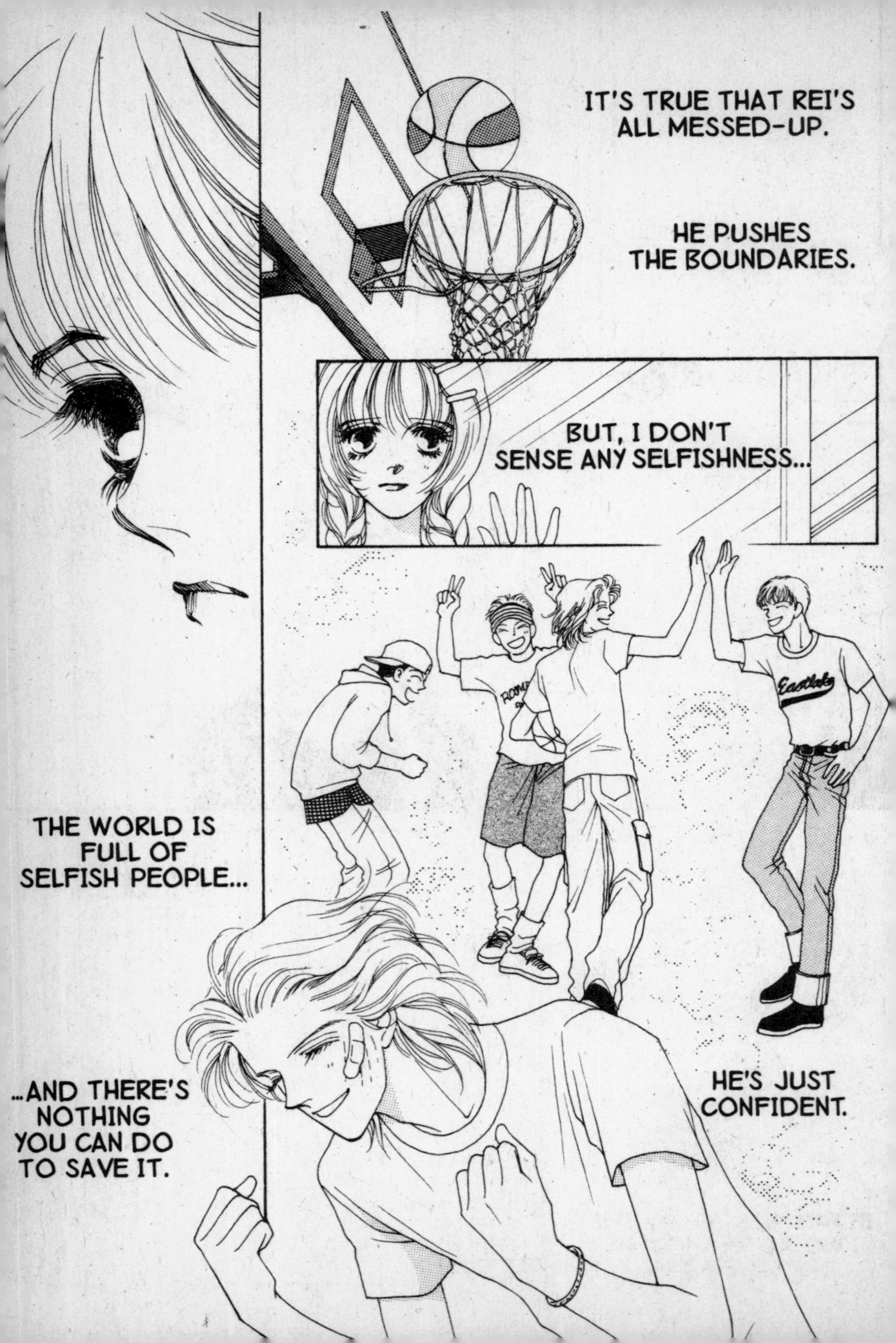
IT'S TRUE THAT REI'S ALL MESSED-UP.
HE PUSHES THE BOUNDARIES.
BUT, I DON'T SENSE ANY SELFISHNESS...
HE'S JUST CONFIDENT.
THE WORLD IS FULL OF SELFISH PEOPLE...
...AND THERE'S NOTHING YOU CAN DO TO SAVE IT.

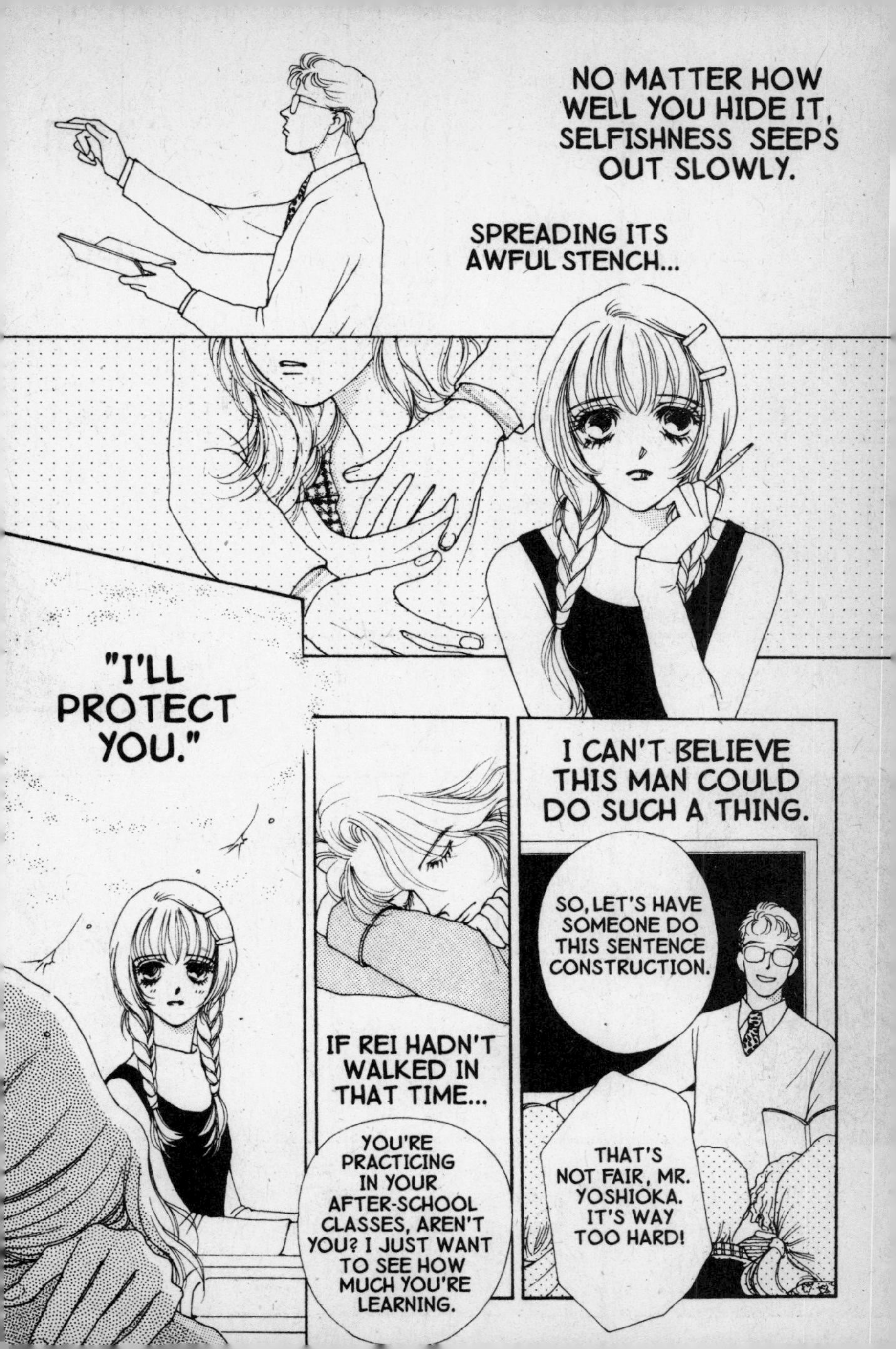
NO MATTER HOW WELL YOU HIDE IT, SELFISHNESS SEEPS OUT SLOWLY.
SPREADING ITS AWFUL STENCH...
I CAN'T BELIEVE THIS MAN COULD DO SUCH A THING.
SO, LET'S HAVE SOMEONE DO THIS SENTENCE CONSTRUCTION.
THAT'S NOT FAIR, MR. YOSHIOKA. IT'S WAY TOO HARD!
IF REI HADN'T WALKED IN THAT TIME...
YOU'RE PRACTICING IN YOUR AFTER-SCHOOL CLASSES, AREN'T YOU? I JUST WANT TO SEE HOW MUCH YOU'RE LEARNING.
"I'LL PROTECT YOU."

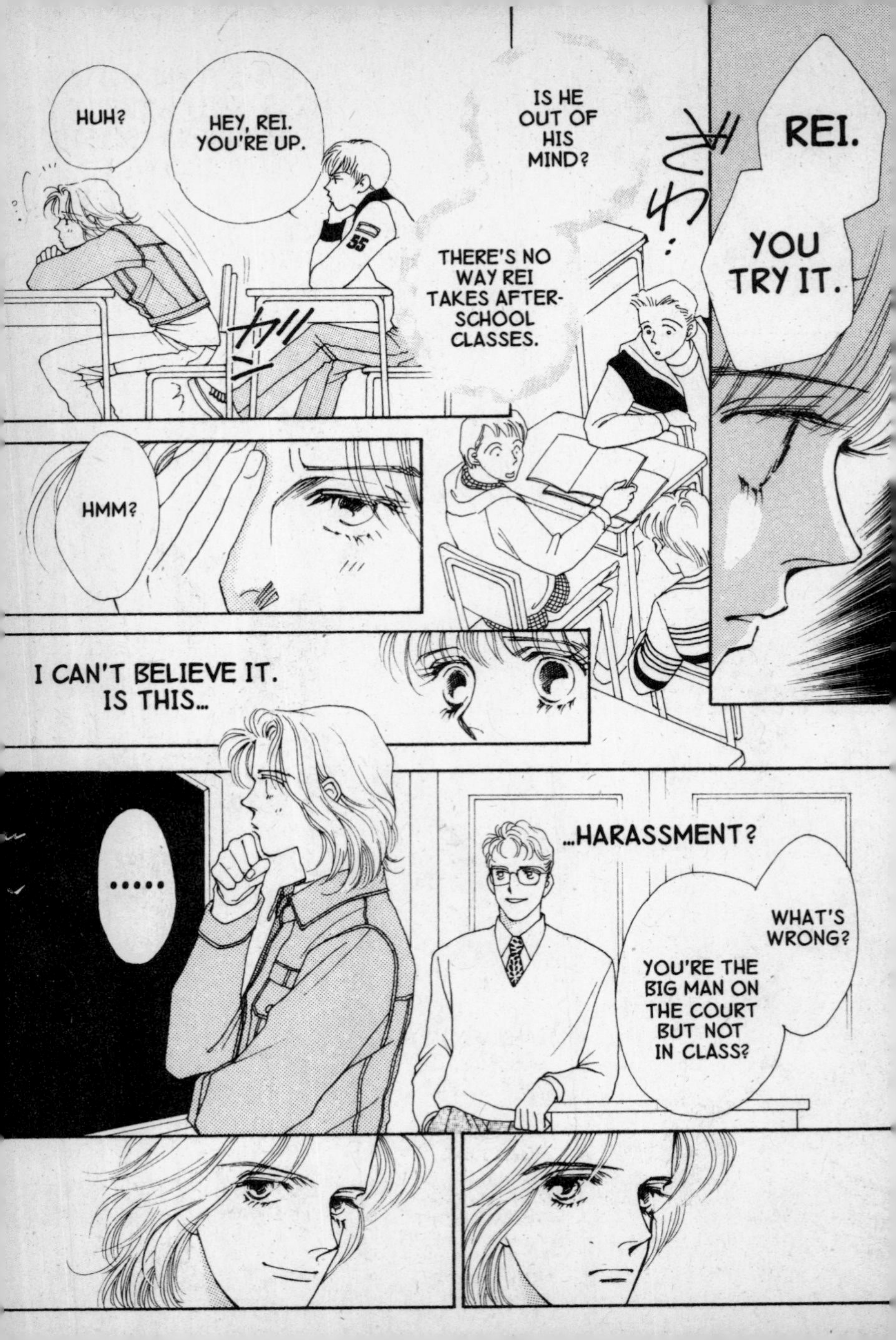
REI.
YOU TRY IT.
ざわ
IS HE OUT OF HIS MIND?
THERE'S NO WAY REI TAKES AFTER-SCHOOL CLASSES.
HEY, REI. YOU'RE UP.
HUH?
HMM?
I CAN'T BELIEVE IT. IS THIS...
...HARASSMENT?
WHAT'S WRONG?
YOU'RE THE BIG MAN ON THE COURT BUT NOT IN CLASS?
.....

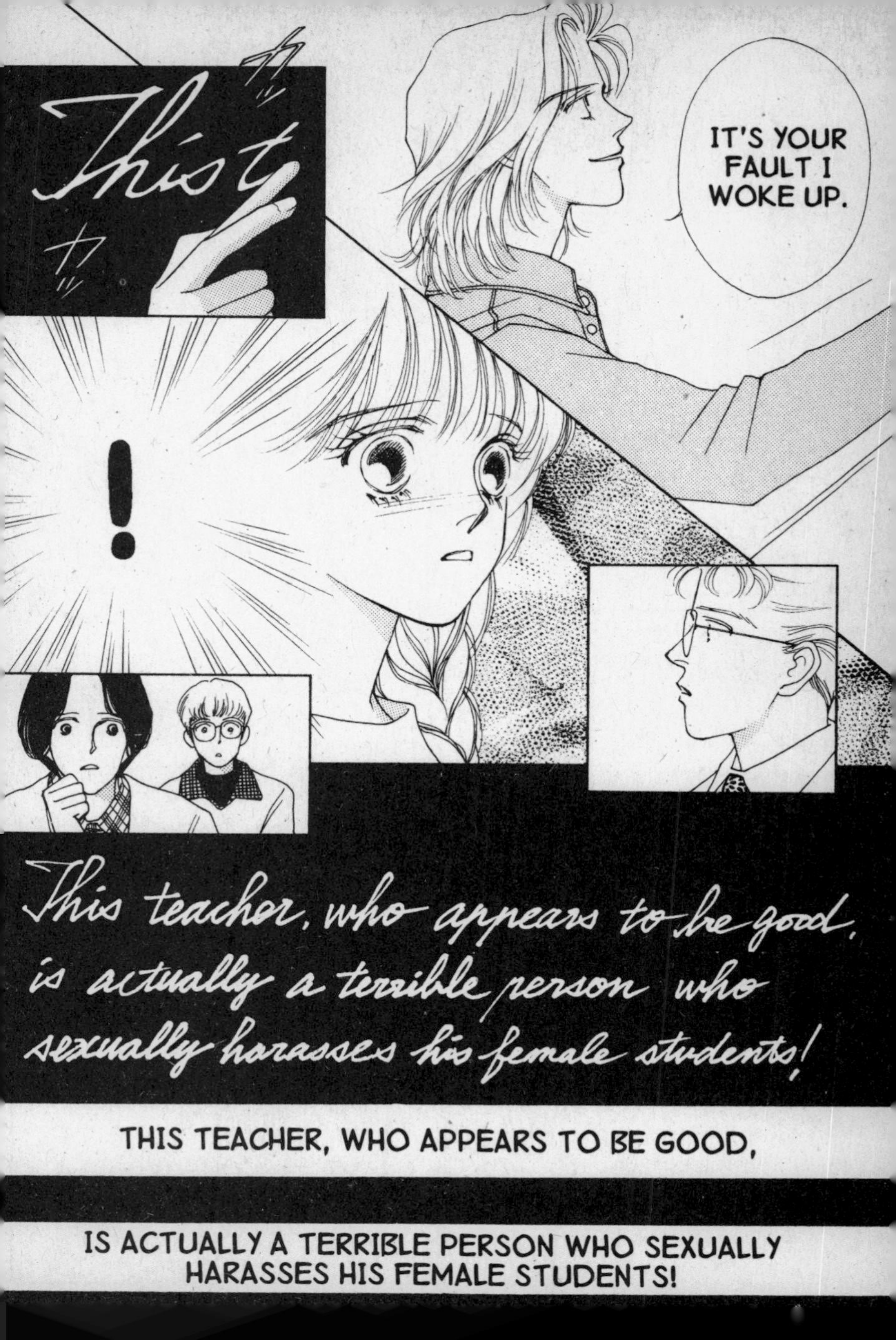
IT'S YOUR FAULT I WOKE UP.
This t
!
This teacher, who appears to be good, is actually a terrible person who sexually harasses his female students!
THIS TEACHER, WHO APPEARS TO BE GOOD,
IS ACTUALLY A TERRIBLE PERSON WHO SEXUALLY HARASSES HIS FEMALE STUDENTS!

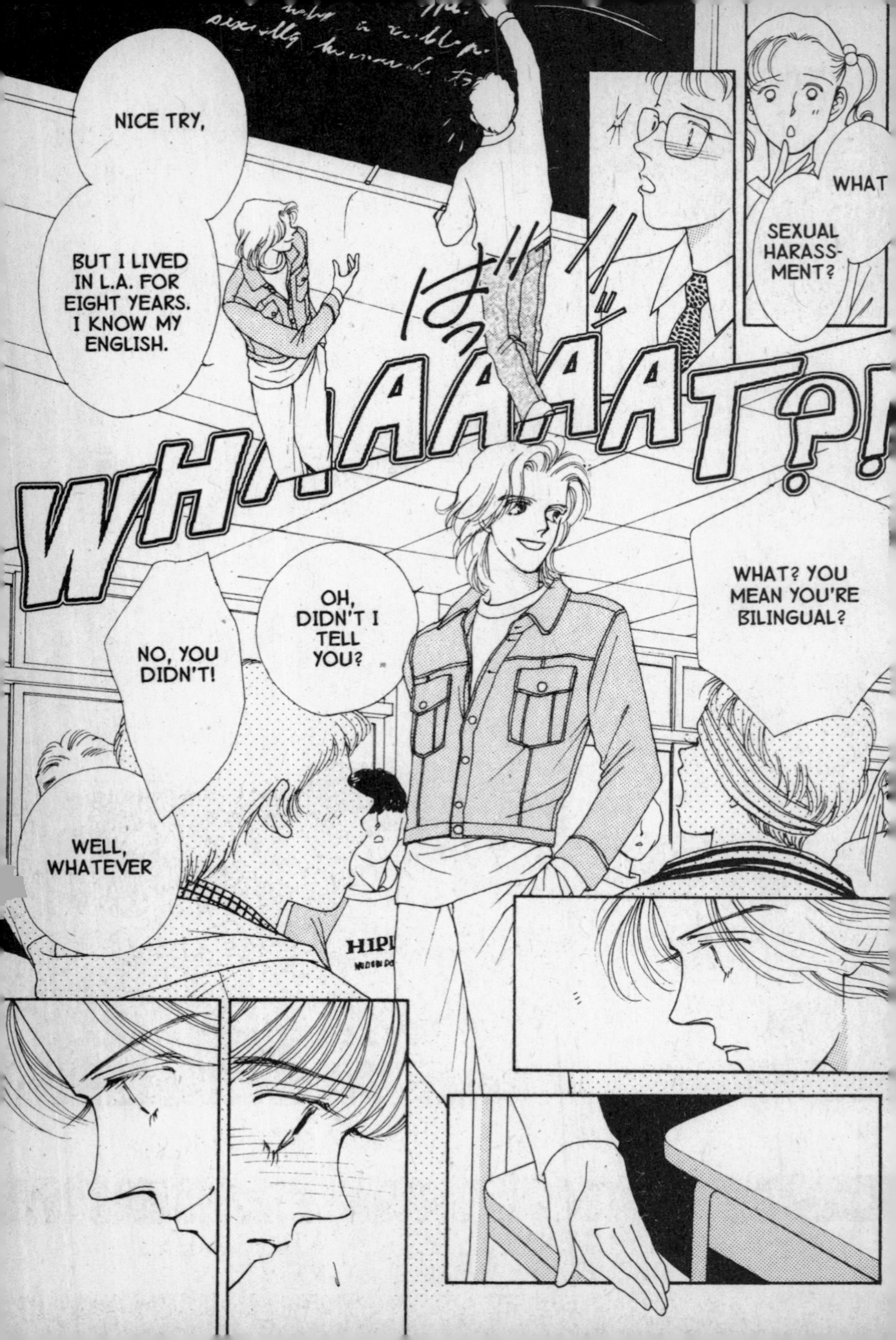

WHAT SEXUAL HARASSMENT?
NICE TRY,
BUT I LIVED IN L.A. FOR EIGHT YEARS. I KNOW MY ENGLISH.
はっ
WHAAAAAT?!
WHAT? YOU MEAN YOU'RE BILINGUAL?
OH, DIDN'T I TELL YOU?
NO, YOU DIDN'T!
WELL, WHATEVER

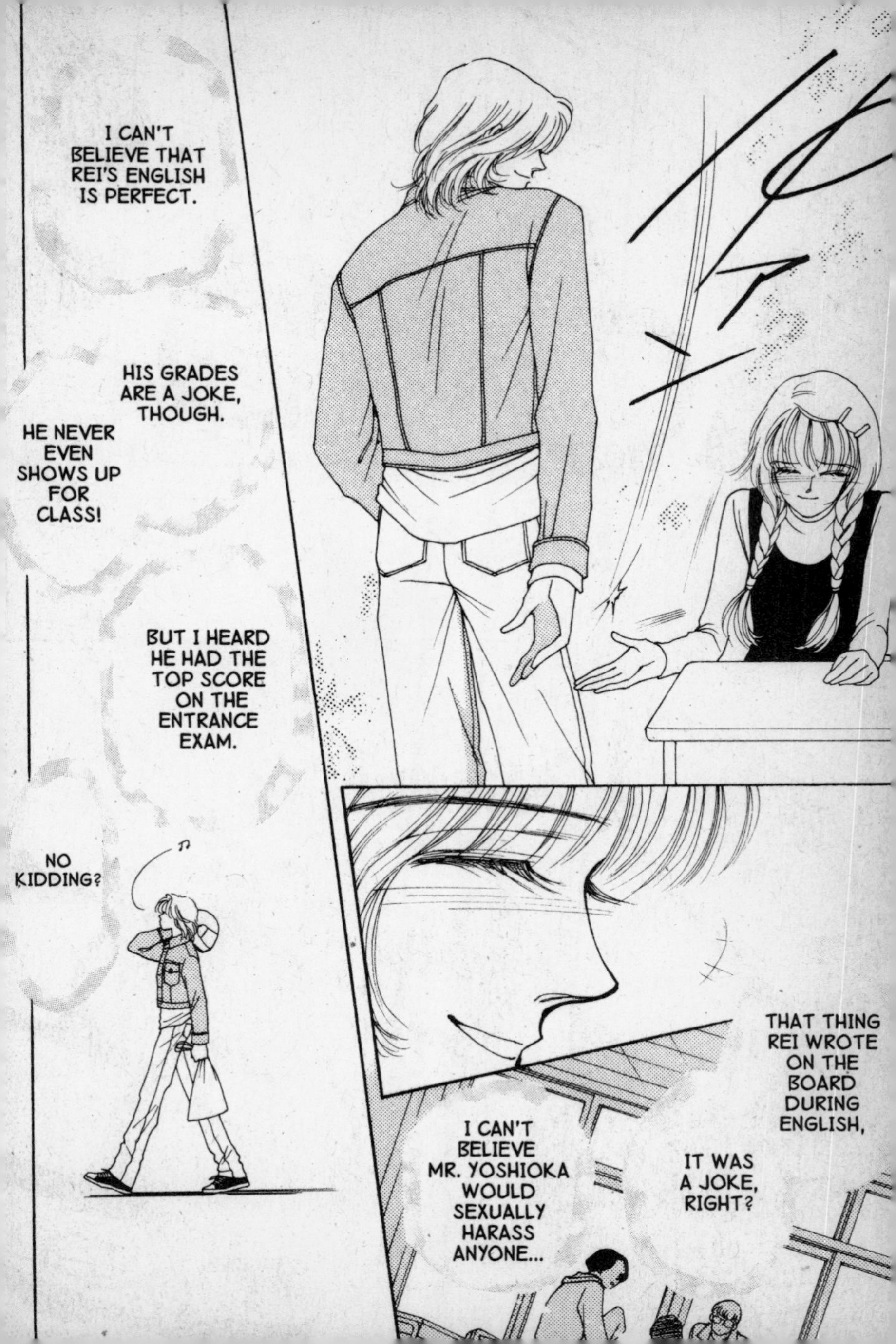
THAT THING REI WROTE ON THE BOARD DURING ENGLISH,
IT WAS A JOKE, RIGHT?
I CAN'T BELIEVE MR. YOSHIOKA WOULD SEXUALLY HARASS ANYONE...
I CAN'T BELIEVE THAT REI'S ENGLISH IS PERFECT.
HIS GRADES ARE A JOKE, THOUGH.
HE NEVER EVEN SHOWS UP FOR CLASS!
BUT I HEARD HE HAD THE TOP SCORE ON THE ENTRANCE EXAM.
NO KIDDING?

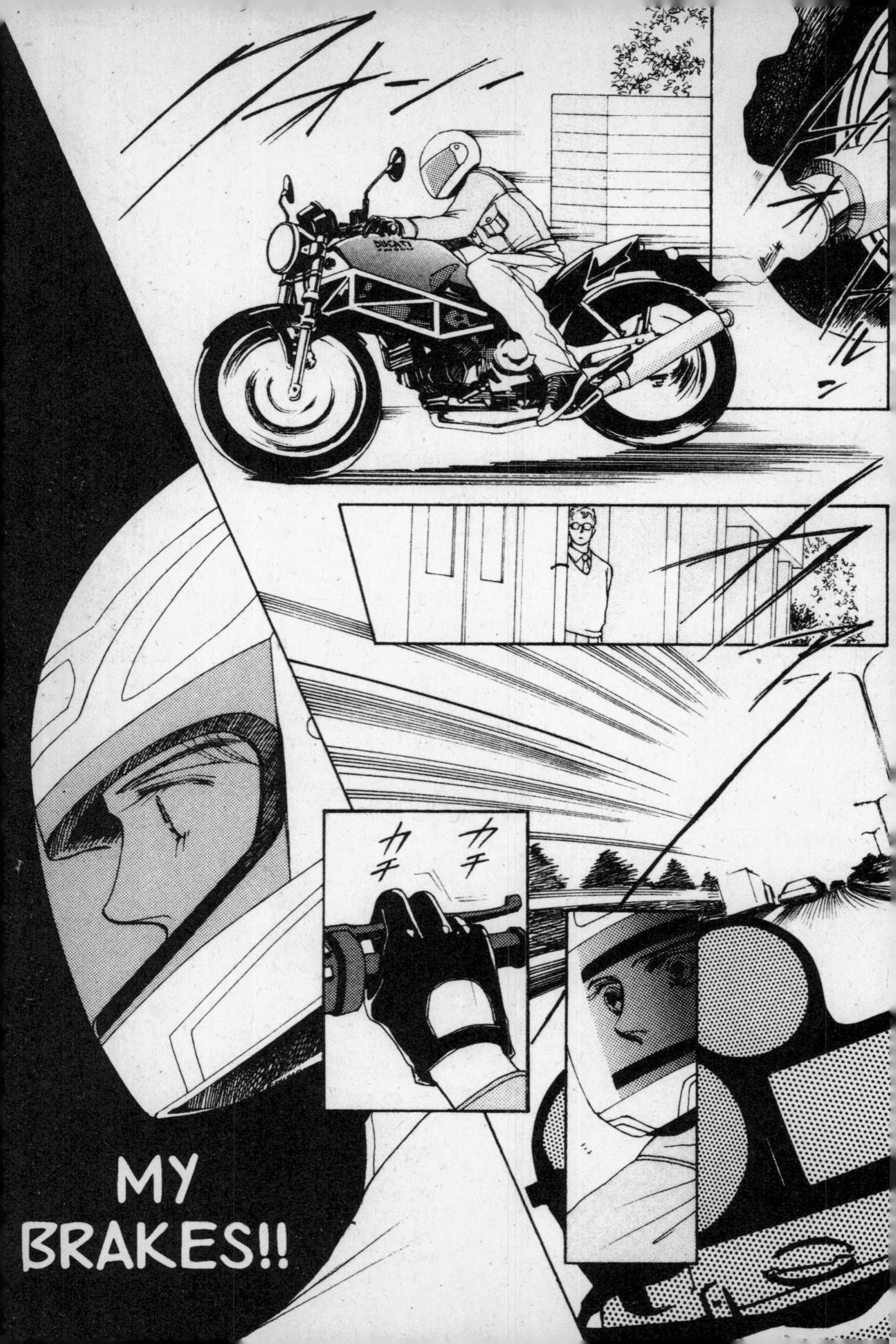
カチ カチ
MY BRAKES!!

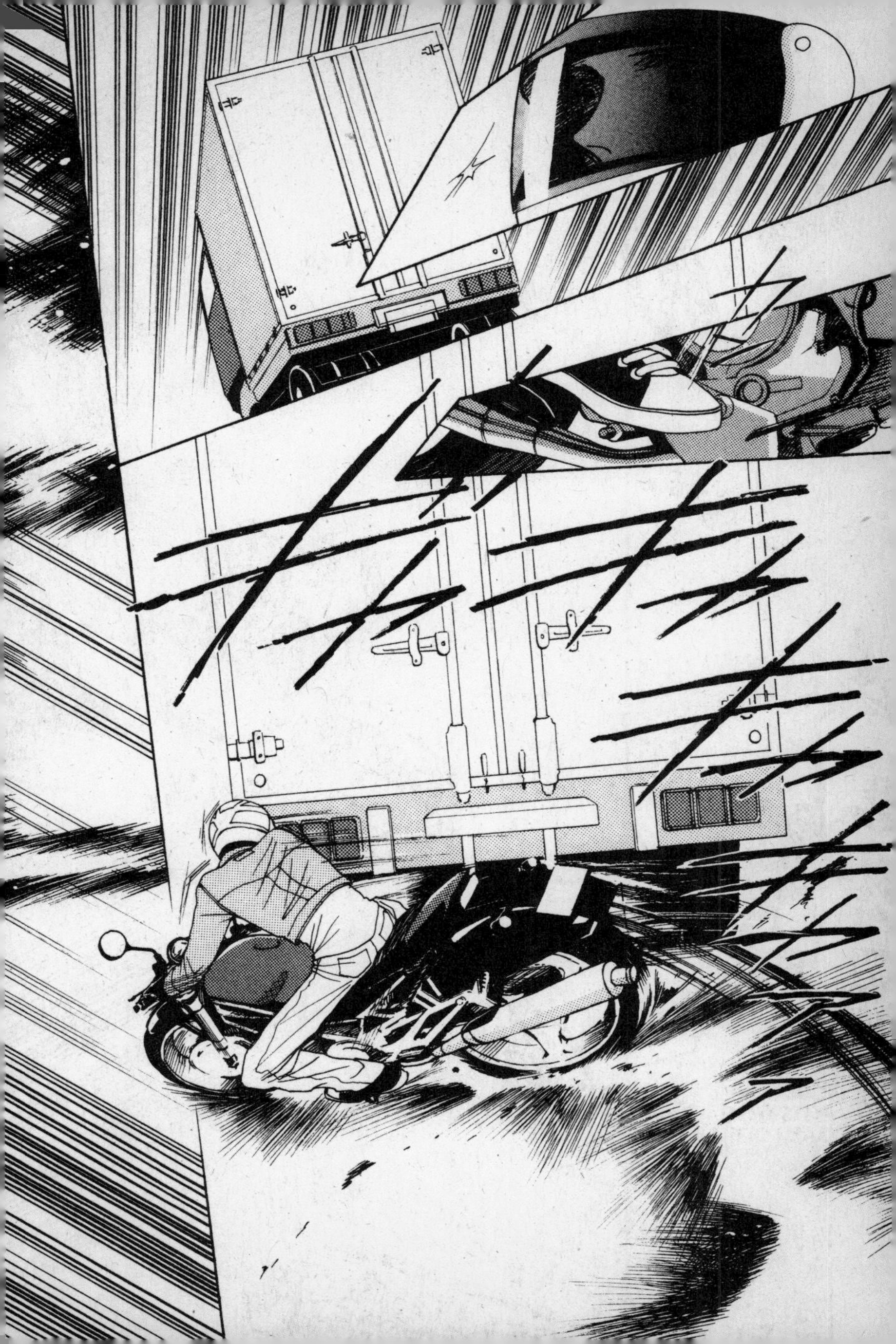

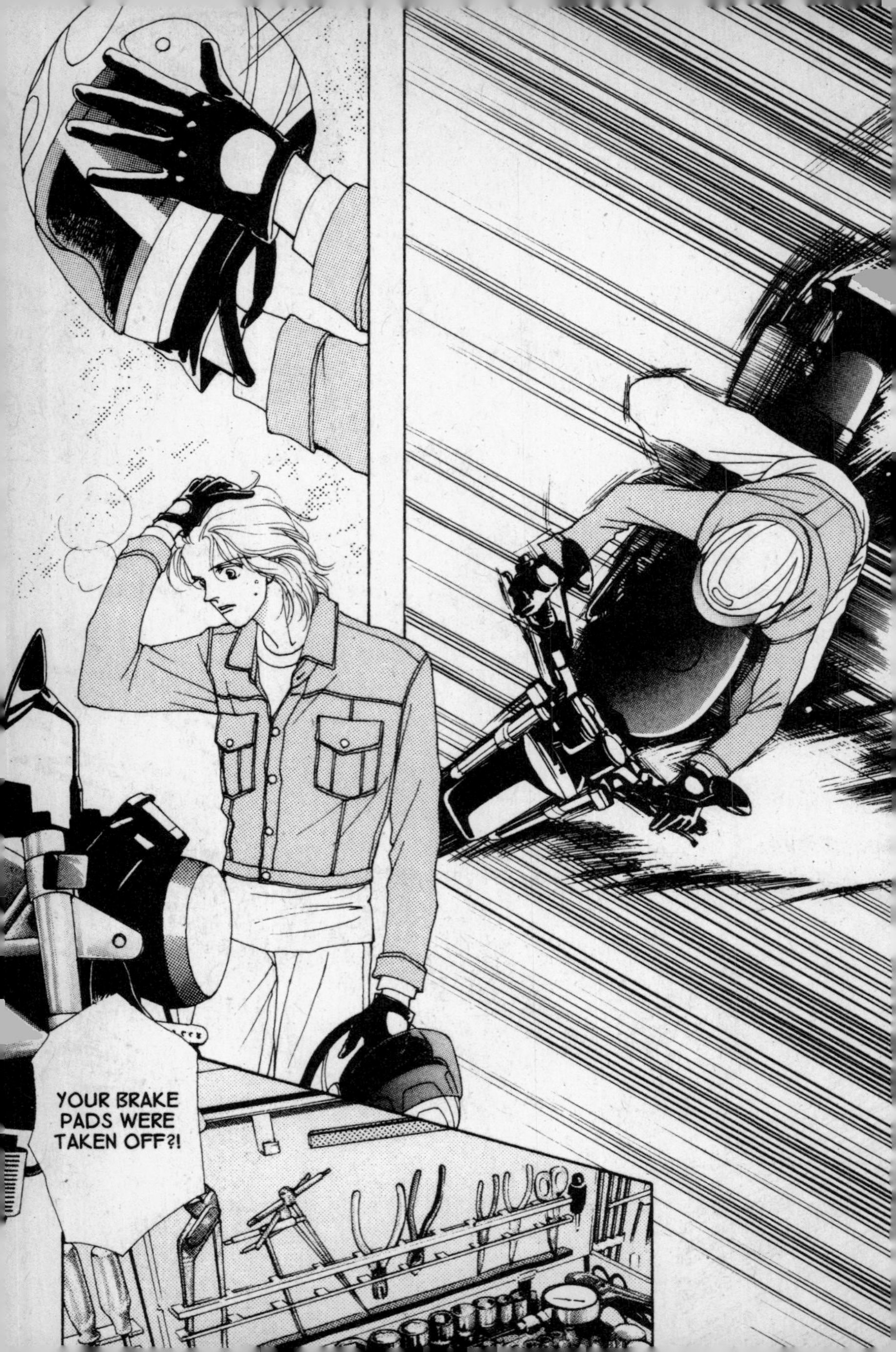
YOUR BRAKE PADS WERE TAKEN OFF?!

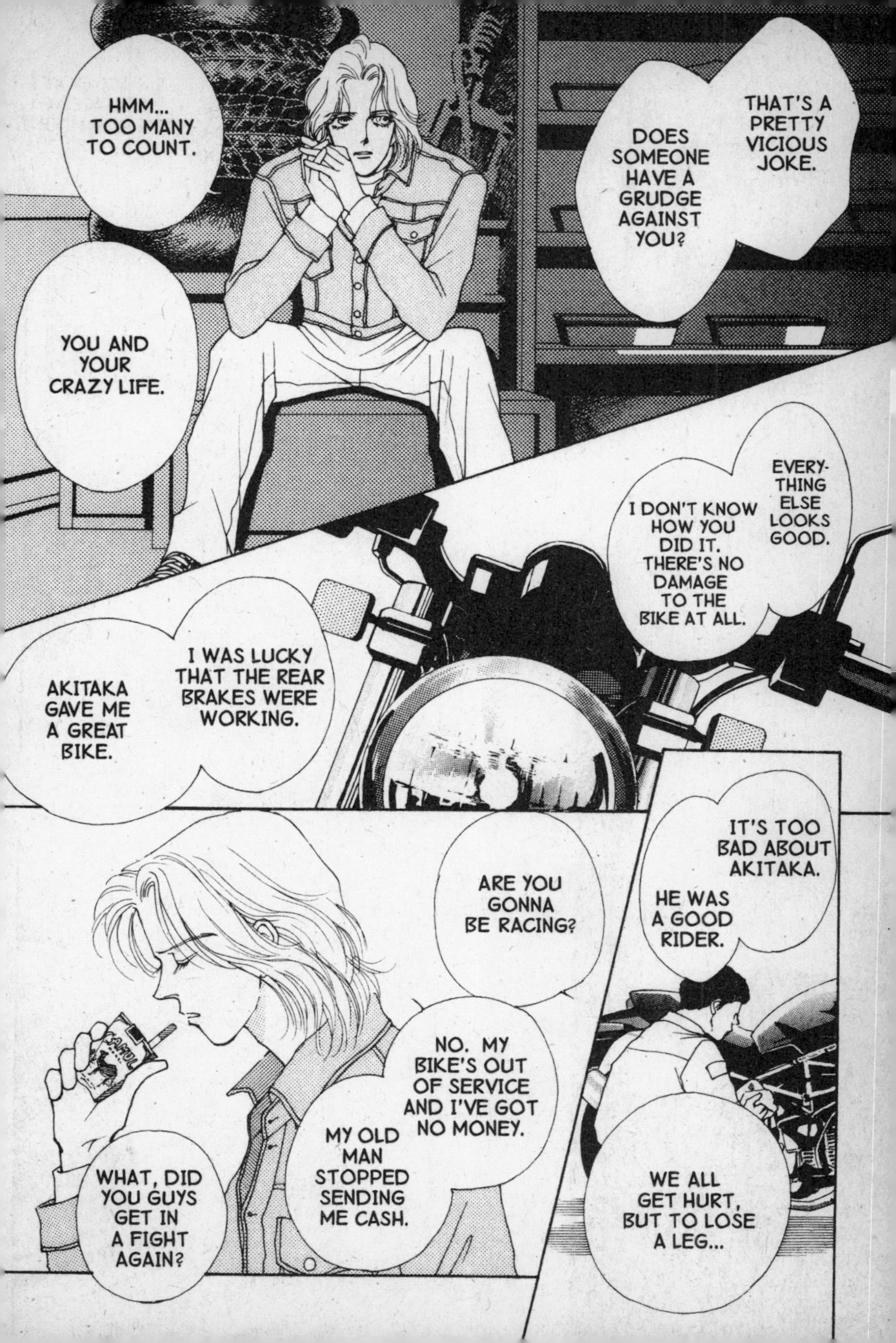
THAT'S A PRETTY VICIOUS JOKE.
DOES SOMEONE HAVE A GRUDGE AGAINST YOU?
HMM... TOO MANY TO COUNT.
YOU AND YOUR CRAZY LIFE.
EVERY-THING ELSE LOOKS GOOD.
I DON'T KNOW HOW YOU DID IT. THERE'S NO DAMAGE TO THE BIKE AT ALL.
I WAS LUCKY THAT THE REAR BRAKES WERE WORKING.
AKITAKA GAVE ME A GREAT BIKE.
IT'S TOO BAD ABOUT AKITAKA.
HE WAS A GOOD RIDER.
WE ALL GET HURT, BUT TO LOSE A LEG...
ARE YOU GONNA BE RACING?
NO. MY BIKE'S OUT OF SERVICE AND I'VE GOT NO MONEY.
MY OLD MAN STOPPED SENDING ME CASH.
WHAT, DID YOU GUYS GET IN A FIGHT AGAIN?

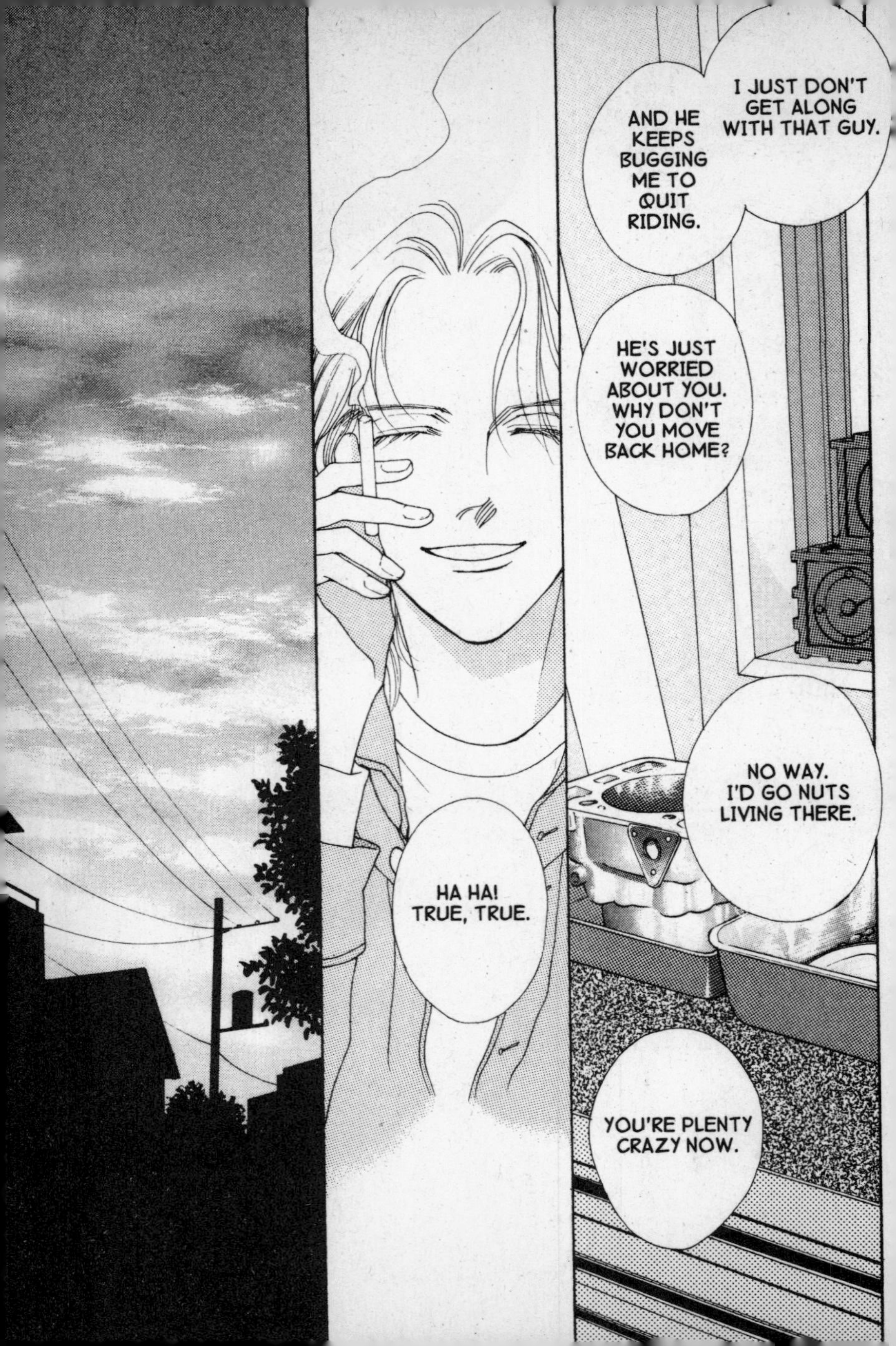
I JUST DON'T GET ALONG WITH THAT GUY.
AND HE KEEPS BUGGING ME TO QUIT RIDING.
HE'S JUST WORRIED ABOUT YOU. WHY DON'T YOU MOVE BACK HOME?
NO WAY. I'D GO NUTS LIVING THERE.
YOU'RE PLENTY CRAZY NOW.
HA HA! TRUE, TRUE.

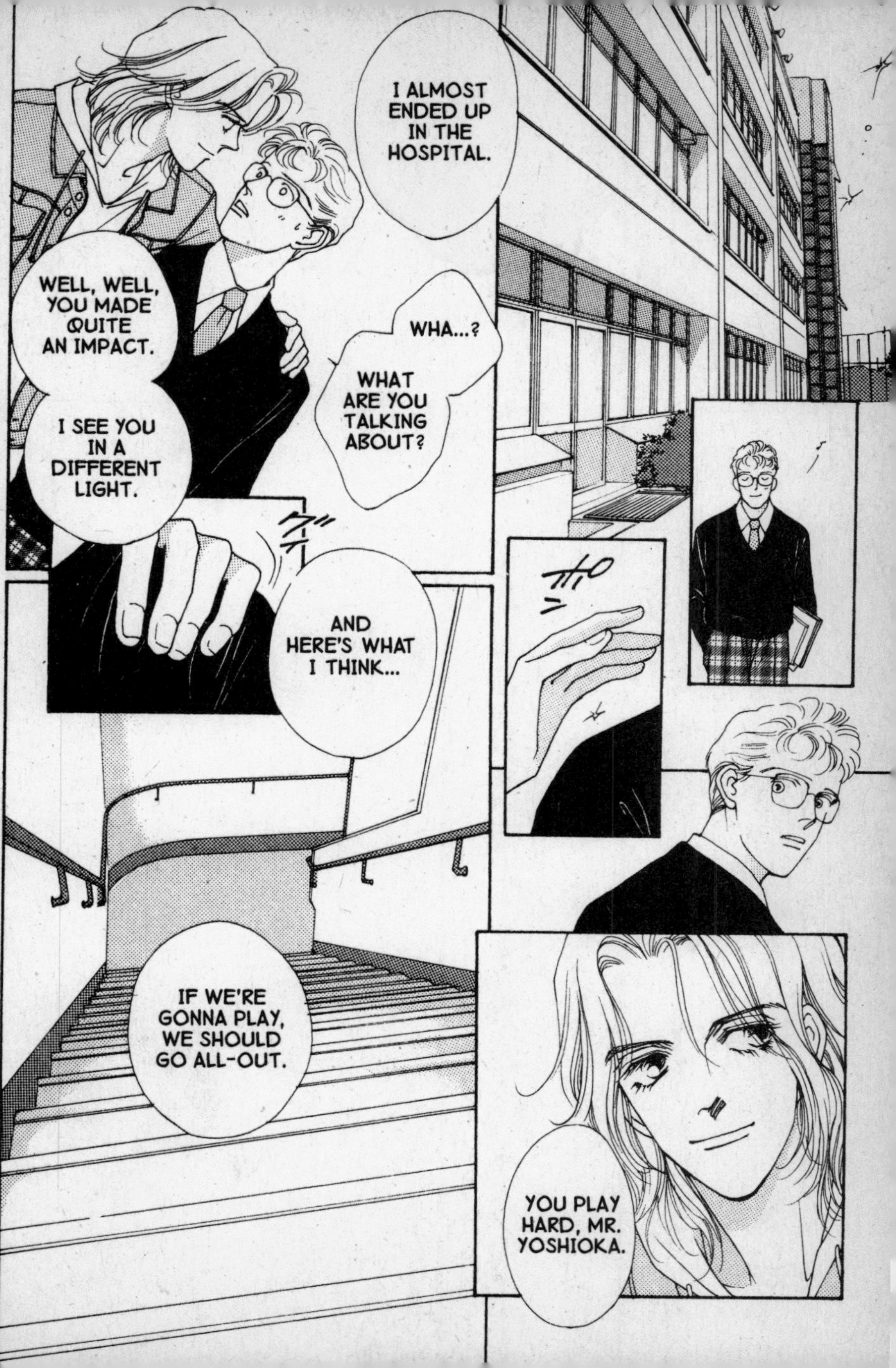
YOU PLAY HARD, MR. YOSHIOKA.
I ALMOST ENDED UP IN THE HOSPITAL.
WHA...?
WHAT ARE YOU TALKING ABOUT?
WELL, WELL, YOU MADE QUITE AN IMPACT.
I SEE YOU IN A DIFFERENT LIGHT.
AND HERE'S WHAT I THINK...
IF WE'RE GONNA PLAY, WE SHOULD GO ALL-OUT.

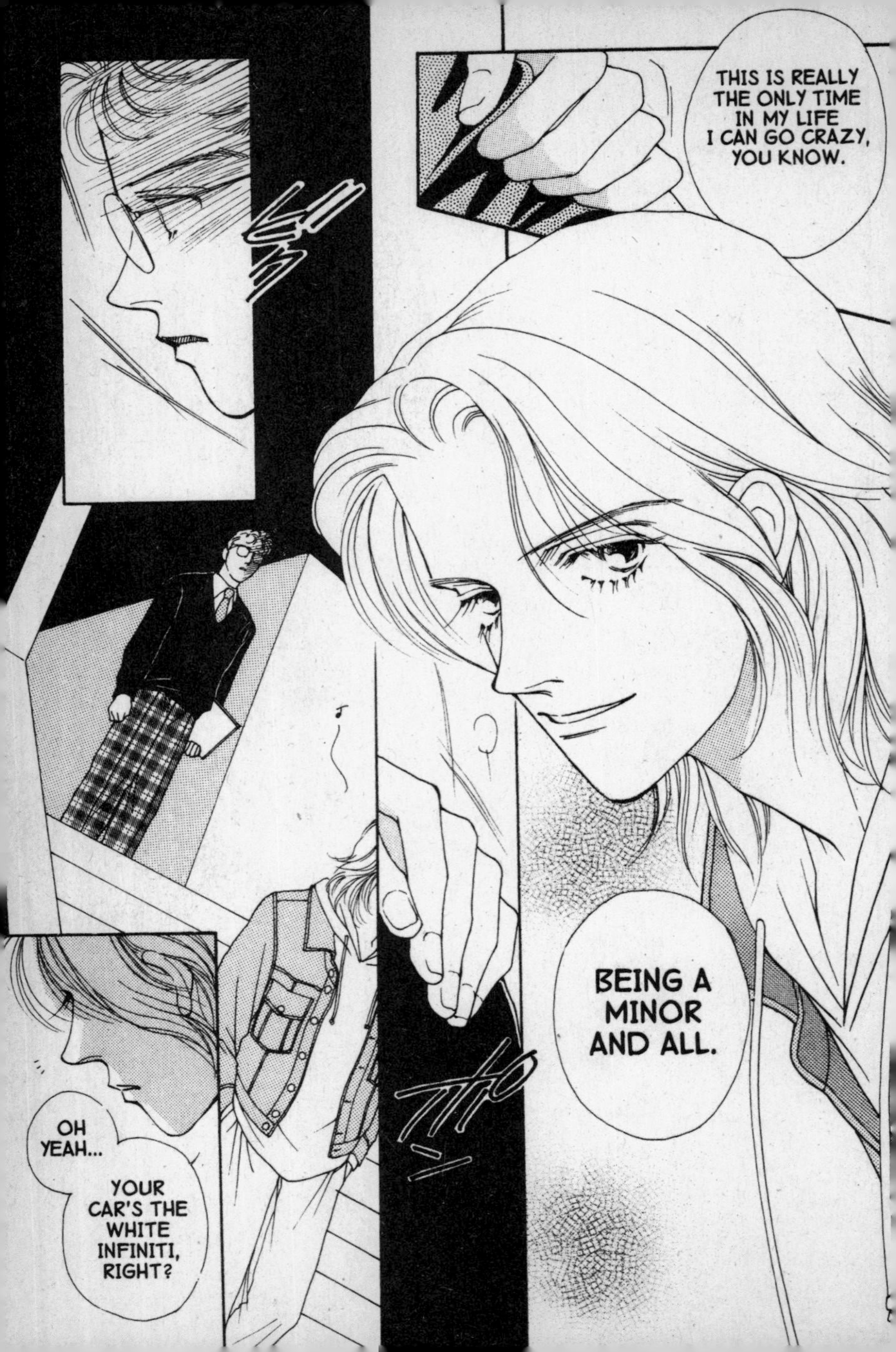
THIS IS REALLY THE ONLY TIME IN MY LIFE I CAN GO CRAZY, YOU KNOW.
BEING A MINOR AND ALL.
OH YEAH...
YOUR CAR'S THE WHITE INFINITI, RIGHT?

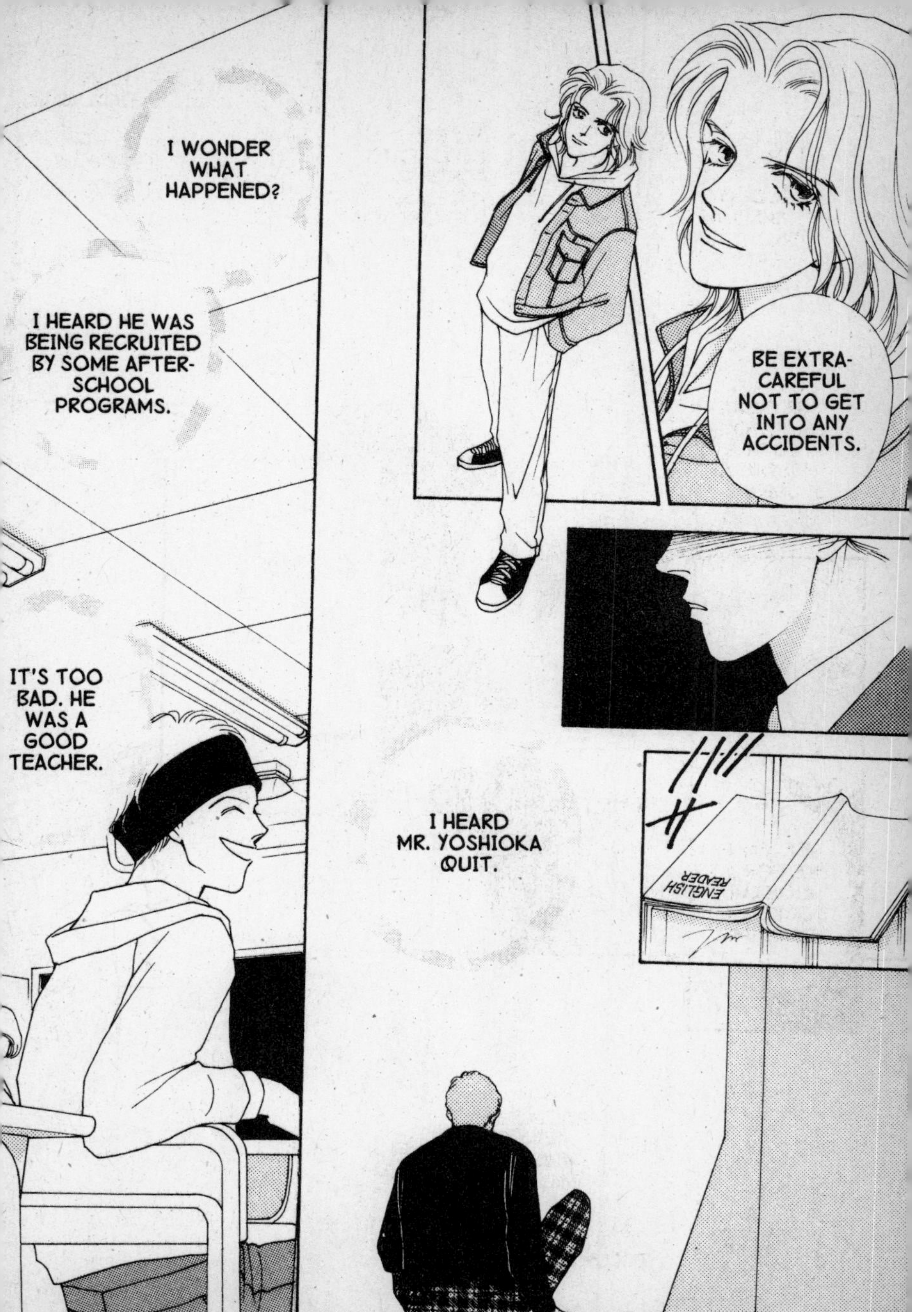
BE EXTRA-CAREFUL NOT TO GET INTO ANY ACCIDENTS.
ENGLISH READER
I HEARD MR. YOSHIOKA QUIT.
I WONDER WHAT HAPPENED?
I HEARD HE WAS BEING RECRUITED BY SOME AFTER-SCHOOL PROGRAMS.
IT'S TOO BAD. HE WAS A GOOD TEACHER.

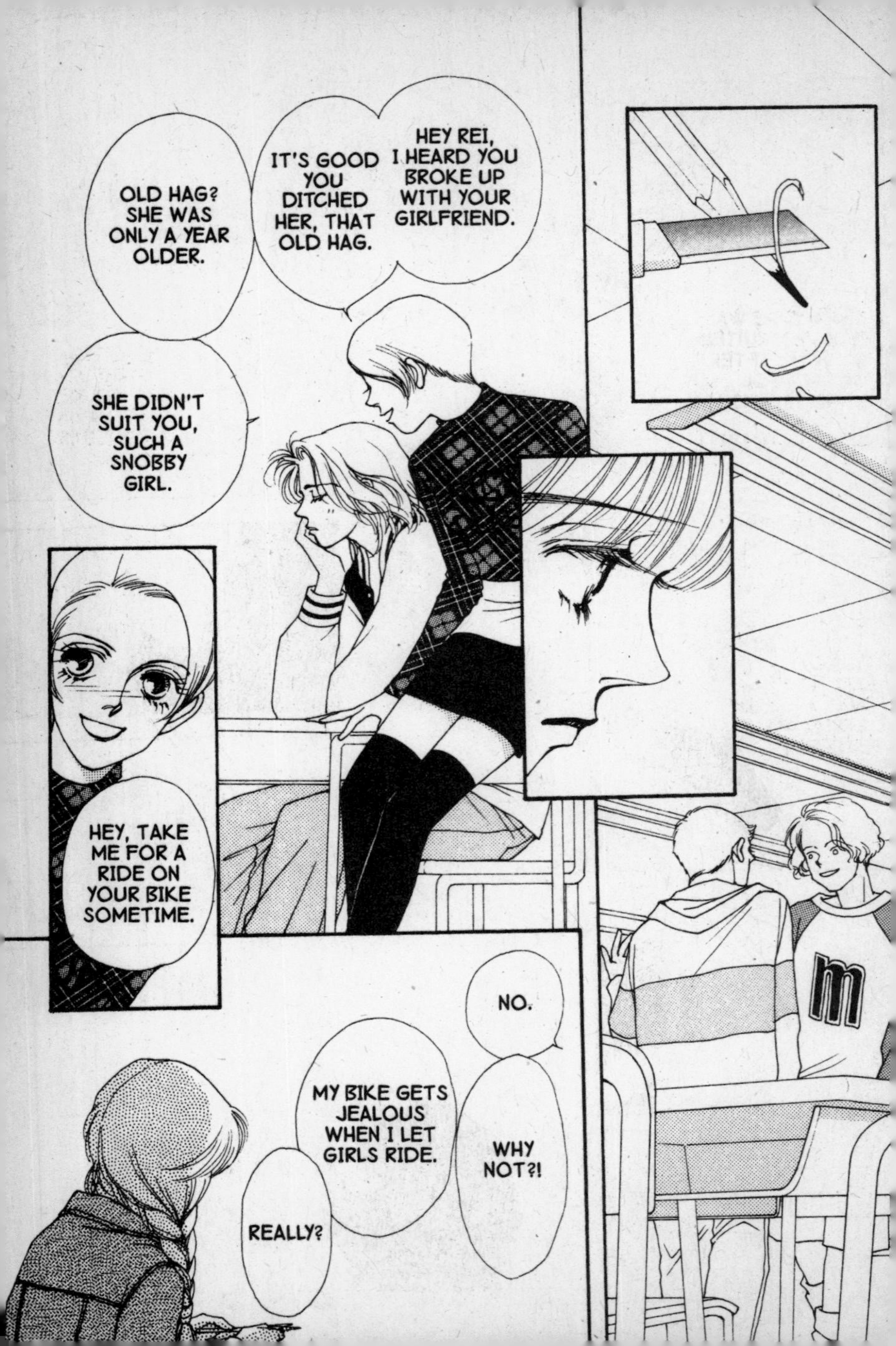
HEY REI, I HEARD YOU BROKE UP WITH YOUR GIRLFRIEND.
IT'S GOOD YOU DITCHED HER, THAT OLD HAG.
OLD HAG? SHE WAS ONLY A YEAR OLDER.
SHE DIDN'T SUIT YOU, SUCH A SNOBBY GIRL.
HEY, TAKE ME FOR A RIDE ON YOUR BIKE SOMETIME.
NO.
WHY NOT?!
MY BIKE GETS JEALOUS WHEN I LET GIRLS RIDE.
REALLY?

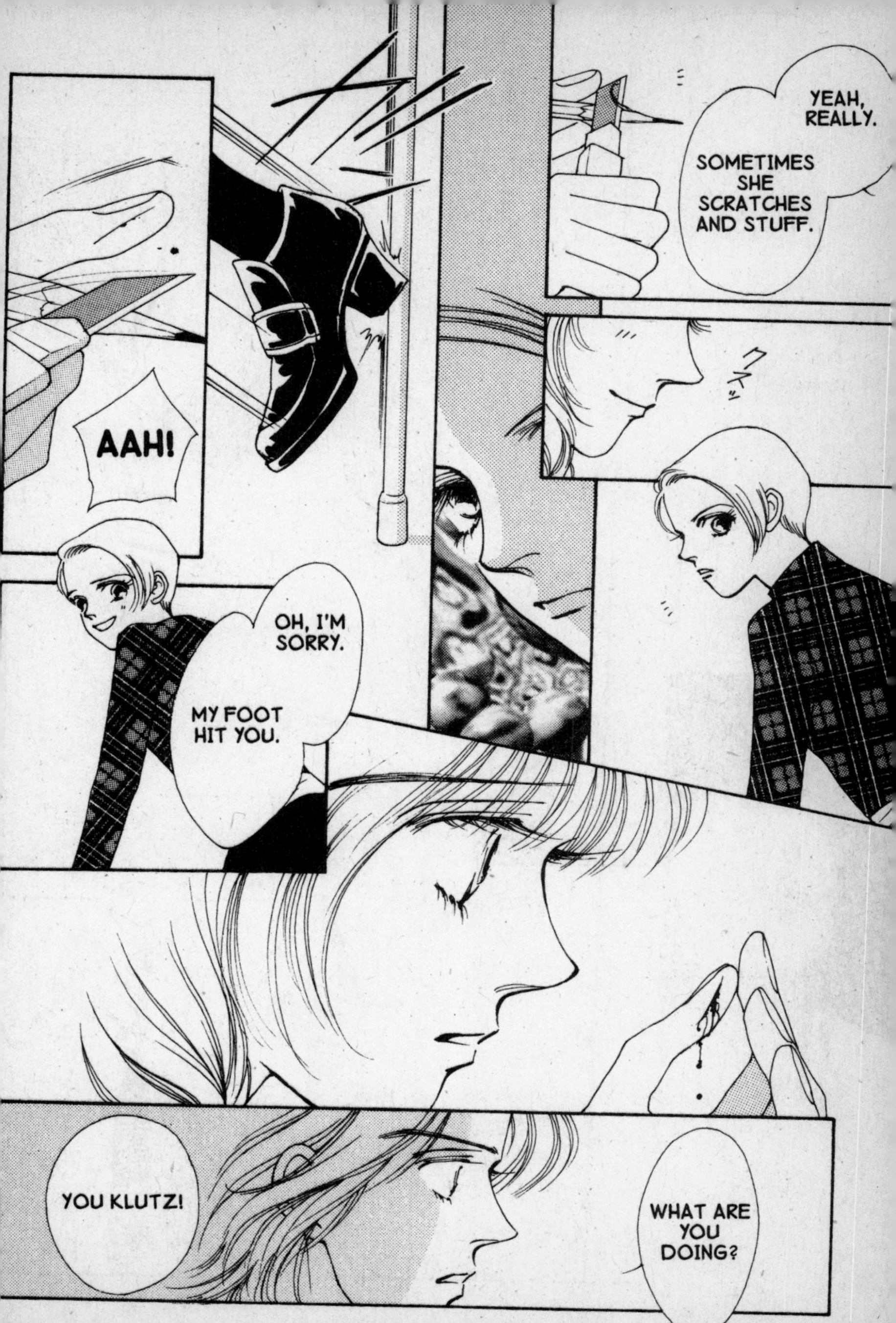
YEAH, REALLY.
SOMETIMES SHE SCRATCHES AND STUFF.
AAH!
クスッ
OH, I'M SORRY.
MY FOOT HIT YOU.
WHAT ARE YOU DOING?
YOU KLUTZ!

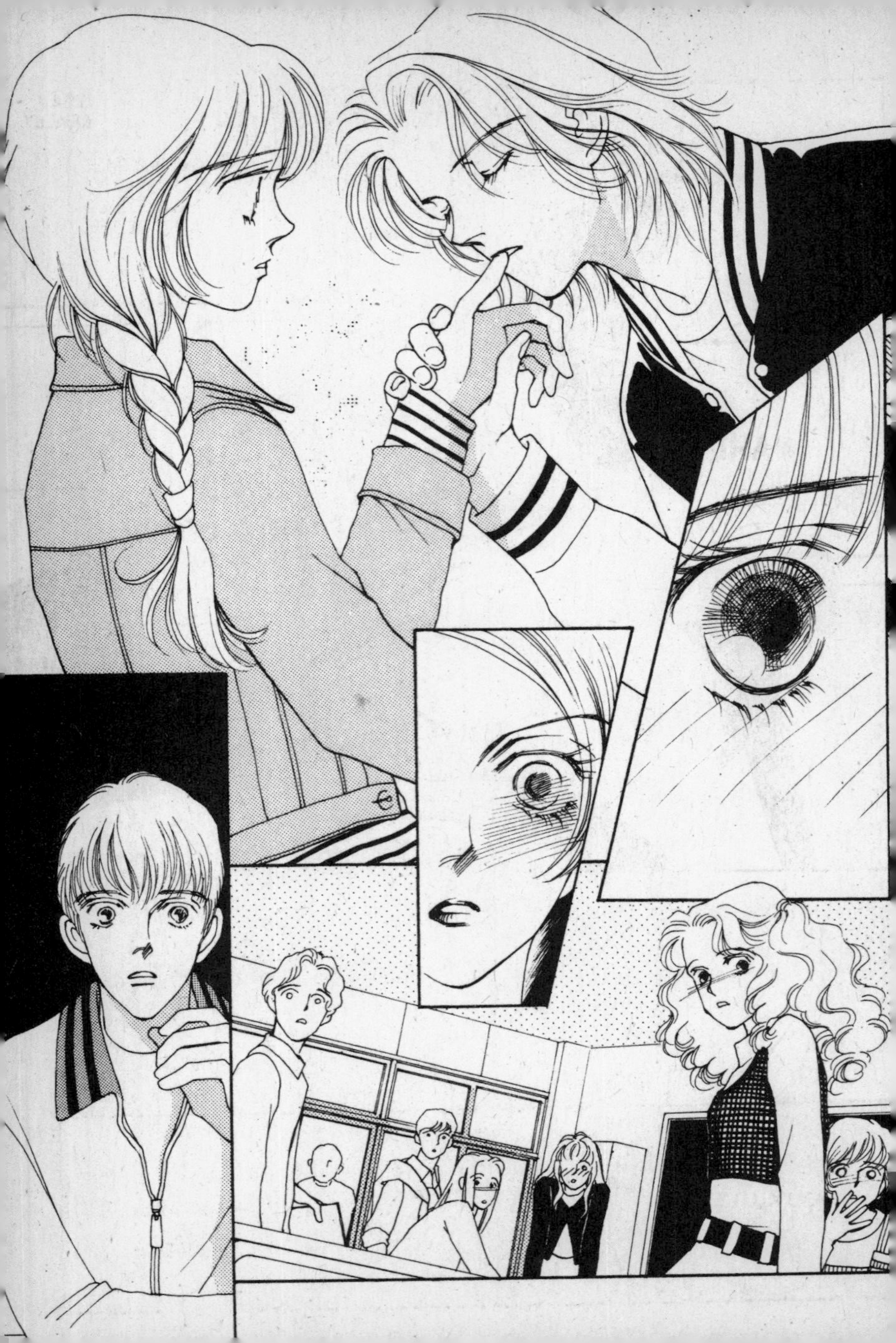

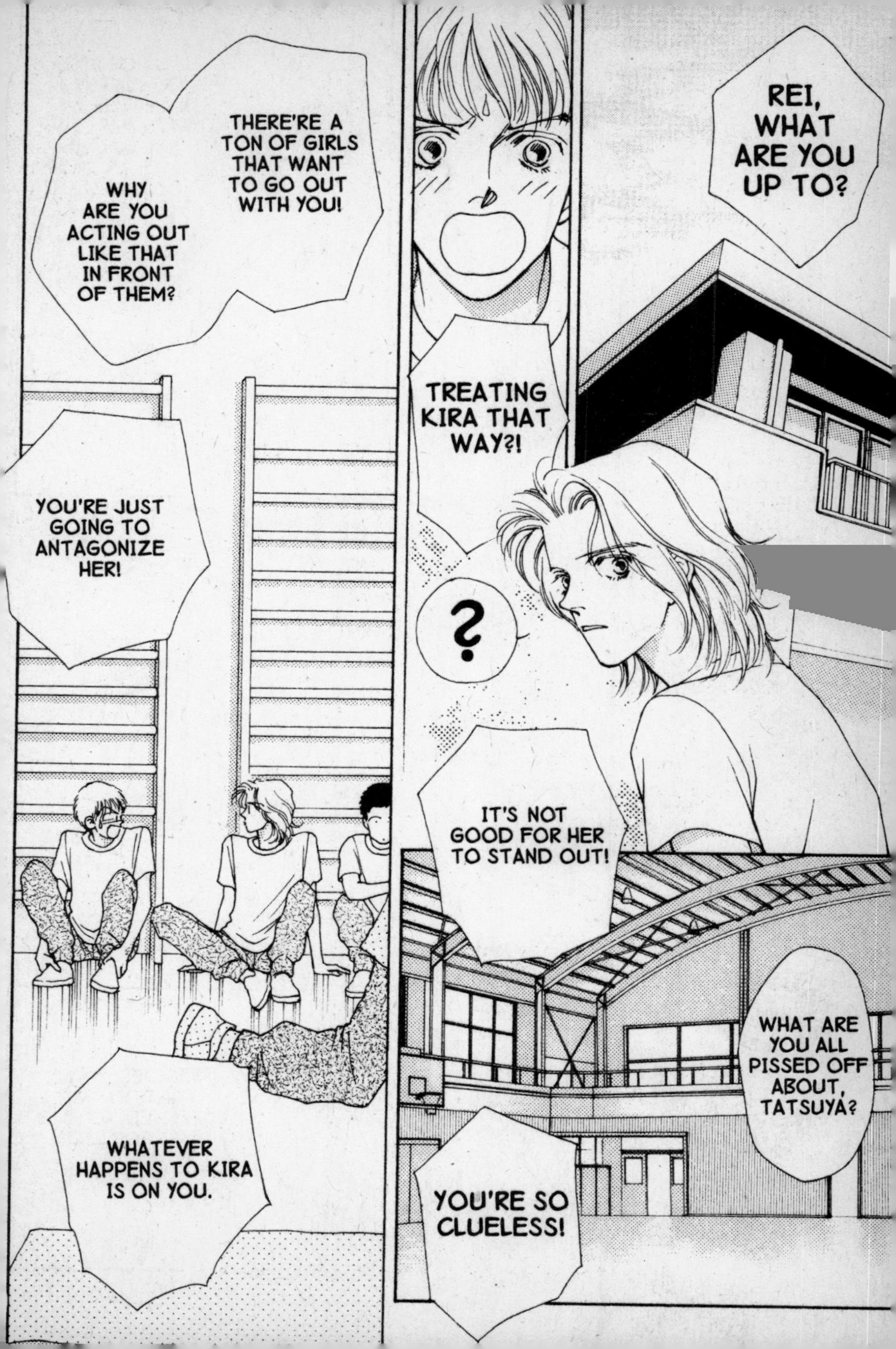
REI, WHAT ARE YOU UP TO?
TREATING KIRA THAT WAY?!
?
IT'S NOT GOOD FOR HER TO STAND OUT!
WHAT ARE YOU ALL PISSED OFF ABOUT, TATSUYA?
YOU'RE SO CLUELESS!
THERE'RE A TON OF GIRLS THAT WANT TO GO OUT WITH YOU!
WHY ARE YOU ACTING OUT LIKE THAT IN FRONT OF THEM?
YOU'RE JUST GOING TO ANTAGONIZE HER!
WHATEVER HAPPENS TO KIRA IS ON YOU.

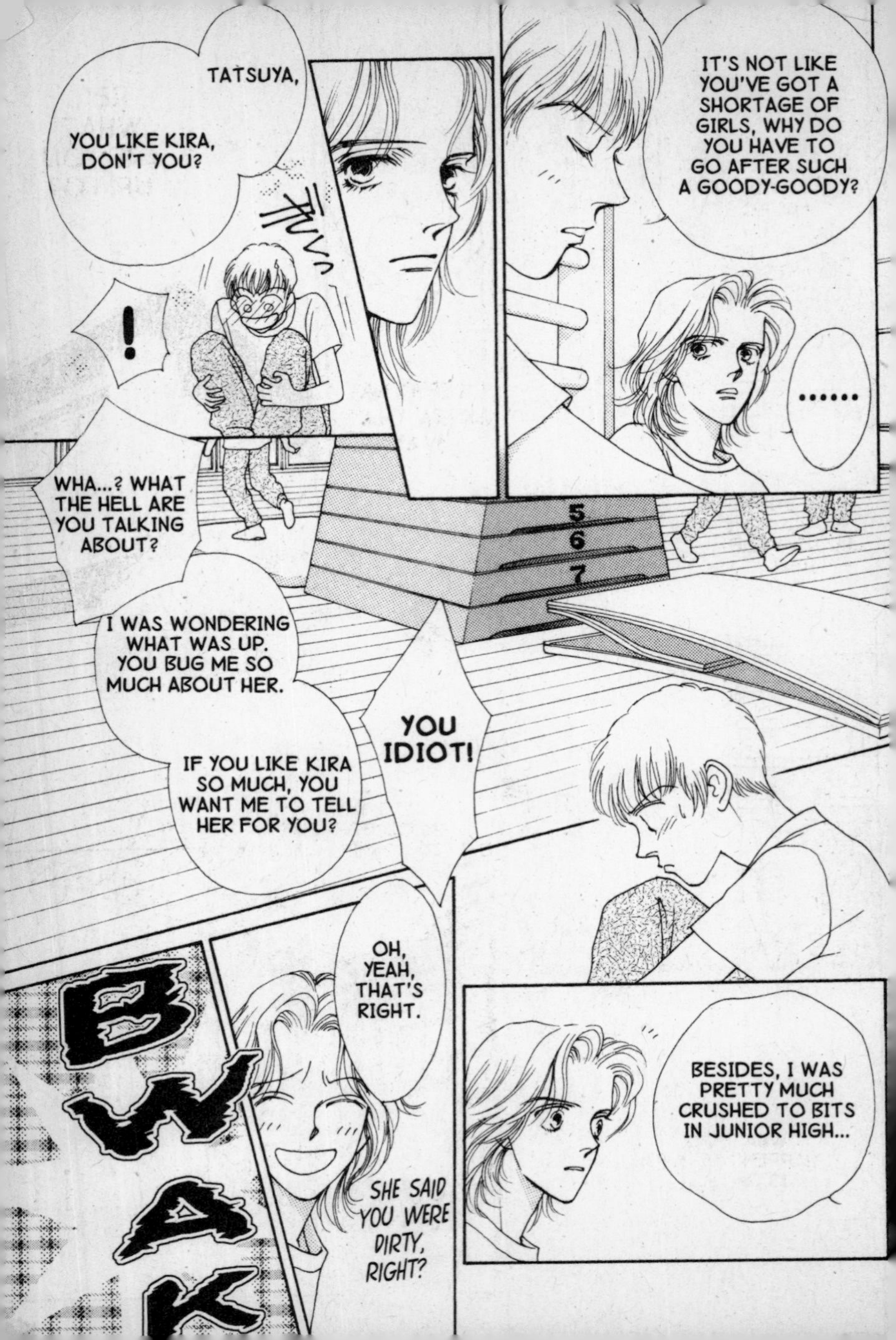
IT'S NOT LIKE YOU'VE GOT A SHORTAGE OF GIRLS, WHY DO YOU HAVE TO GO AFTER SUCH A GOODY-GOODY?
......
TATSUYA,
YOU LIKE KIRA, DON'T YOU?
!
WHA...? WHAT THE HELL ARE YOU TALKING ABOUT?
I WAS WONDERING WHAT WAS UP. YOU BUG ME SO MUCH ABOUT HER.
IF YOU LIKE KIRA SO MUCH, YOU WANT ME TO TELL HER FOR YOU?
YOU IDIOT!
5
6
7
BESIDES, I WAS PRETTY MUCH CRUSHED TO BITS IN JUNIOR HIGH...
OH, YEAH, THAT'S RIGHT.
SHE SAID YOU WERE DIRTY, RIGHT?
BWAK

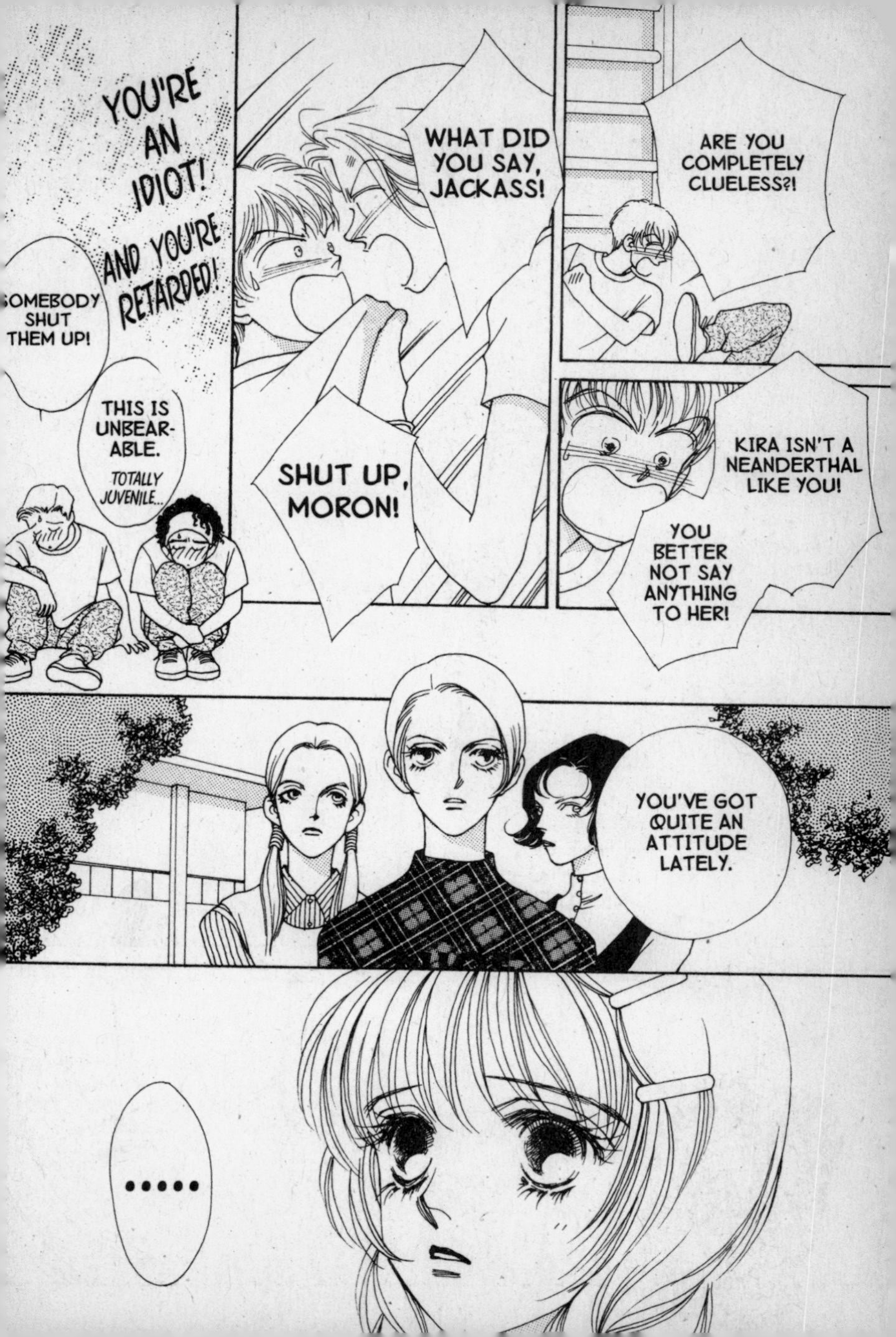

ARE YOU COMPLETELY CLUELESS?!
KIRA ISN'T A NEANDERTHAL LIKE YOU!
YOU BETTER NOT SAY ANYTHING TO HER!
WHAT DID YOU SAY, JACKASS!
SHUT UP, MORON!
YOU'RE AN IDIOT!
AND YOU'RE RETARDED!
SOMEBODY SHUT THEM UP!
THIS IS UNBEAR-ABLE.
TOTALLY JUVENILE...
YOU'VE GOT QUITE AN ATTITUDE LATELY.
.....

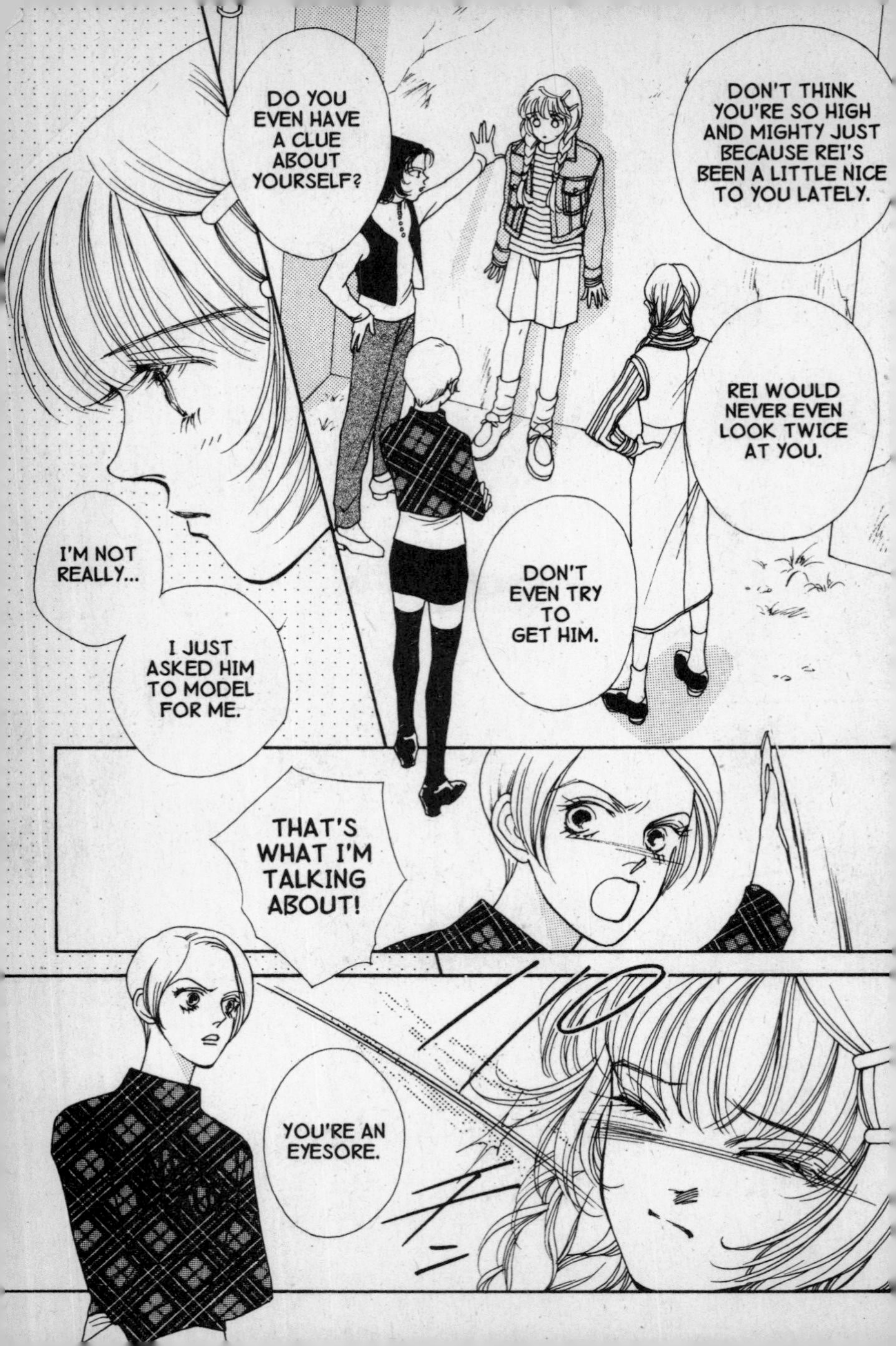
DON'T THINK YOU'RE SO HIGH AND MIGHTY JUST BECAUSE REI'S BEEN A LITTLE NICE TO YOU LATELY.
DO YOU EVEN HAVE A CLUE ABOUT YOURSELF?
REI WOULD NEVER EVEN LOOK TWICE AT YOU.
DON'T EVEN TRY TO GET HIM.
I'M NOT REALLY...
I JUST ASKED HIM TO MODEL FOR ME.
THAT'S WHAT I'M TALKING ABOUT!
YOU'RE AN EYESORE.

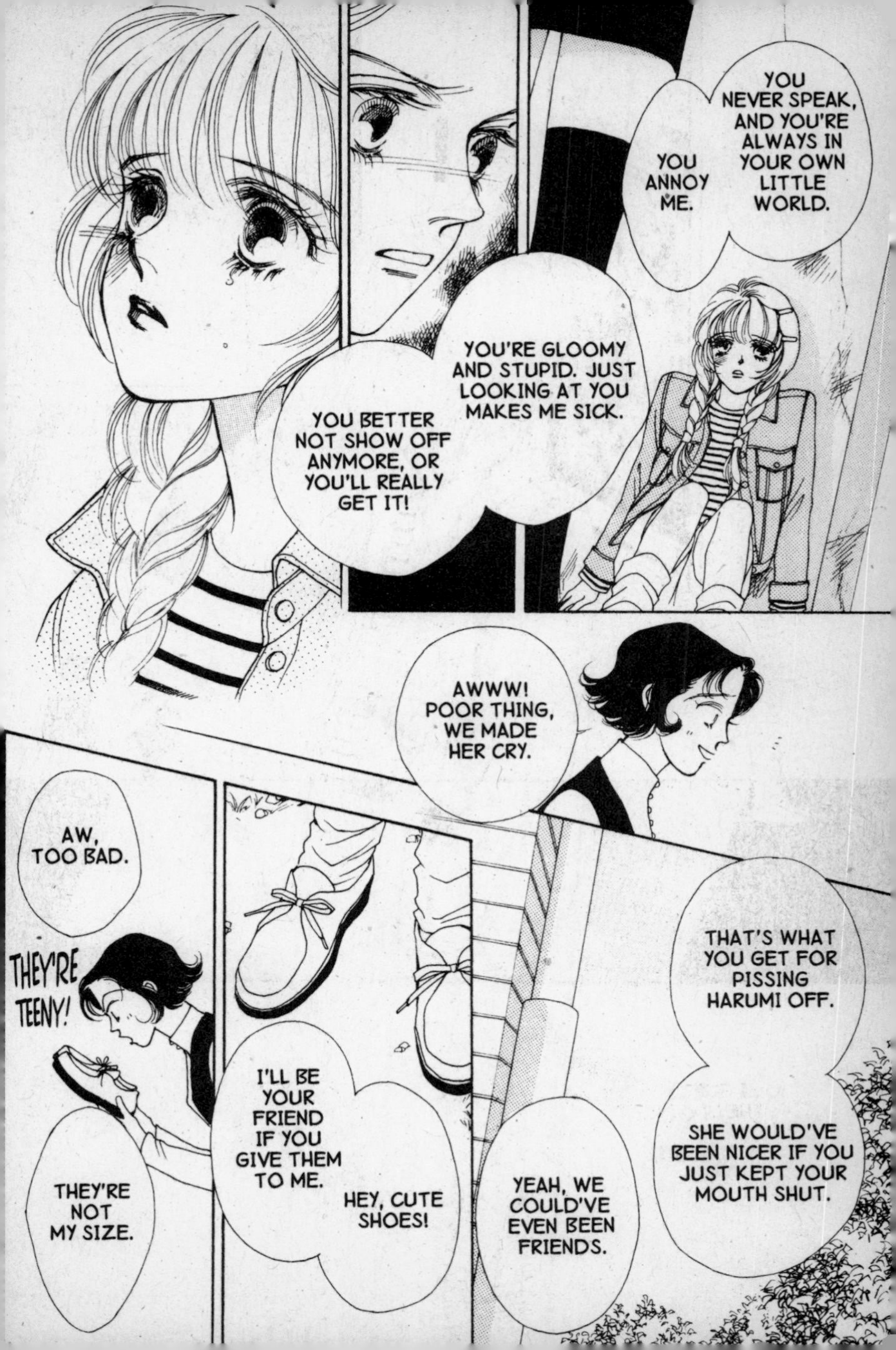
YOU NEVER SPEAK, AND YOU'RE ALWAYS IN YOUR OWN LITTLE WORLD.
YOU ANNOY ME.
YOU'RE GLOOMY AND STUPID. JUST LOOKING AT YOU MAKES ME SICK.
YOU BETTER NOT SHOW OFF ANYMORE, OR YOU'LL REALLY GET IT!
AWWW! POOR THING, WE MADE HER CRY.
THAT'S WHAT YOU GET FOR PISSING HARUMI OFF.
SHE WOULD'VE BEEN NICER IF YOU JUST KEPT YOUR MOUTH SHUT.
YEAH, WE COULD'VE EVEN BEEN FRIENDS.
HEY, CUTE SHOES!
I'LL BE YOUR FRIEND IF YOU GIVE THEM TO ME.
AW, TOO BAD.
THEY'RE TEENY!
THEY'RE NOT MY SIZE.

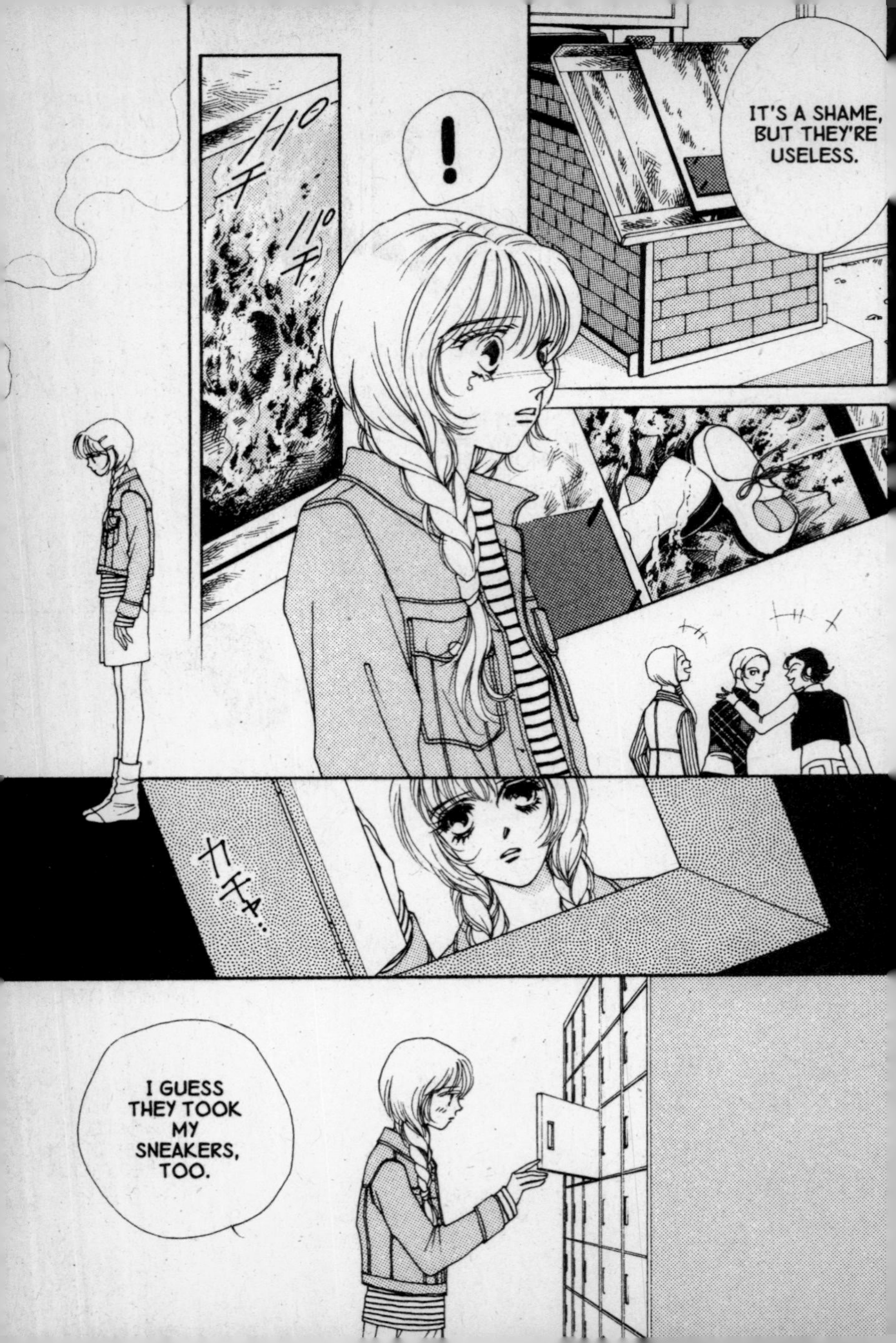
IT'S A SHAME, BUT THEY'RE USELESS.
!
パチ パチ
カチャ…
I GUESS THEY TOOK MY SNEAKERS, TOO.

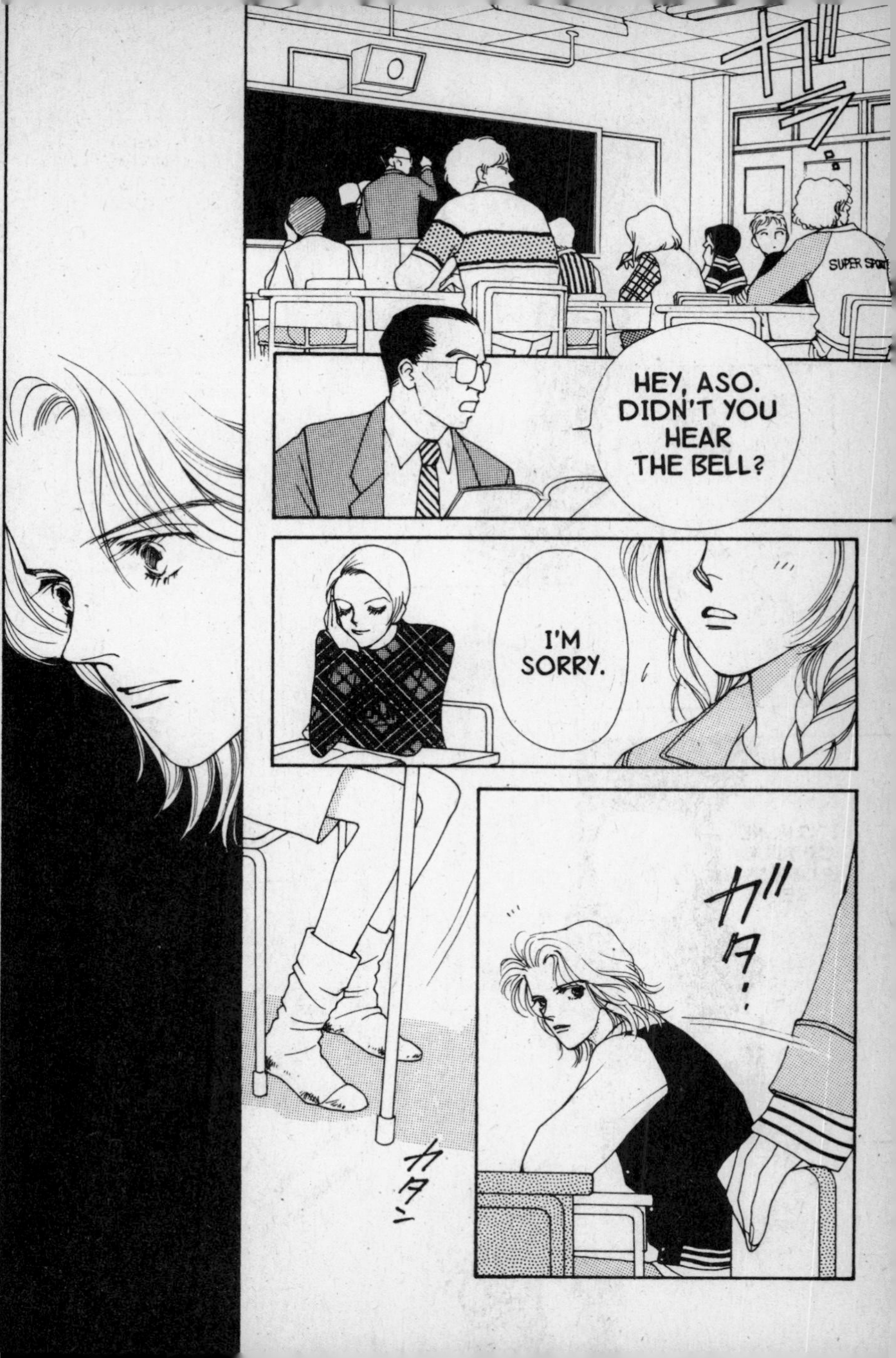
ガラ
HEY, ASO. DIDN'T YOU HEAR THE BELL?
I'M SORRY.
ガタ！
カタン

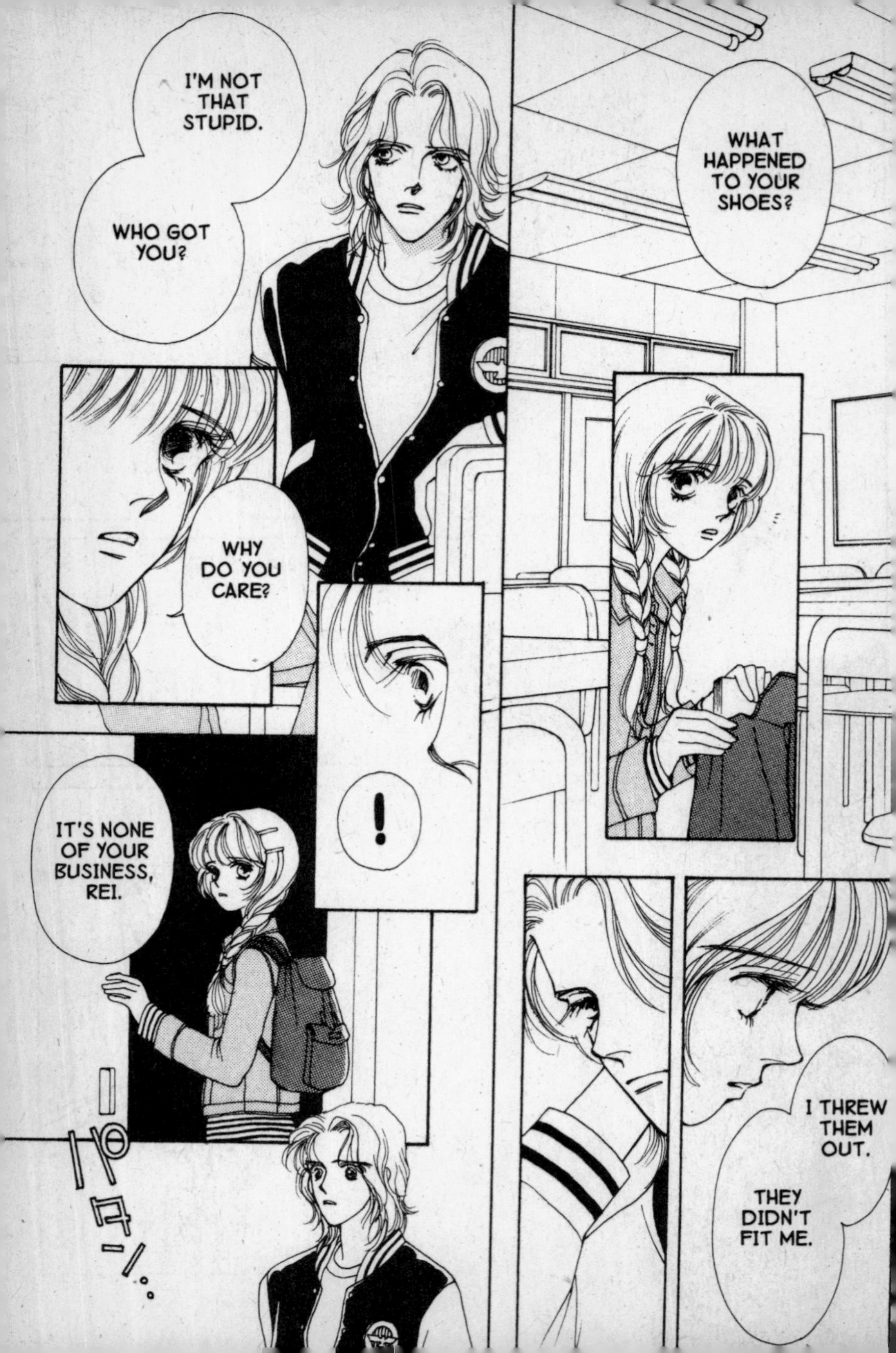
WHAT HAPPENED TO YOUR SHOES?
I THREW THEM OUT.
THEY DIDN'T FIT ME.
I'M NOT THAT STUPID.
WHO GOT YOU?
WHY DO YOU CARE?
!
IT'S NONE OF YOUR BUSINESS, REI.

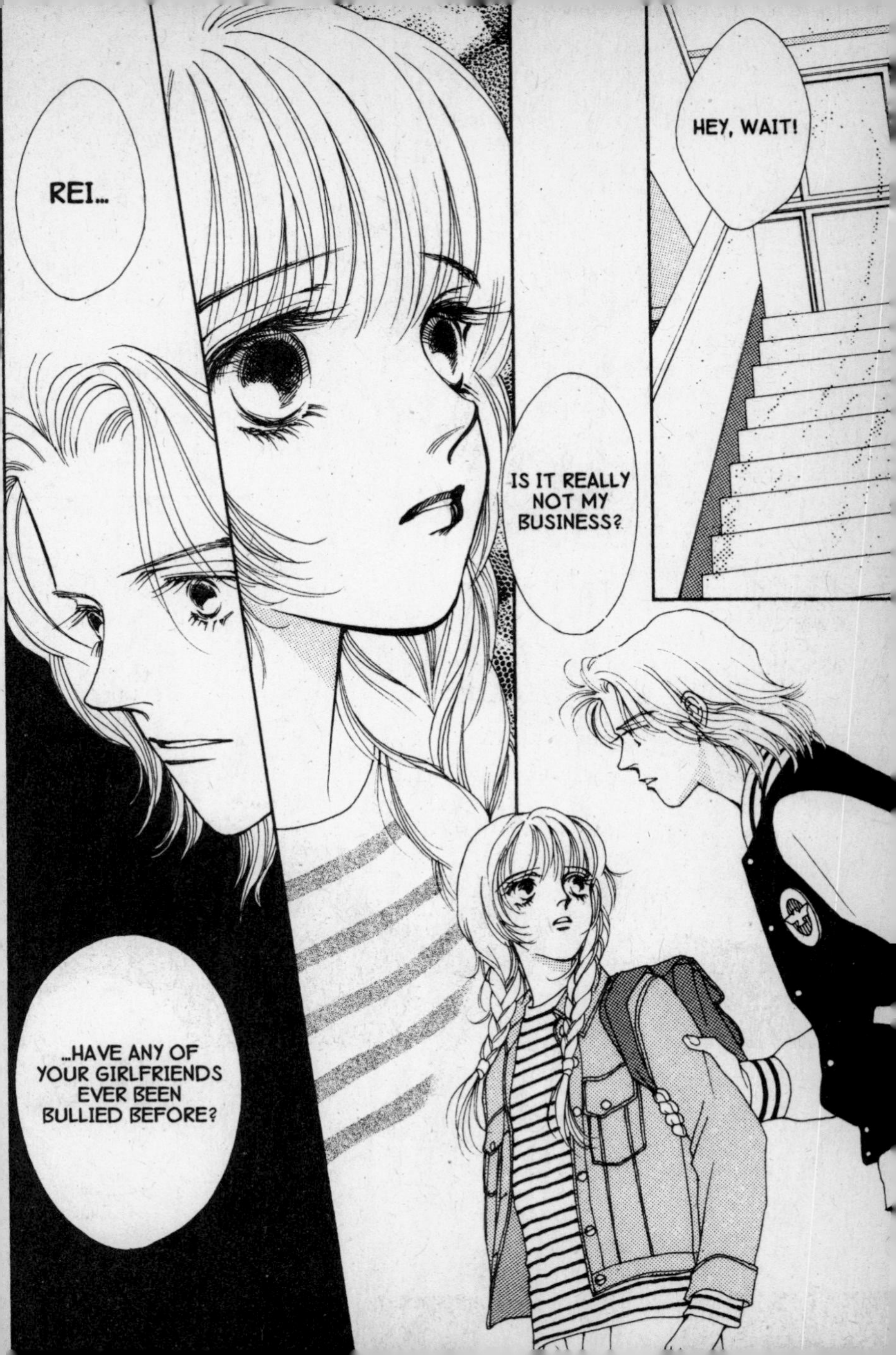
HEY, WAIT!
IS IT REALLY NOT MY BUSINESS?
REI...
...HAVE ANY OF YOUR GIRLFRIENDS EVER BEEN BULLIED BEFORE?

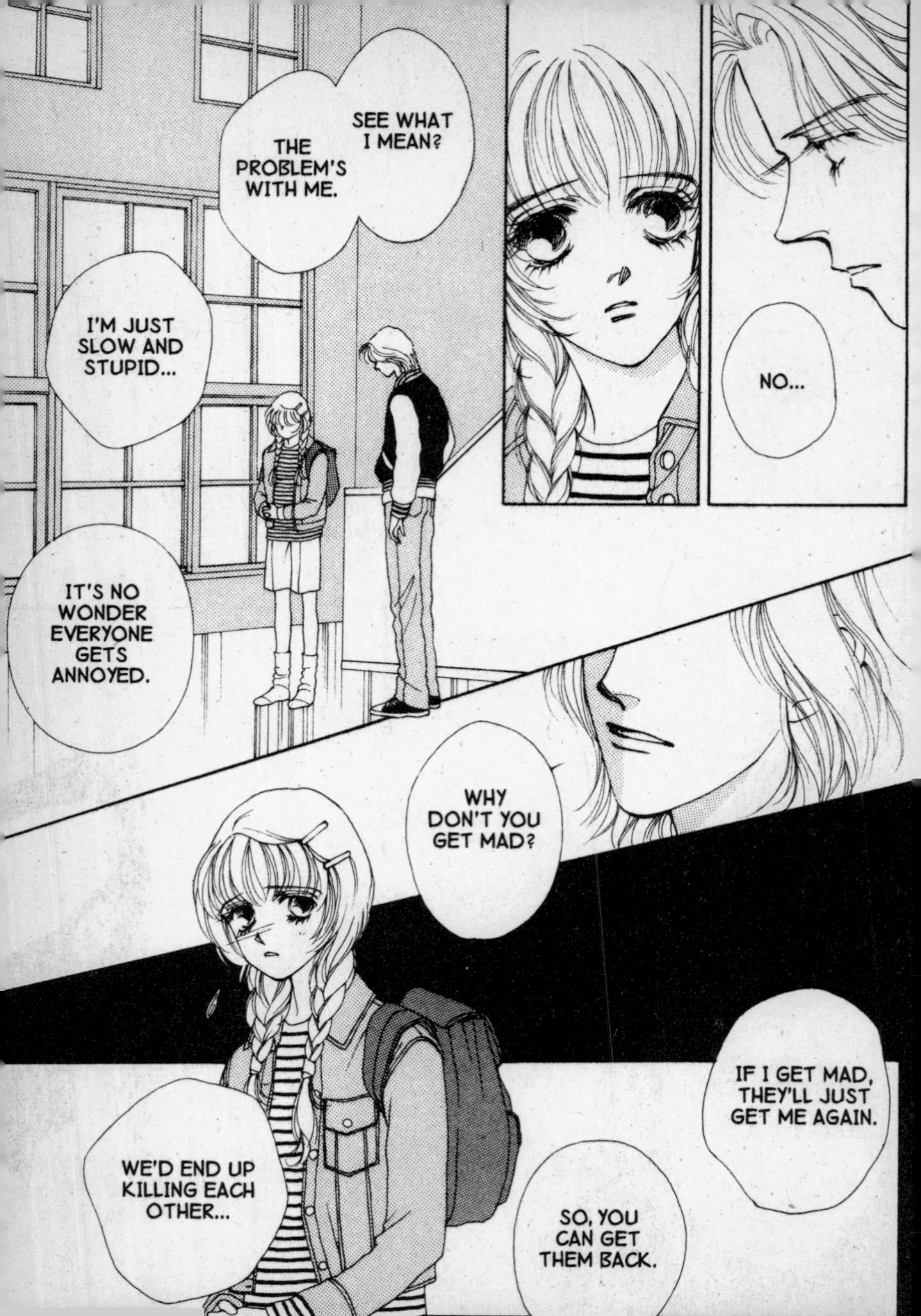
NO...
SEE WHAT I MEAN?
THE PROBLEM'S WITH ME.
I'M JUST SLOW AND STUPID...
IT'S NO WONDER EVERYONE GETS ANNOYED.
WHY DON'T YOU GET MAD?
IF I GET MAD, THEY'LL JUST GET ME AGAIN.
SO, YOU CAN GET THEM BACK.
WE'D END UP KILLING EACH OTHER...

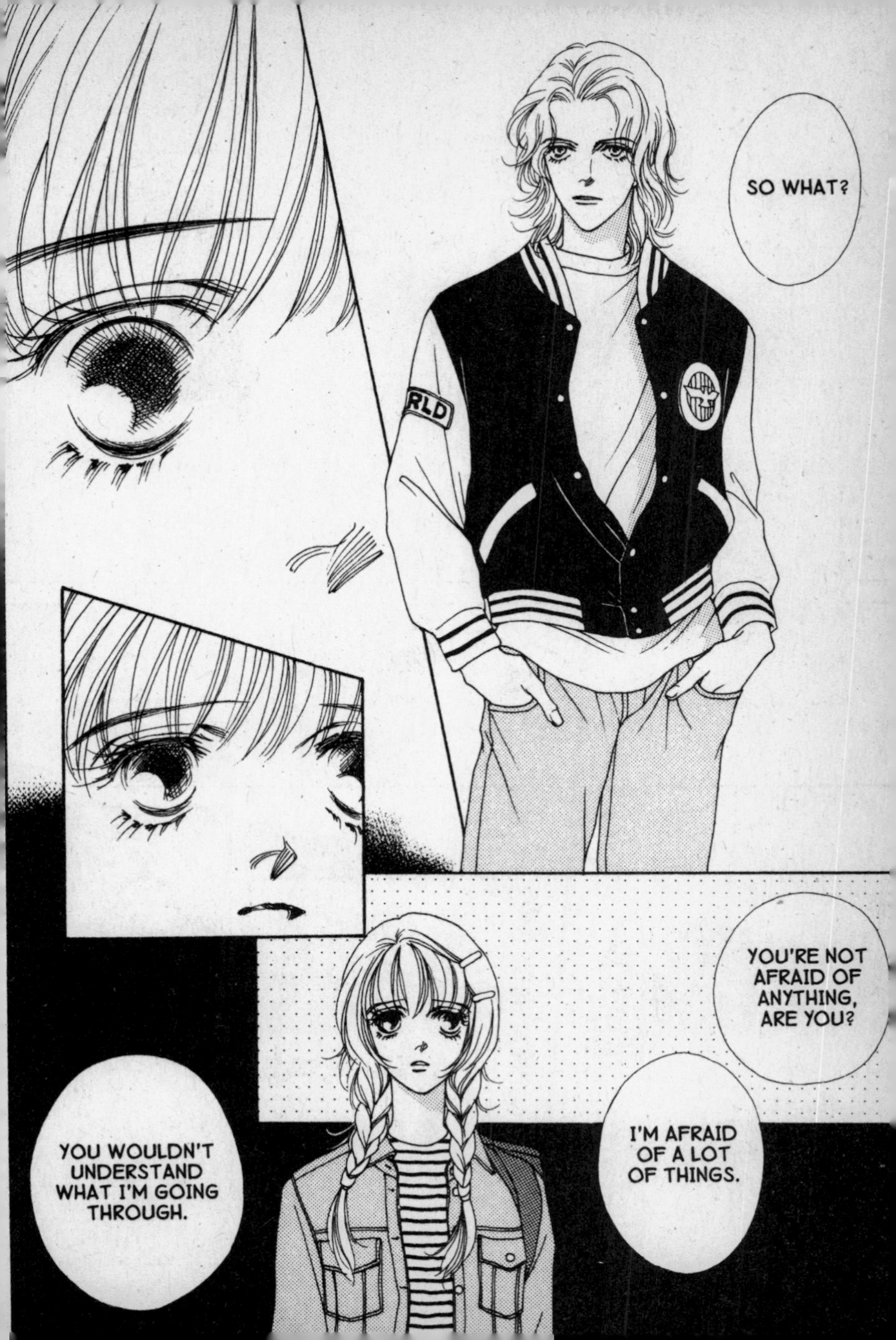
SO WHAT?
RLD
YOU'RE NOT AFRAID OF ANYTHING, ARE YOU?
I'M AFRAID OF A LOT OF THINGS.
YOU WOULDN'T UNDERSTAND WHAT I'M GOING THROUGH.

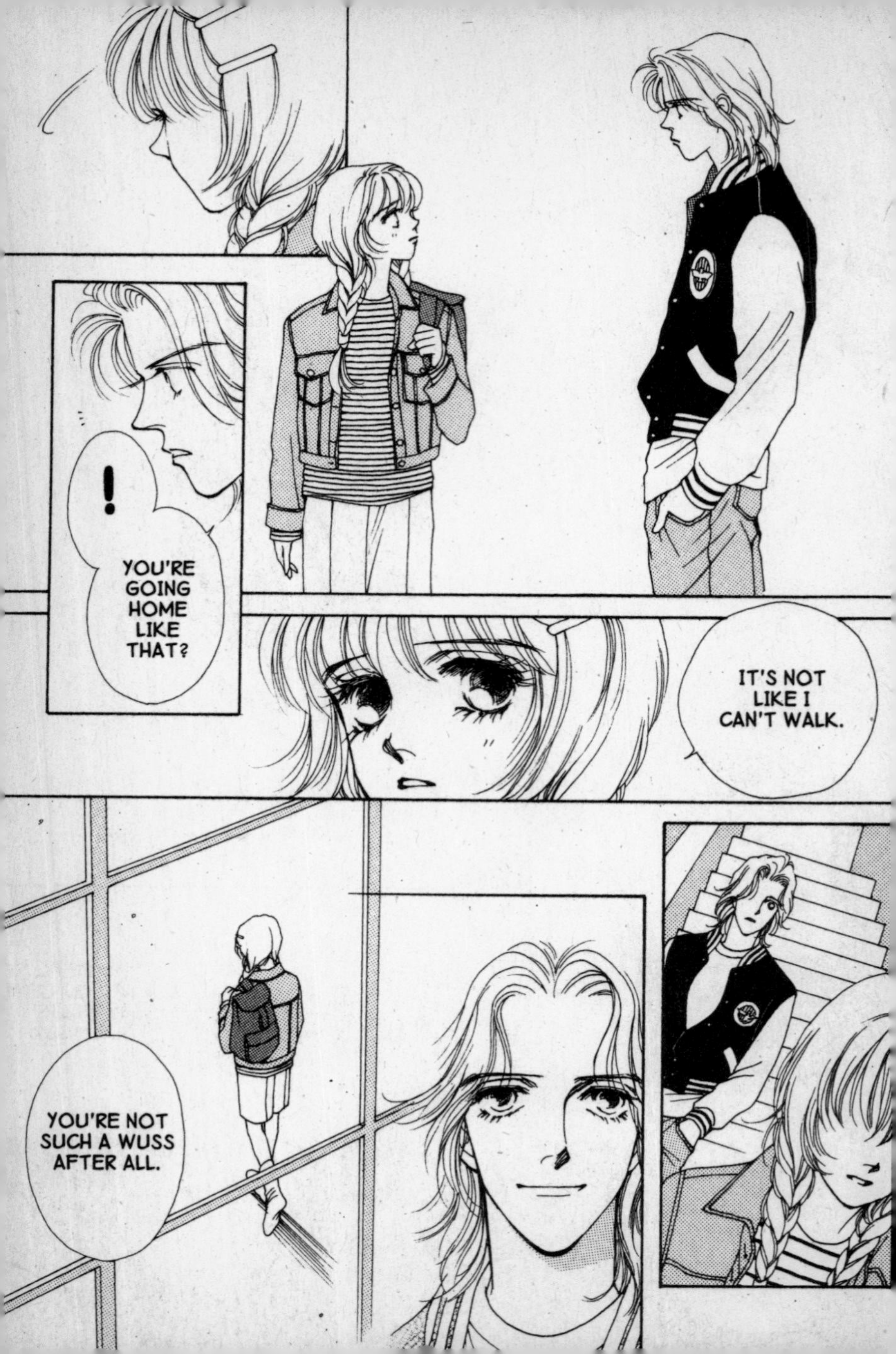
!
YOU'RE GOING HOME LIKE THAT?
IT'S NOT LIKE I CAN'T WALK.
YOU'RE NOT SUCH A WUSS AFTER ALL.

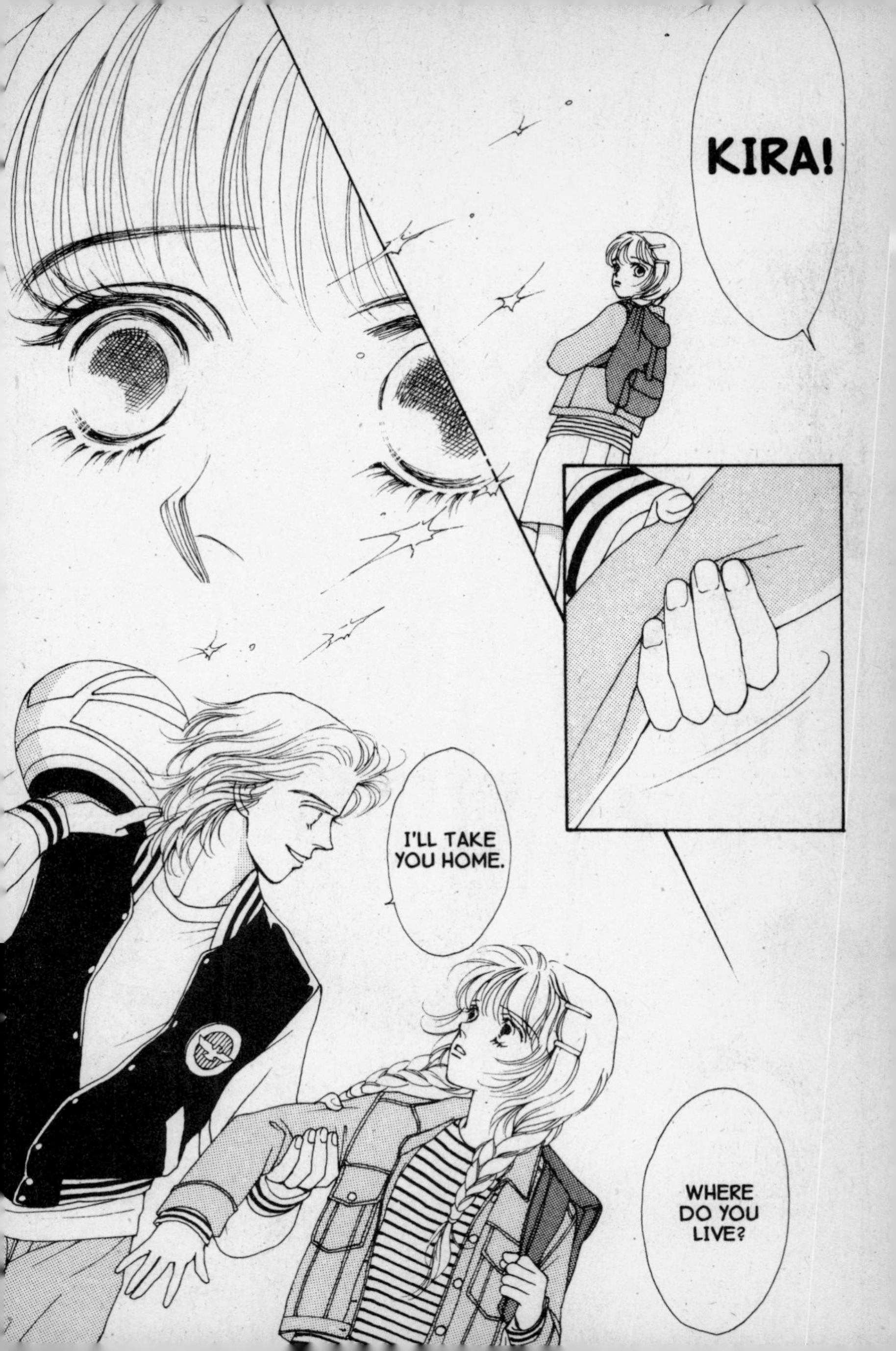
KIRA!
I'LL TAKE YOU HOME.
WHERE DO YOU LIVE?

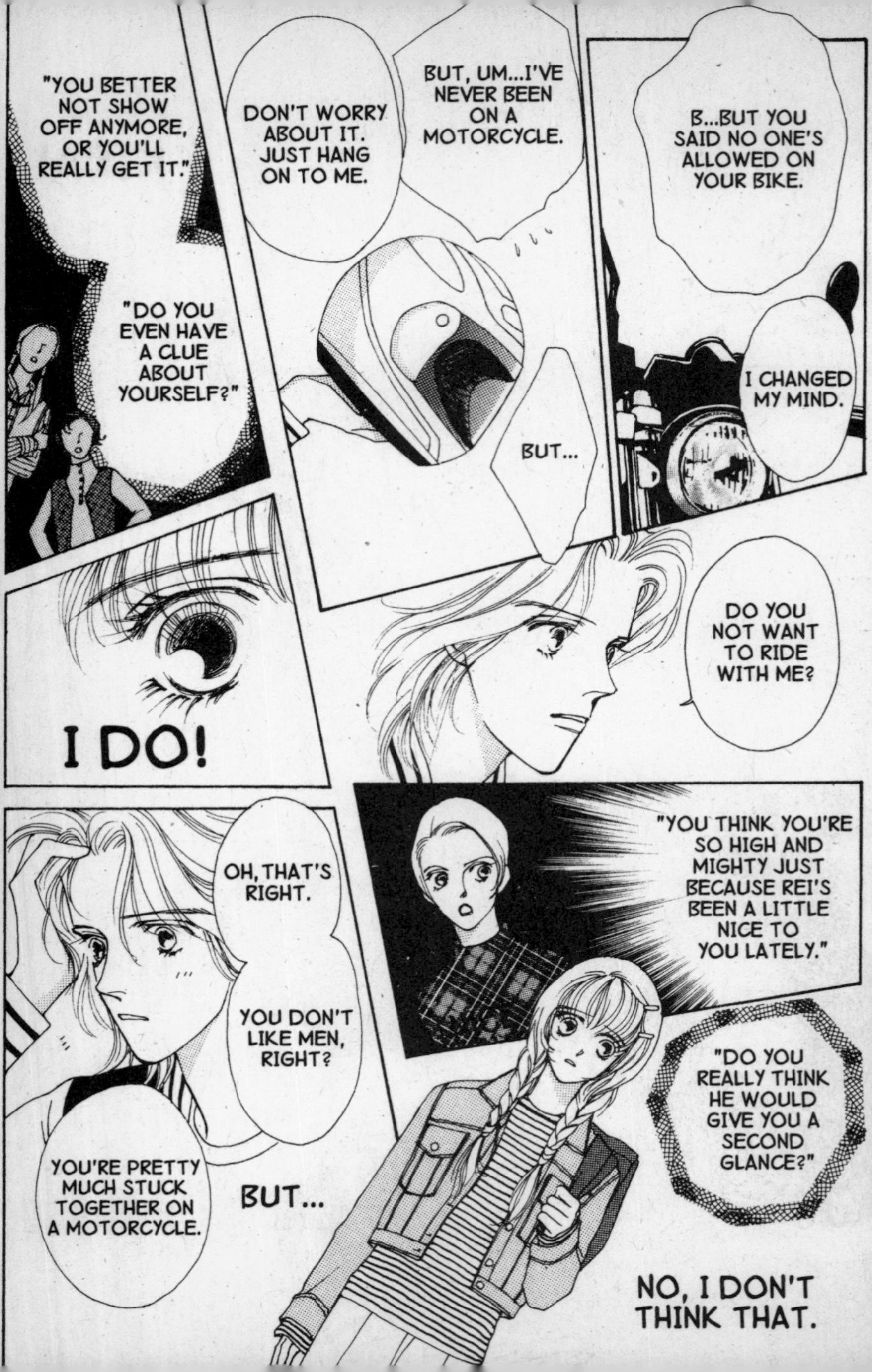
B...BUT YOU SAID NO ONE'S ALLOWED ON YOUR BIKE.
I CHANGED MY MIND.
BUT, UM...I'VE NEVER BEEN ON A MOTORCYCLE.
DON'T WORRY ABOUT IT. JUST HANG ON TO ME.
BUT...
"YOU BETTER NOT SHOW OFF ANYMORE, OR YOU'LL REALLY GET IT."
"DO YOU EVEN HAVE A CLUE ABOUT YOURSELF?"
DO YOU NOT WANT TO RIDE WITH ME?
I DO!
"YOU THINK YOU'RE SO HIGH AND MIGHTY JUST BECAUSE REI'S BEEN A LITTLE NICE TO YOU LATELY."
"DO YOU REALLY THINK HE WOULD GIVE YOU A SECOND GLANCE?"
NO, I DON'T THINK THAT.
OH, THAT'S RIGHT.
YOU DON'T LIKE MEN, RIGHT?
YOU'RE PRETTY MUCH STUCK TOGETHER ON A MOTORCYCLE.
BUT...

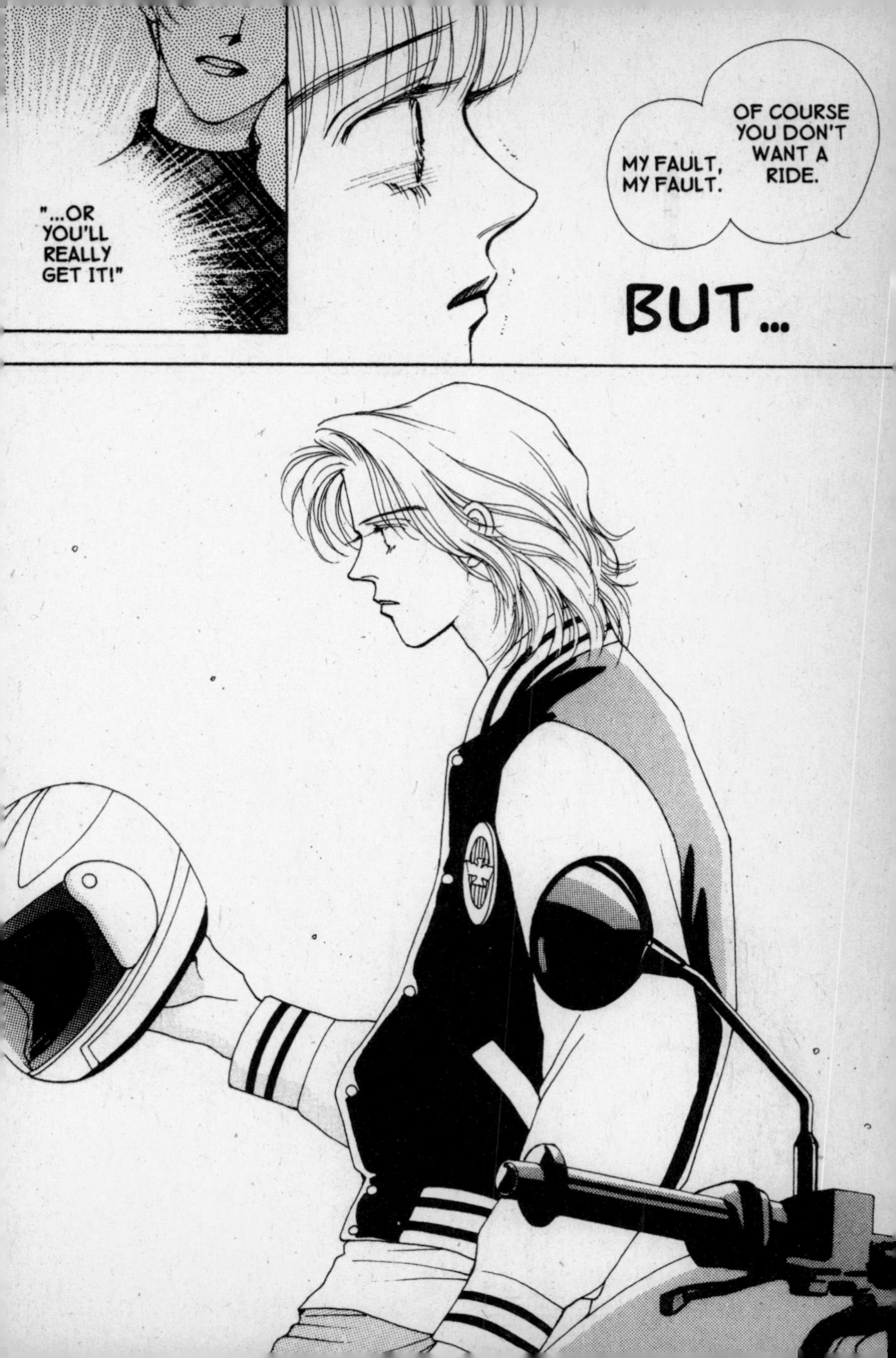
OF COURSE YOU DON'T WANT A RIDE.
MY FAULT, MY FAULT.
BUT...
"...OR YOU'LL REALLY GET IT!"

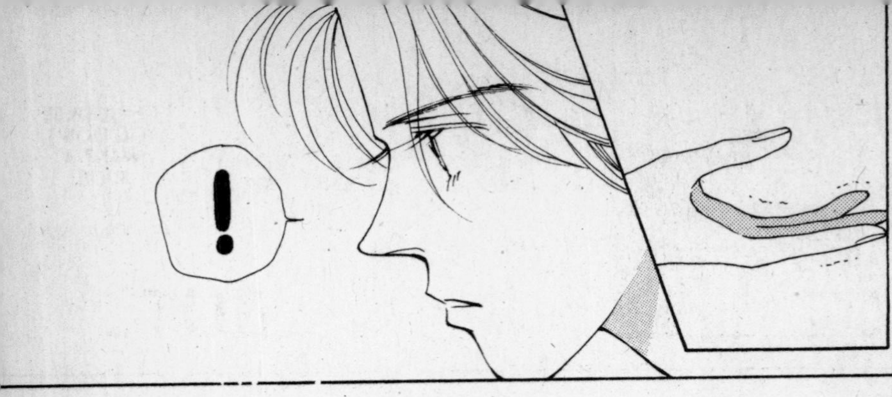
!
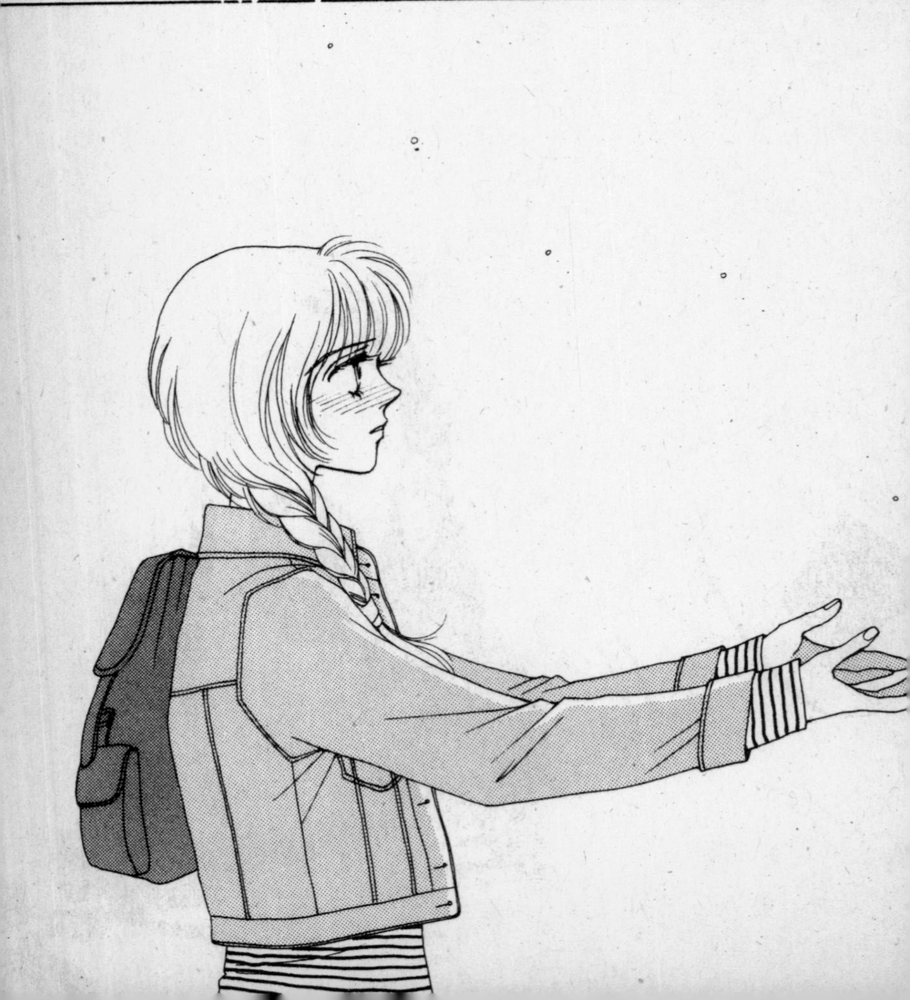

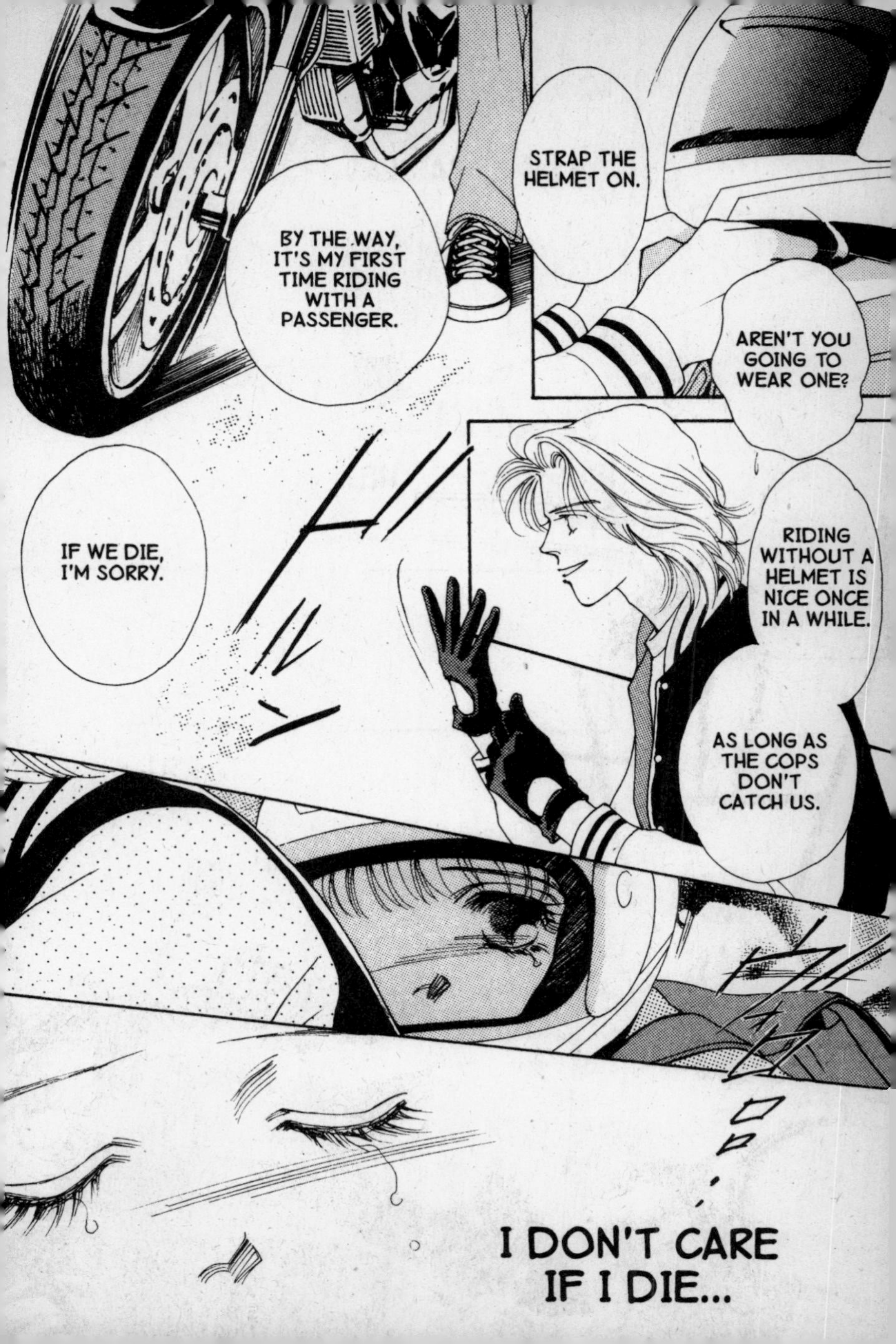
STRAP THE HELMET ON.
AREN'T YOU GOING TO WEAR ONE?
RIDING WITHOUT A HELMET IS NICE ONCE IN A WHILE.
AS LONG AS THE COPS DON'T CATCH US.
BY THE WAY, IT'S MY FIRST TIME RIDING WITH A PASSENGER.
IF WE DIE, I'M SORRY.
I DON'T CARE IF I DIE...

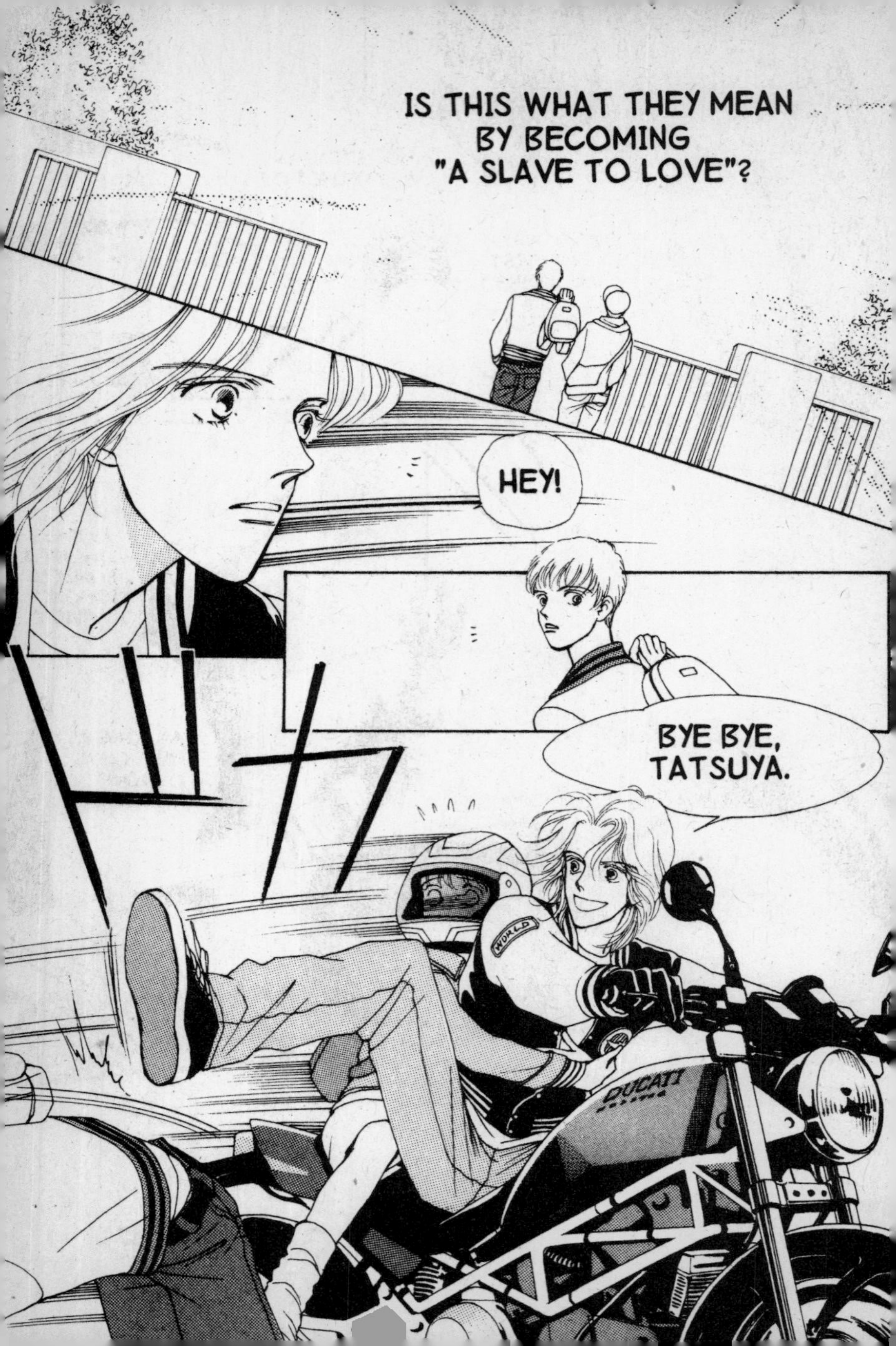
IS THIS WHAT THEY MEAN BY BECOMING "A SLAVE TO LOVE"?
HEY!
BYE BYE, TATSUYA.

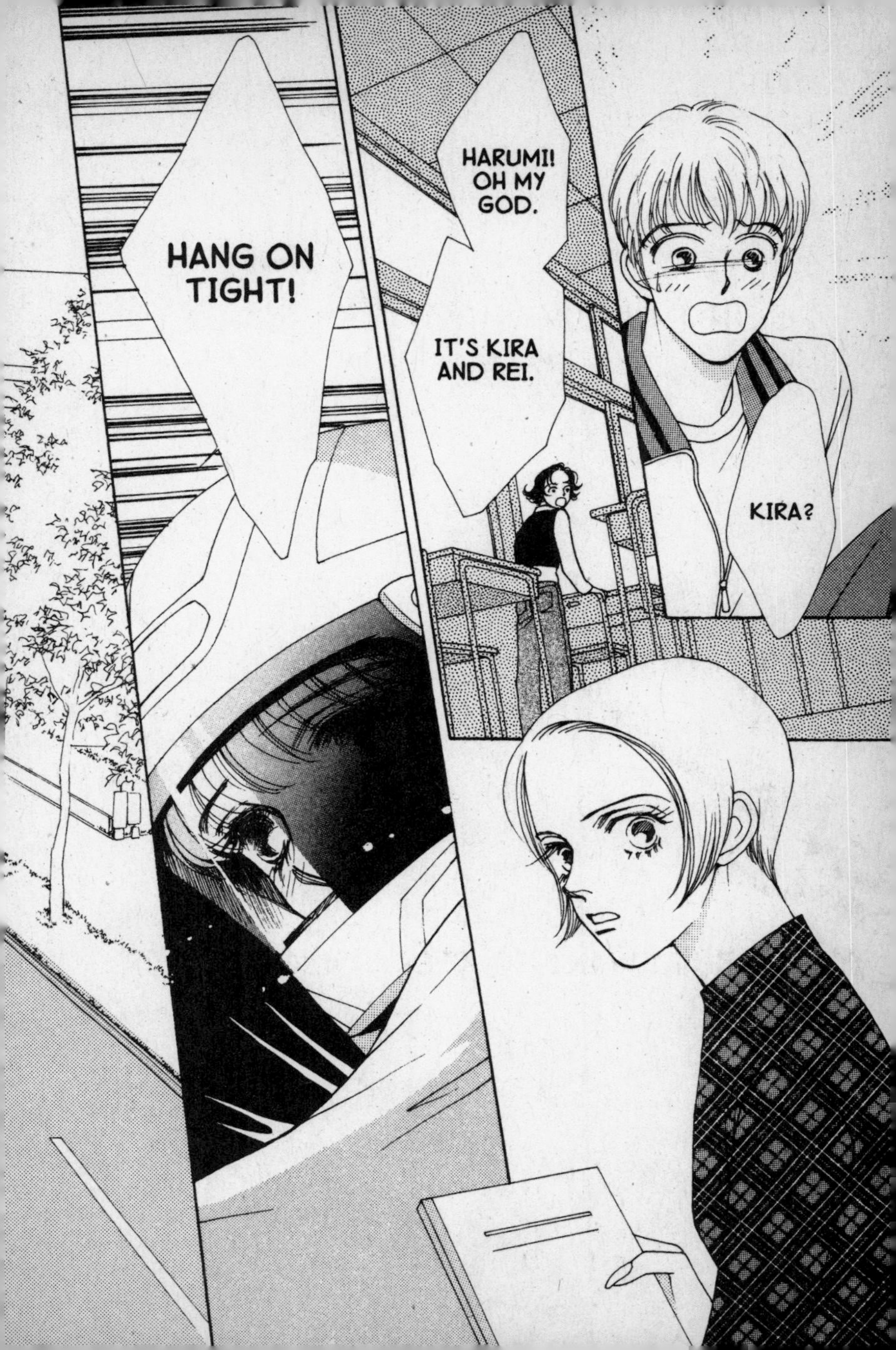
KIRA?
HARUMI! OH MY GOD.
IT'S KIRA AND REI.
HANG ON TIGHT!

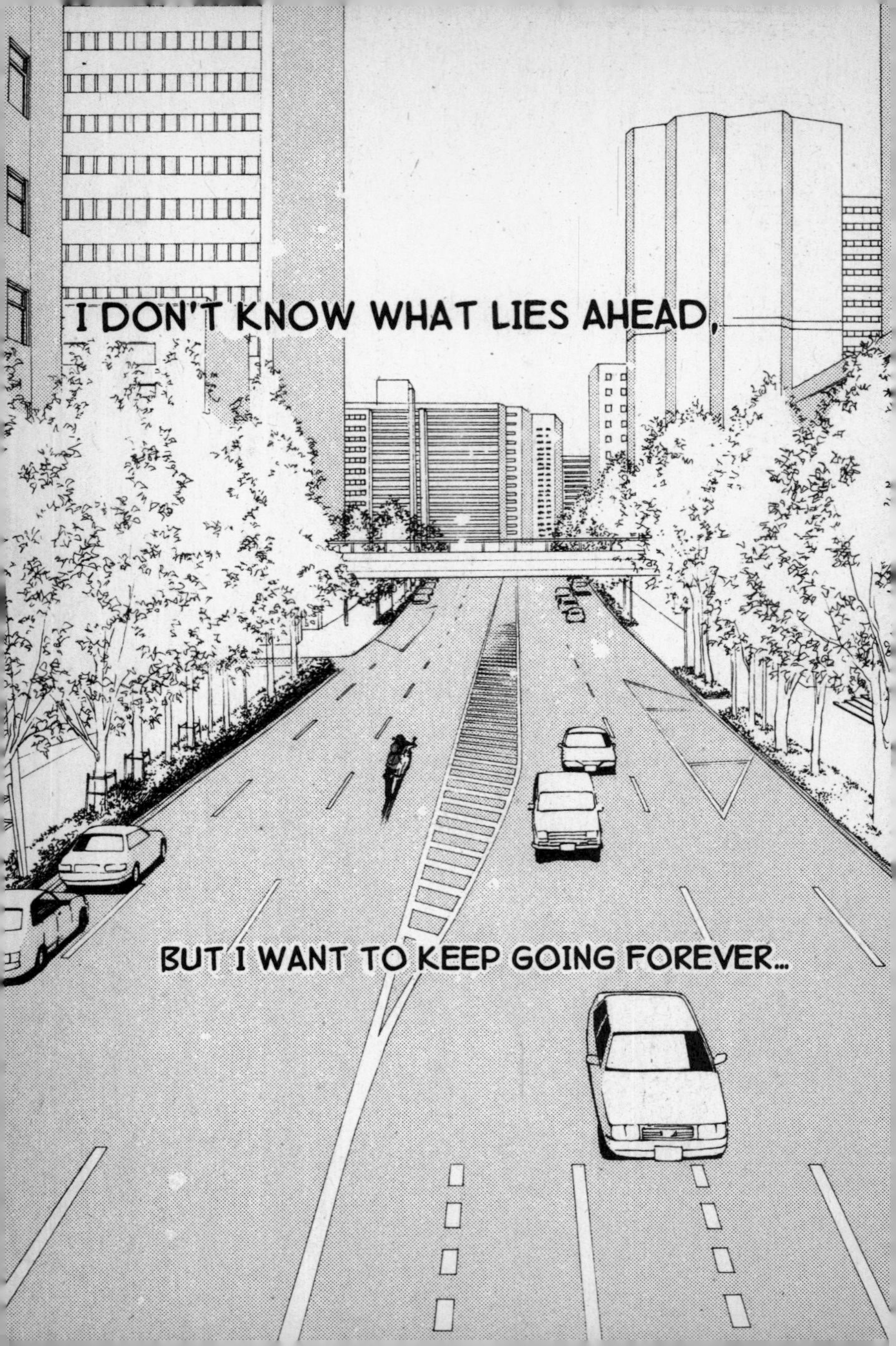
I DON'T KNOW WHAT LIES AHEAD,
BUT I WANT TO KEEP GOING FOREVER...

MARS

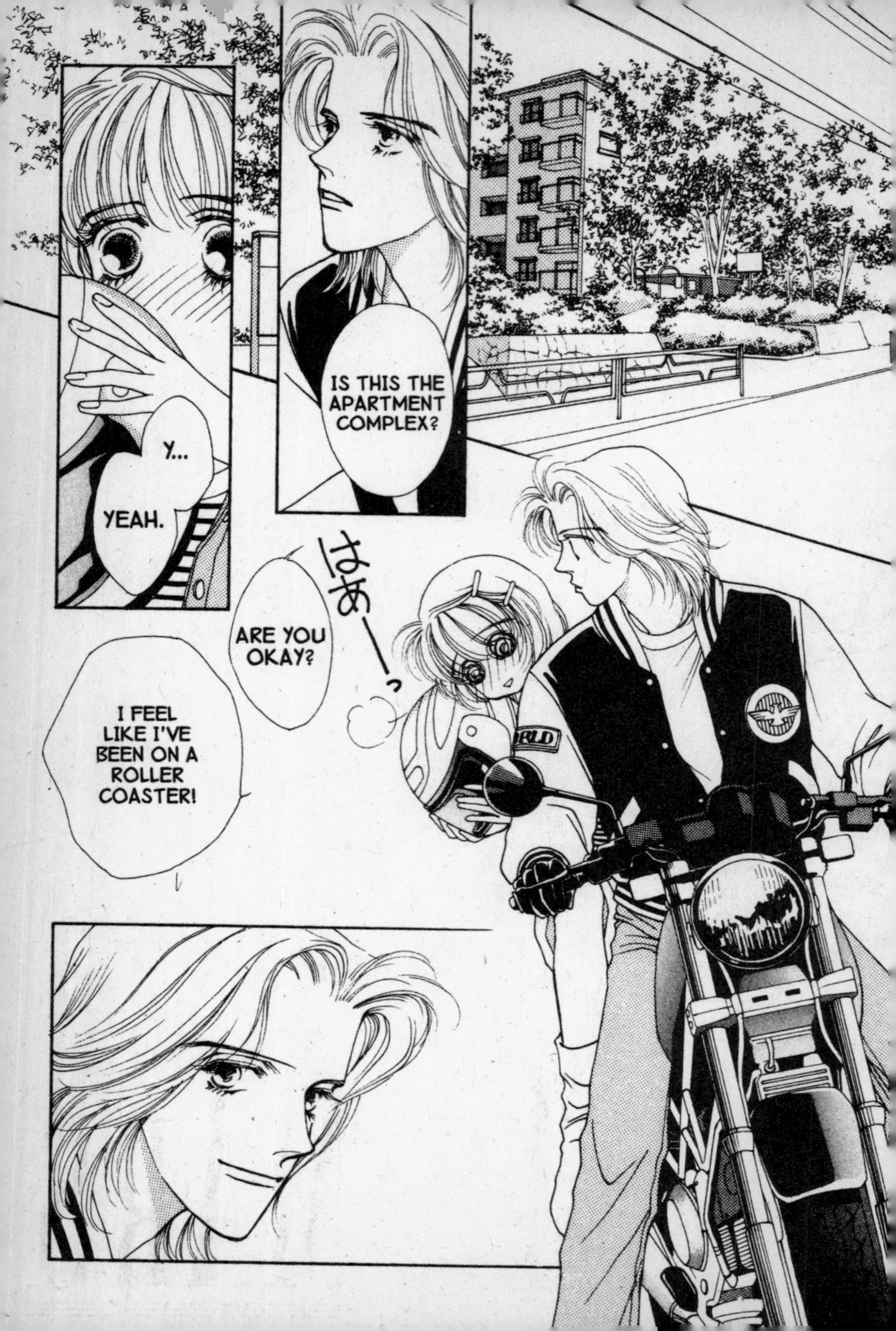
はあー
ARE YOU OKAY?
I FEEL LIKE I'VE BEEN ON A ROLLER COASTER!
IS THIS THE APARTMENT COMPLEX?
Y... YEAH.

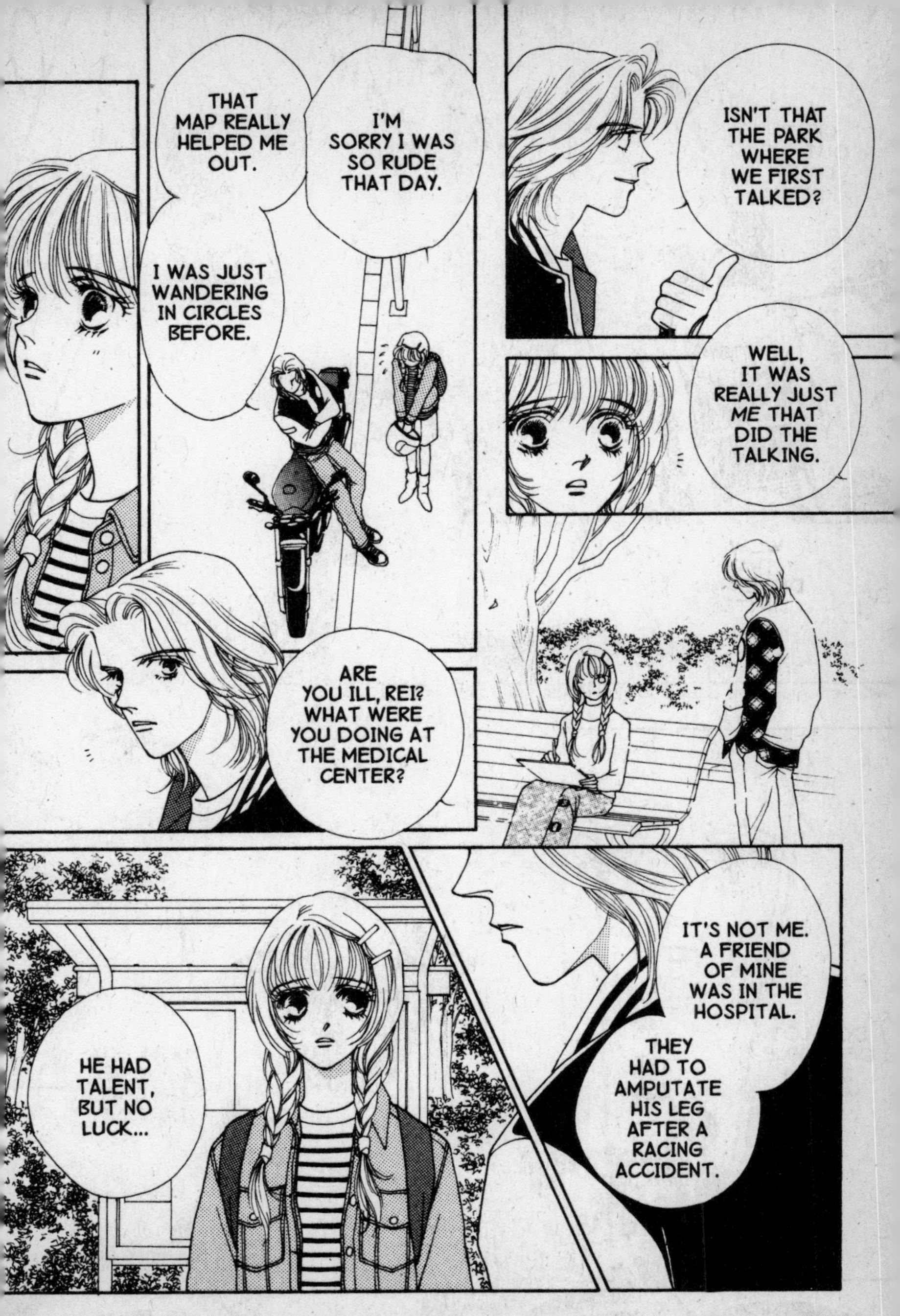
ISN'T THAT THE PARK WHERE WE FIRST TALKED?
WELL, IT WAS REALLY JUST *ME* THAT DID THE TALKING.
I'M SORRY I WAS SO RUDE THAT DAY.
THAT MAP REALLY HELPED ME OUT.
I WAS JUST WANDERING IN CIRCLES BEFORE.
ARE YOU ILL, REI? WHAT WERE YOU DOING AT THE MEDICAL CENTER?
IT'S NOT ME. A FRIEND OF MINE WAS IN THE HOSPITAL.
THEY HAD TO AMPUTATE HIS LEG AFTER A RACING ACCIDENT.
HE HAD TALENT, BUT NO LUCK...

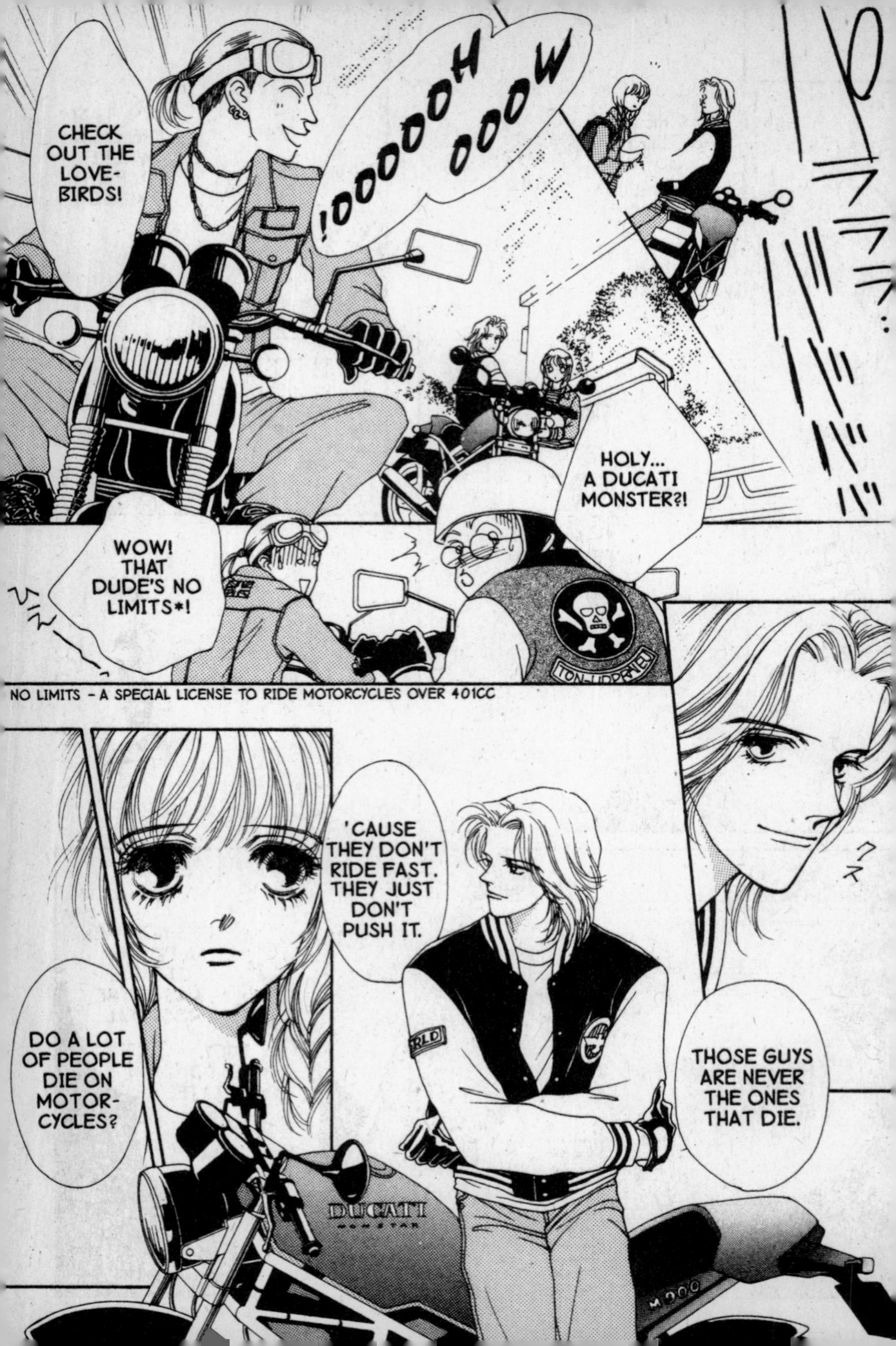
WOOOO HOOOOOO!
CHECK OUT THE LOVE-BIRDS!
HOLY... A DUCATI MONSTER?!
WOW! THAT DUDE'S NO LIMITS*!
NO LIMITS - A SPECIAL LICENSE TO RIDE MOTORCYCLES OVER 401CC
THOSE GUYS ARE NEVER THE ONES THAT DIE.
'CAUSE THEY DON'T RIDE FAST. THEY JUST DON'T PUSH IT.
DO A LOT OF PEOPLE DIE ON MOTOR-CYCLES?
DUCATI

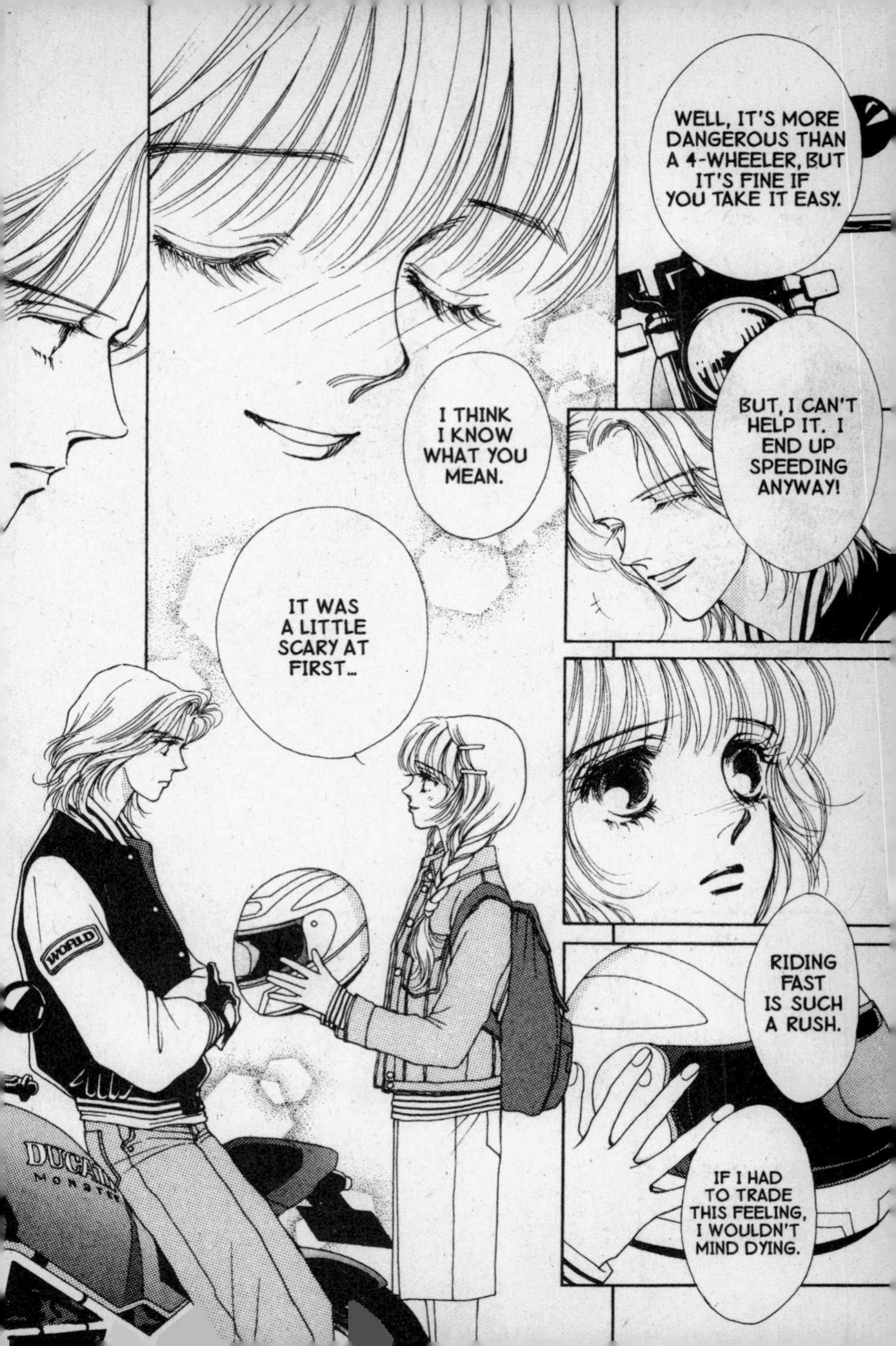
WELL, IT'S MORE DANGEROUS THAN A 4-WHEELER, BUT IT'S FINE IF YOU TAKE IT EASY.
BUT, I CAN'T HELP IT. I END UP SPEEDING ANYWAY!
RIDING FAST IS SUCH A RUSH.
IF I HAD TO TRADE THIS FEELING, I WOULDN'T MIND DYING.
I THINK I KNOW WHAT YOU MEAN.
IT WAS A LITTLE SCARY AT FIRST...

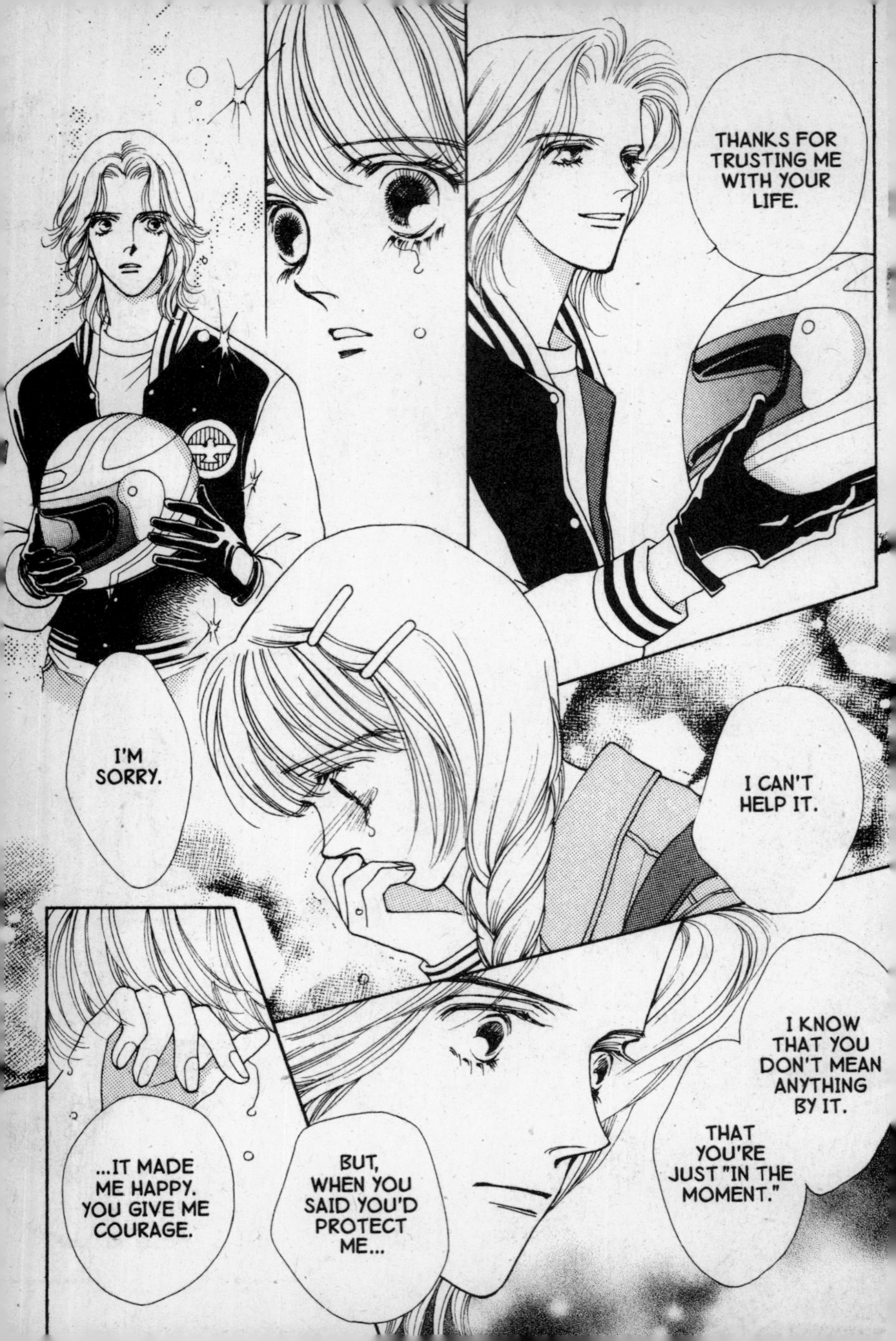
THANKS FOR TRUSTING ME WITH YOUR LIFE.
I CAN'T HELP IT.
I'M SORRY.
I KNOW THAT YOU DON'T MEAN ANYTHING BY IT.
THAT YOU'RE JUST "IN THE MOMENT."
BUT, WHEN YOU SAID YOU'D PROTECT ME...
...IT MADE ME HAPPY. YOU GIVE ME COURAGE.

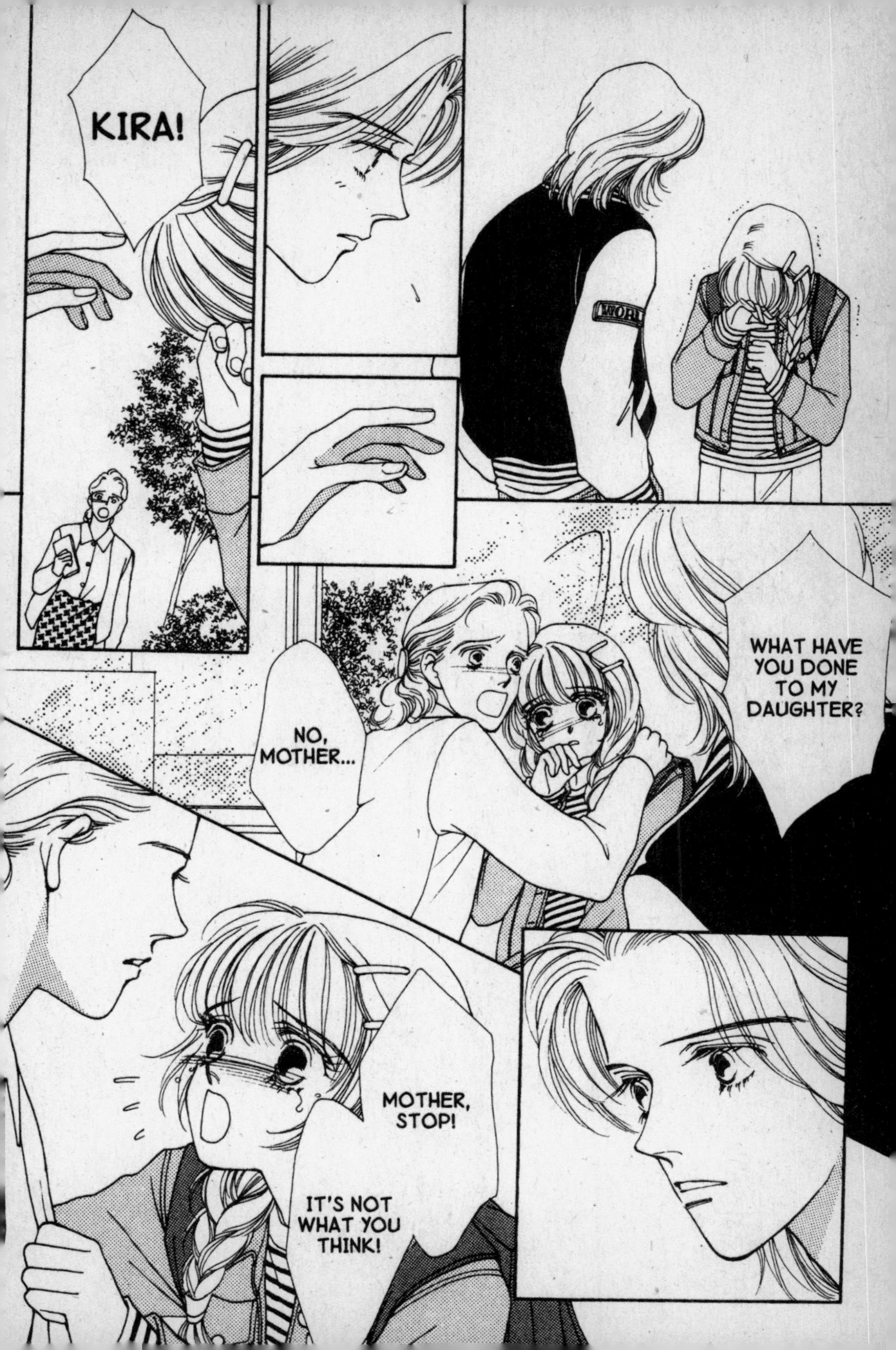
KIRA!
WHAT HAVE YOU DONE TO MY DAUGHTER?
NO, MOTHER...
MOTHER, STOP!
IT'S NOT WHAT YOU THINK!

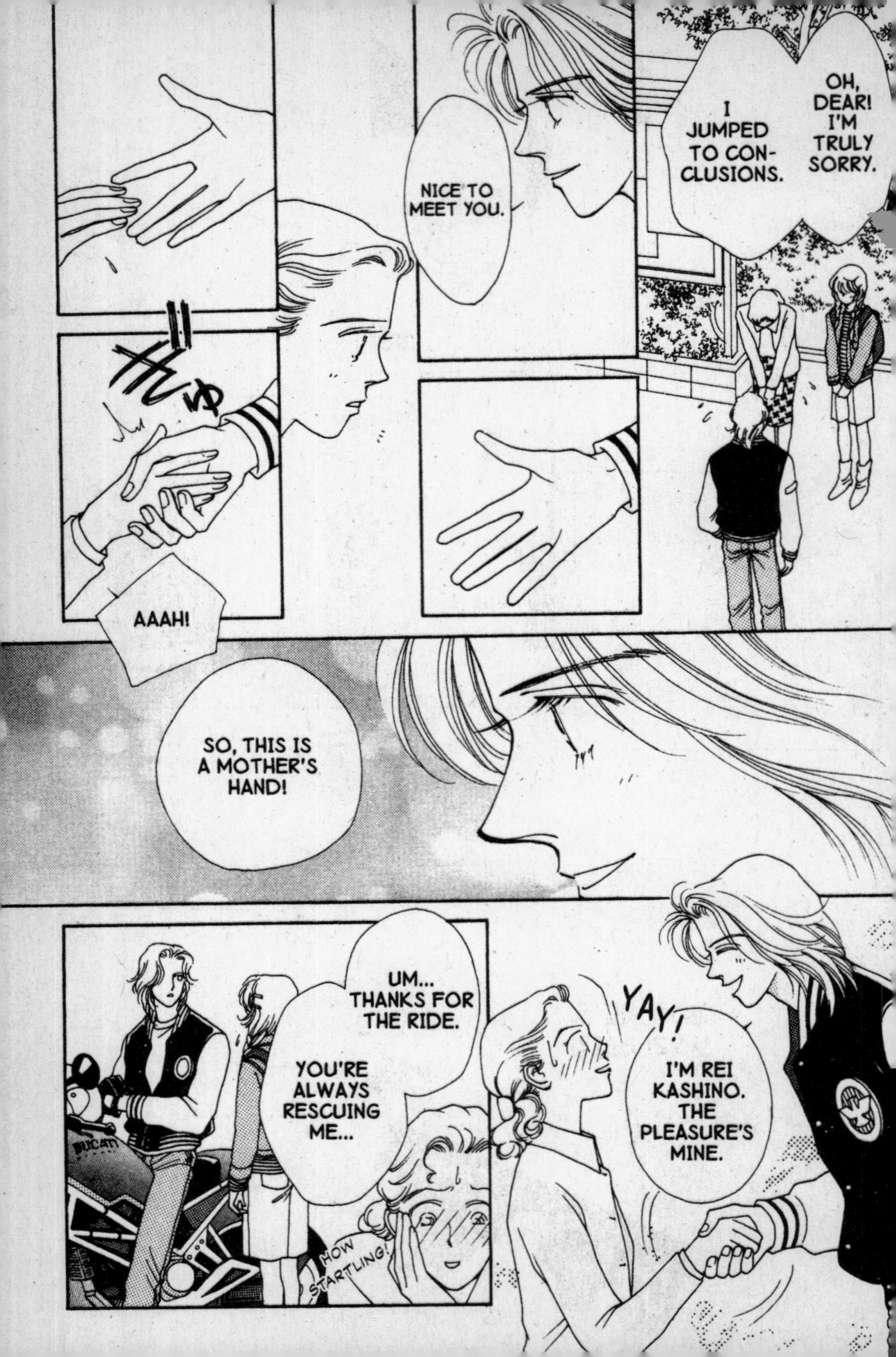
OH, DEAR! I'M TRULY SORRY.
I JUMPED TO CONCLUSIONS.
NICE TO MEET YOU.
AAAH!
SO, THIS IS A MOTHER'S HAND!
YAY!
I'M REI KASHINO. THE PLEASURE'S MINE.
UM... THANKS FOR THE RIDE.
YOU'RE ALWAYS RESCUING ME...
HOW STARTLING!

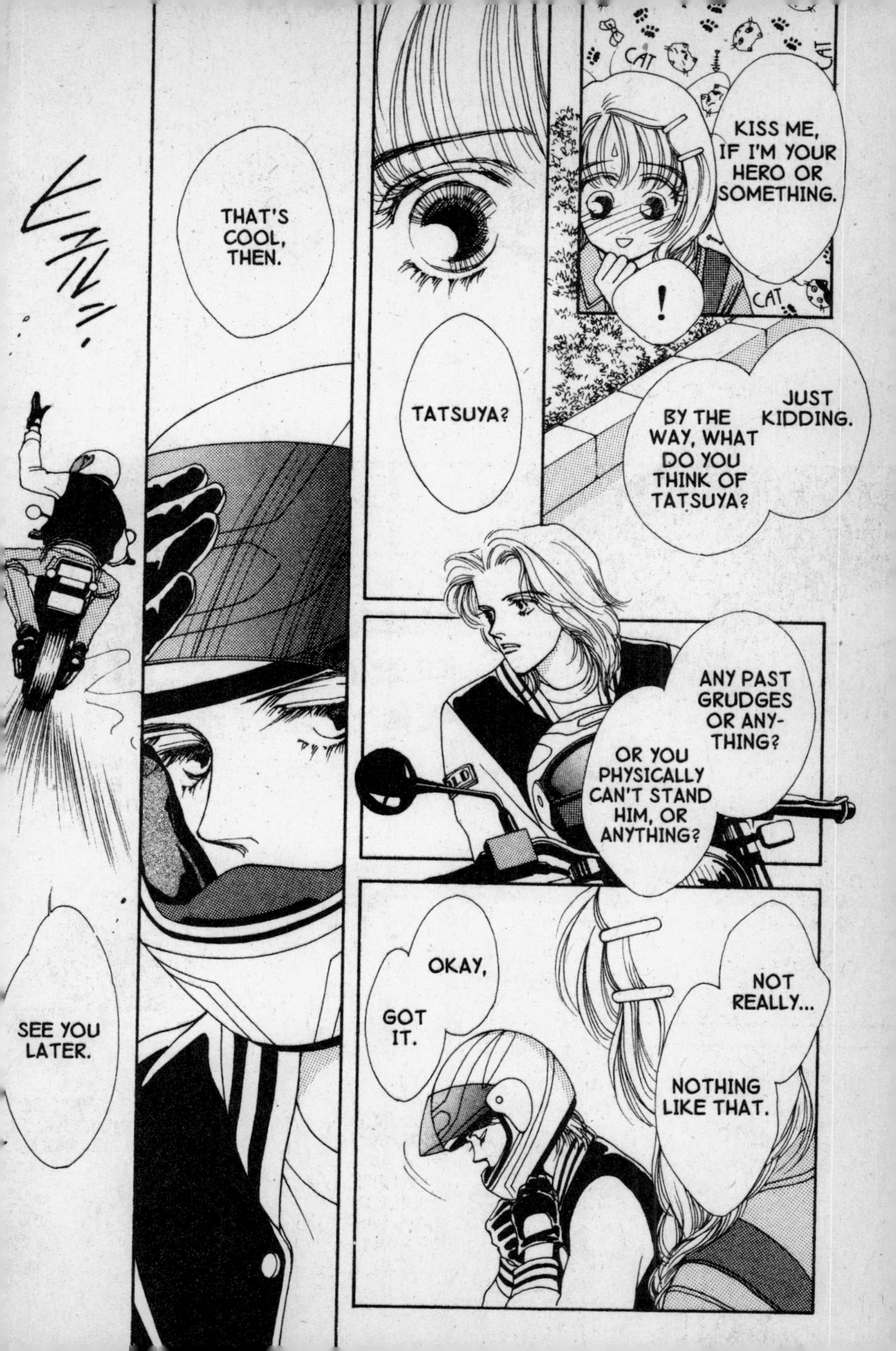
KISS ME, IF I'M YOUR HERO OR SOMETHING.
!
JUST KIDDING.
BY THE WAY, WHAT DO YOU THINK OF TATSUYA?
TATSUYA?
ANY PAST GRUDGES OR ANY-THING?
OR YOU PHYSICALLY CAN'T STAND HIM, OR ANYTHING?
NOT REALLY...
NOTHING LIKE THAT.
OKAY,
GOT IT.
THAT'S COOL, THEN.
SEE YOU LATER.

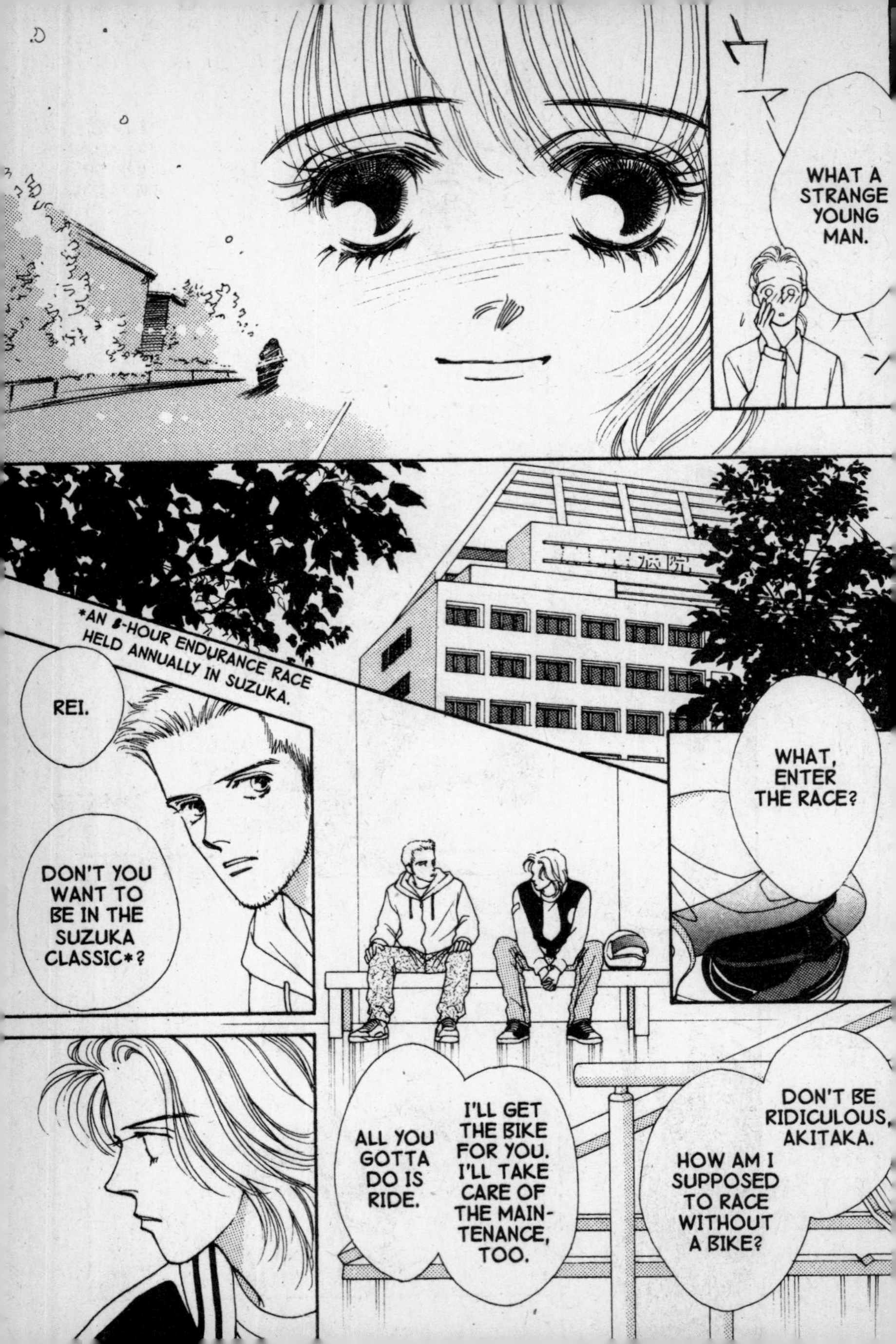
WHAT A STRANGE YOUNG MAN.
REI.
DON'T YOU WANT TO BE IN THE SUZUKA CLASSIC*?
*AN 8-HOUR ENDURANCE RACE HELD ANNUALLY IN SUZUKA.
WHAT, ENTER THE RACE?
DON'T BE RIDICULOUS, AKITAKA.
HOW AM I SUPPOSED TO RACE WITHOUT A BIKE?
I'LL GET THE BIKE FOR YOU. I'LL TAKE CARE OF THE MAINTENANCE, TOO.
ALL YOU GOTTA DO IS RIDE.

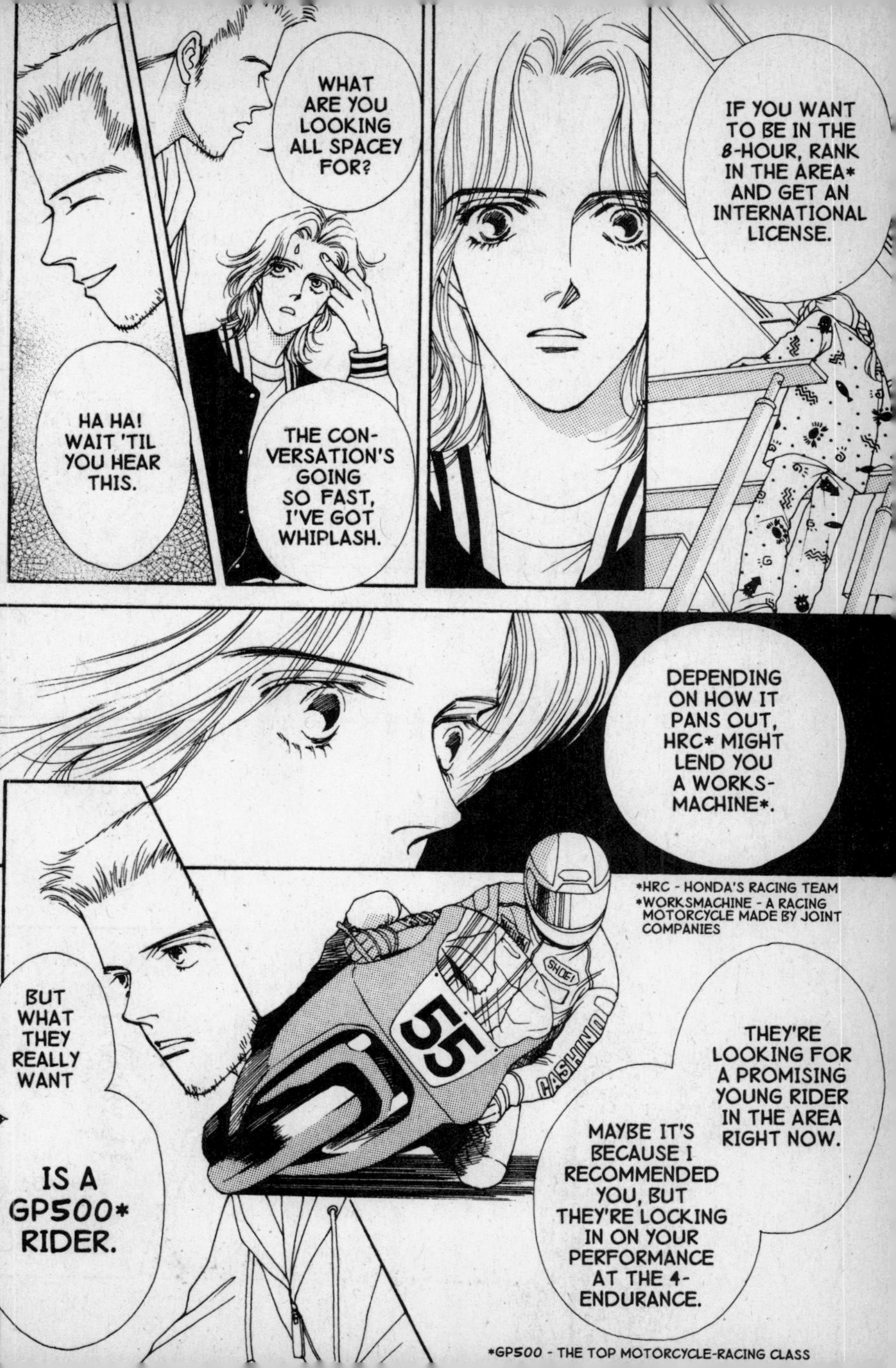
IF YOU WANT TO BE IN THE 8-HOUR, RANK IN THE AREA* AND GET AN INTERNATIONAL LICENSE.
WHAT ARE YOU LOOKING ALL SPACEY FOR?
THE CON-VERSATION'S GOING SO FAST, I'VE GOT WHIPLASH.
HA HA! WAIT 'TIL YOU HEAR THIS.
DEPENDING ON HOW IT PANS OUT, HRC* MIGHT LEND YOU A WORKS-MACHINE*.
*HRC - HONDA'S RACING TEAM
*WORKSMACHINE - A RACING MOTORCYCLE MADE BY JOINT COMPANIES
SHOEI
55
THEY'RE LOOKING FOR A PROMISING YOUNG RIDER IN THE AREA RIGHT NOW.
MAYBE IT'S BECAUSE I RECOMMENDED YOU, BUT THEY'RE LOCKING IN ON YOUR PERFORMANCE AT THE 4-ENDURANCE.
BUT WHAT THEY REALLY WANT
IS A GP500* RIDER.
*GP500 - THE TOP MOTORCYCLE-RACING CLASS

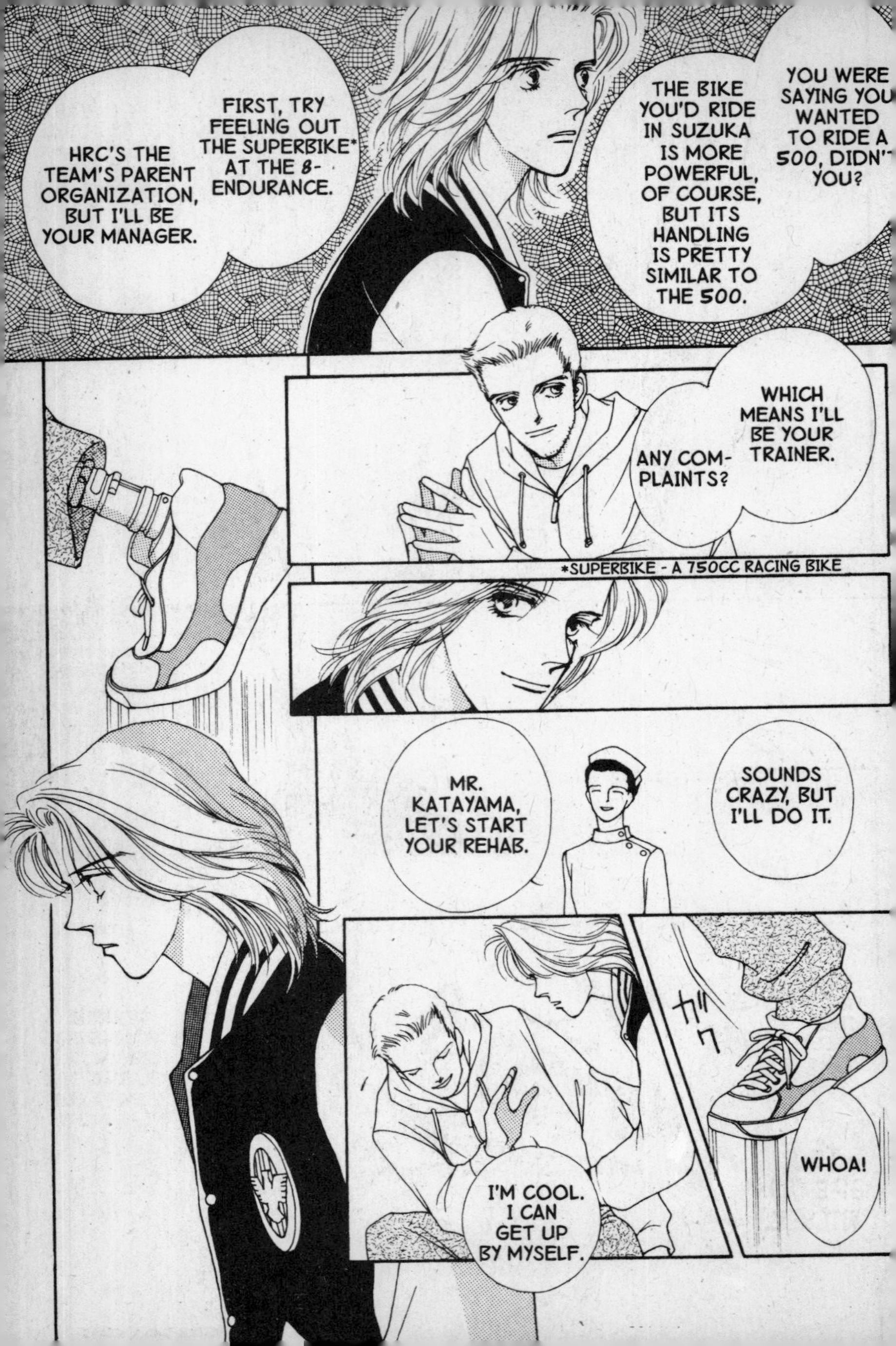
YOU WERE SAYING YOU WANTED TO RIDE A 500, DIDN'T YOU?
THE BIKE YOU'D RIDE IN SUZUKA IS MORE POWERFUL, OF COURSE, BUT ITS HANDLING IS PRETTY SIMILAR TO THE 500.
FIRST, TRY FEELING OUT THE SUPERBIKE* AT THE 8-ENDURANCE.
HRC'S THE TEAM'S PARENT ORGANIZATION, BUT I'LL BE YOUR MANAGER.
WHICH MEANS I'LL BE YOUR TRAINER.
ANY COMPLAINTS?
*SUPERBIKE - A 750CC RACING BIKE
SOUNDS CRAZY, BUT I'LL DO IT.
MR. KATAYAMA, LET'S START YOUR REHAB.
ガック
WHOA!
I'M COOL. I CAN GET UP BY MYSELF.

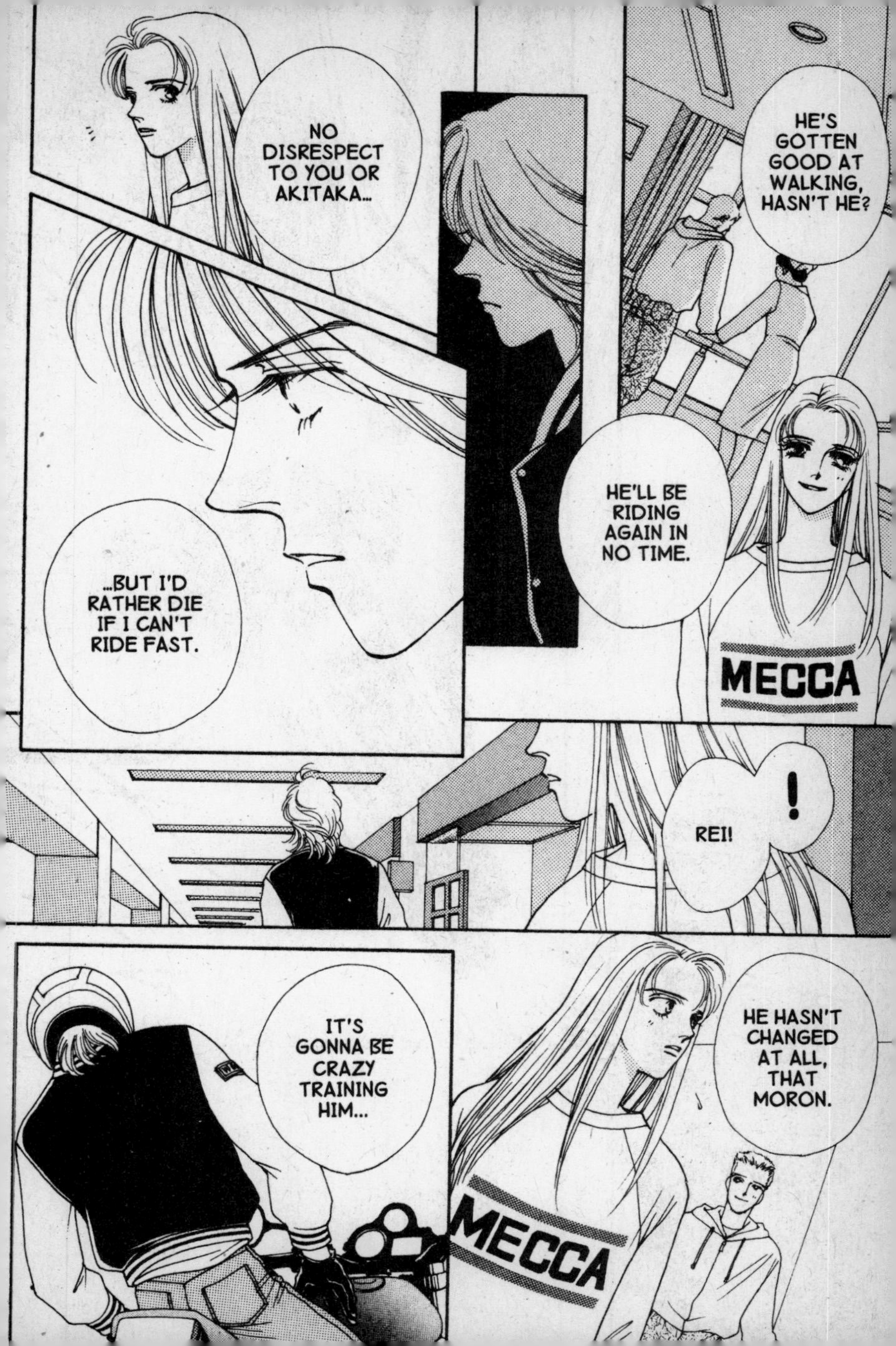
HE'S GOTTEN GOOD AT WALKING, HASN'T HE?
HE'LL BE RIDING AGAIN IN NO TIME.
MECCA
NO DISRESPECT TO YOU OR AKITAKA...
...BUT I'D RATHER DIE IF I CAN'T RIDE FAST.
!
REI!
HE HASN'T CHANGED AT ALL, THAT MORON.
MECCA
IT'S GONNA BE CRAZY TRAINING HIM...

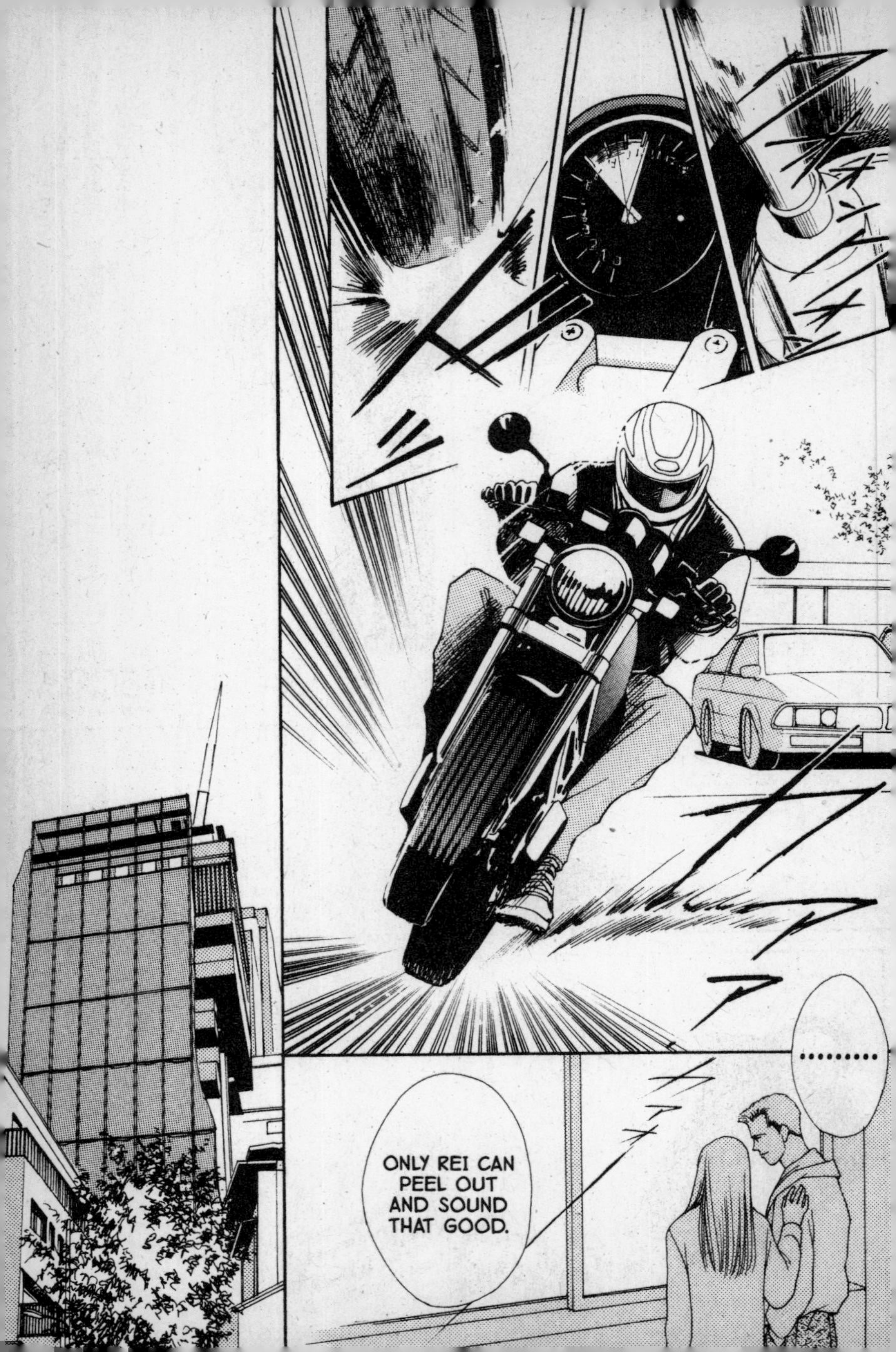
....
ONLY REI CAN PEEL OUT AND SOUND THAT GOOD.

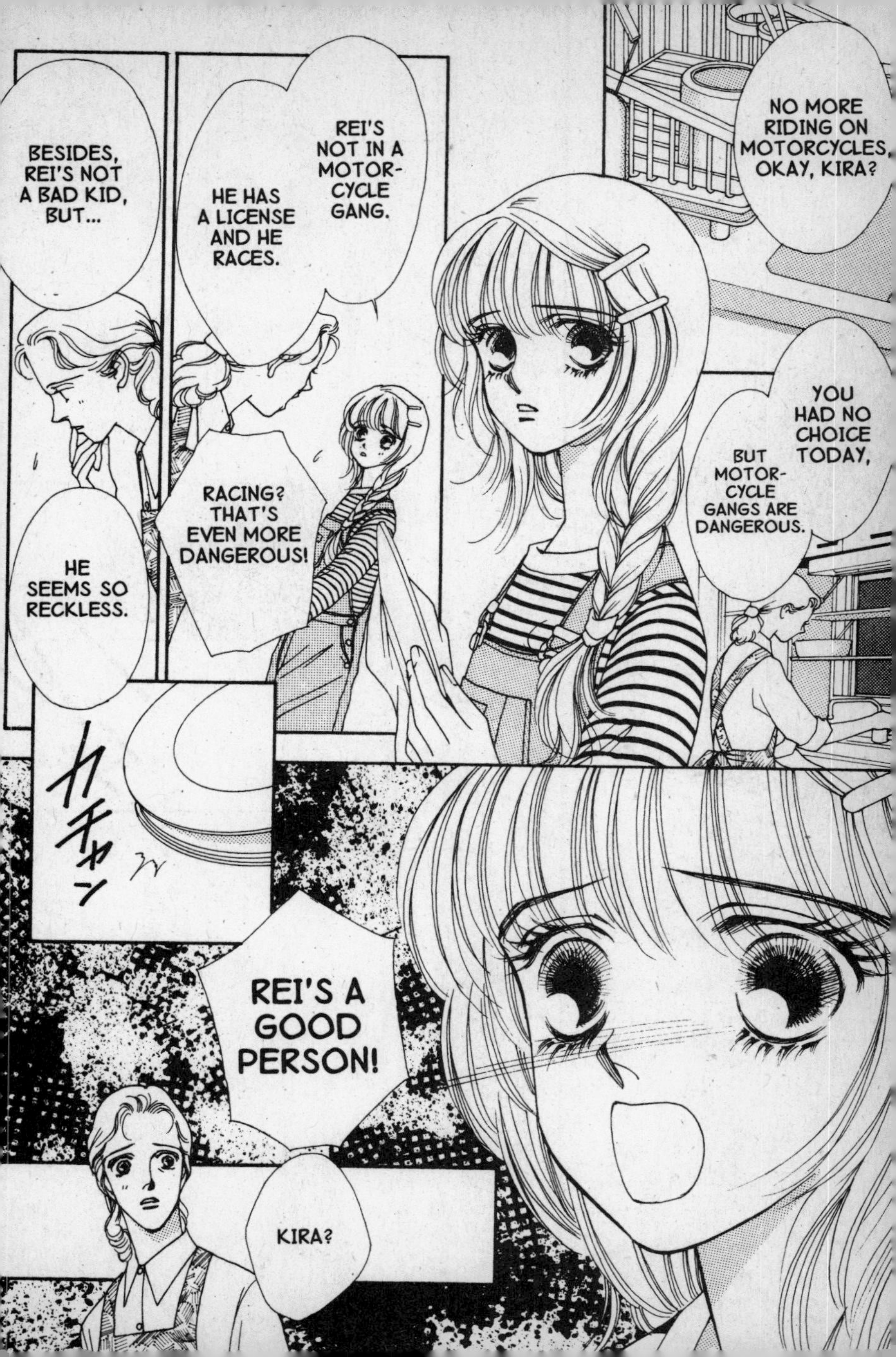
NO MORE RIDING ON MOTORCYCLES, OKAY, KIRA?
YOU HAD NO CHOICE TODAY,
BUT MOTORCYCLE GANGS ARE DANGEROUS.
REI'S NOT IN A MOTORCYCLE GANG.
HE HAS A LICENSE AND HE RACES.
RACING? THAT'S EVEN MORE DANGEROUS!
BESIDES, REI'S NOT A BAD KID, BUT...
HE SEEMS SO RECKLESS.
REI'S A GOOD PERSON!
カチャン
KIRA?

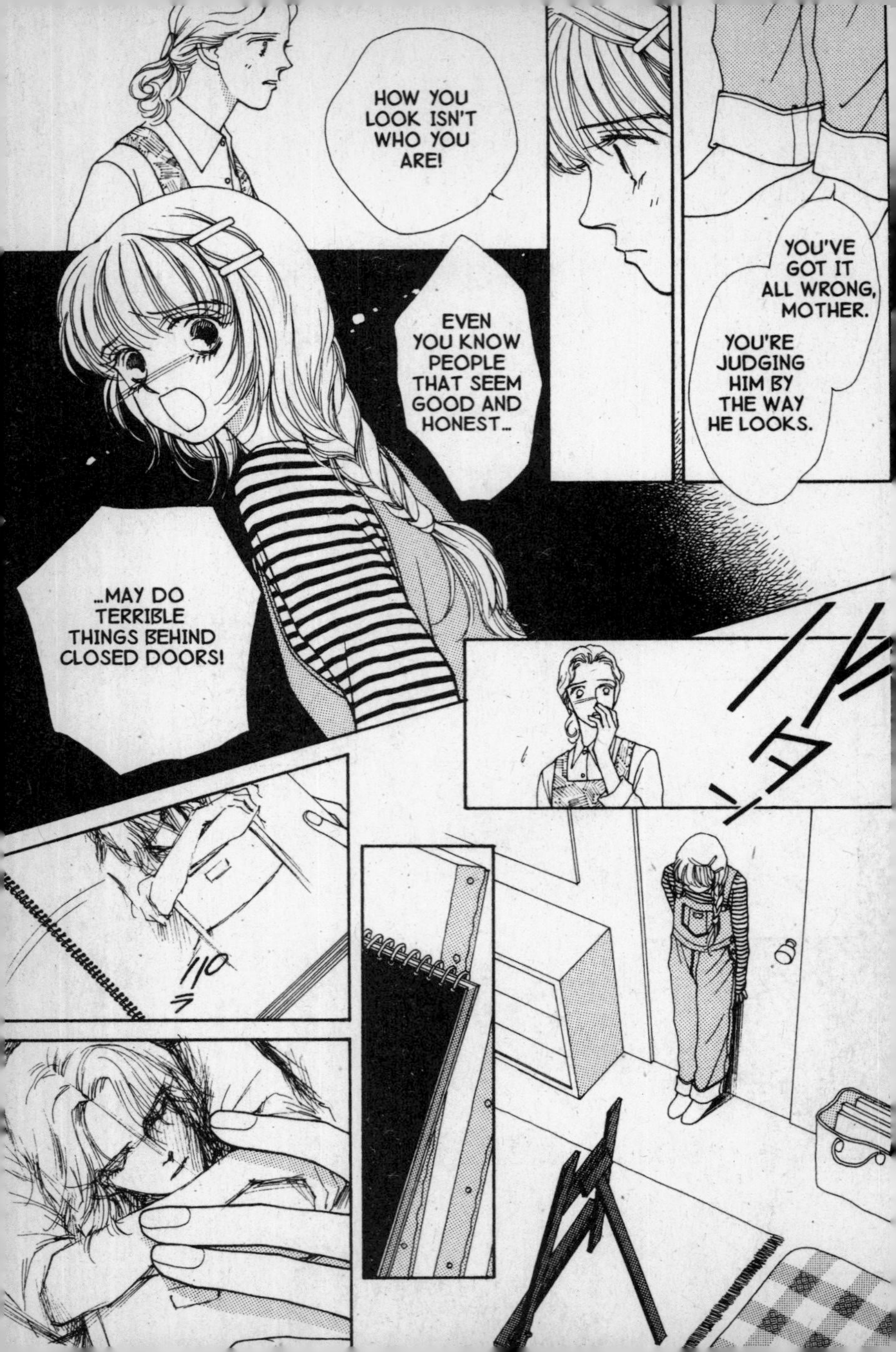
YOU'VE GOT IT ALL WRONG, MOTHER.
YOU'RE JUDGING HIM BY THE WAY HE LOOKS.
HOW YOU LOOK ISN'T WHO YOU ARE!
EVEN YOU KNOW PEOPLE THAT SEEM GOOD AND HONEST...
...MAY DO TERRIBLE THINGS BEHIND CLOSED DOORS!
バタン

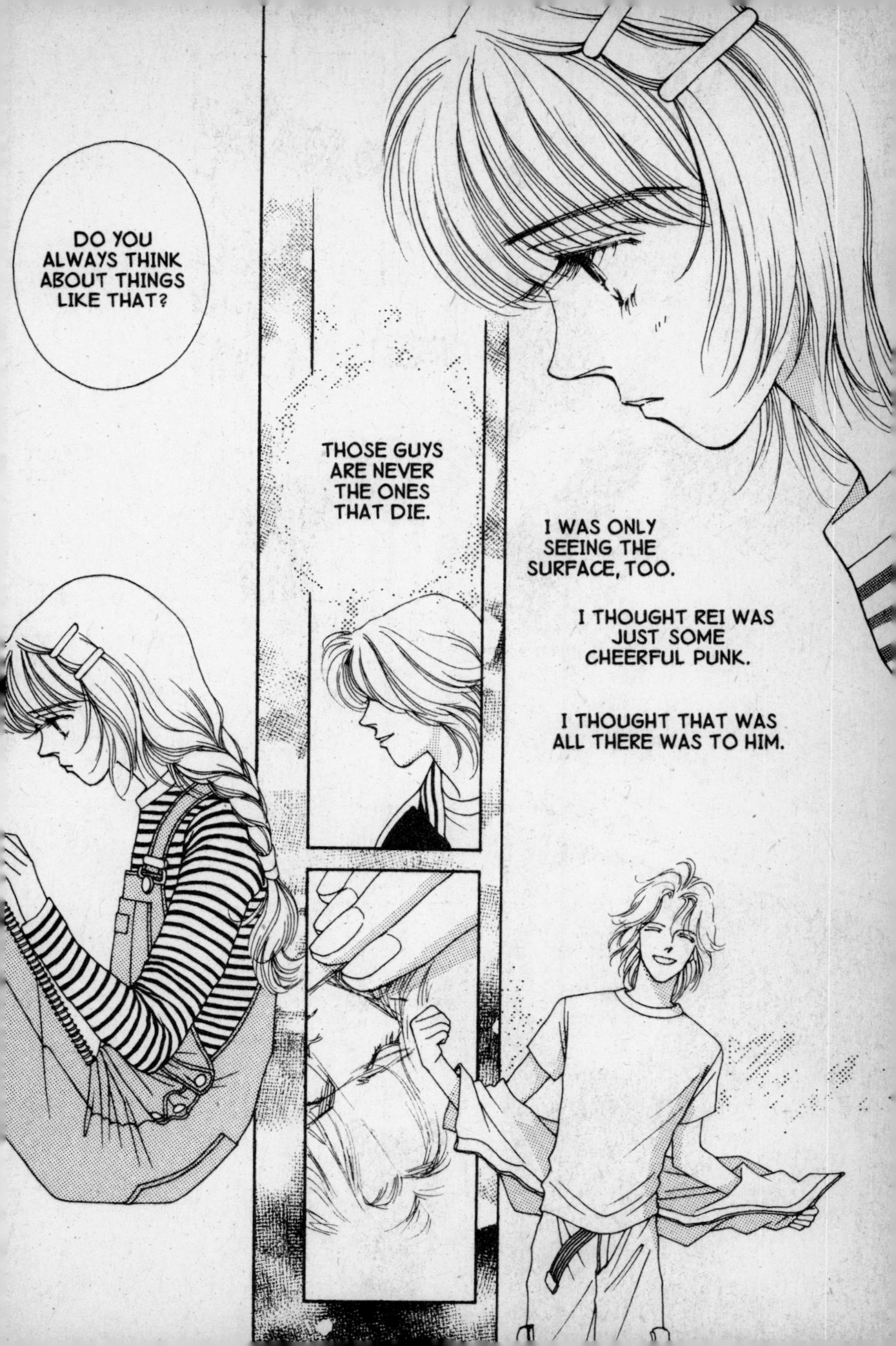
I WAS ONLY SEEING THE SURFACE, TOO.
I THOUGHT REI WAS JUST SOME CHEERFUL PUNK.
I THOUGHT THAT WAS ALL THERE WAS TO HIM.
THOSE GUYS ARE NEVER THE ONES THAT DIE.
DO YOU ALWAYS THINK ABOUT THINGS LIKE THAT?

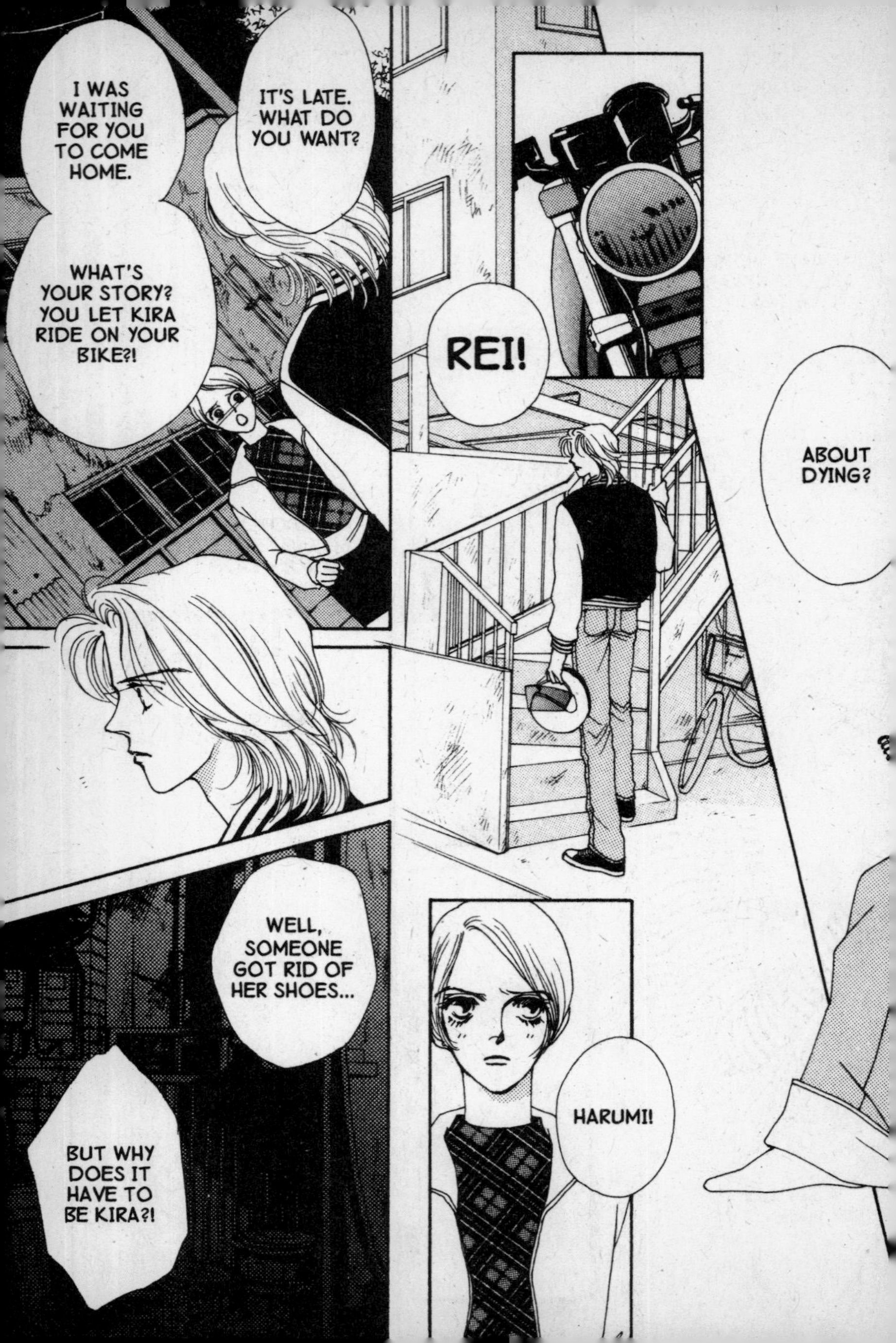
ABOUT DYING?
REI!
HARUMI!
IT'S LATE. WHAT DO YOU WANT?
I WAS WAITING FOR YOU TO COME HOME.
WHAT'S YOUR STORY? YOU LET KIRA RIDE ON YOUR BIKE?!
WELL, SOMEONE GOT RID OF HER SHOES...
BUT WHY DOES IT HAVE TO BE KIRA?!

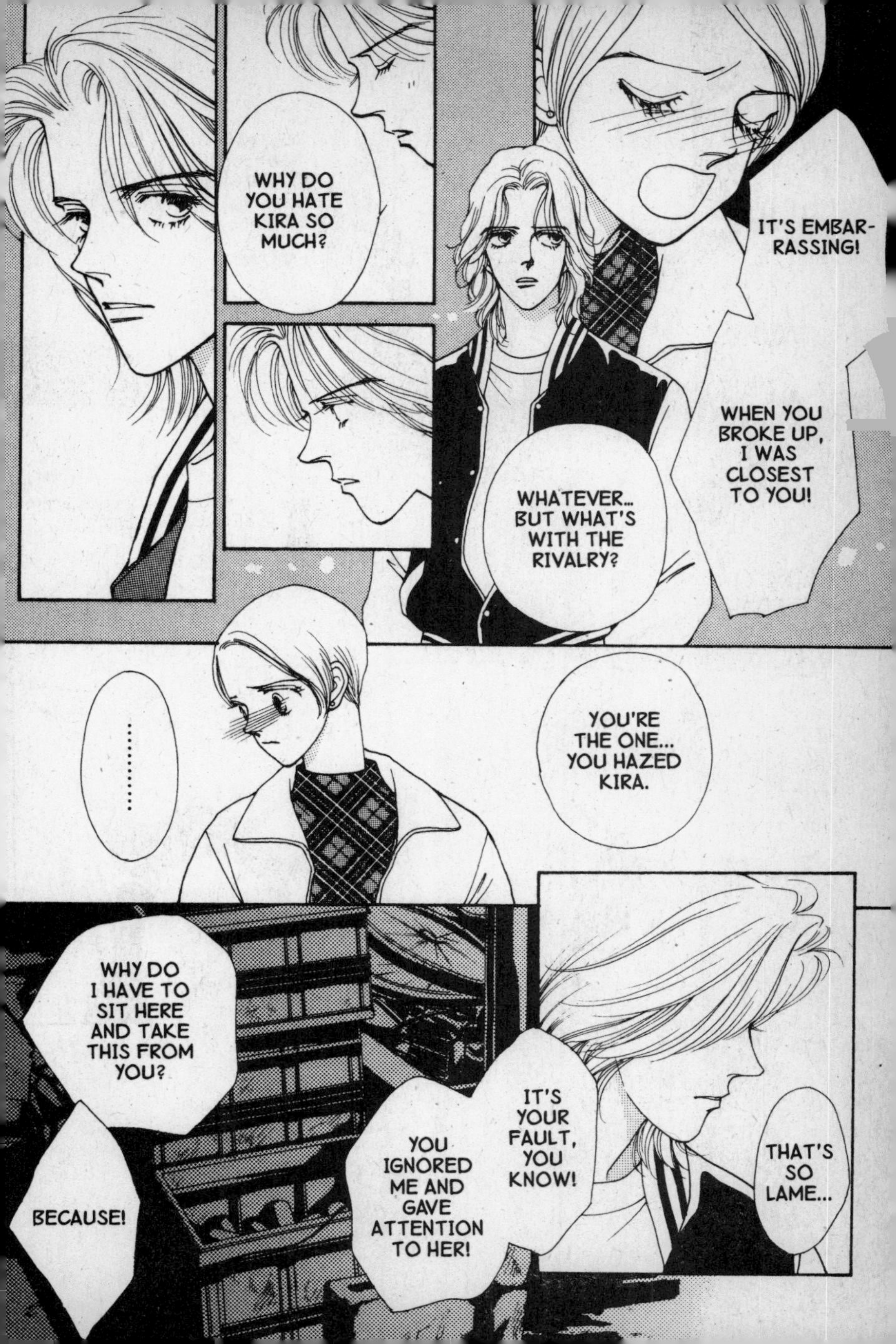
IT'S EMBARRASSING!
WHEN YOU BROKE UP, I WAS CLOSEST TO YOU!
WHATEVER... BUT WHAT'S WITH THE RIVALRY?
WHY DO YOU HATE KIRA SO MUCH?
YOU'RE THE ONE... YOU HAZED KIRA.
....
THAT'S SO LAME...
WHY DO I HAVE TO SIT HERE AND TAKE THIS FROM YOU?
BECAUSE!
IT'S YOUR FAULT, YOU KNOW!
YOU IGNORED ME AND GAVE ATTENTION TO HER!

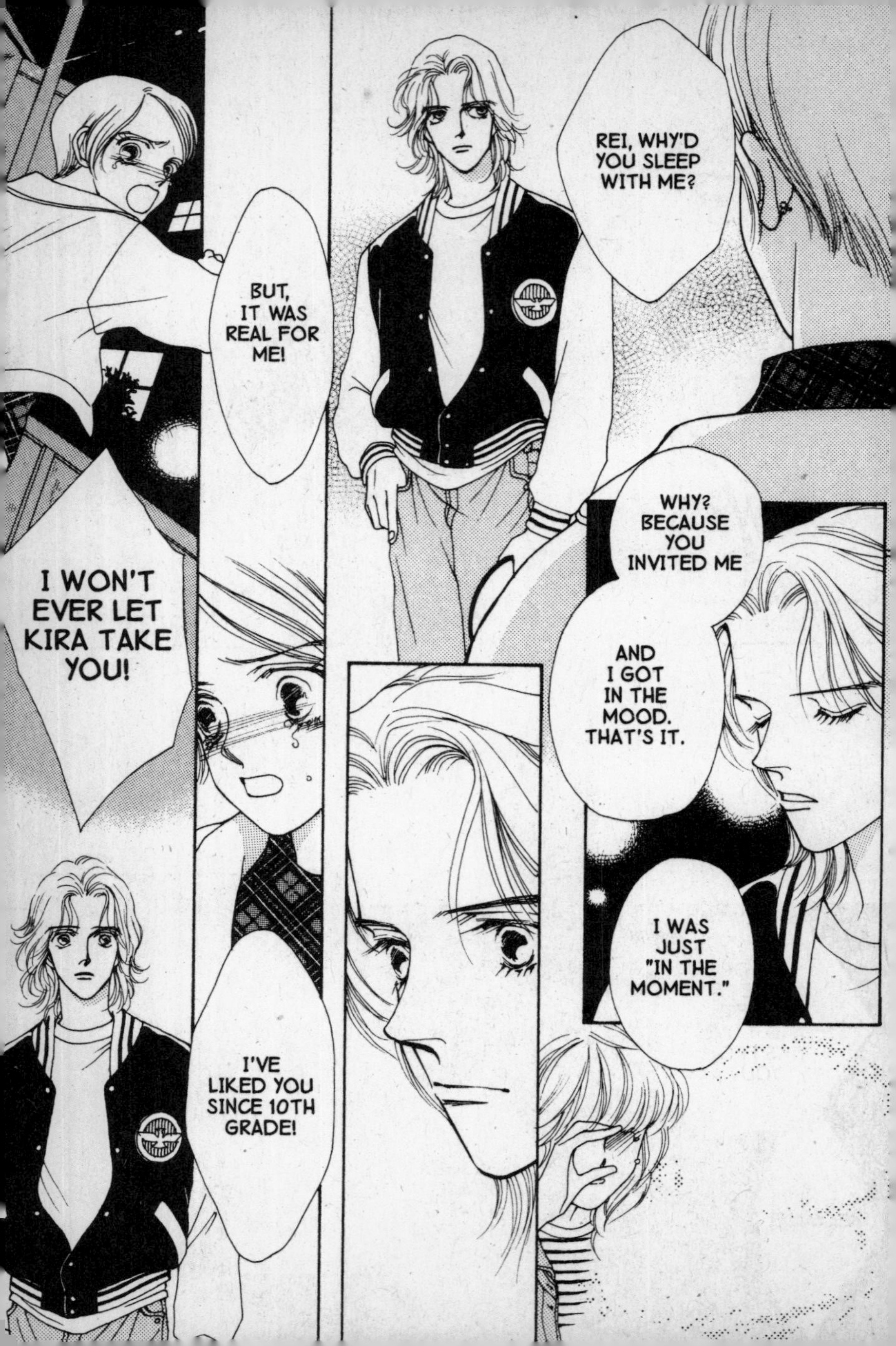
REI, WHY'D YOU SLEEP WITH ME?
WHY? BECAUSE YOU INVITED ME
AND I GOT IN THE MOOD. THAT'S IT.
I WAS JUST "IN THE MOMENT."
BUT, IT WAS REAL FOR ME!
I'VE LIKED YOU SINCE 10TH GRADE!
I WON'T EVER LET KIRA TAKE YOU!

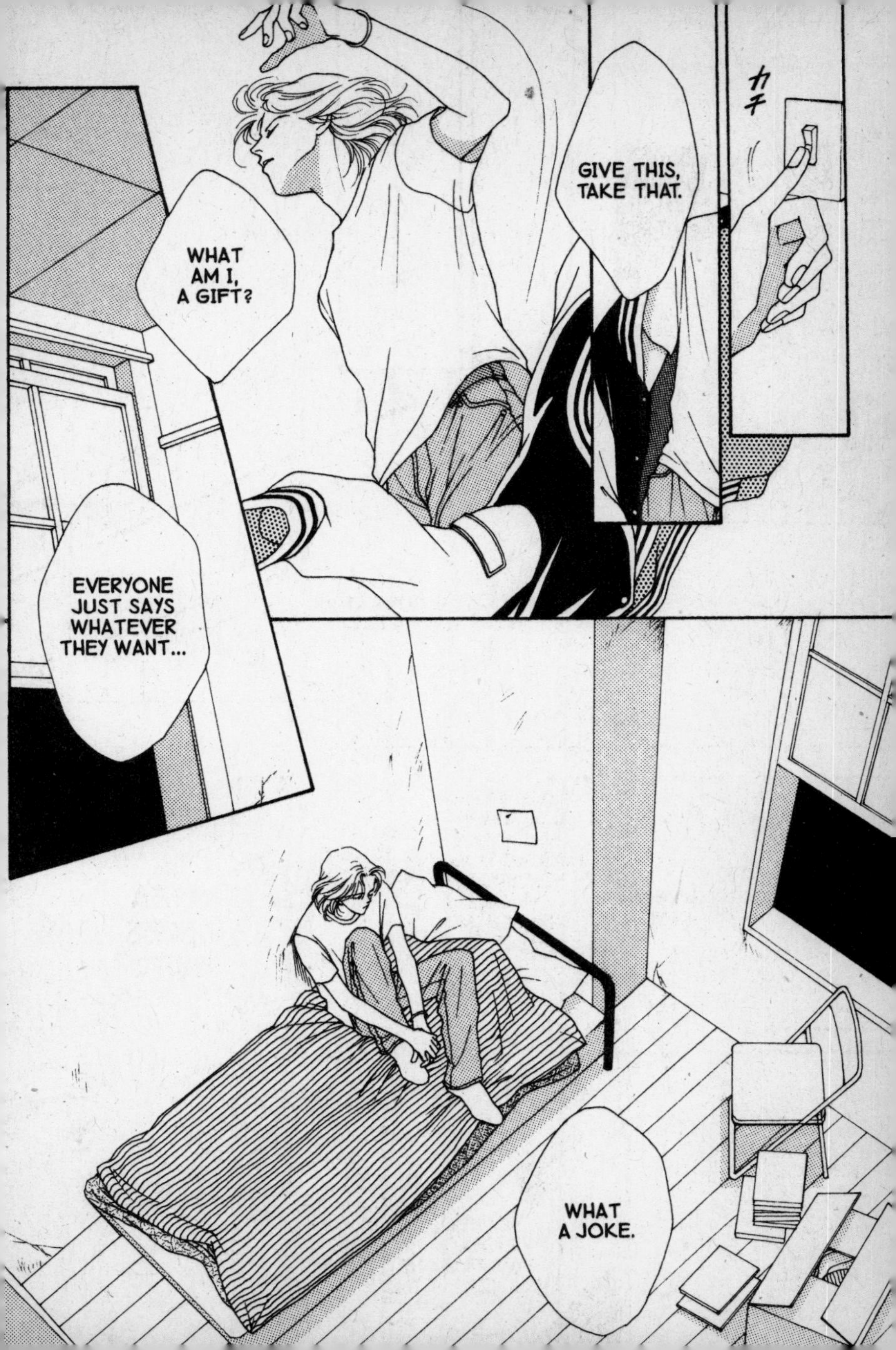
カチ
GIVE THIS, TAKE THAT.
WHAT AM I, A GIFT?
EVERYONE JUST SAYS WHATEVER THEY WANT...
WHAT A JOKE.

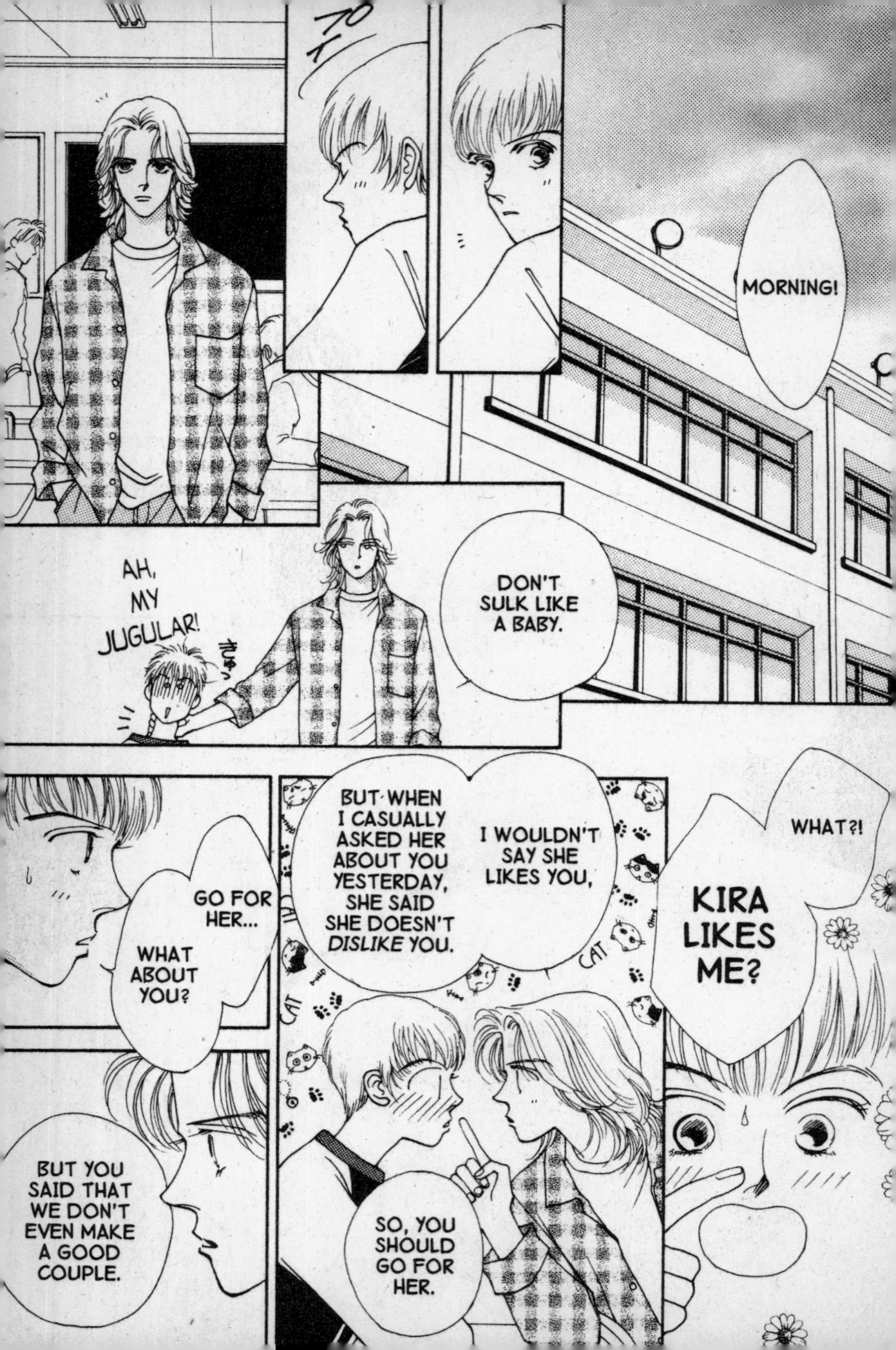
MORNING!
DON'T SULK LIKE A BABY.
AH, MY JUGULAR!
WHAT?!
KIRA LIKES ME?
I WOULDN'T SAY SHE LIKES YOU,
BUT WHEN I CASUALLY ASKED HER ABOUT YOU YESTERDAY, SHE SAID SHE DOESN'T *DISLIKE* YOU.
SO, YOU SHOULD GO FOR HER.
GO FOR HER...
WHAT ABOUT YOU?
BUT YOU SAID THAT WE DON'T EVEN MAKE A GOOD COUPLE.

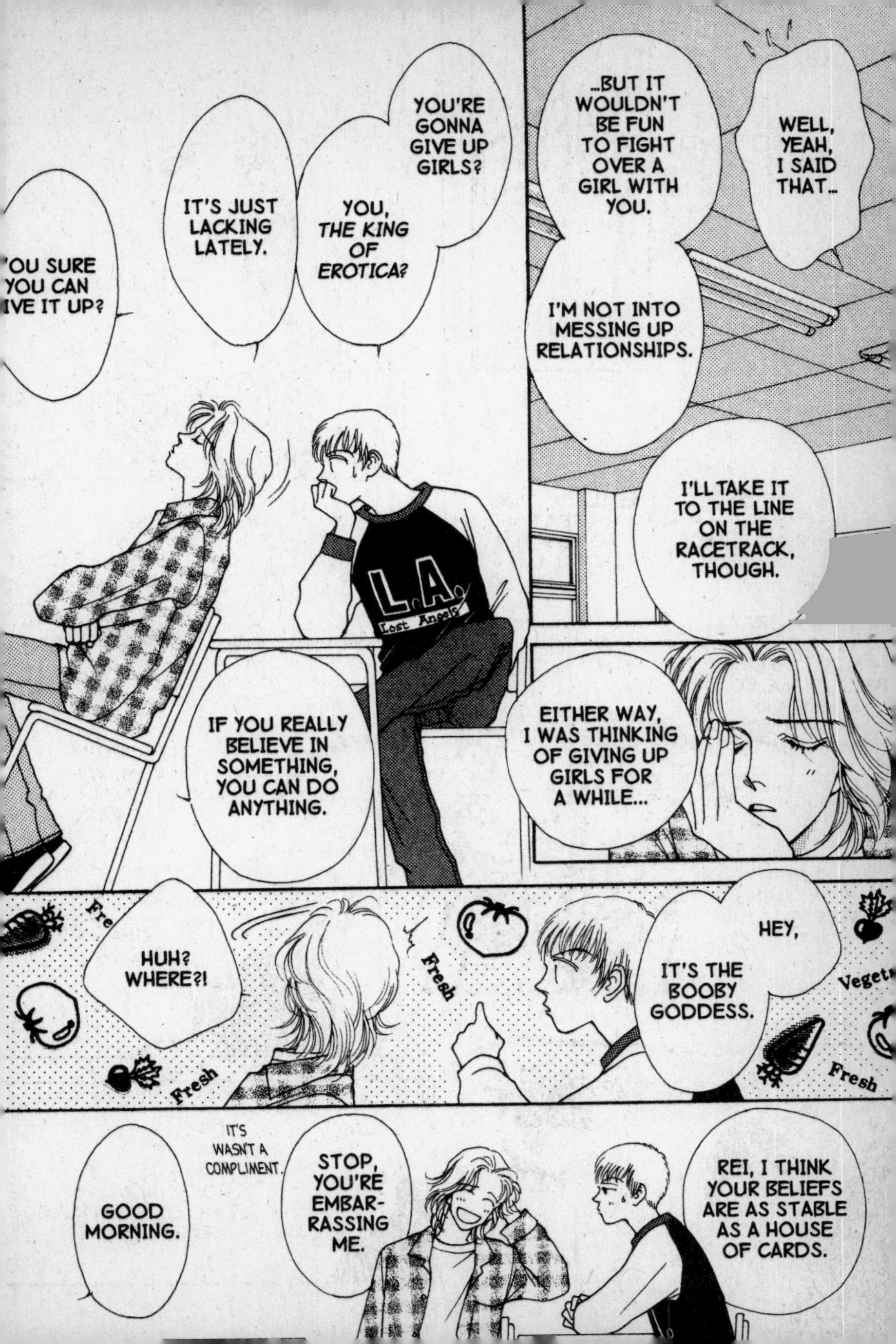
WELL, YEAH, I SAID THAT...
...BUT IT WOULDN'T BE FUN TO FIGHT OVER A GIRL WITH YOU.
I'M NOT INTO MESSING UP RELATIONSHIPS.
I'LL TAKE IT TO THE LINE ON THE RACETRACK, THOUGH.
EITHER WAY, I WAS THINKING OF GIVING UP GIRLS FOR A WHILE...
YOU'RE GONNA GIVE UP GIRLS?
YOU, THE KING OF EROTICA?
IT'S JUST LACKING LATELY.
OU SURE YOU CAN IVE IT UP?
IF YOU REALLY BELIEVE IN SOMETHING, YOU CAN DO ANYTHING.
HEY, IT'S THE BOOBY GODDESS.
HUH? WHERE?!
REI, I THINK YOUR BELIEFS ARE AS STABLE AS A HOUSE OF CARDS.
STOP, YOU'RE EMBARRASSING ME.
IT'S WASN'T A COMPLIMENT.
GOOD MORNING.

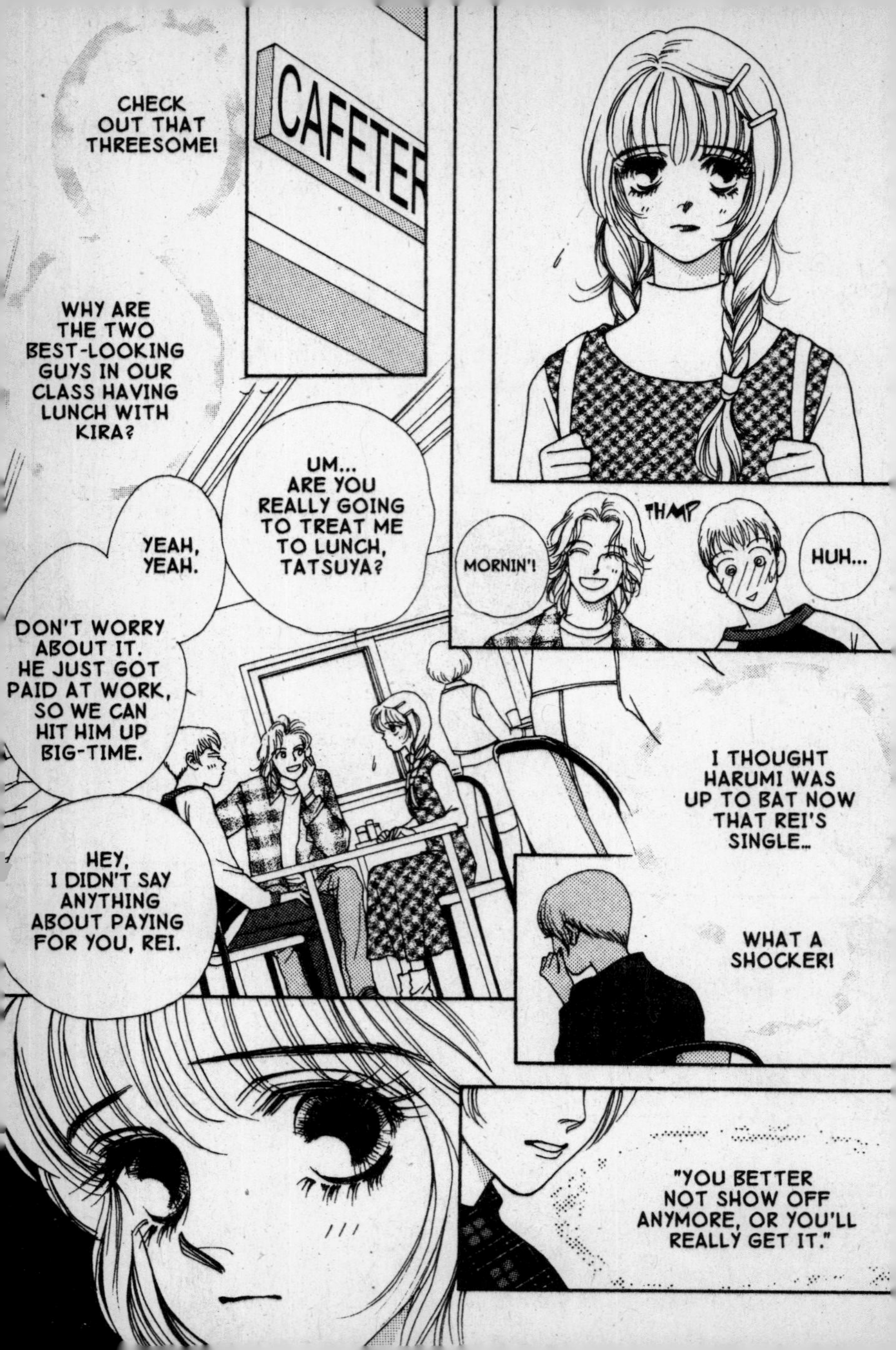
CAFETER
CHECK OUT THAT THREESOME!
THMP
MORNIN'!
HUH...
WHY ARE THE TWO BEST-LOOKING GUYS IN OUR CLASS HAVING LUNCH WITH KIRA?
UM... ARE YOU REALLY GOING TO TREAT ME TO LUNCH, TATSUYA?
YEAH, YEAH.
DON'T WORRY ABOUT IT. HE JUST GOT PAID AT WORK, SO WE CAN HIT HIM UP BIG-TIME.
HEY, I DIDN'T SAY ANYTHING ABOUT PAYING FOR YOU, REI.
I THOUGHT HARUMI WAS UP TO BAT NOW THAT REI'S SINGLE...
WHAT A SHOCKER!
"YOU BETTER NOT SHOW OFF ANYMORE, OR YOU'LL REALLY GET IT."

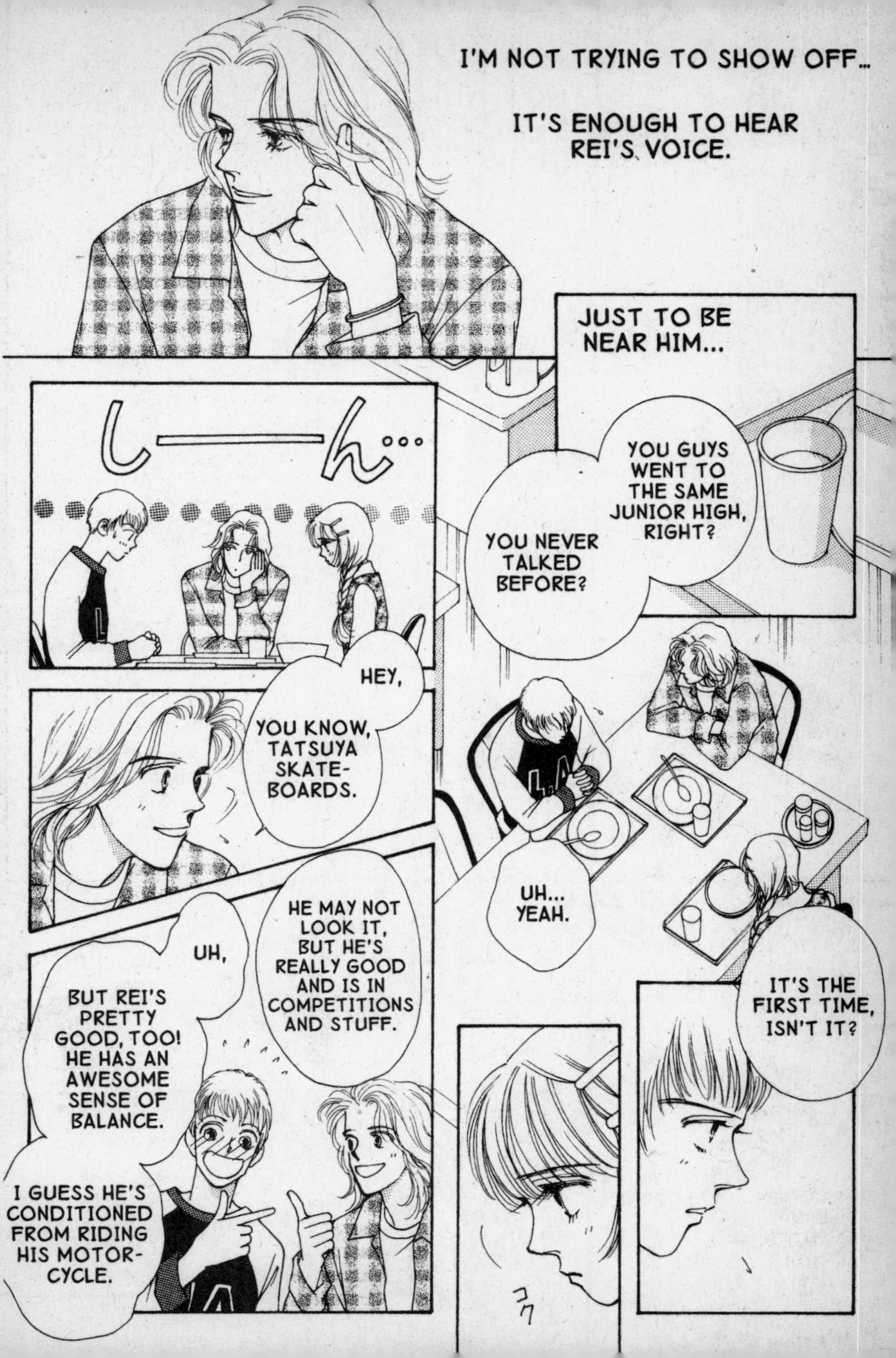
I'M NOT TRYING TO SHOW OFF...
IT'S ENOUGH TO HEAR REI'S VOICE.
JUST TO BE NEAR HIM...
YOU GUYS WENT TO THE SAME JUNIOR HIGH, RIGHT?
YOU NEVER TALKED BEFORE?
UH... YEAH.
IT'S THE FIRST TIME, ISN'T IT?
コク
しーん...
HEY,
YOU KNOW, TATSUYA SKATE-BOARDS.
HE MAY NOT LOOK IT, BUT HE'S REALLY GOOD AND IS IN COMPETITIONS AND STUFF.
UH,
BUT REI'S PRETTY GOOD, TOO! HE HAS AN AWESOME SENSE OF BALANCE.
I GUESS HE'S CONDITIONED FROM RIDING HIS MOTOR-CYCLE.

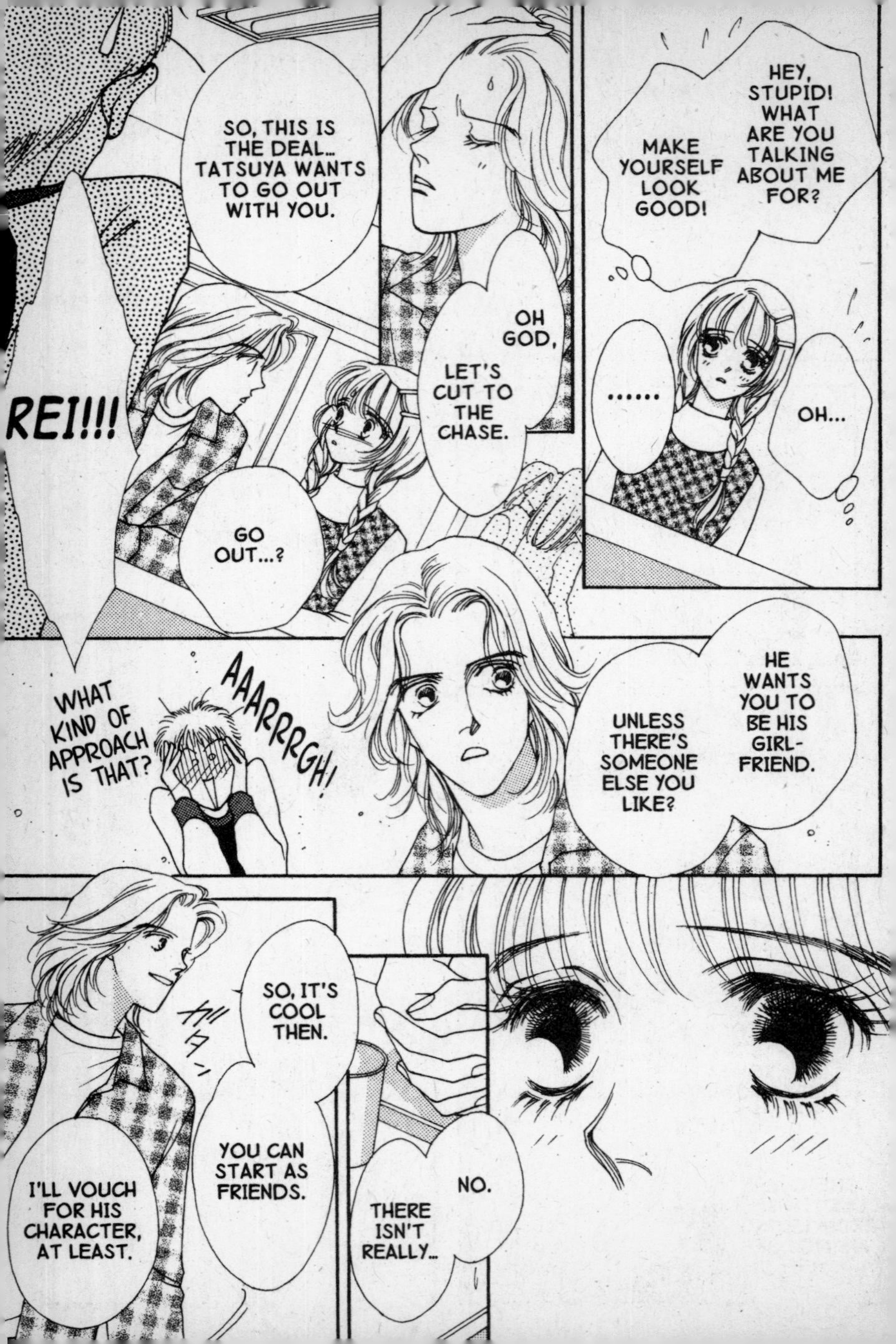
HEY, STUPID! WHAT ARE YOU TALKING ABOUT ME FOR?
MAKE YOURSELF LOOK GOOD!
OH...
......
OH GOD,
LET'S CUT TO THE CHASE.
SO, THIS IS THE DEAL... TATSUYA WANTS TO GO OUT WITH YOU.
GO OUT...?
REI!!!
HE WANTS YOU TO BE HIS GIRL-FRIEND.
UNLESS THERE'S SOMEONE ELSE YOU LIKE?
AAARRRGH!
WHAT KIND OF APPROACH IS THAT?
NO.
THERE ISN'T REALLY...
SO, IT'S COOL THEN.
YOU CAN START AS FRIENDS.
I'LL VOUCH FOR HIS CHARACTER, AT LEAST.

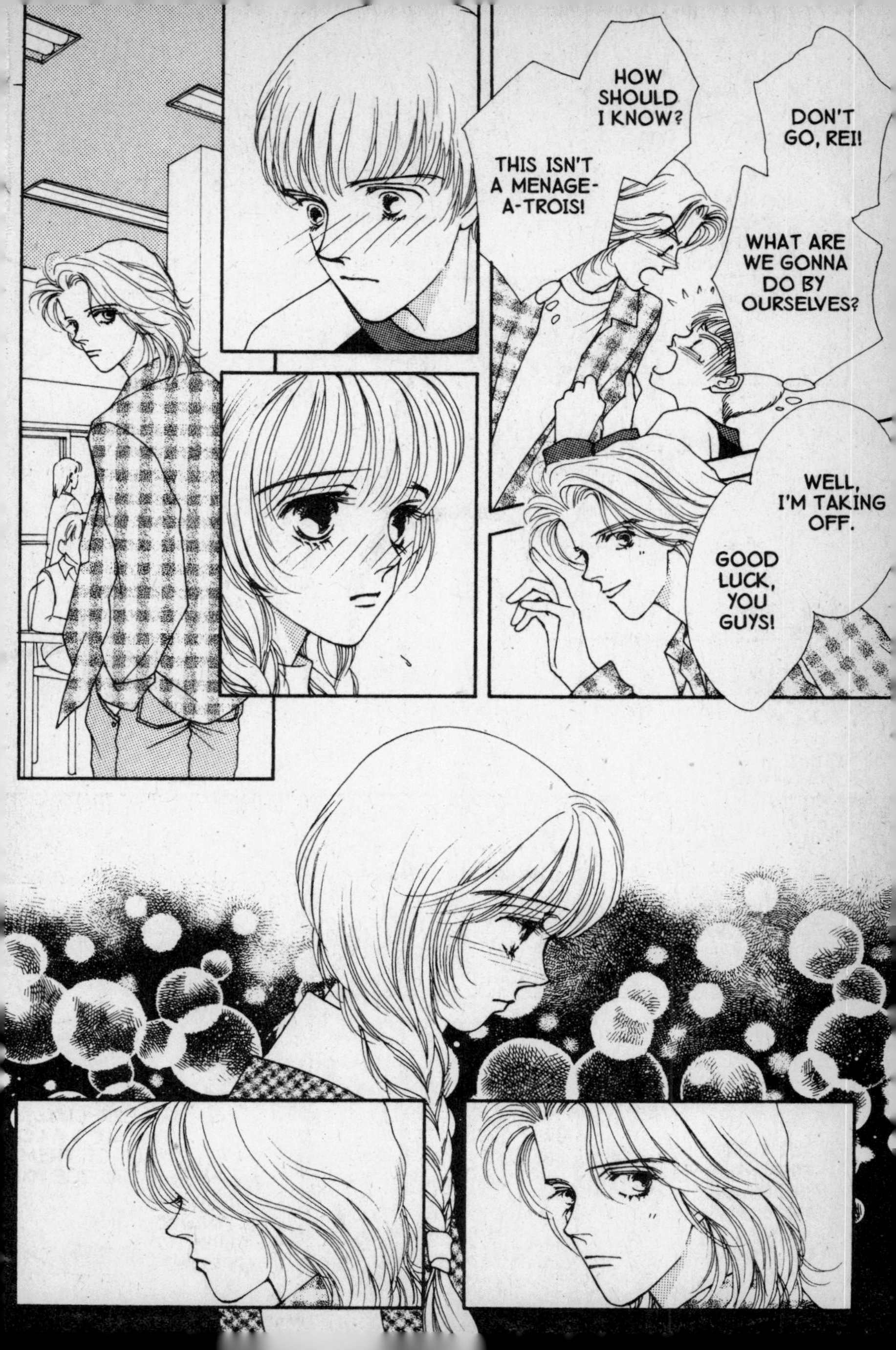
DON'T GO, REI!
WHAT ARE WE GONNA DO BY OURSELVES?
HOW SHOULD I KNOW?
THIS ISN'T A MENAGE-A-TROIS!
WELL, I'M TAKING OFF.
GOOD LUCK, YOU GUYS!

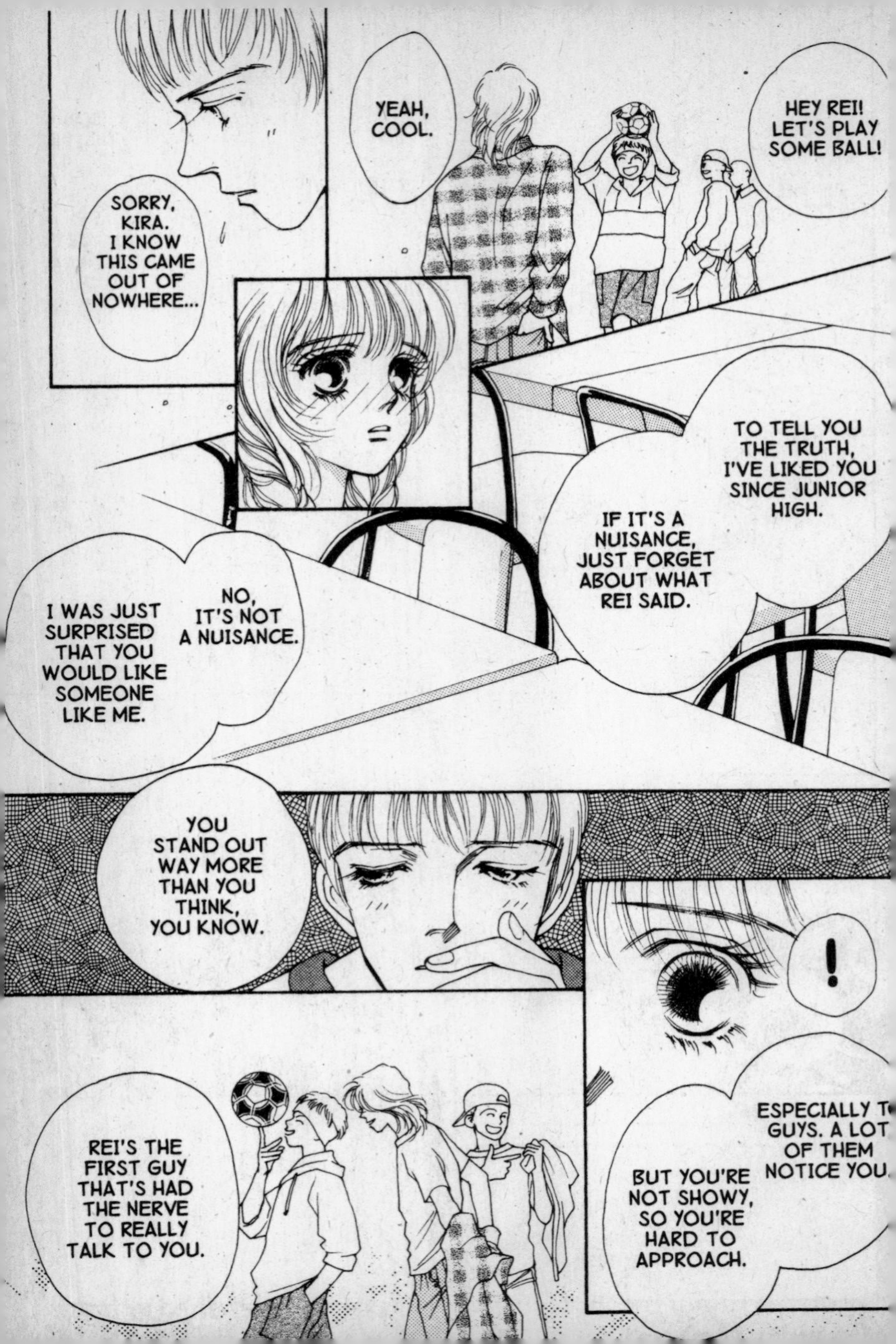
HEY REI! LET'S PLAY SOME BALL!
YEAH, COOL.
SORRY, KIRA. I KNOW THIS CAME OUT OF NOWHERE...
TO TELL YOU THE TRUTH, I'VE LIKED YOU SINCE JUNIOR HIGH.
IF IT'S A NUISANCE, JUST FORGET ABOUT WHAT REI SAID.
NO, IT'S NOT A NUISANCE.
I WAS JUST SURPRISED THAT YOU WOULD LIKE SOMEONE LIKE ME.
YOU STAND OUT WAY MORE THAN YOU THINK, YOU KNOW.
!
ESPECIALLY T GUYS. A LOT OF THEM NOTICE YOU.
BUT YOU'RE NOT SHOWY, SO YOU'RE HARD TO APPROACH.
REI'S THE FIRST GUY THAT'S HAD THE NERVE TO REALLY TALK TO YOU.

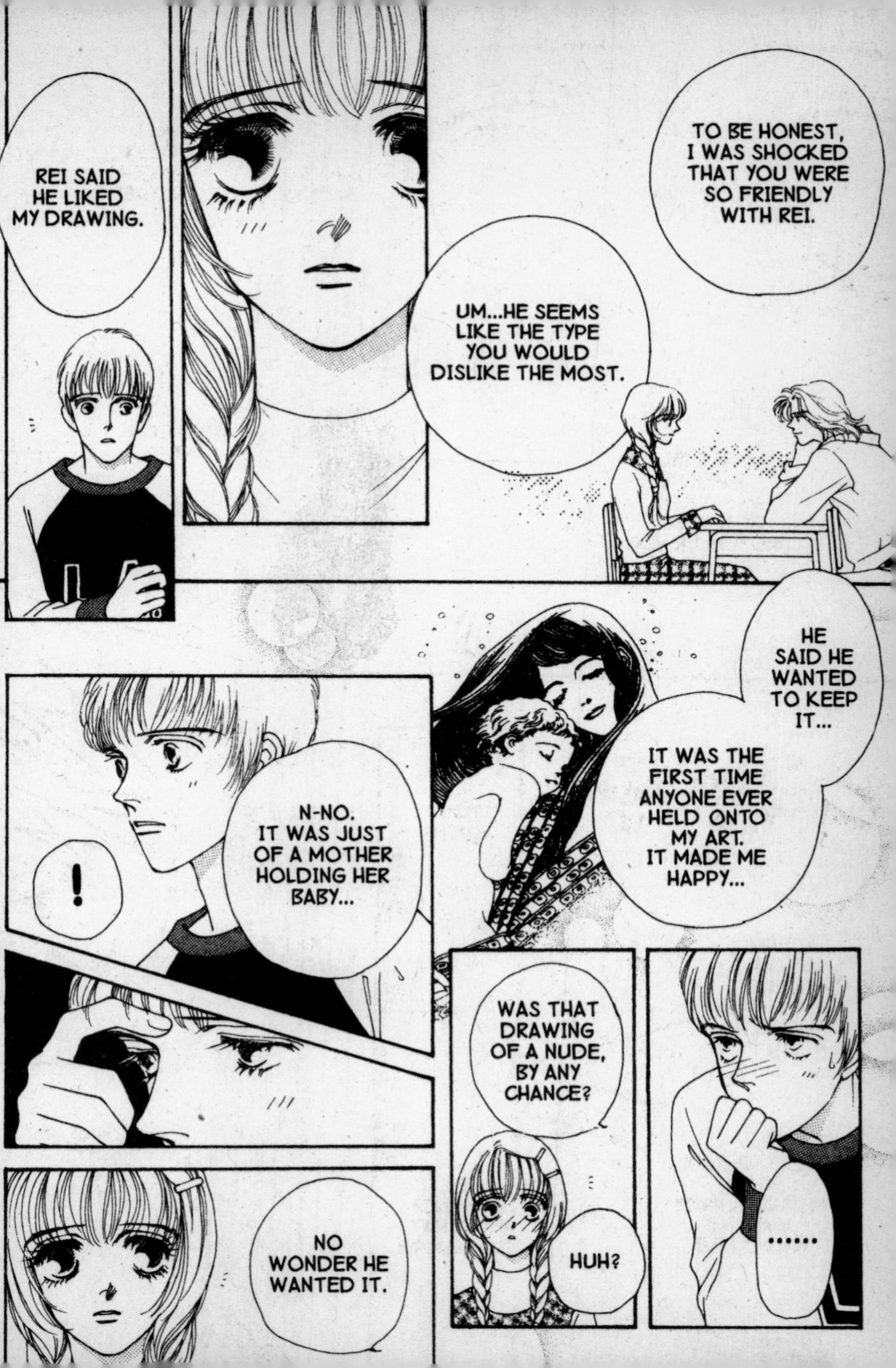
TO BE HONEST, I WAS SHOCKED THAT YOU WERE SO FRIENDLY WITH REI.
UM...HE SEEMS LIKE THE TYPE YOU WOULD DISLIKE THE MOST.
REI SAID HE LIKED MY DRAWING.
HE SAID HE WANTED TO KEEP IT...
IT WAS THE FIRST TIME ANYONE EVER HELD ONTO MY ART. IT MADE ME HAPPY...
......
WAS THAT DRAWING OF A NUDE, BY ANY CHANCE?
HUH?
N-NO. IT WAS JUST OF A MOTHER HOLDING HER BABY...
!
NO WONDER HE WANTED IT.

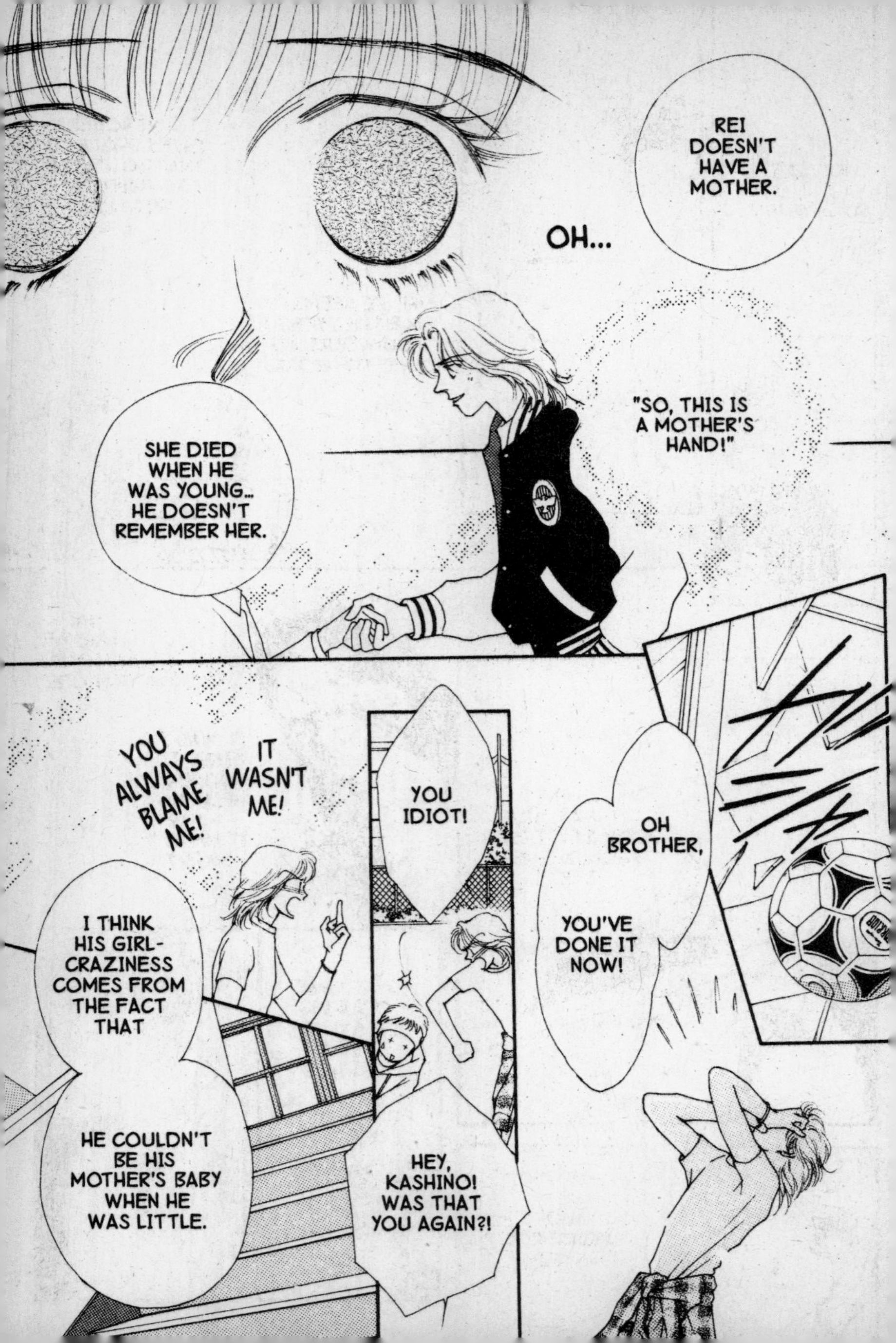
REI DOESN'T HAVE A MOTHER.
OH...
"SO, THIS IS A MOTHER'S HAND!"
SHE DIED WHEN HE WAS YOUNG... HE DOESN'T REMEMBER HER.
OH BROTHER,
YOU'VE DONE IT NOW!
YOU IDIOT!
HEY, KASHINO! WAS THAT YOU AGAIN?!
IT WASN'T ME!
YOU ALWAYS BLAME ME!
I THINK HIS GIRL-CRAZINESS COMES FROM THE FACT THAT
HE COULDN'T BE HIS MOTHER'S BABY WHEN HE WAS LITTLE.

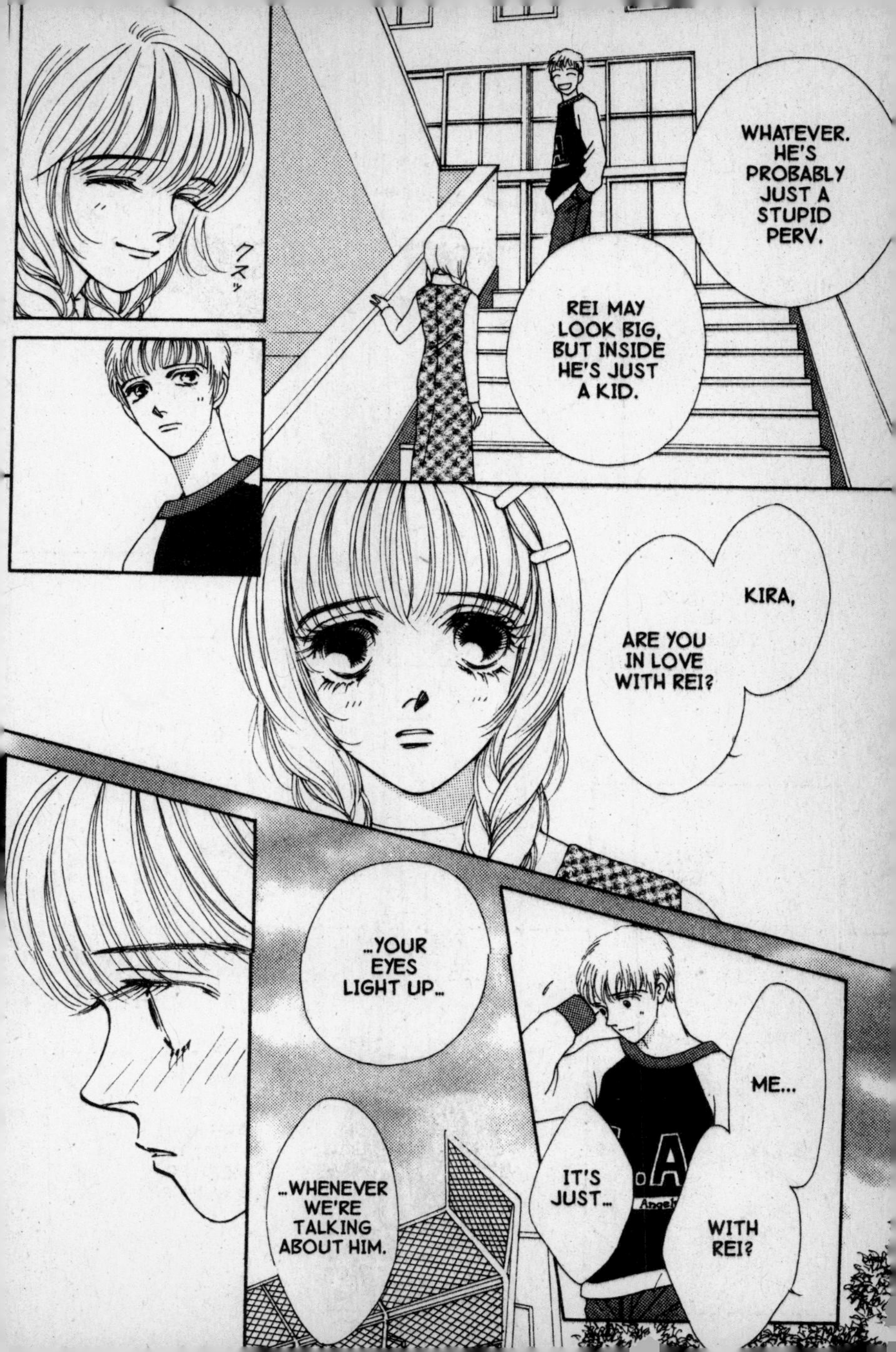
WHATEVER. HE'S PROBABLY JUST A STUPID PERV.
REI MAY LOOK BIG, BUT INSIDE HE'S JUST A KID.
クスッ
KIRA,
ARE YOU IN LOVE WITH REI?
ME...
WITH REI?
IT'S JUST...
...YOUR EYES LIGHT UP...
...WHENEVER WE'RE TALKING ABOUT HIM.

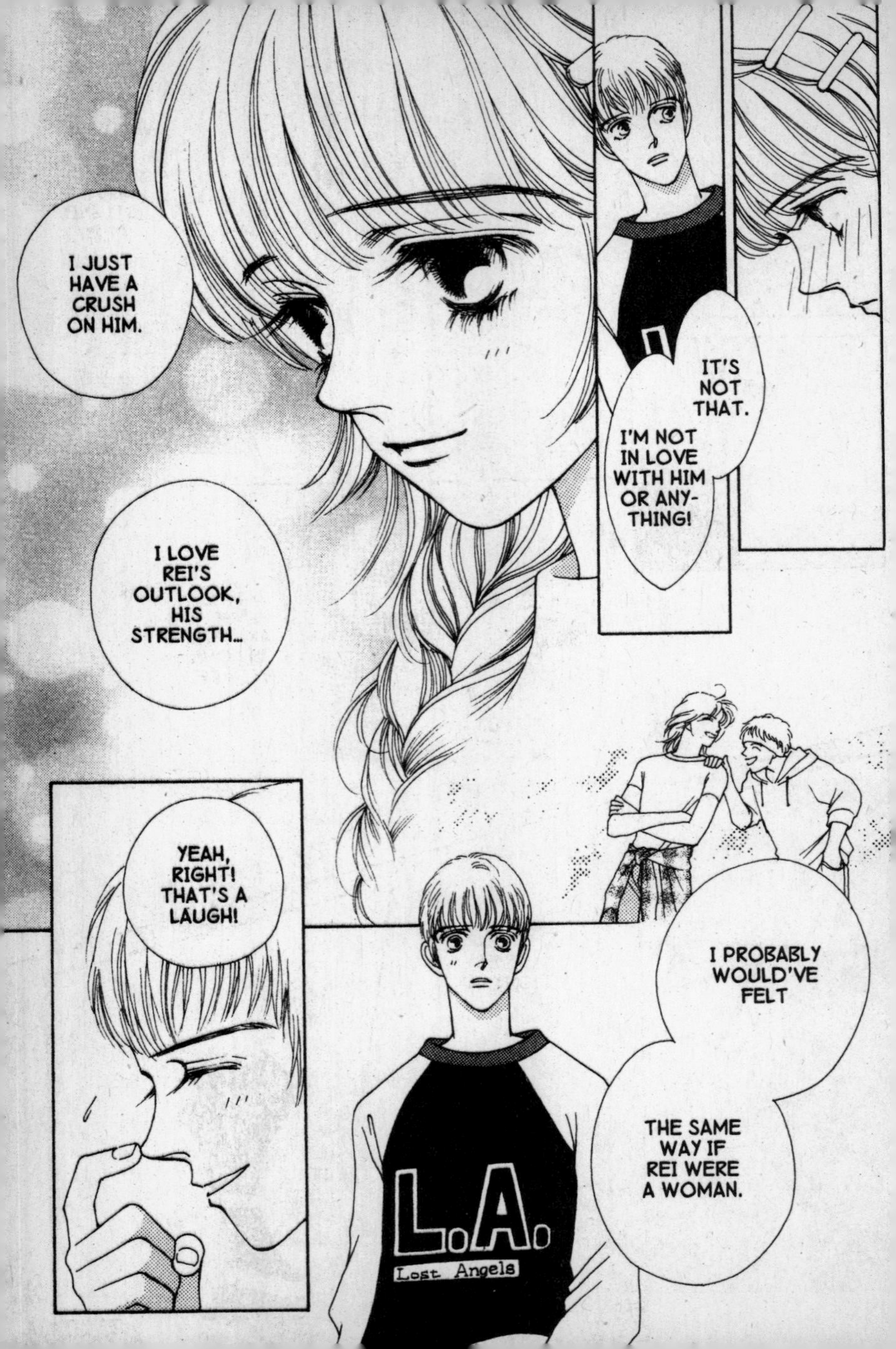
IT'S NOT THAT.
I'M NOT IN LOVE WITH HIM OR ANY-THING!
I JUST HAVE A CRUSH ON HIM.
I LOVE REI'S OUTLOOK, HIS STRENGTH...
I PROBABLY WOULD'VE FELT
THE SAME WAY IF REI WERE A WOMAN.
L.A.
Lost Angels
YEAH, RIGHT! THAT'S A LAUGH!

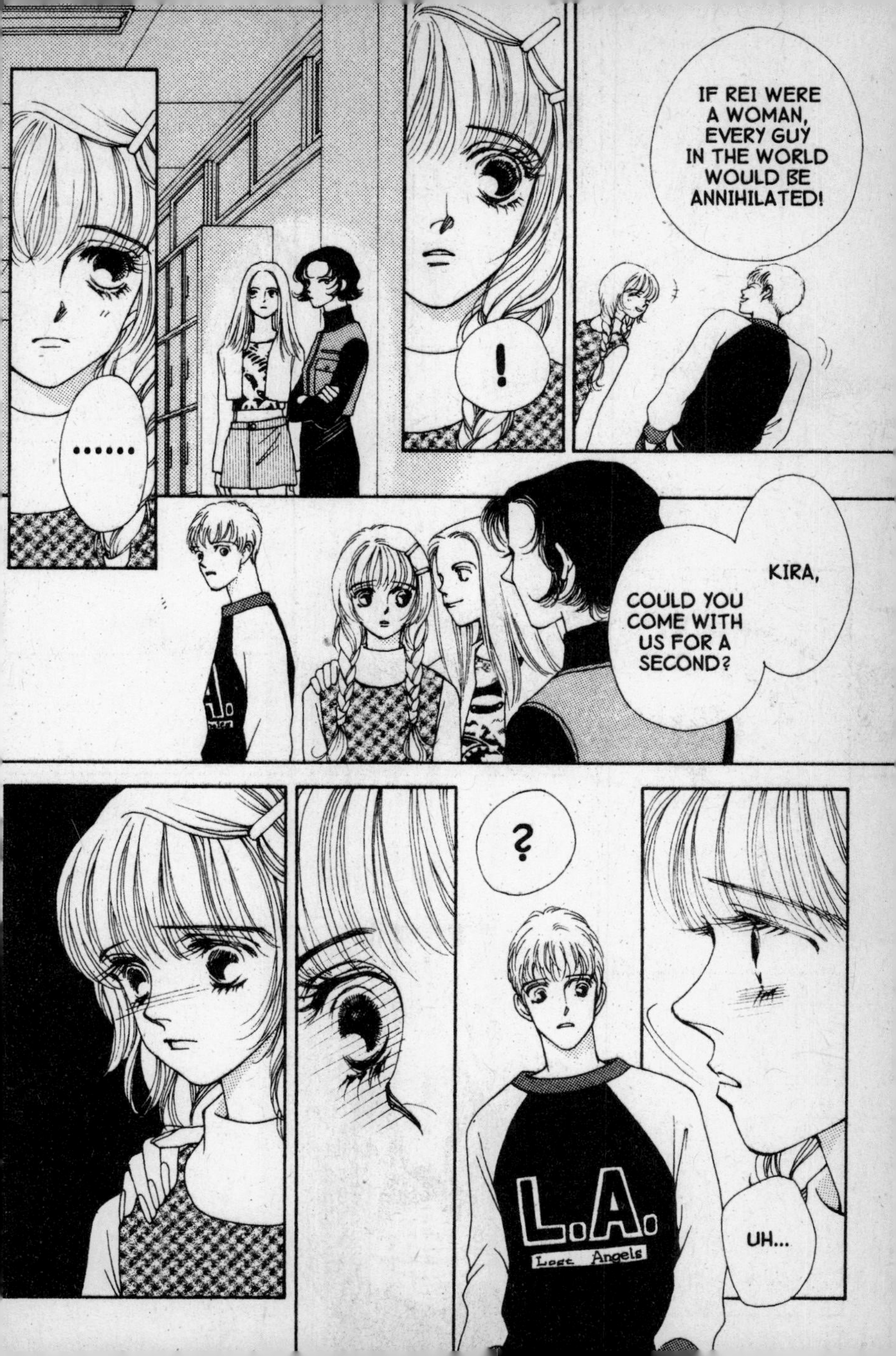
IF REI WERE A WOMAN, EVERY GUY IN THE WORLD WOULD BE ANNIHILATED!
!
......
KIRA,
COULD YOU COME WITH US FOR A SECOND?
UH...
?
L.A.
Lost Angels

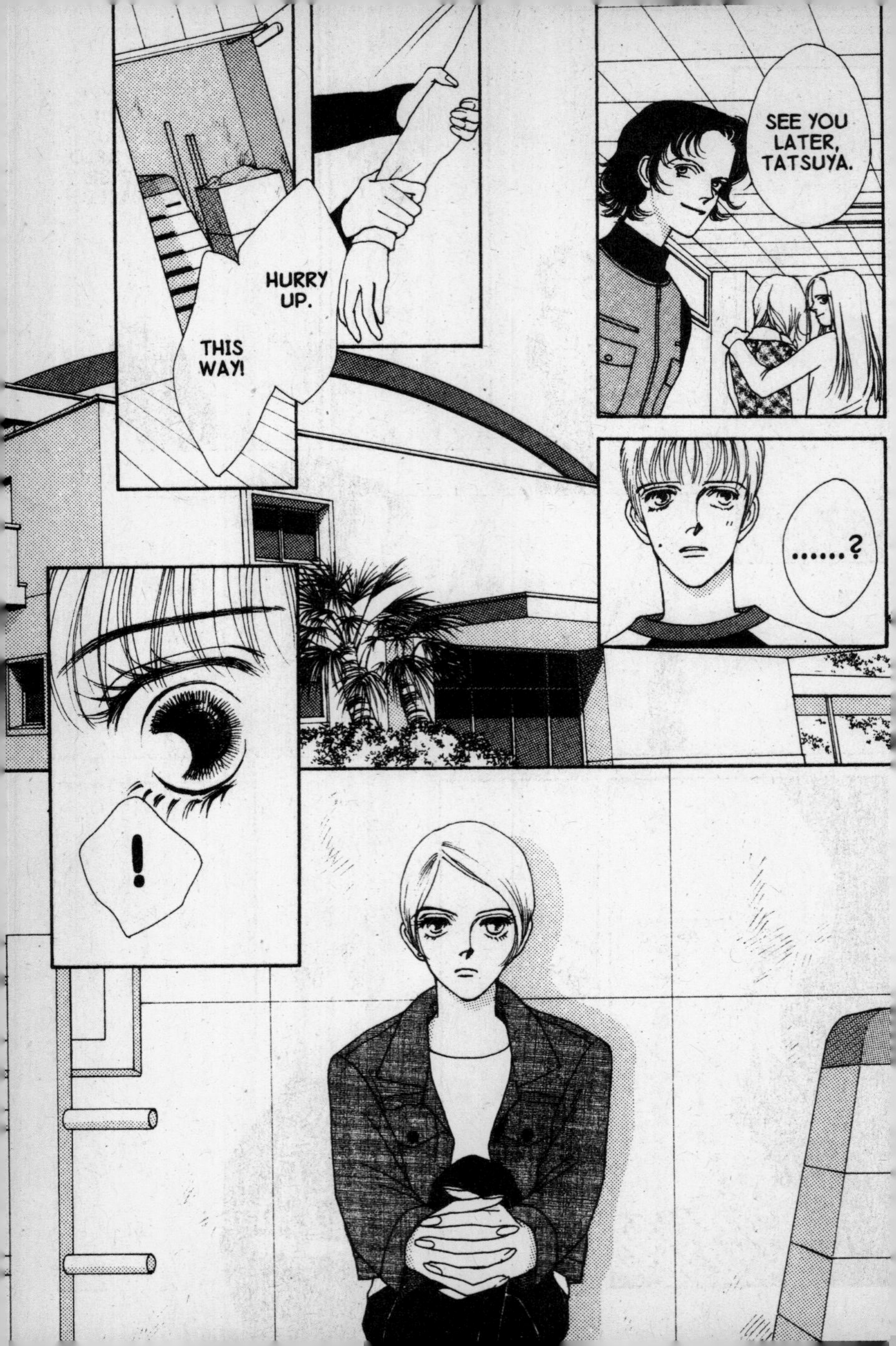
SEE YOU LATER, TATSUYA.
HURRY UP.
THIS WAY!
......?
!

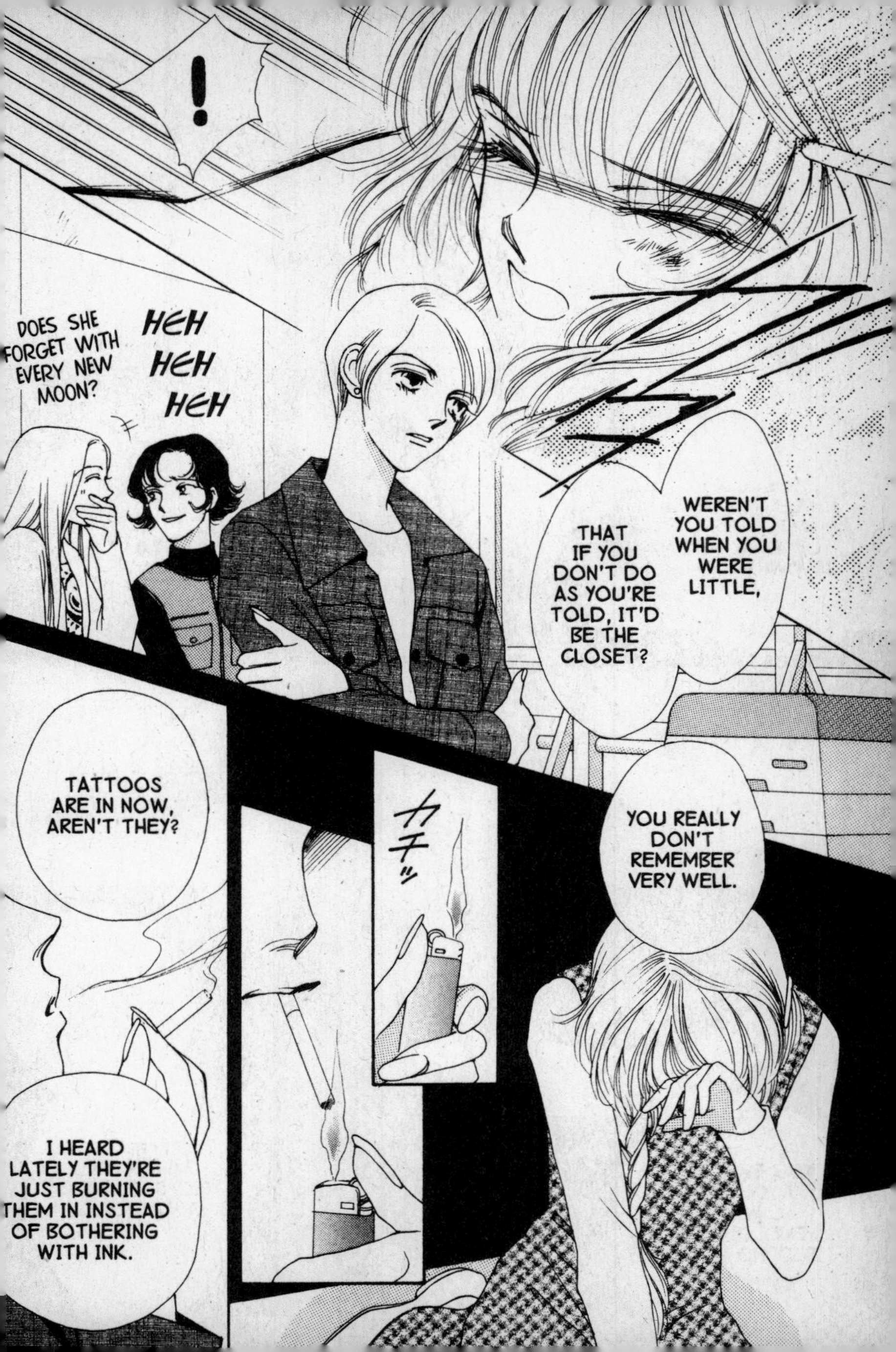
!
WEREN'T YOU TOLD WHEN YOU WERE LITTLE,
THAT IF YOU DON'T DO AS YOU'RE TOLD, IT'D BE THE CLOSET?
DOES SHE FORGET WITH EVERY NEW MOON?
HEH HEH HEH
YOU REALLY DON'T REMEMBER VERY WELL.
カチッ
TATTOOS ARE IN NOW, AREN'T THEY?
I HEARD LATELY THEY'RE JUST BURNING THEM IN INSTEAD OF BOTHERING WITH INK.

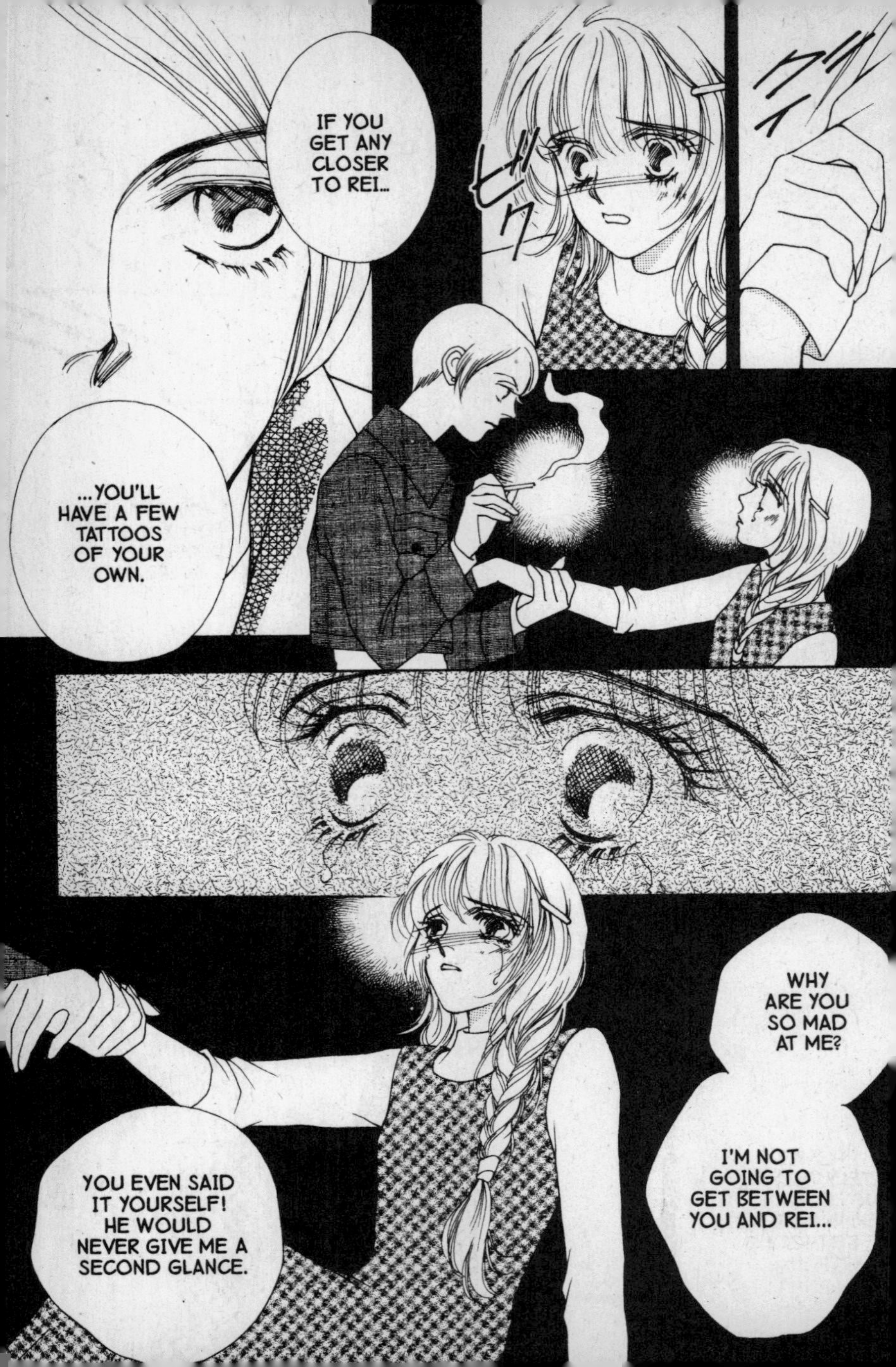
IF YOU GET ANY CLOSER TO REI...
...YOU'LL HAVE A FEW TATTOOS OF YOUR OWN.
WHY ARE YOU SO MAD AT ME?
I'M NOT GOING TO GET BETWEEN YOU AND REI...
YOU EVEN SAID IT YOURSELF! HE WOULD NEVER GIVE ME A SECOND GLANCE.

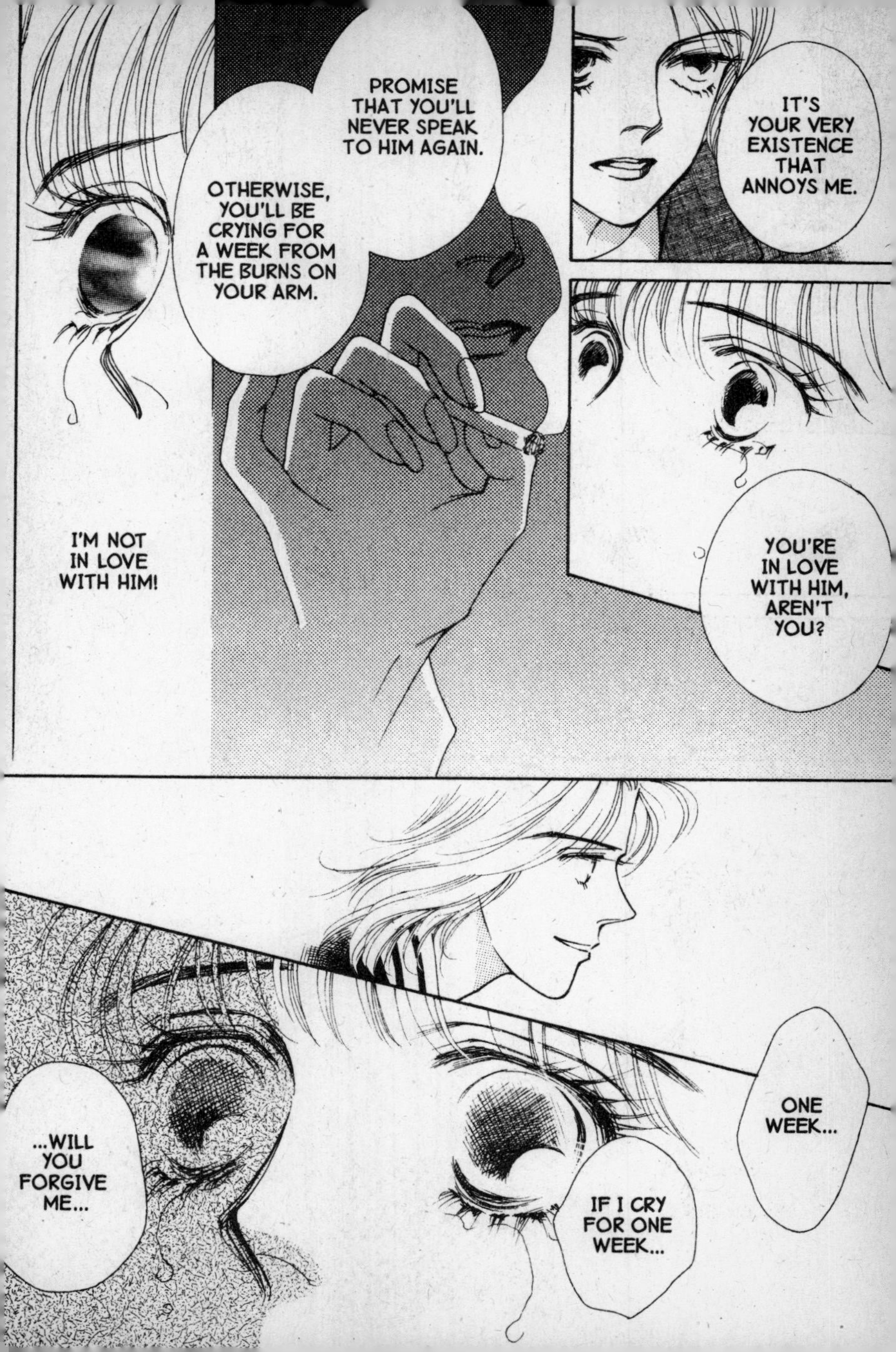
IT'S YOUR VERY EXISTENCE THAT ANNOYS ME.
YOU'RE IN LOVE WITH HIM, AREN'T YOU?
PROMISE THAT YOU'LL NEVER SPEAK TO HIM AGAIN.
OTHERWISE, YOU'LL BE CRYING FOR A WEEK FROM THE BURNS ON YOUR ARM.
I'M NOT IN LOVE WITH HIM!
ONE WEEK...
IF I CRY FOR ONE WEEK...
...WILL YOU FORGIVE ME...

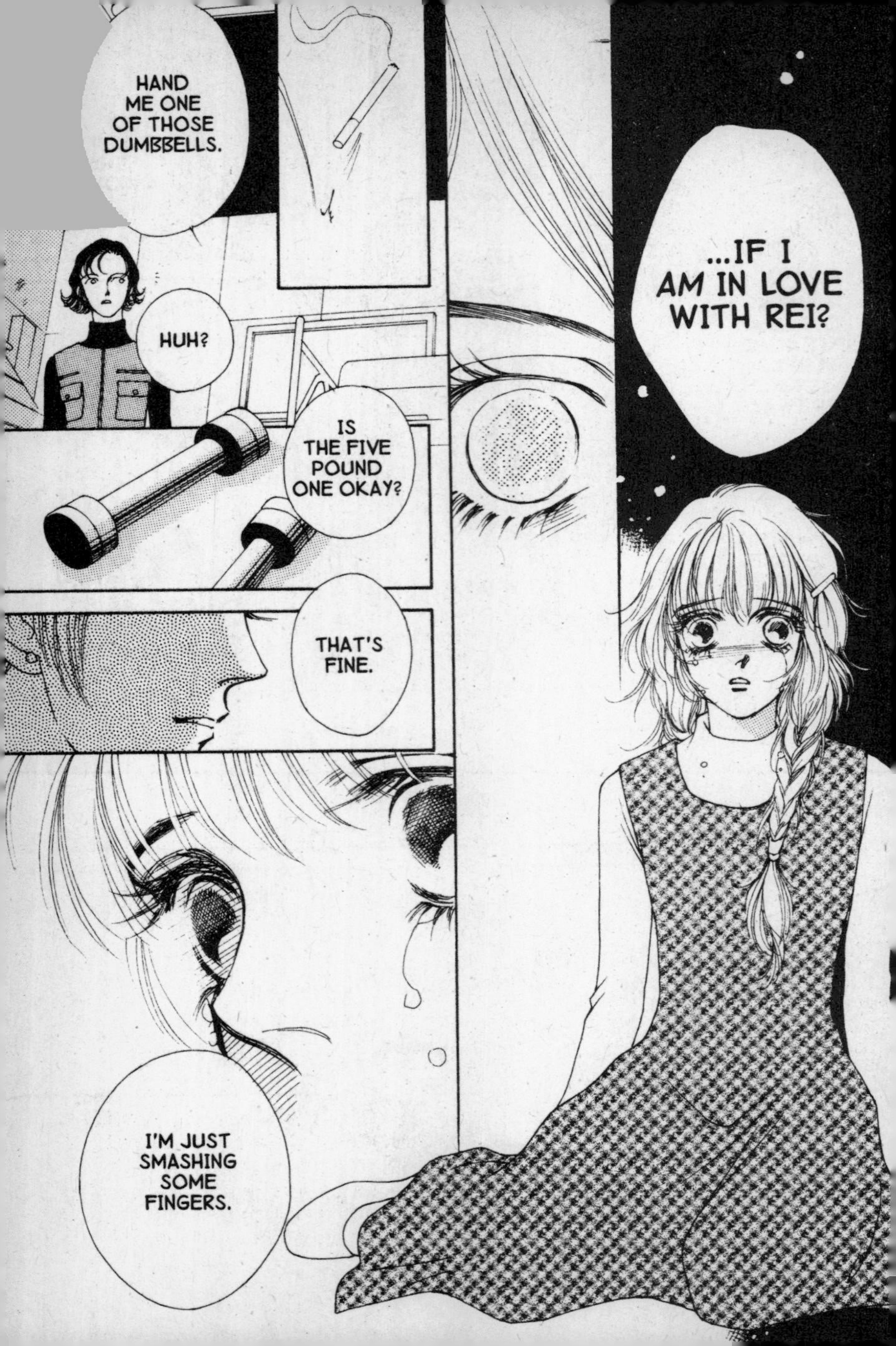
...IF I AM IN LOVE WITH REI?
HAND ME ONE OF THOSE DUMBBELLS.
HUH?
IS THE FIVE POUND ONE OKAY?
THAT'S FINE.
I'M JUST SMASHING SOME FINGERS.

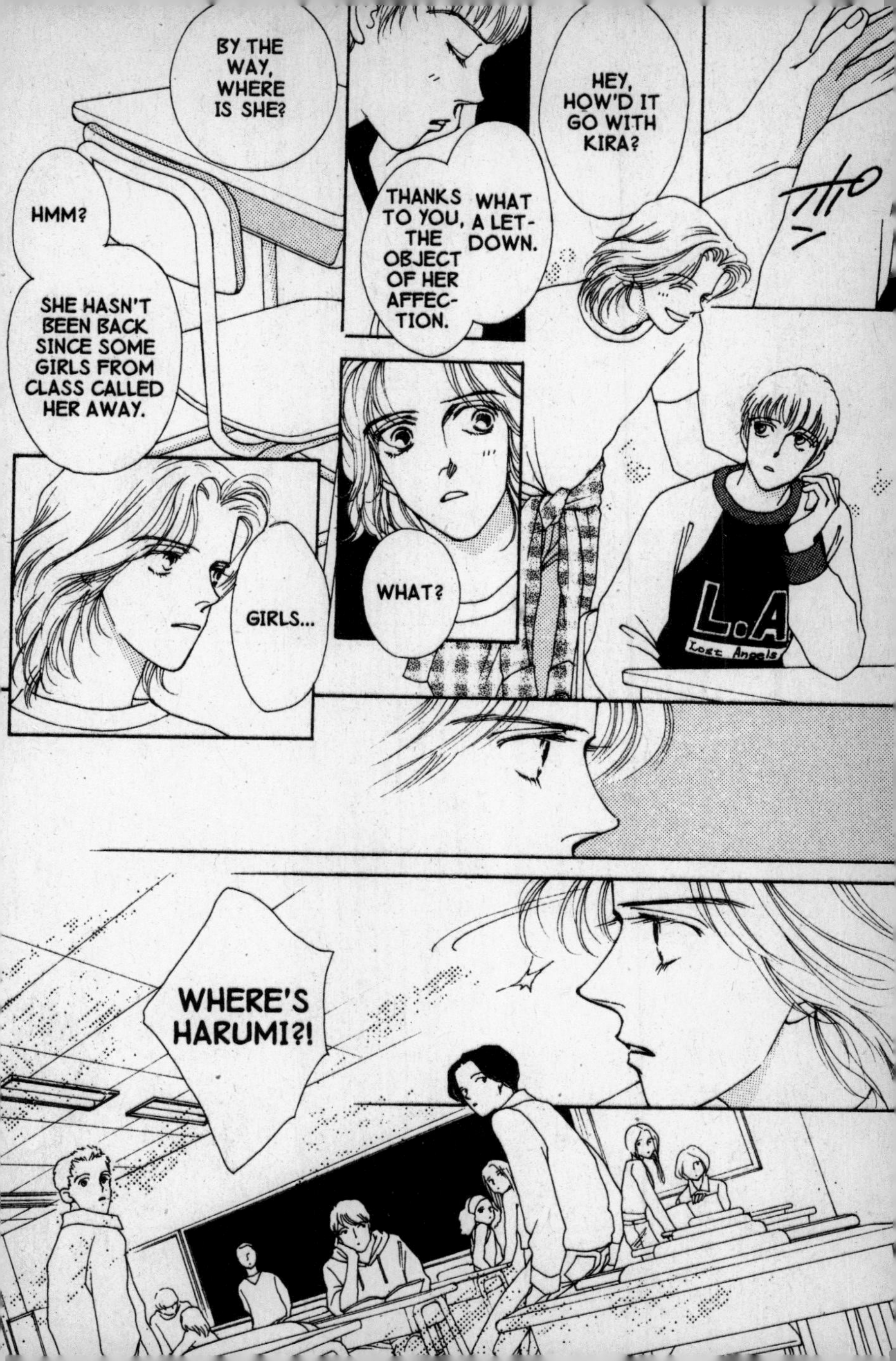
HEY, HOW'D IT GO WITH KIRA?
WHAT A LET-DOWN.
THANKS TO YOU, THE OBJECT OF HER AFFECTION.
BY THE WAY, WHERE IS SHE?
HMM?
SHE HASN'T BEEN BACK SINCE SOME GIRLS FROM CLASS CALLED HER AWAY.
WHAT?
GIRLS...
WHERE'S HARUMI?!

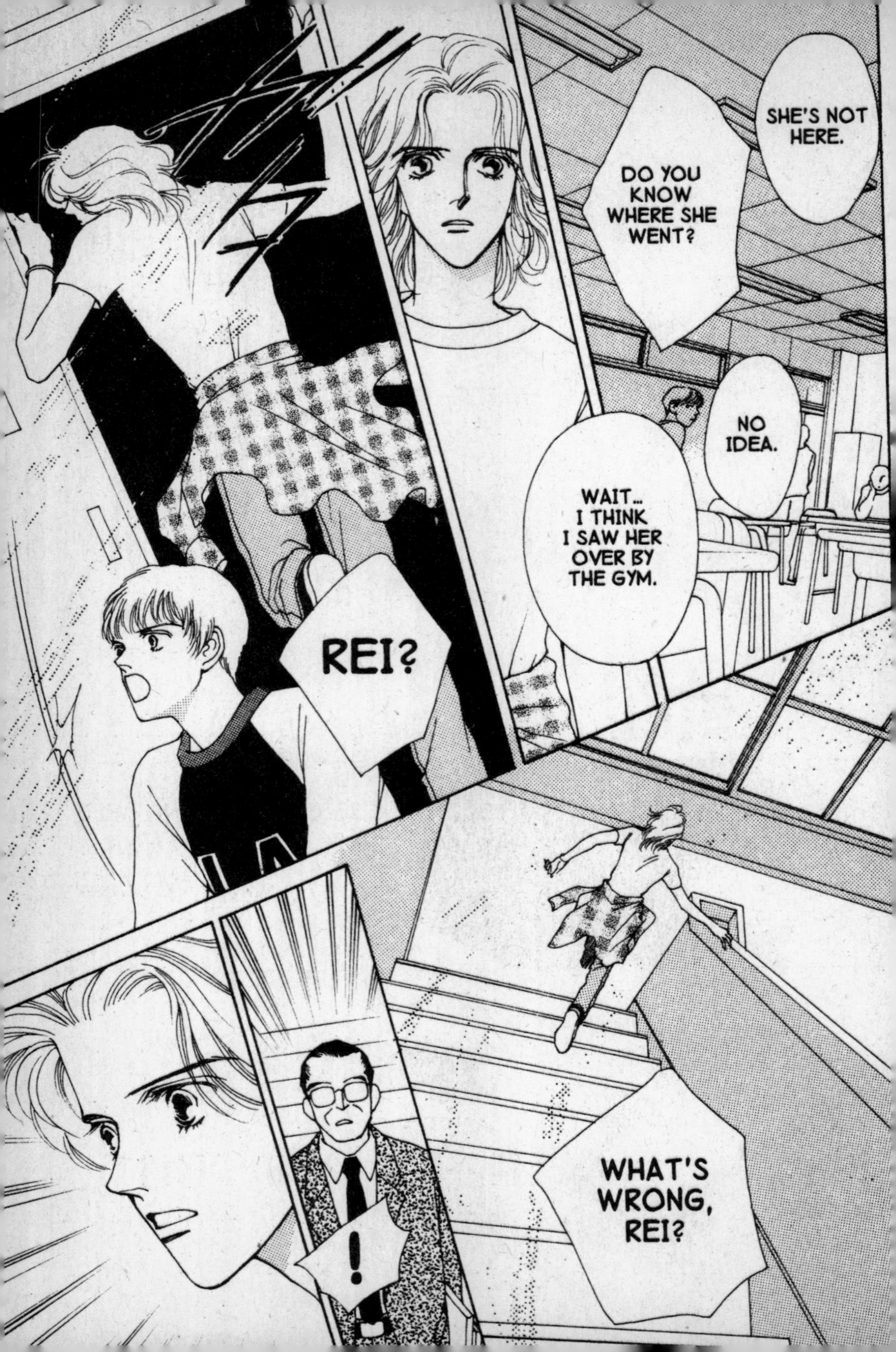
SHE'S NOT HERE.
DO YOU KNOW WHERE SHE WENT?
NO IDEA.
WAIT... I THINK I SAW HER OVER BY THE GYM.
REI?
WHAT'S WRONG, REI?
!

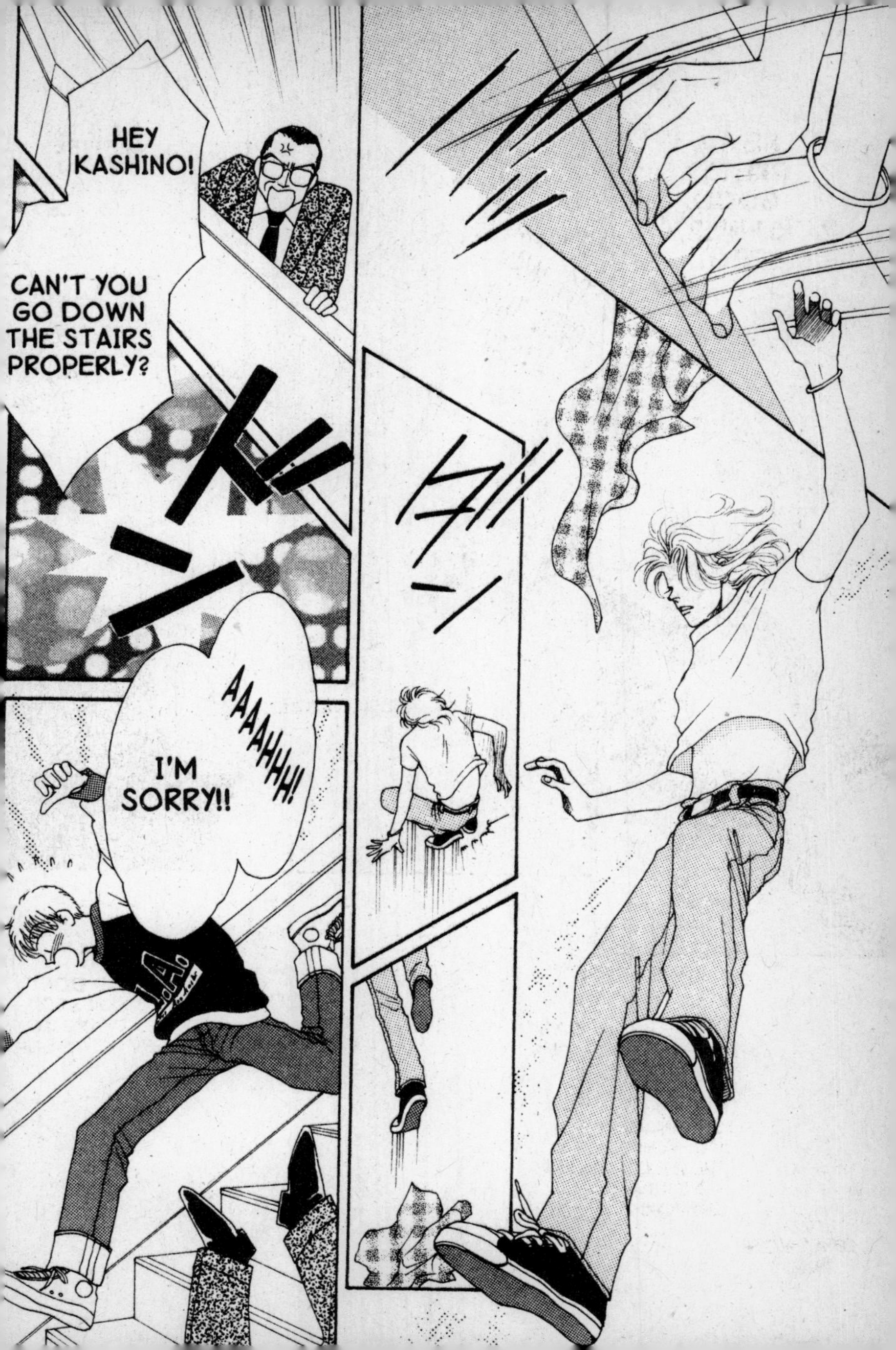
HEY KASHINO!
CAN'T YOU GO DOWN THE STAIRS PROPERLY?
AAAAHHH!
I'M SORRY!!

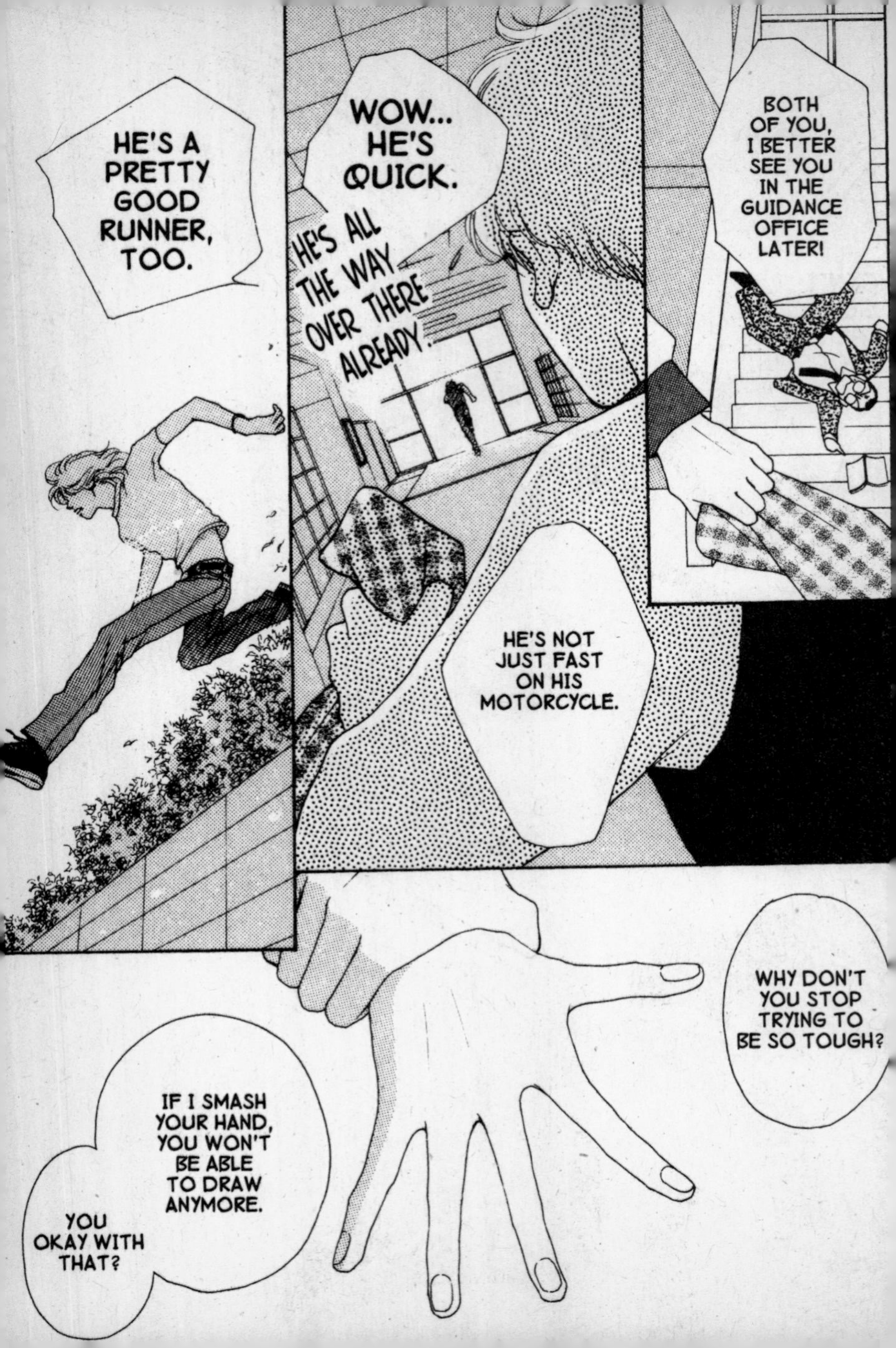
BOTH OF YOU, I BETTER SEE YOU IN THE GUIDANCE OFFICE LATER!
WOW... HE'S QUICK.
HE'S ALL THE WAY OVER THERE ALREADY.
HE'S NOT JUST FAST ON HIS MOTORCYCLE.
HE'S A PRETTY GOOD RUNNER, TOO.
WHY DON'T YOU STOP TRYING TO BE SO TOUGH?
IF I SMASH YOUR HAND, YOU WON'T BE ABLE TO DRAW ANYMORE.
YOU OKAY WITH THAT?

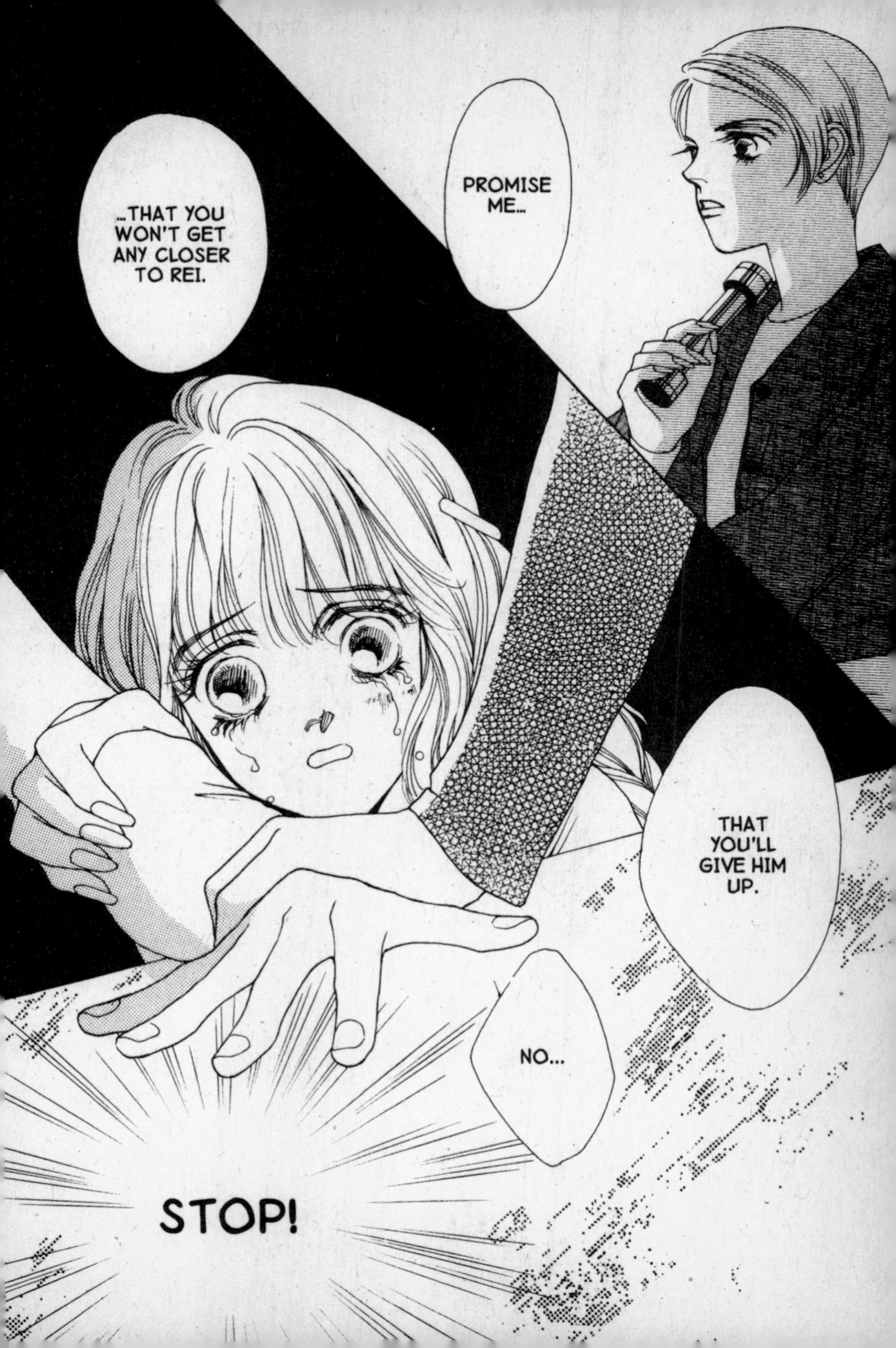
PROMISE ME...
...THAT YOU WON'T GET ANY CLOSER TO REI.
THAT YOU'LL GIVE HIM UP.
NO...
STOP!

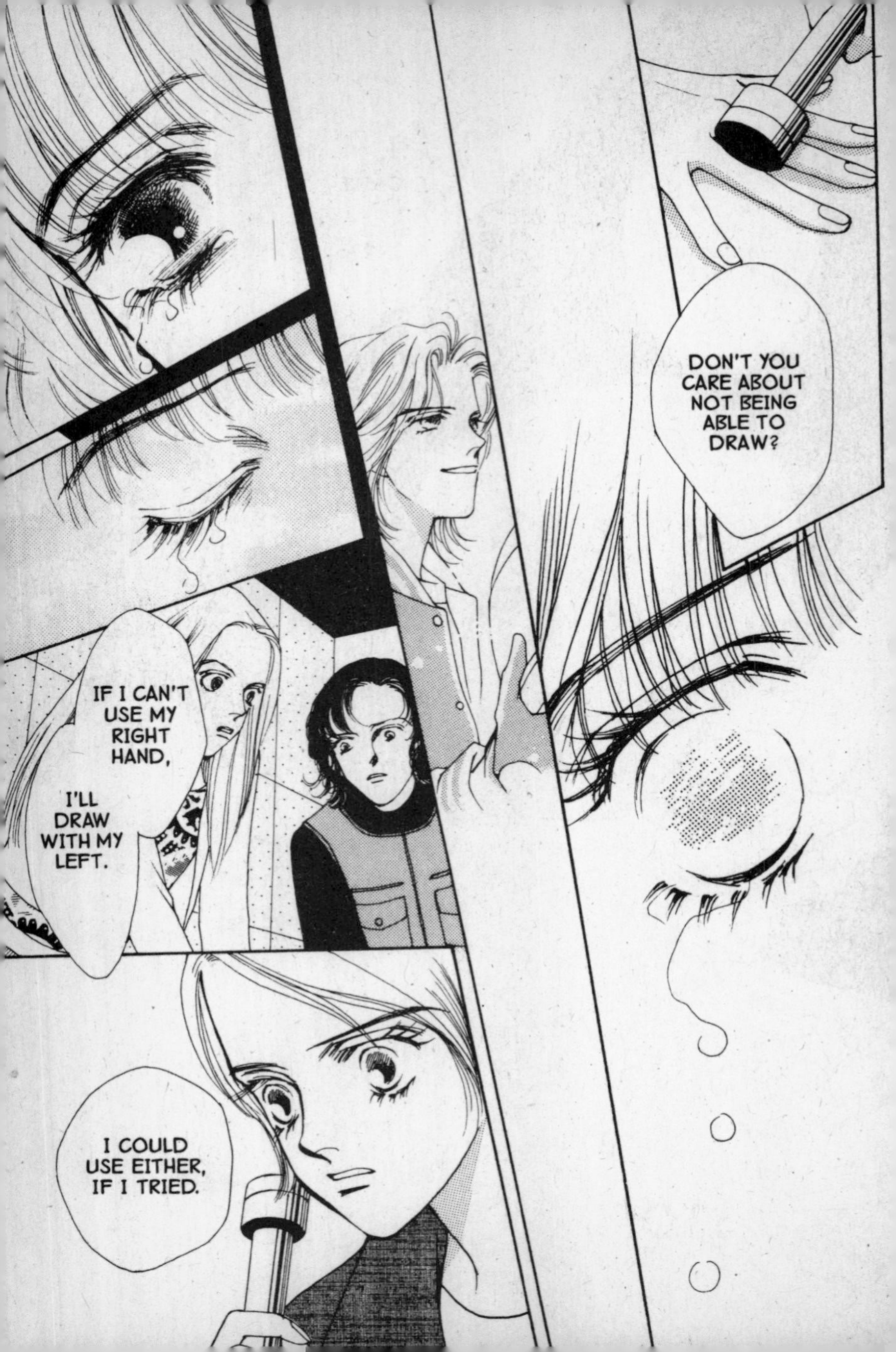
DON'T YOU CARE ABOUT NOT BEING ABLE TO DRAW?
IF I CAN'T USE MY RIGHT HAND,
I'LL DRAW WITH MY LEFT.
I COULD USE EITHER, IF I TRIED.

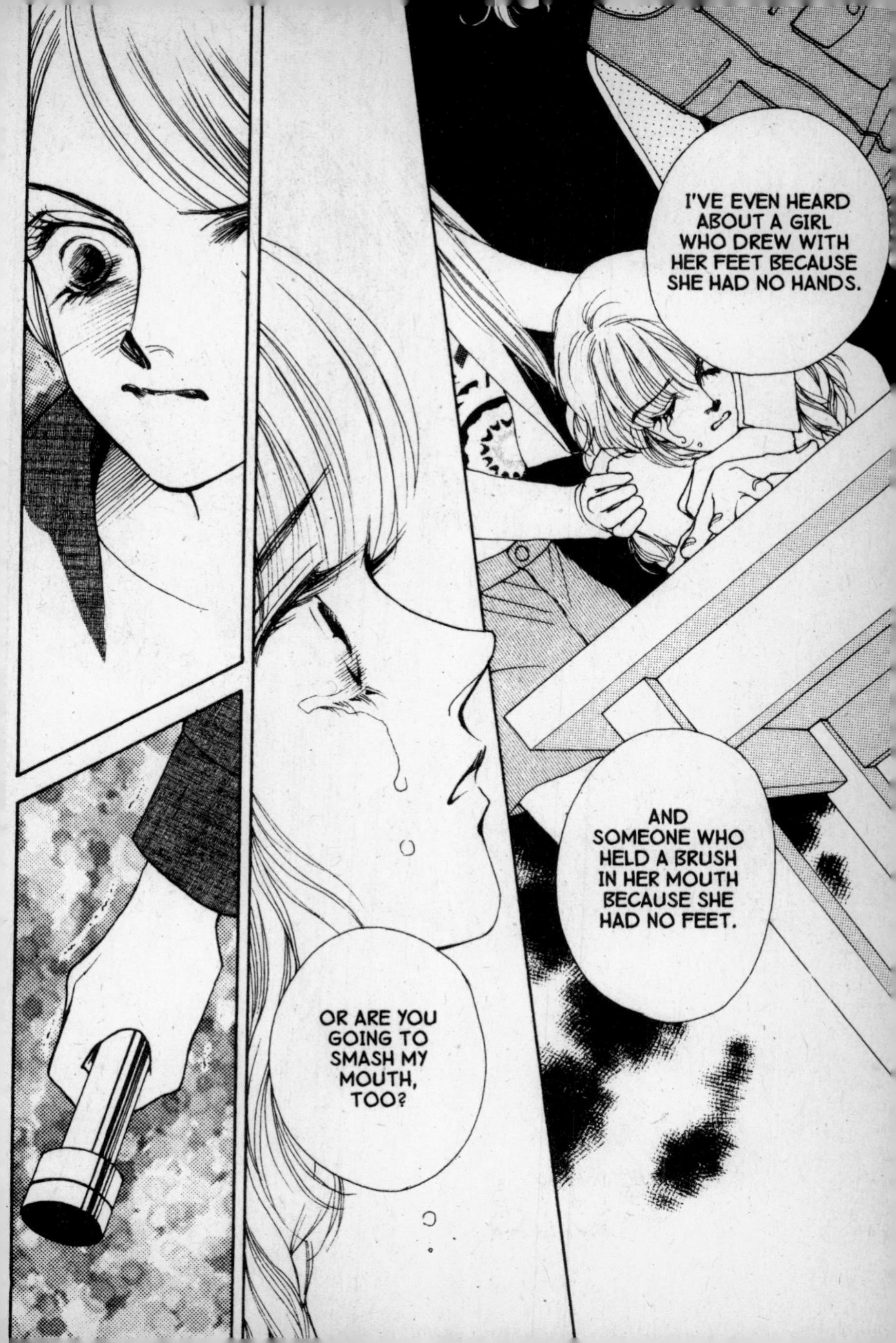
I'VE EVEN HEARD ABOUT A GIRL WHO DREW WITH HER FEET BECAUSE SHE HAD NO HANDS.
AND SOMEONE WHO HELD A BRUSH IN HER MOUTH BECAUSE SHE HAD NO FEET.
OR ARE YOU GOING TO SMASH MY MOUTH, TOO?

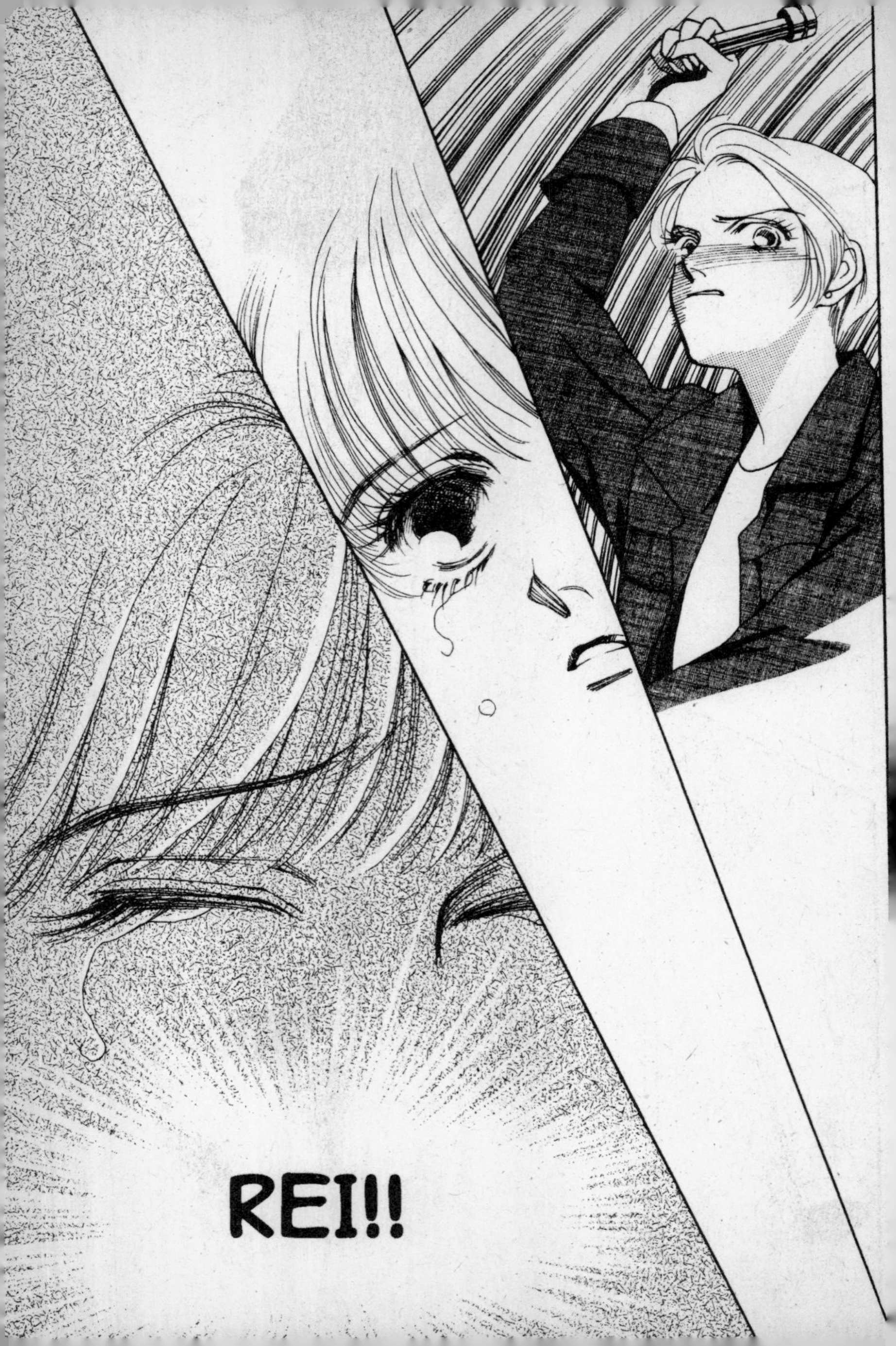
REI!!

MARS

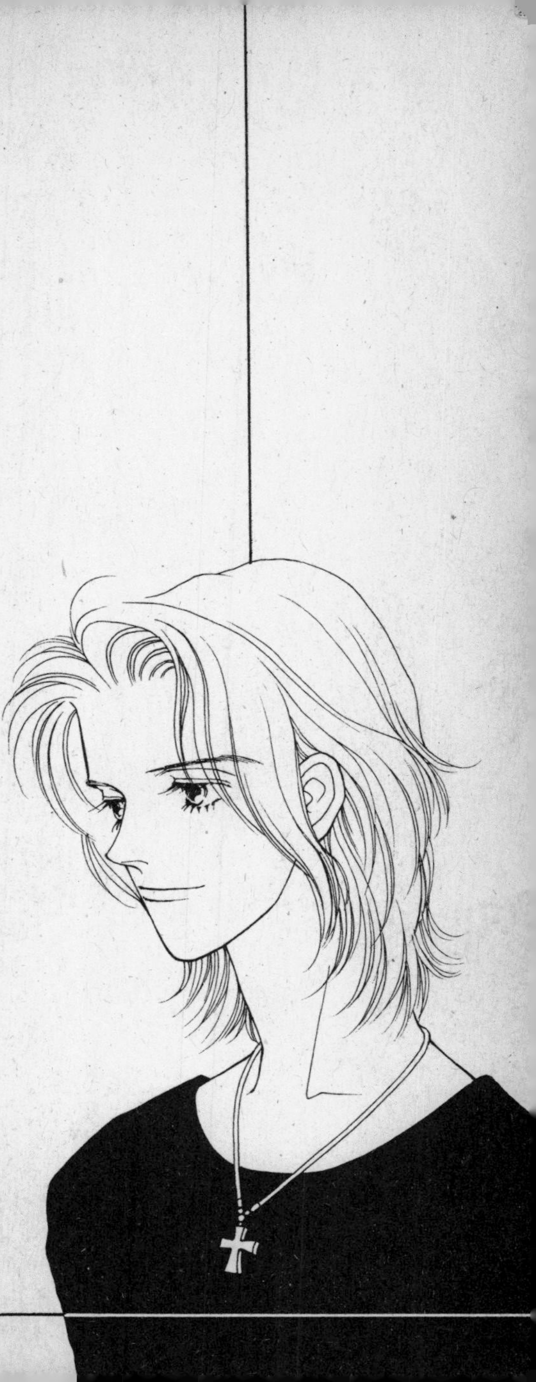

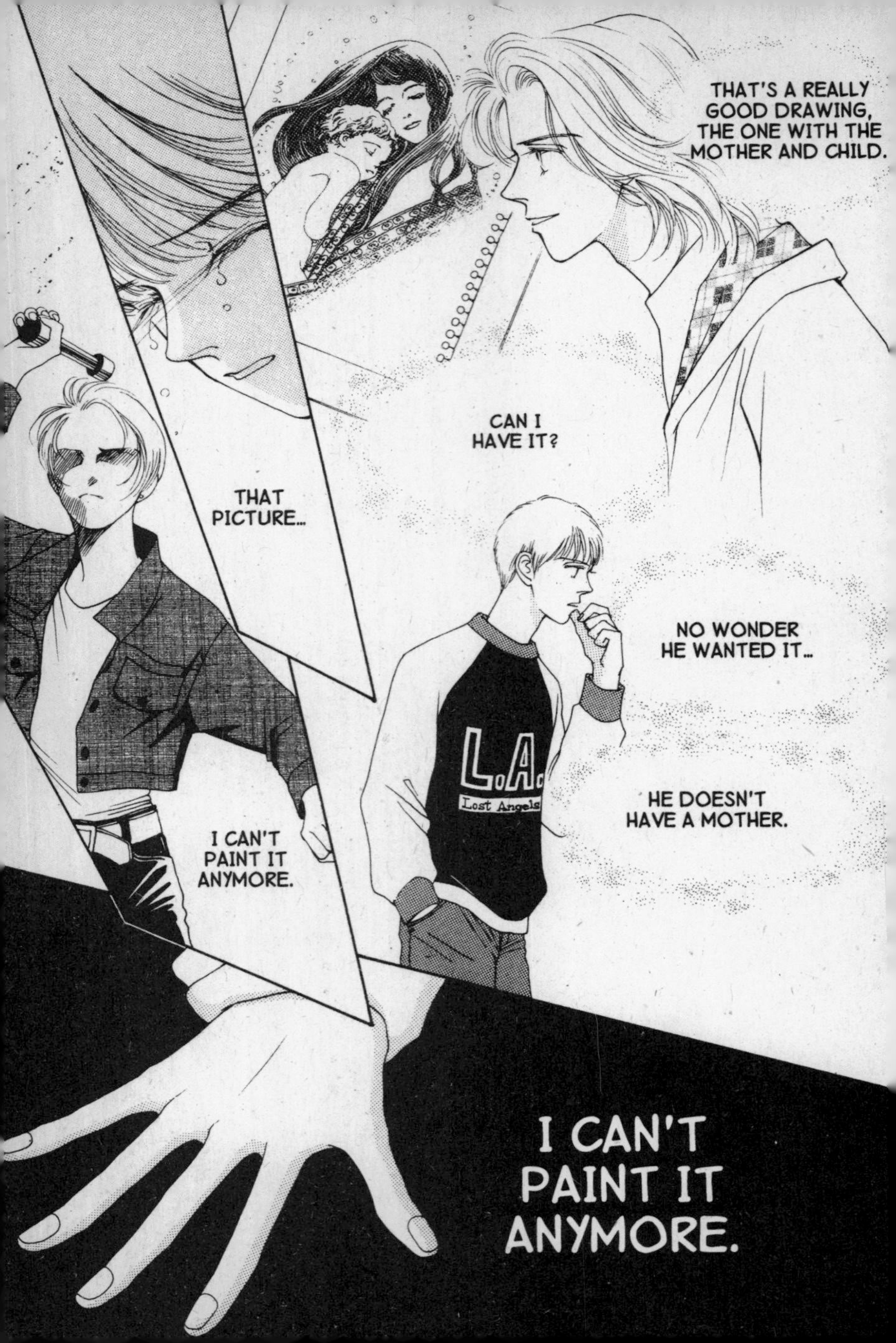
THAT'S A REALLY GOOD DRAWING, THE ONE WITH THE MOTHER AND CHILD.
CAN I HAVE IT?
NO WONDER HE WANTED IT...
HE DOESN'T HAVE A MOTHER.
L.A. Lost Angels
THAT PICTURE...
I CAN'T PAINT IT ANYMORE.
I CAN'T PAINT IT ANYMORE.

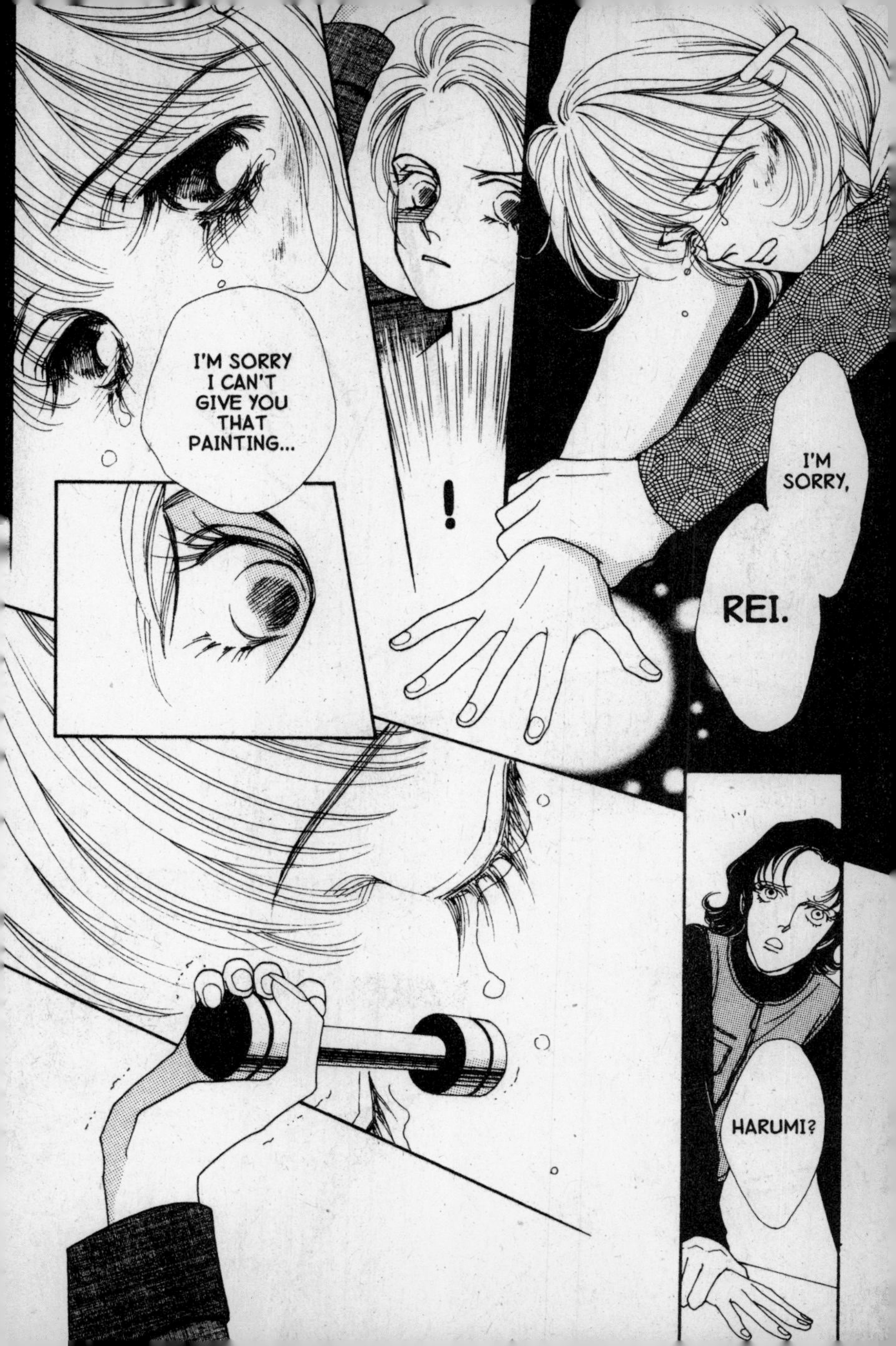
I'M SORRY,
REI.
!
I'M SORRY I CAN'T GIVE YOU THAT PAINTING...
HARUMI?

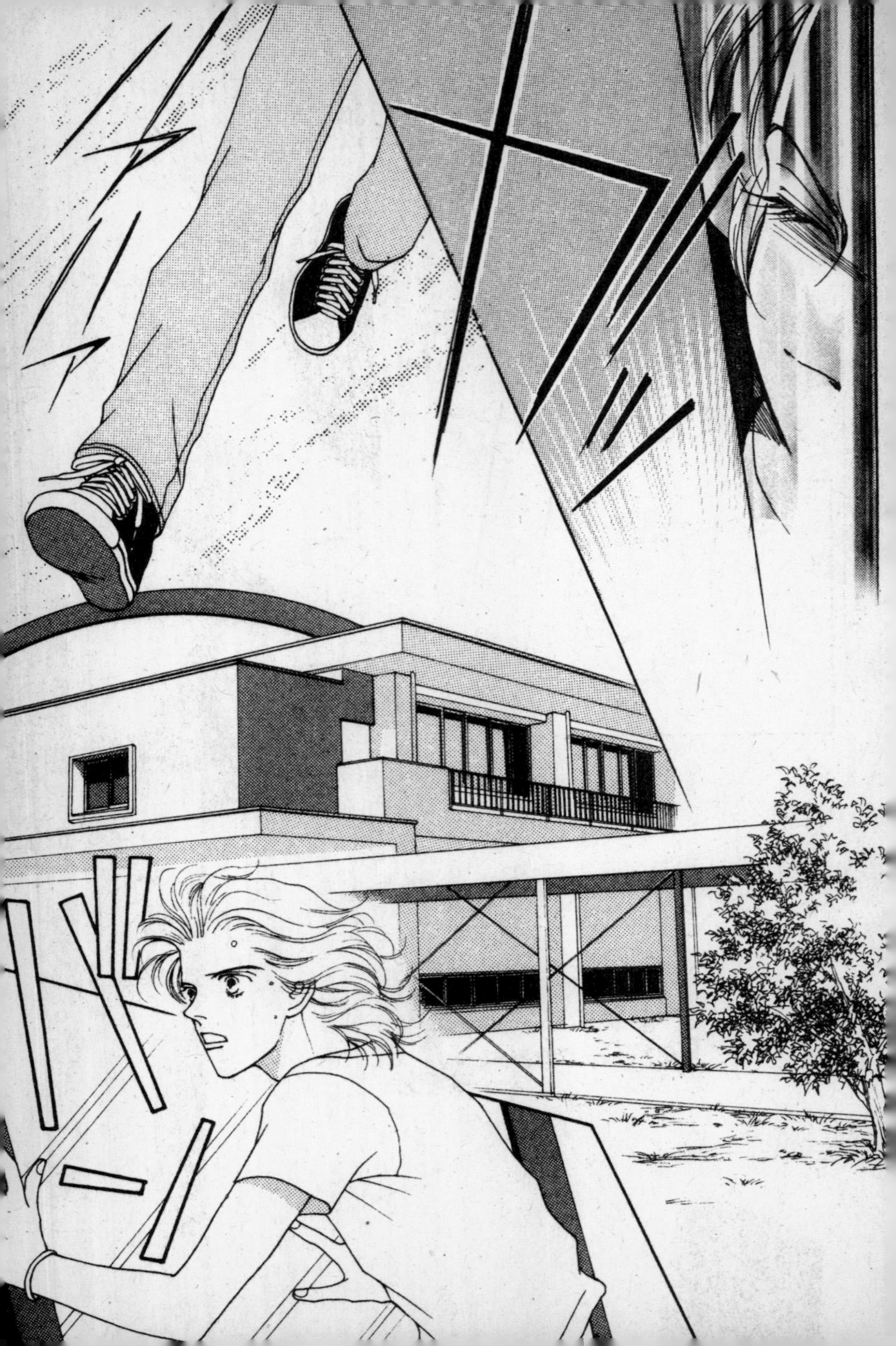

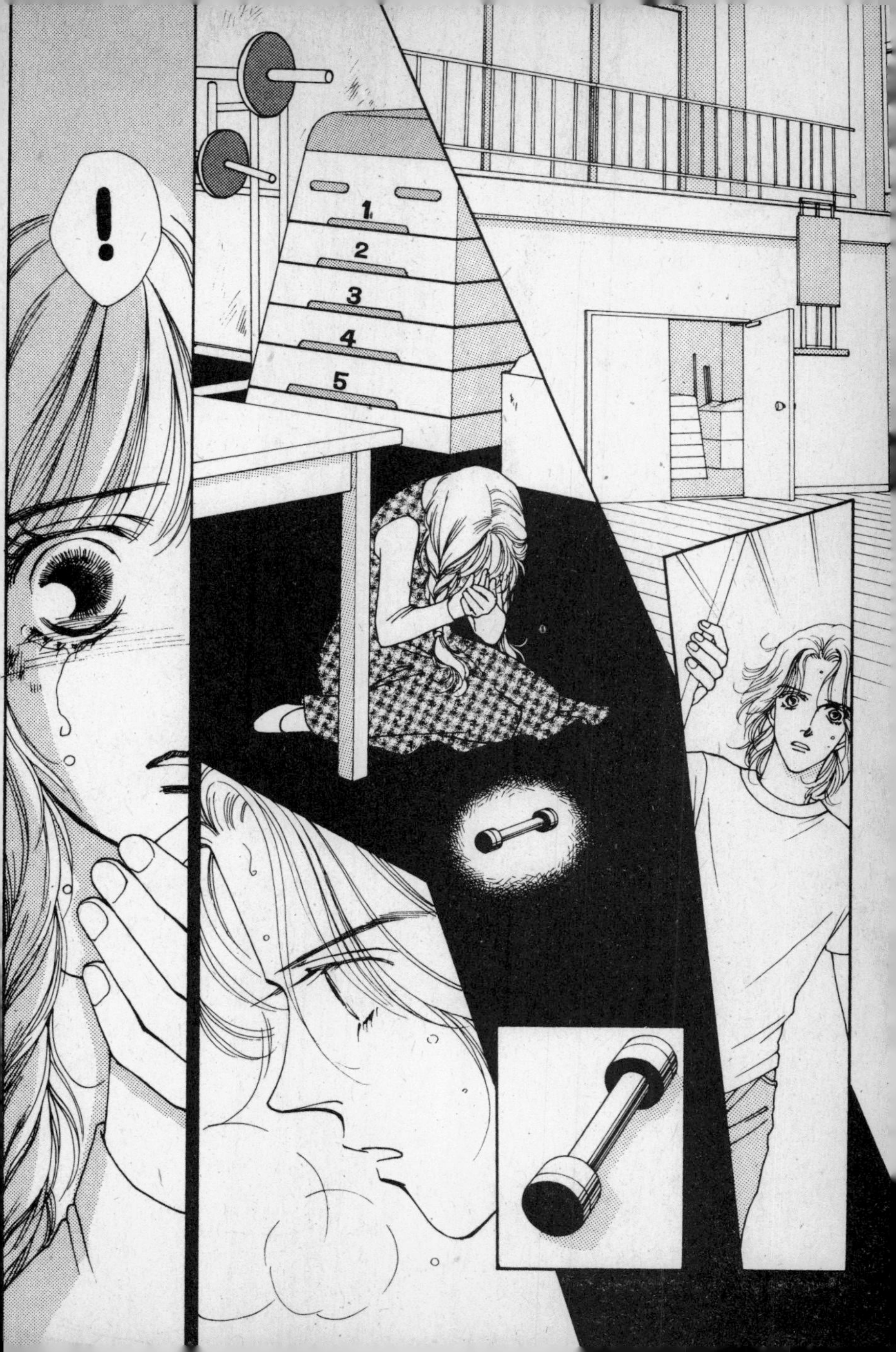
!

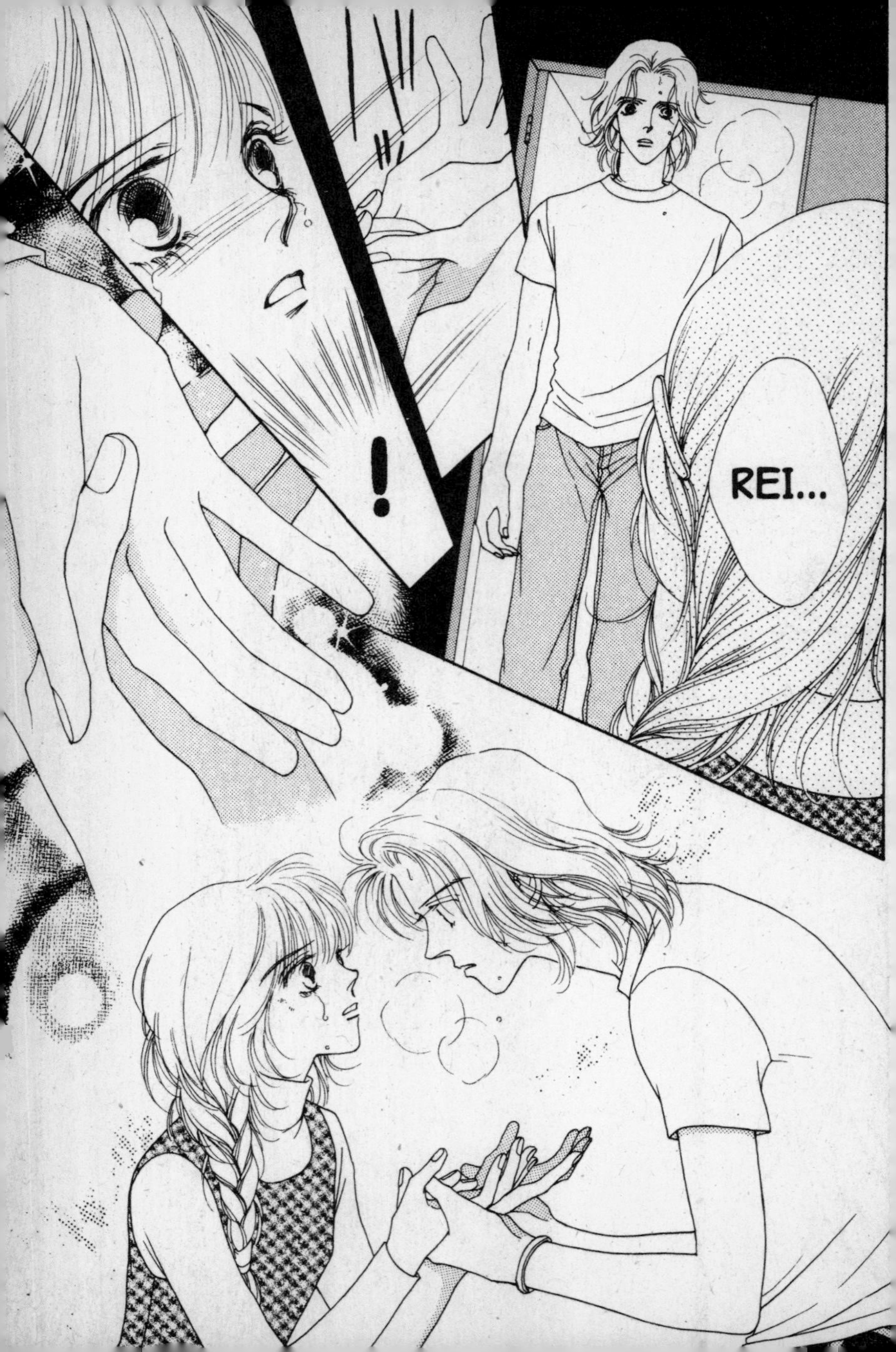
REI...
!

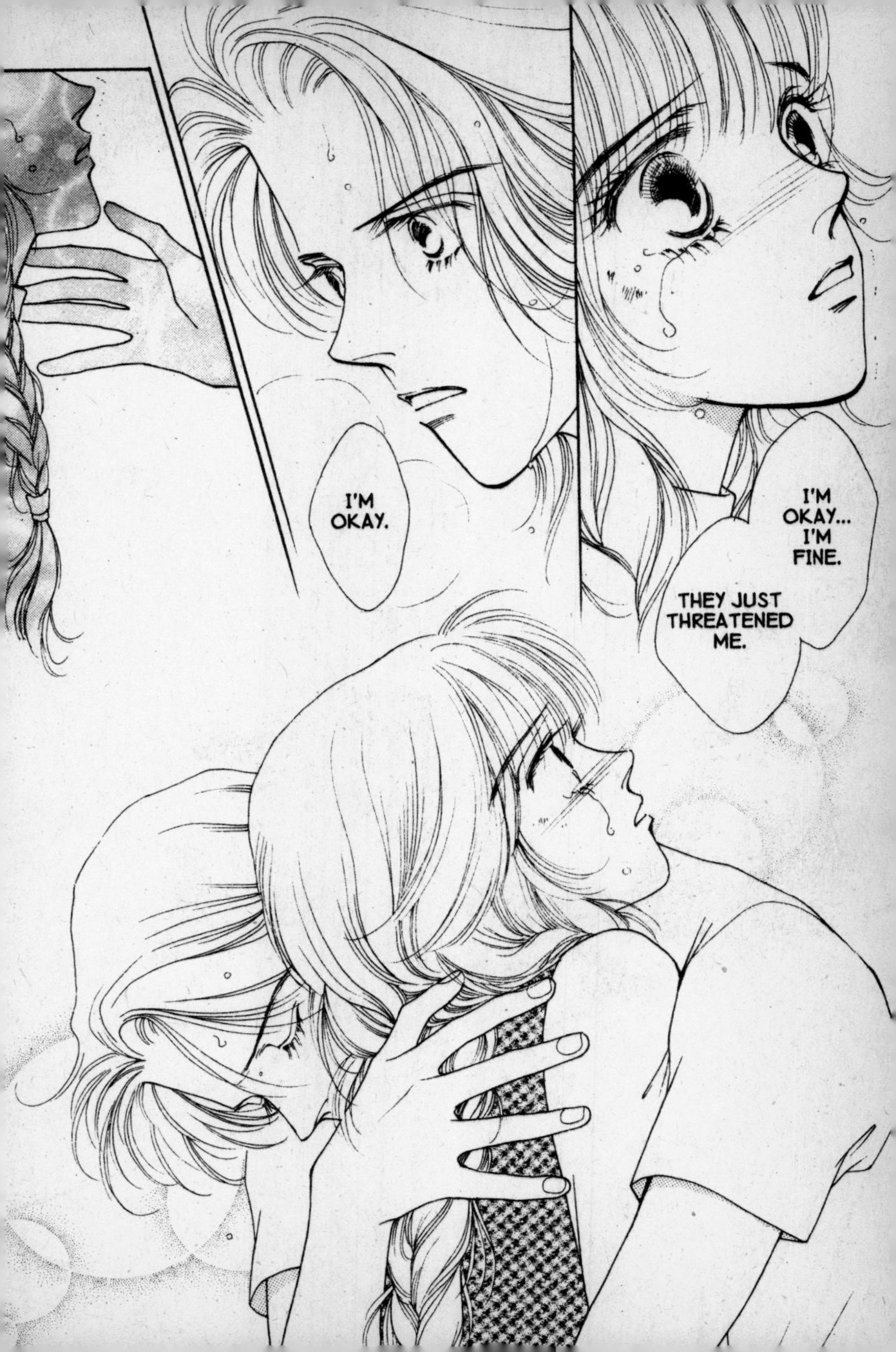
I'M OKAY... I'M FINE.
THEY JUST THREATENED ME.
I'M OKAY.

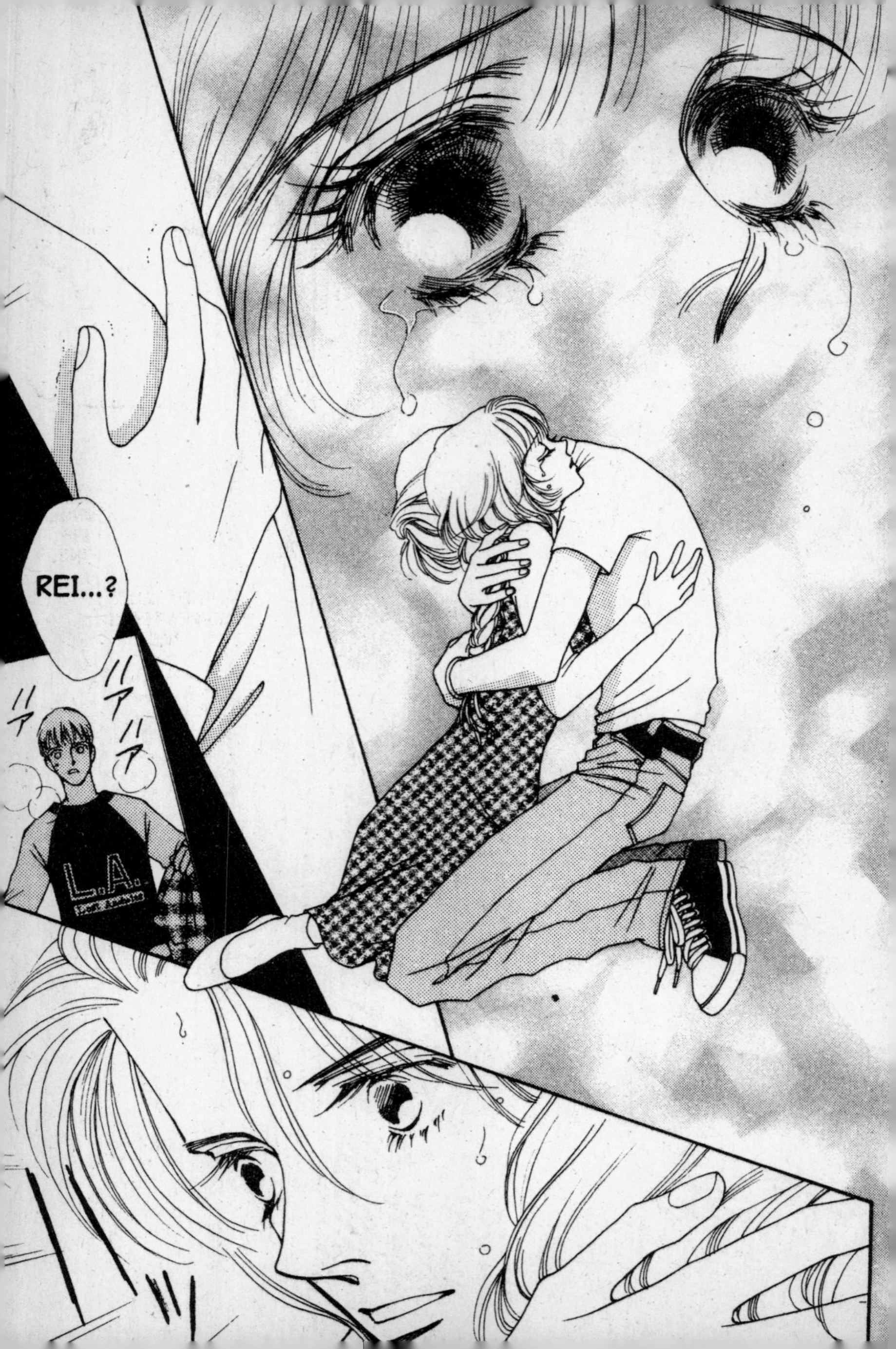
REI...?
ハアハア
ハア

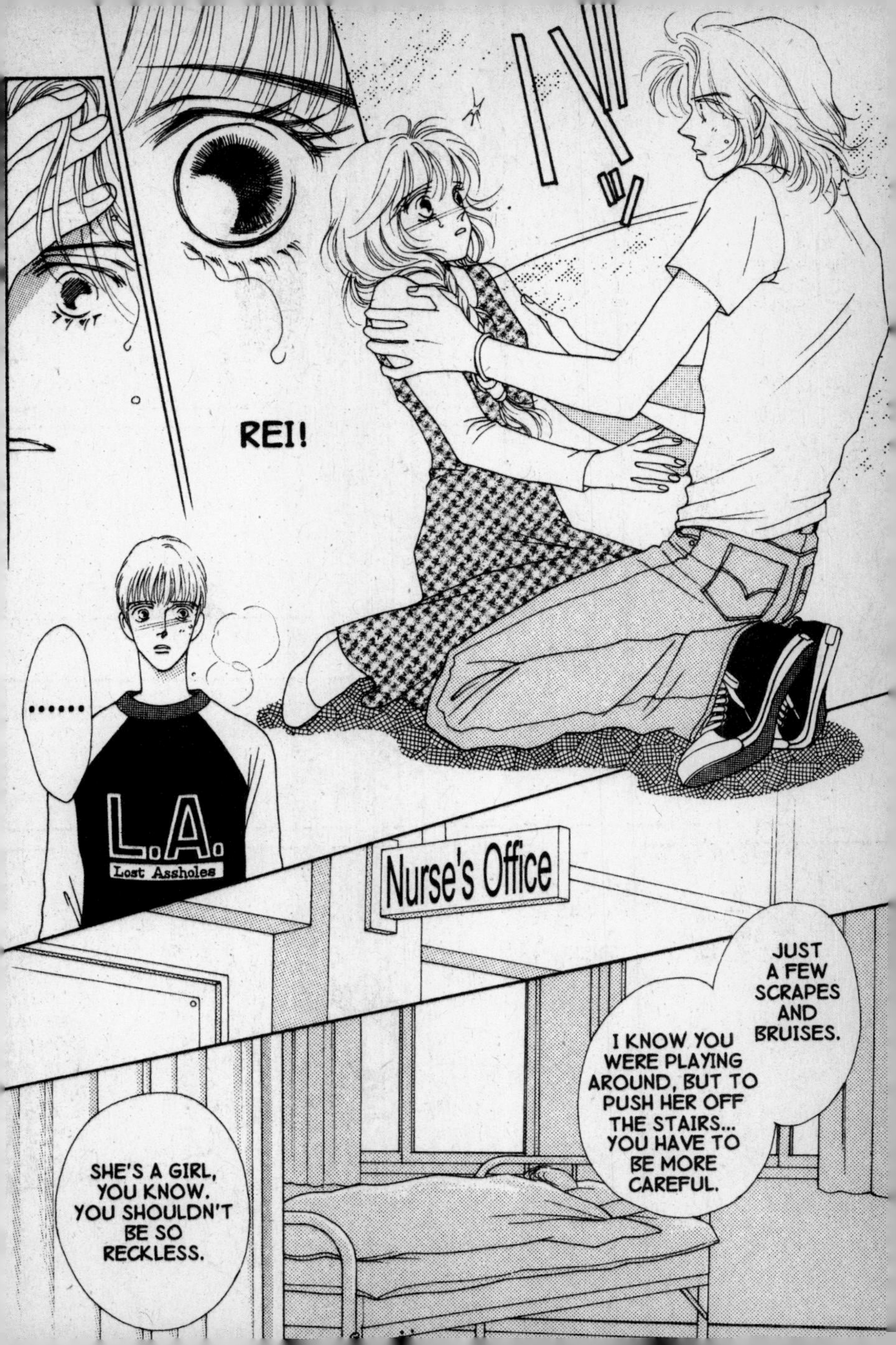
REI!
......
L.A.
Lost Assholes
Nurse's Office
JUST A FEW SCRAPES AND BRUISES.
I KNOW YOU WERE PLAYING AROUND, BUT TO PUSH HER OFF THE STAIRS... YOU HAVE TO BE MORE CAREFUL.
SHE'S A GIRL, YOU KNOW. YOU SHOULDN'T BE SO RECKLESS.

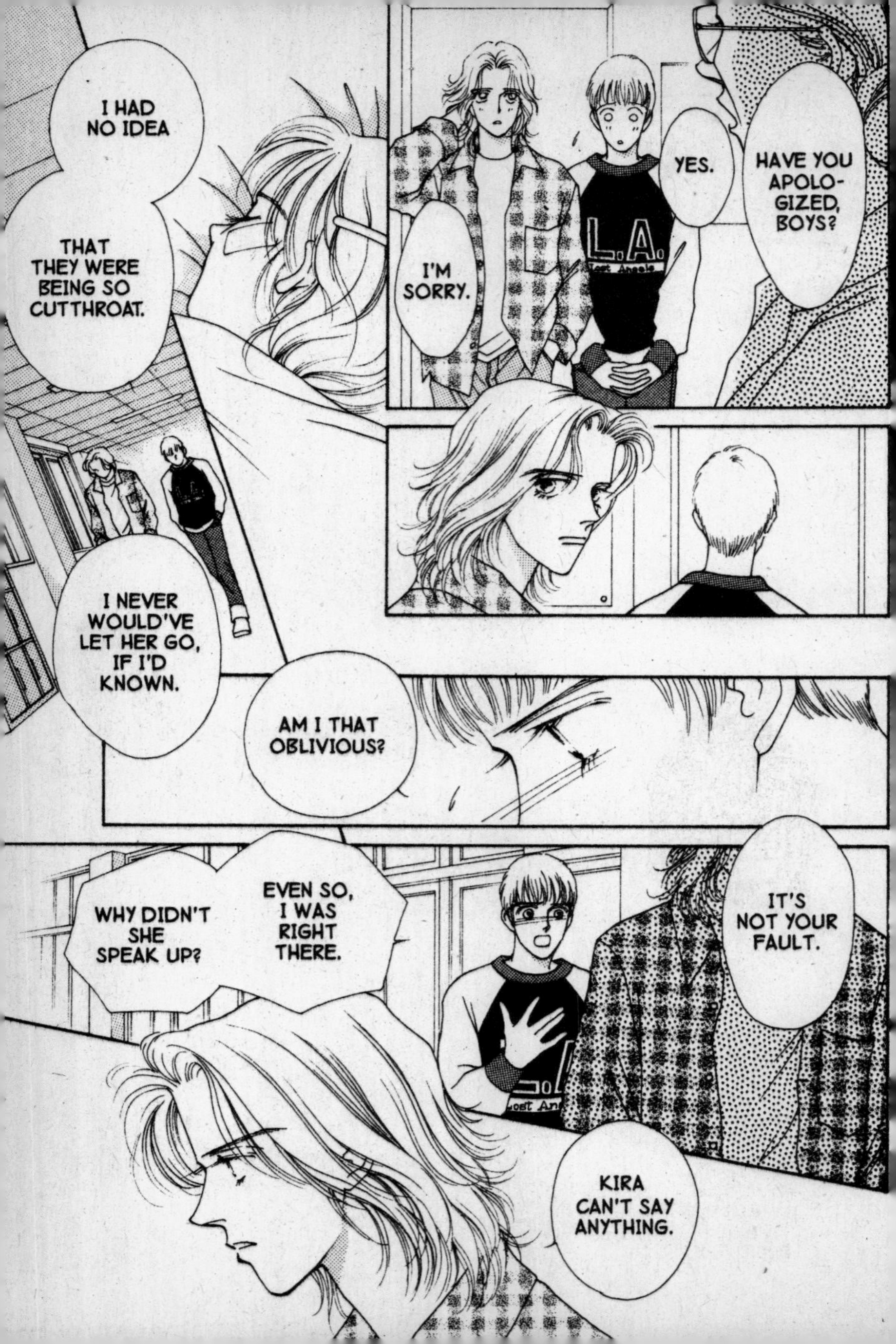
HAVE YOU APOLOGIZED, BOYS?
YES.
I'M SORRY.
I HAD NO IDEA
THAT THEY WERE BEING SO CUTTHROAT.
I NEVER WOULD'VE LET HER GO, IF I'D KNOWN.
AM I THAT OBLIVIOUS?
IT'S NOT YOUR FAULT.
EVEN SO, I WAS RIGHT THERE.
WHY DIDN'T SHE SPEAK UP?
KIRA CAN'T SAY ANYTHING.

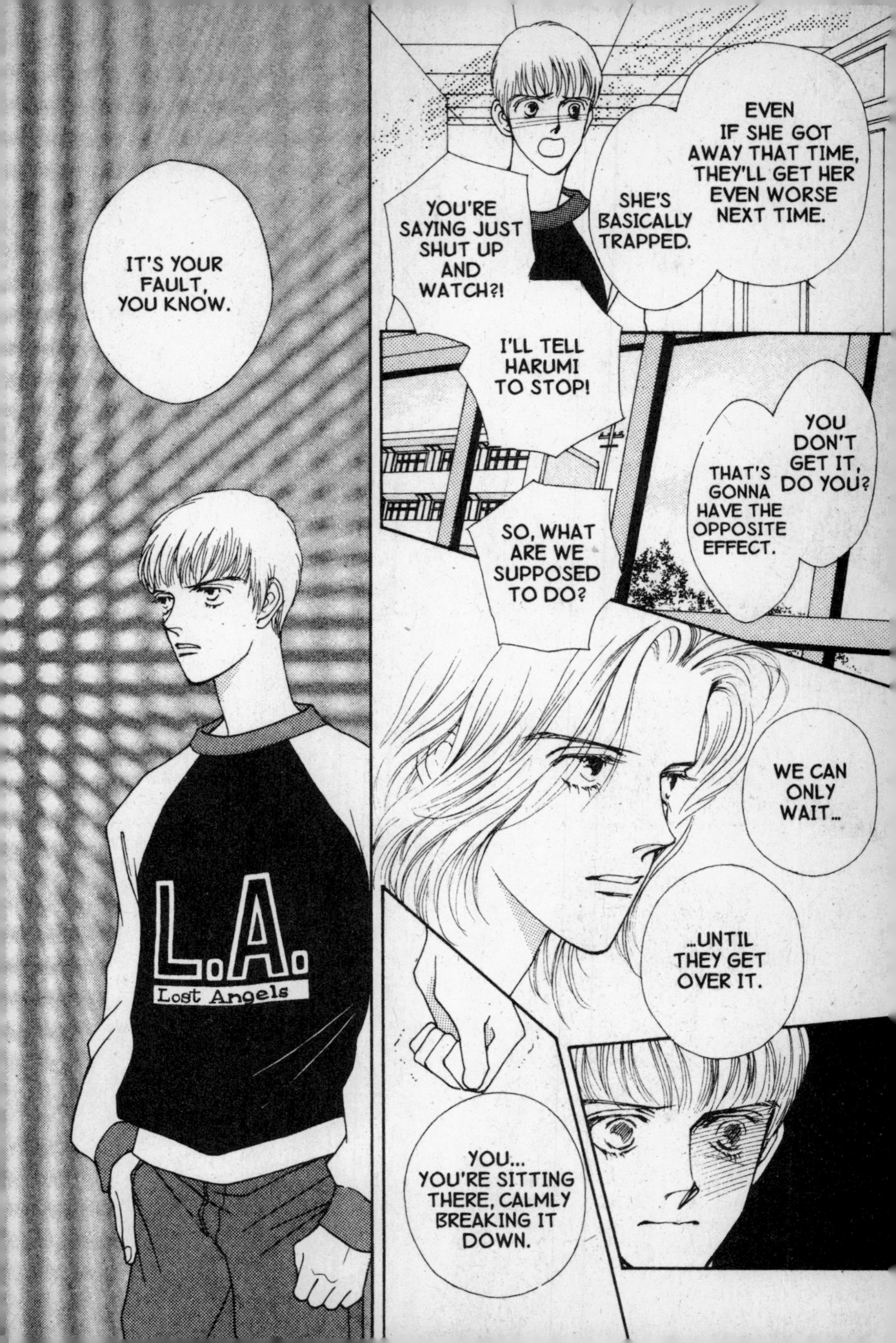
EVEN IF SHE GOT AWAY THAT TIME, THEY'LL GET HER EVEN WORSE NEXT TIME.
SHE'S BASICALLY TRAPPED.
YOU'RE SAYING JUST SHUT UP AND WATCH?!
I'LL TELL HARUMI TO STOP!
YOU DON'T GET IT, DO YOU?
THAT'S GONNA HAVE THE OPPOSITE EFFECT.
SO, WHAT ARE WE SUPPOSED TO DO?
WE CAN ONLY WAIT...
...UNTIL THEY GET OVER IT.
YOU... YOU'RE SITTING THERE, CALMLY BREAKING IT DOWN.
IT'S YOUR FAULT, YOU KNOW.
L.A.
Lost Angels

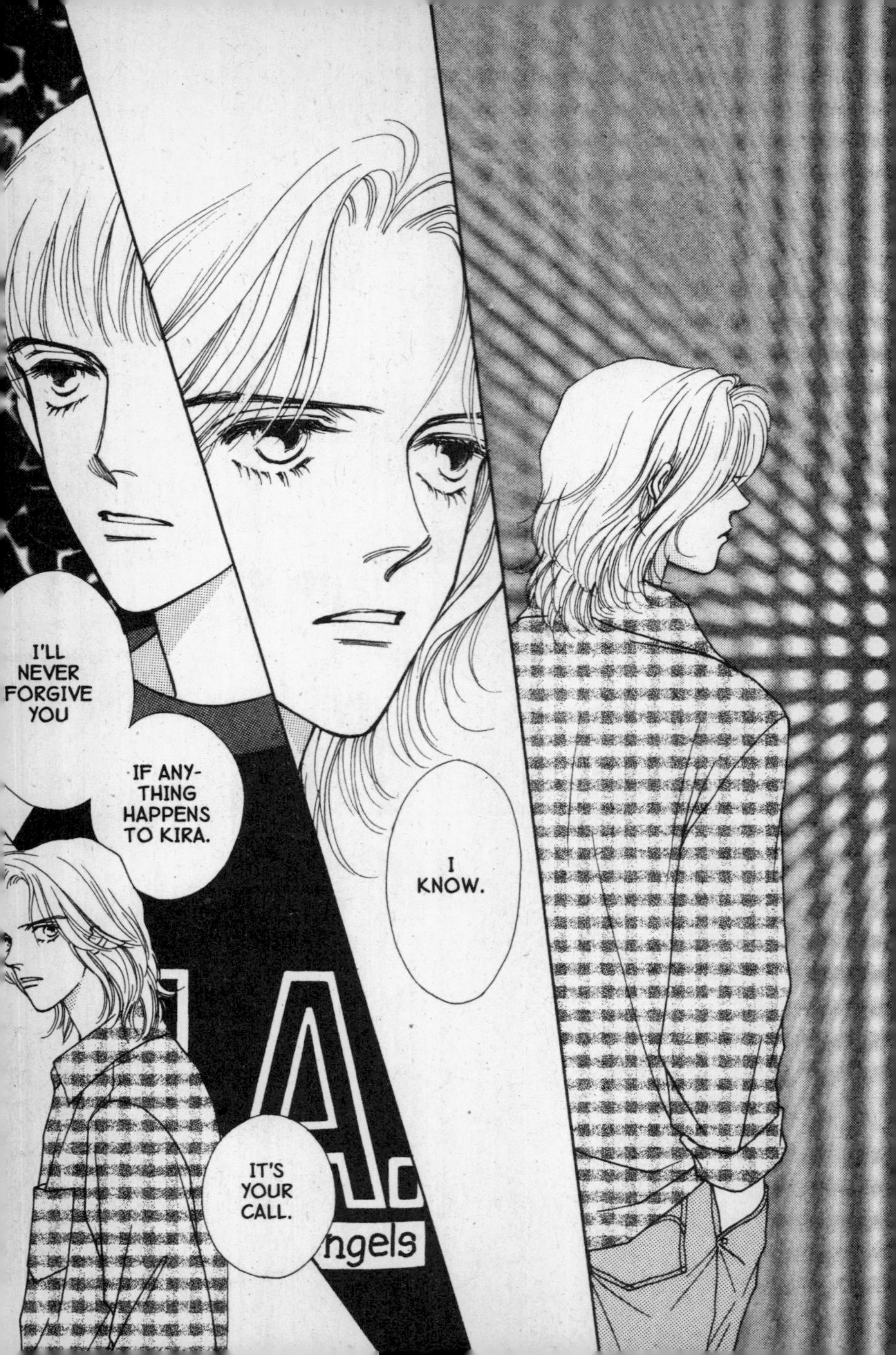
I'LL NEVER FORGIVE YOU
IF ANY-THING HAPPENS TO KIRA.
I KNOW.
IT'S YOUR CALL.

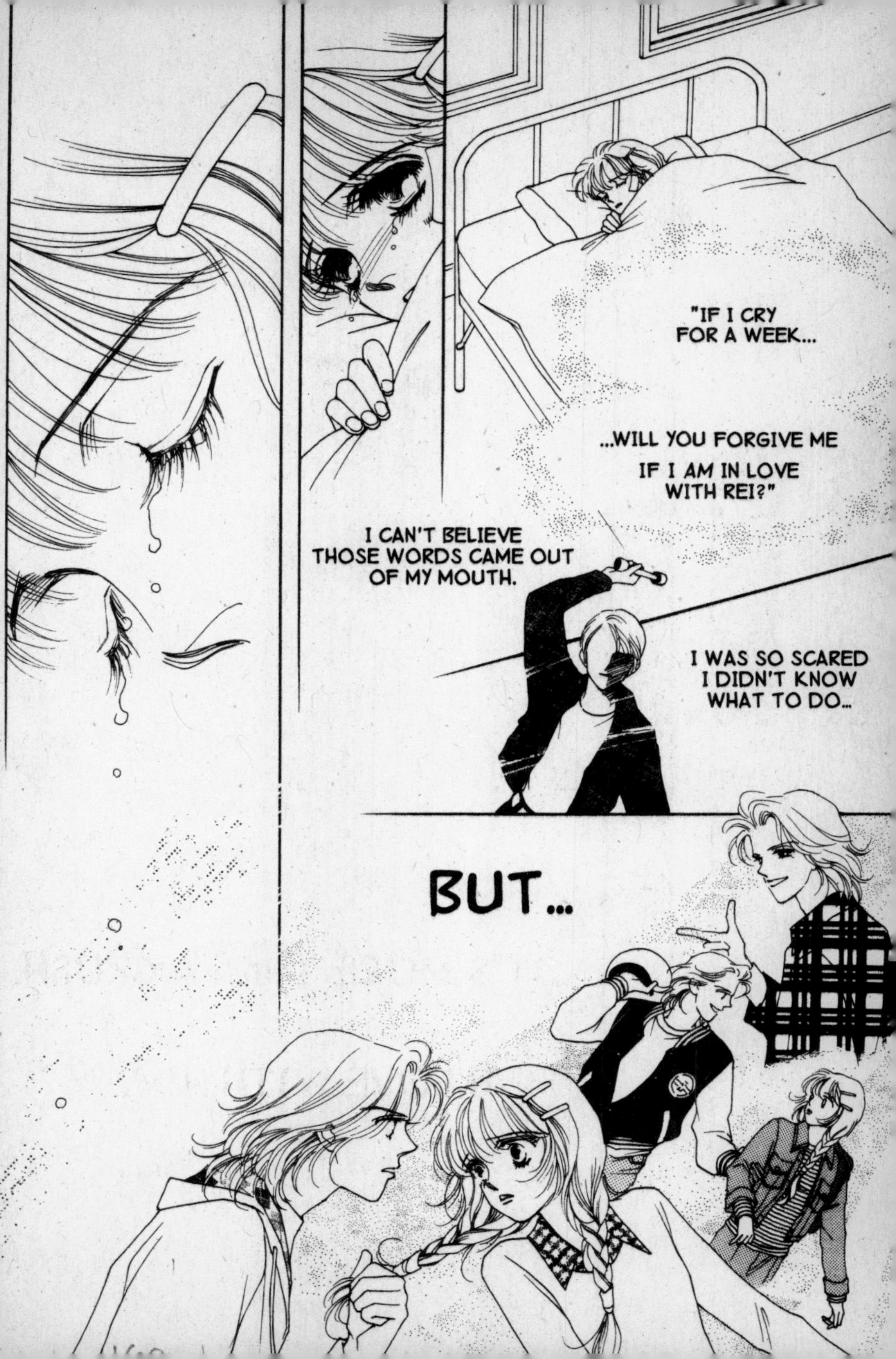
"IF I CRY FOR A WEEK...
...WILL YOU FORGIVE ME
IF I AM IN LOVE WITH REI?"
I CAN'T BELIEVE THOSE WORDS CAME OUT OF MY MOUTH.
I WAS SO SCARED I DIDN'T KNOW WHAT TO DO...
BUT...

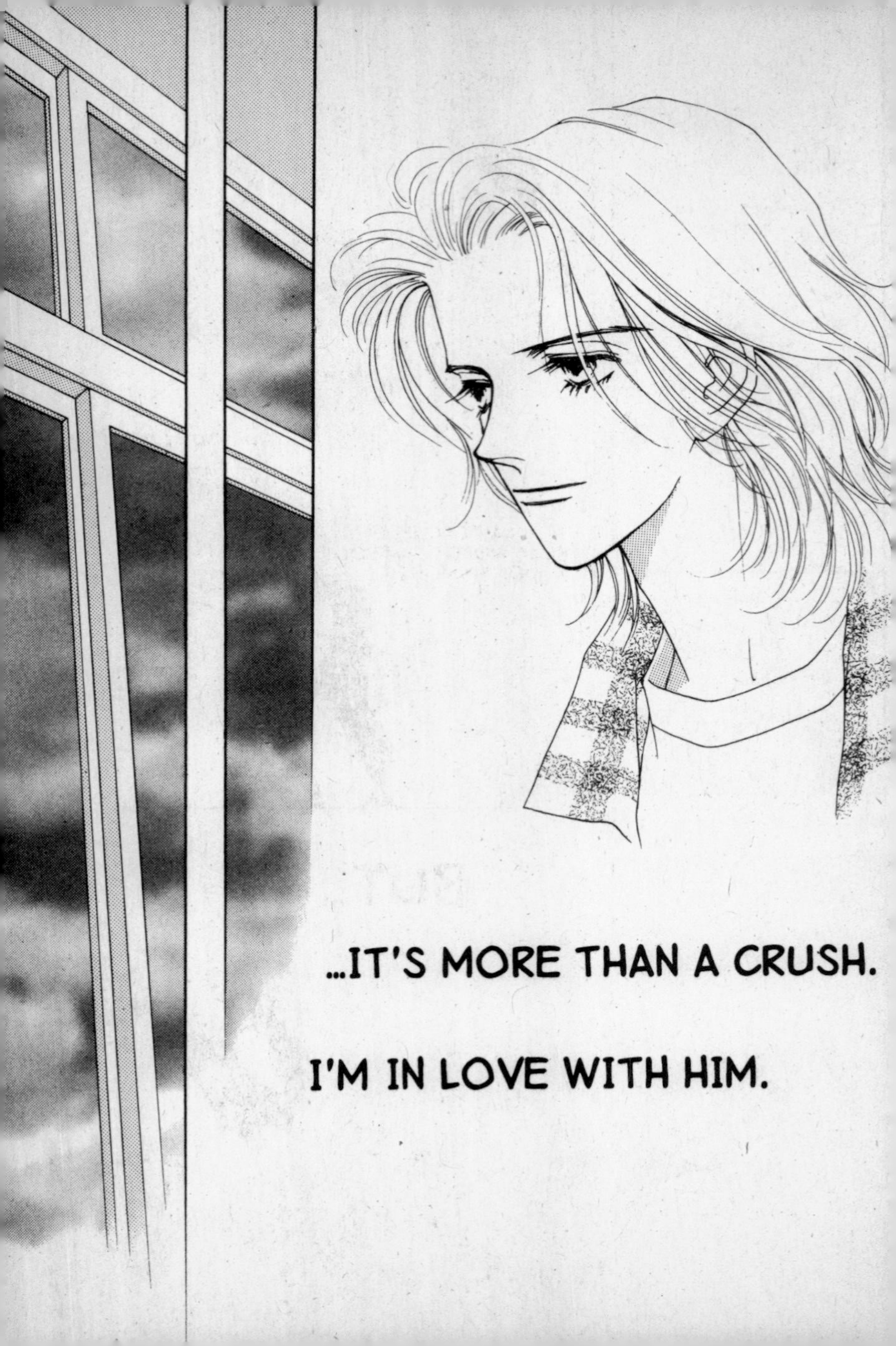

...IT'S MORE THAN A CRUSH.
I'M IN LOVE WITH HIM.

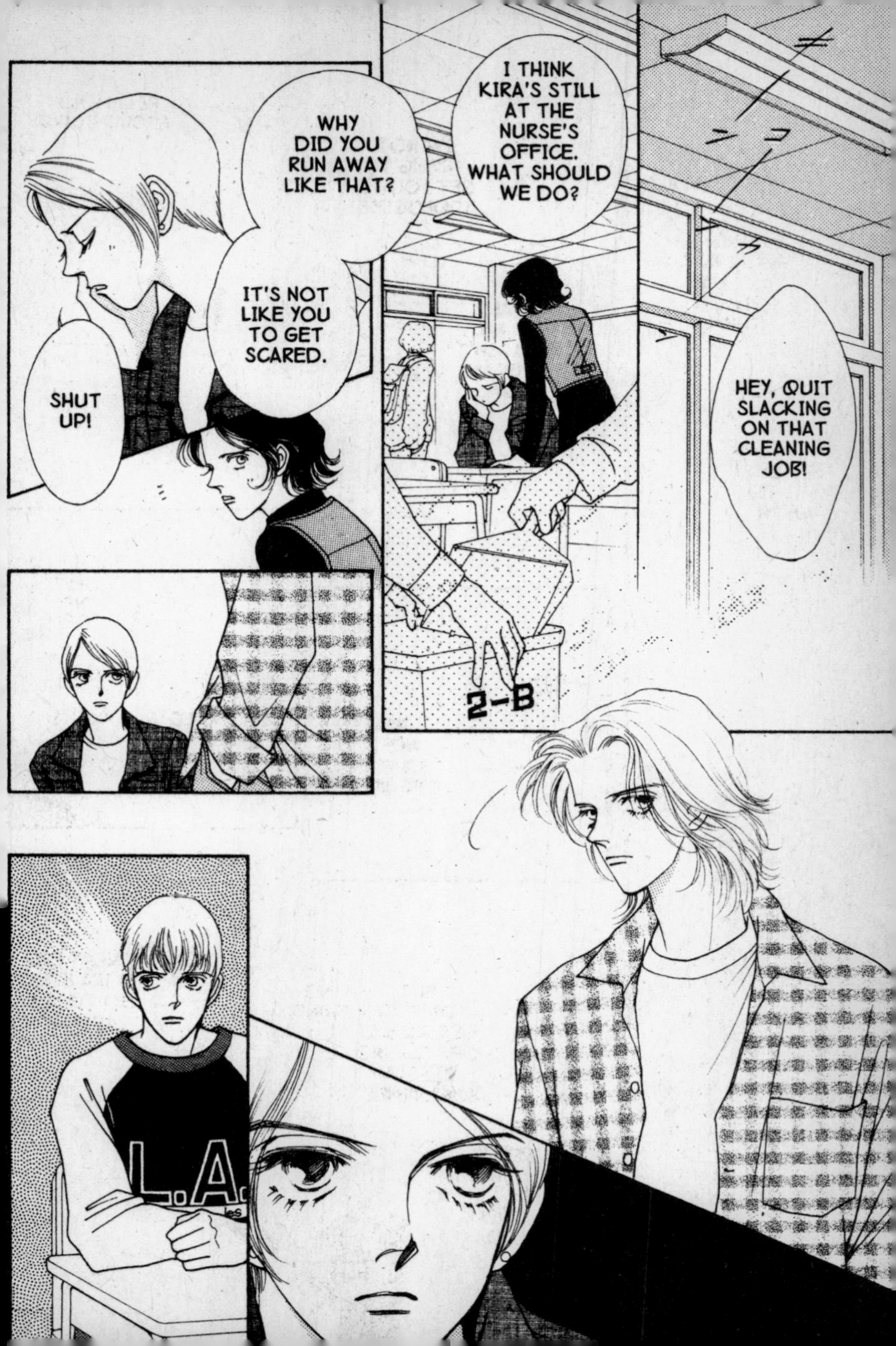
HEY, QUIT SLACKING ON THAT CLEANING JOB!
I THINK KIRA'S STILL AT THE NURSE'S OFFICE. WHAT SHOULD WE DO?
2-B
WHY DID YOU RUN AWAY LIKE THAT?
IT'S NOT LIKE YOU TO GET SCARED.
SHUT UP!
L.A.

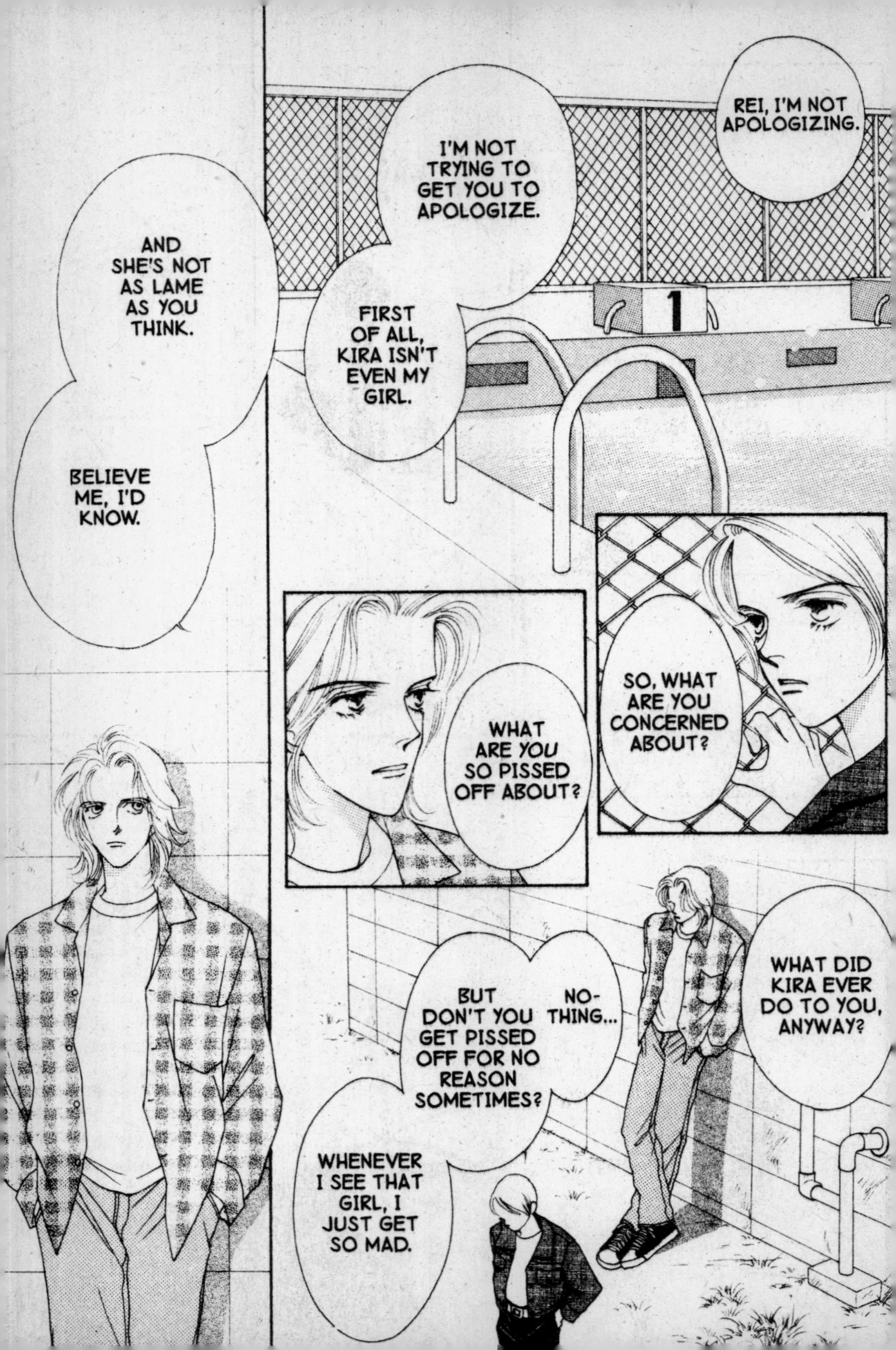
REI, I'M NOT APOLOGIZING.
I'M NOT TRYING TO GET YOU TO APOLOGIZE.
FIRST OF ALL, KIRA ISN'T EVEN MY GIRL.
AND SHE'S NOT AS LAME AS YOU THINK.
BELIEVE ME, I'D KNOW.
SO, WHAT ARE YOU CONCERNED ABOUT?
WHAT ARE *YOU* SO PISSED OFF ABOUT?
WHAT DID KIRA EVER DO TO YOU, ANYWAY?
NO-THING...
BUT DON'T YOU GET PISSED OFF FOR NO REASON SOMETIMES?
WHENEVER I SEE THAT GIRL, I JUST GET SO MAD.

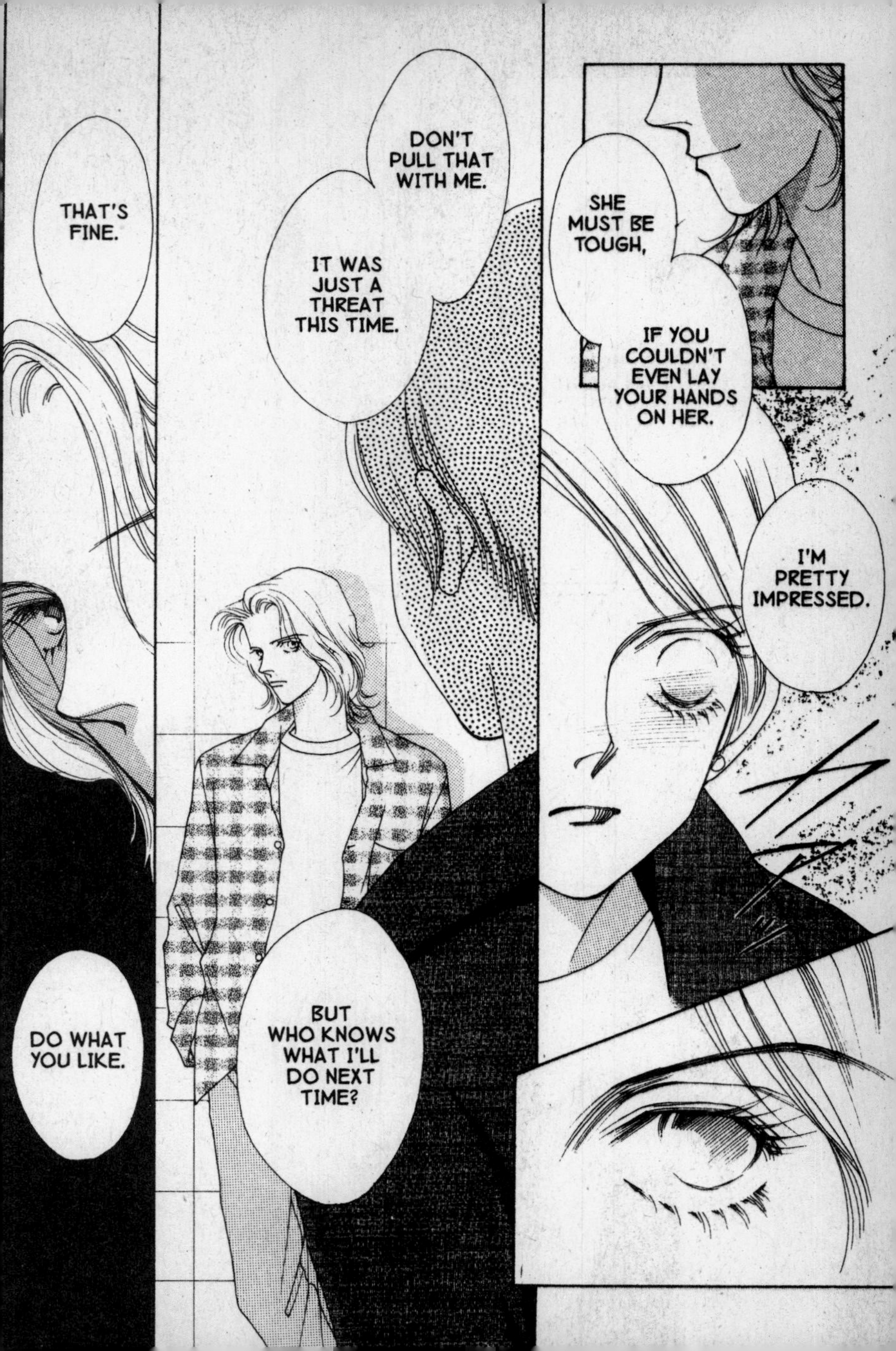
SHE MUST BE TOUGH,
IF YOU COULDN'T EVEN LAY YOUR HANDS ON HER.
I'M PRETTY IMPRESSED.
DON'T PULL THAT WITH ME.
IT WAS JUST A THREAT THIS TIME.
BUT WHO KNOWS WHAT I'LL DO NEXT TIME?
THAT'S FINE.
DO WHAT YOU LIKE.

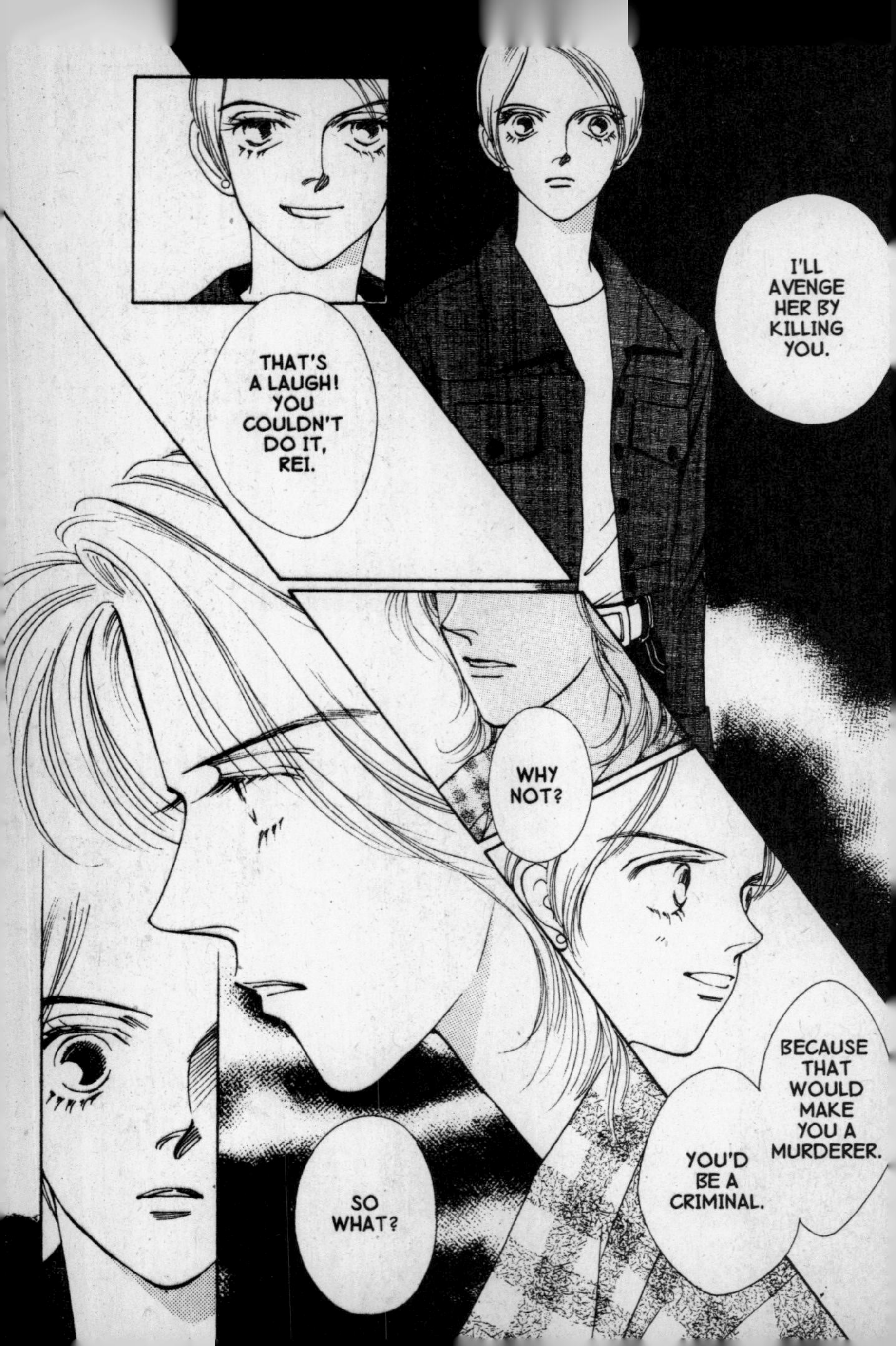
I'LL AVENGE HER BY KILLING YOU.
THAT'S A LAUGH! YOU COULDN'T DO IT, REI.
WHY NOT?
BECAUSE THAT WOULD MAKE YOU A MURDERER.
YOU'D BE A CRIMINAL.
SO WHAT?

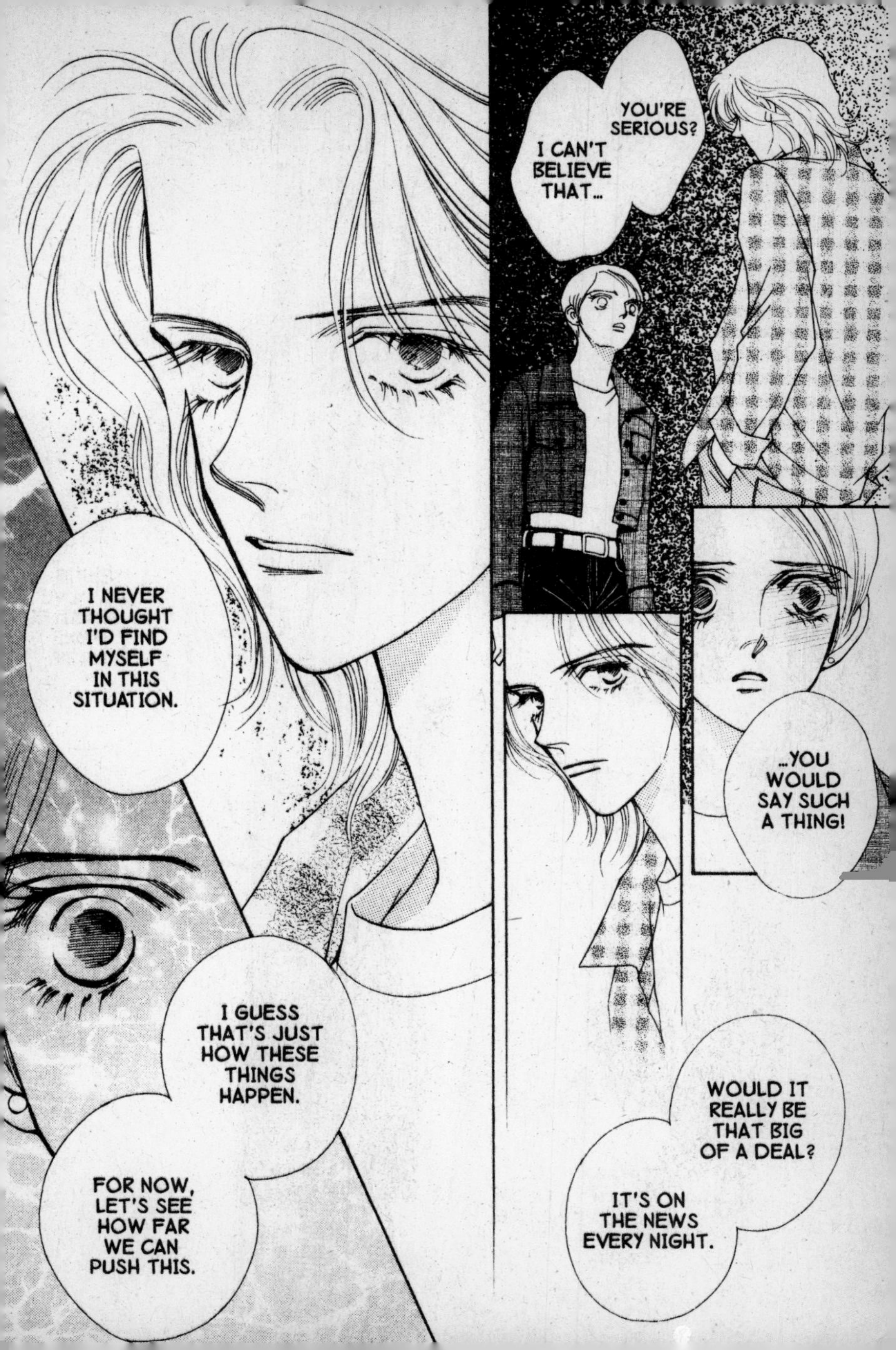
YOU'RE SERIOUS? I CAN'T BELIEVE THAT...
...YOU WOULD SAY SUCH A THING!
WOULD IT REALLY BE THAT BIG OF A DEAL?
IT'S ON THE NEWS EVERY NIGHT.
I NEVER THOUGHT I'D FIND MYSELF IN THIS SITUATION.
I GUESS THAT'S JUST HOW THESE THINGS HAPPEN.
FOR NOW, LET'S SEE HOW FAR WE CAN PUSH THIS.

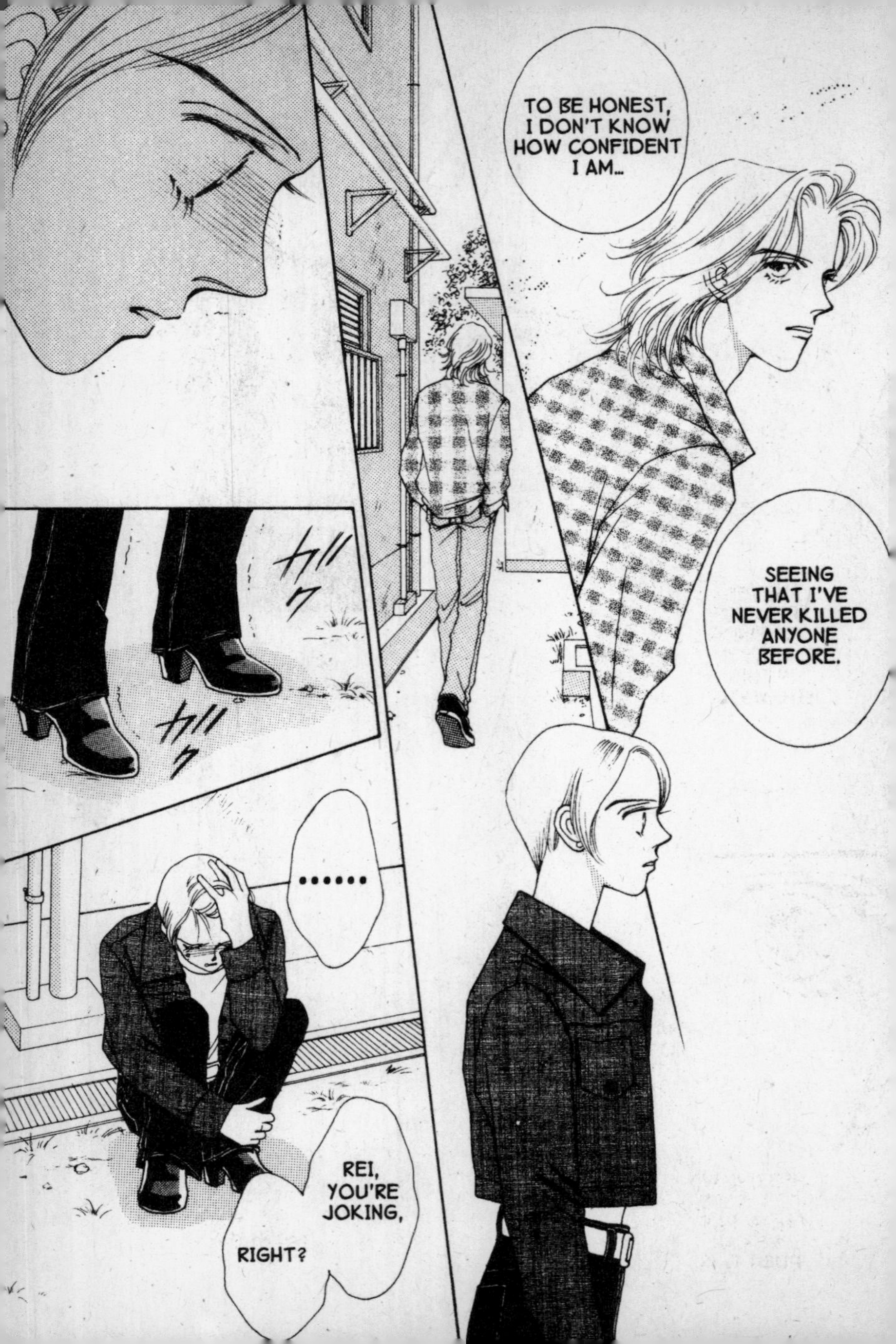

TO BE HONEST, I DON'T KNOW HOW CONFIDENT I AM...
SEEING THAT I'VE NEVER KILLED ANYONE BEFORE.
......
REI, YOU'RE JOKING,
RIGHT?

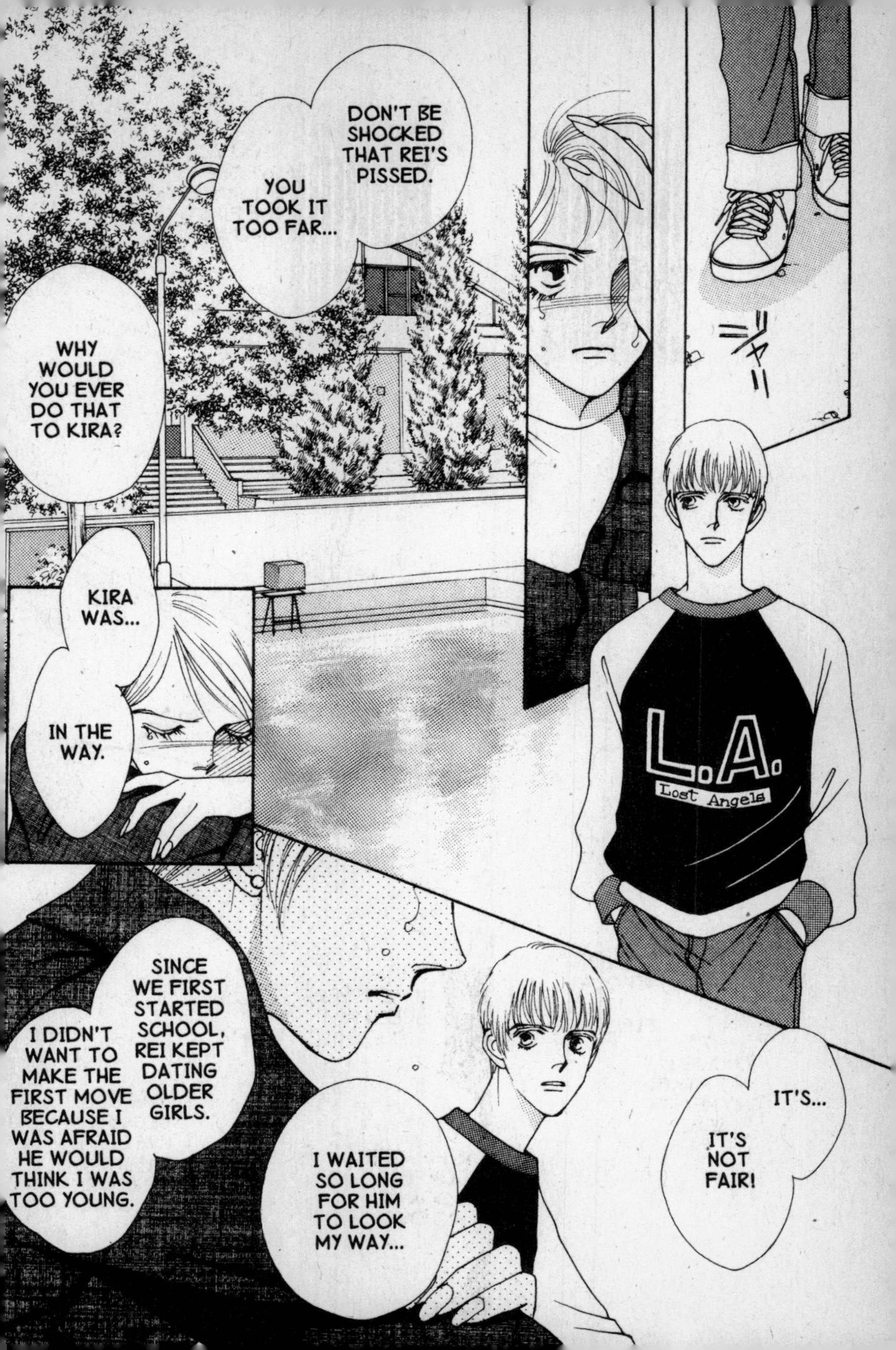
DON'T BE SHOCKED THAT REI'S PISSED.
YOU TOOK IT TOO FAR...
WHY WOULD YOU EVER DO THAT TO KIRA?
L.A. Lost Angels
KIRA WAS...
IN THE WAY.
IT'S...
IT'S NOT FAIR!
I WAITED SO LONG FOR HIM TO LOOK MY WAY...
SINCE WE FIRST STARTED SCHOOL, REI KEPT DATING OLDER GIRLS.
I DIDN'T WANT TO MAKE THE FIRST MOVE BECAUSE I WAS AFRAID HE WOULD THINK I WAS TOO YOUNG.

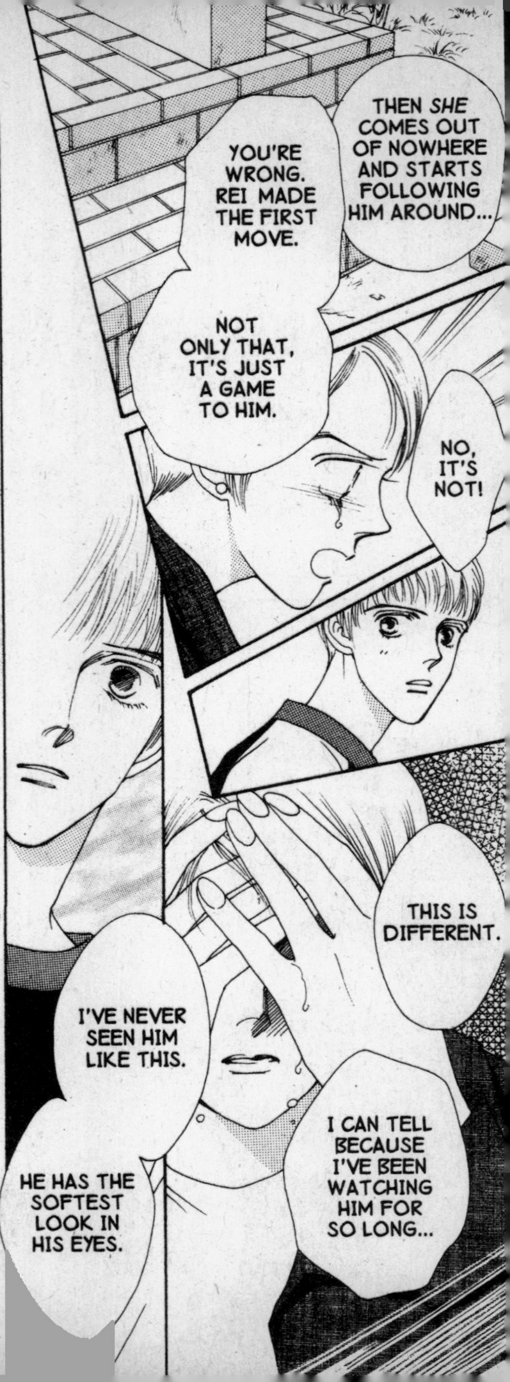
THEN *SHE* COMES OUT OF NOWHERE AND STARTS FOLLOWING HIM AROUND...
YOU'RE WRONG. REI MADE THE FIRST MOVE.
NOT ONLY THAT, IT'S JUST A GAME TO HIM.
NO, IT'S NOT!
THIS IS DIFFERENT.
I'VE NEVER SEEN HIM LIKE THIS.
I CAN TELL BECAUSE I'VE BEEN WATCHING HIM FOR SO LONG...
HE HAS THE SOFTEST LOOK IN HIS EYES.

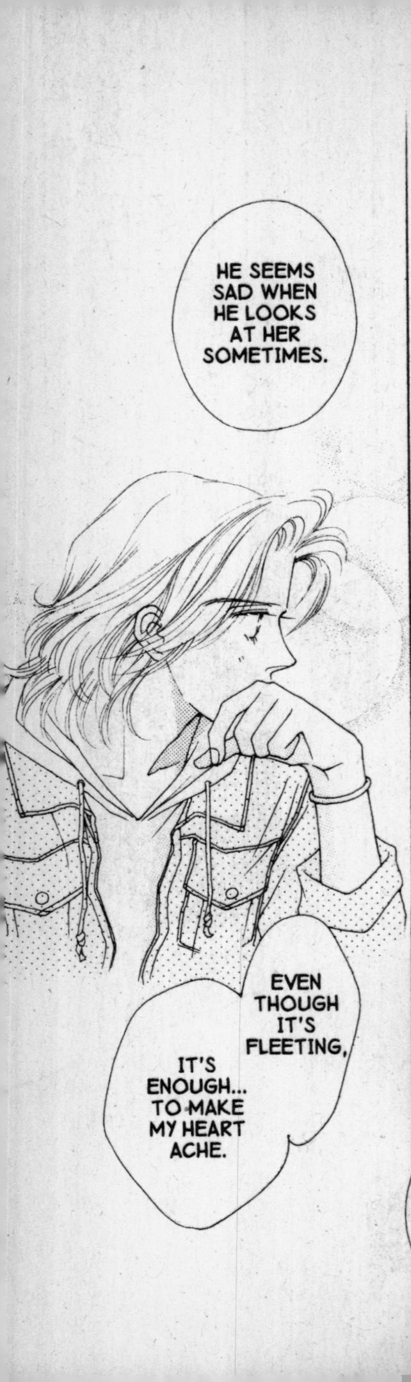
HE SEEMS SAD WHEN HE LOOKS AT HER SOMETIMES.
EVEN THOUGH IT'S FLEETING,
IT'S ENOUGH... TO MAKE MY HEART ACHE.

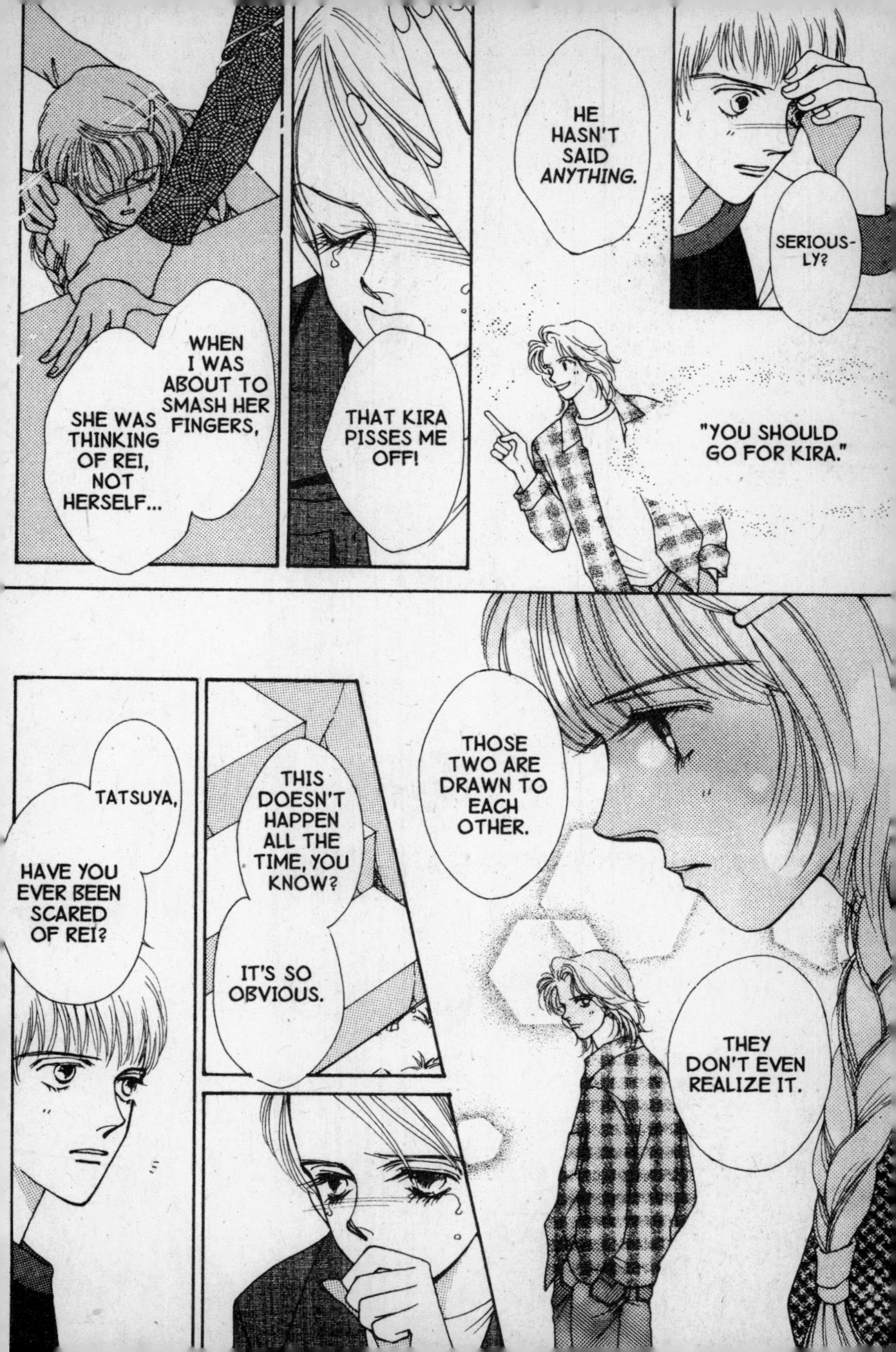
HE HASN'T SAID ANYTHING.
SERIOUS-LY?
"YOU SHOULD GO FOR KIRA."
THAT KIRA PISSES ME OFF!
WHEN I WAS ABOUT TO SMASH HER FINGERS,
SHE WAS THINKING OF REI, NOT HERSELF...
THOSE TWO ARE DRAWN TO EACH OTHER.
THEY DON'T EVEN REALIZE IT.
THIS DOESN'T HAPPEN ALL THE TIME, YOU KNOW?
IT'S SO OBVIOUS.
TATSUYA,
HAVE YOU EVER BEEN SCARED OF REI?

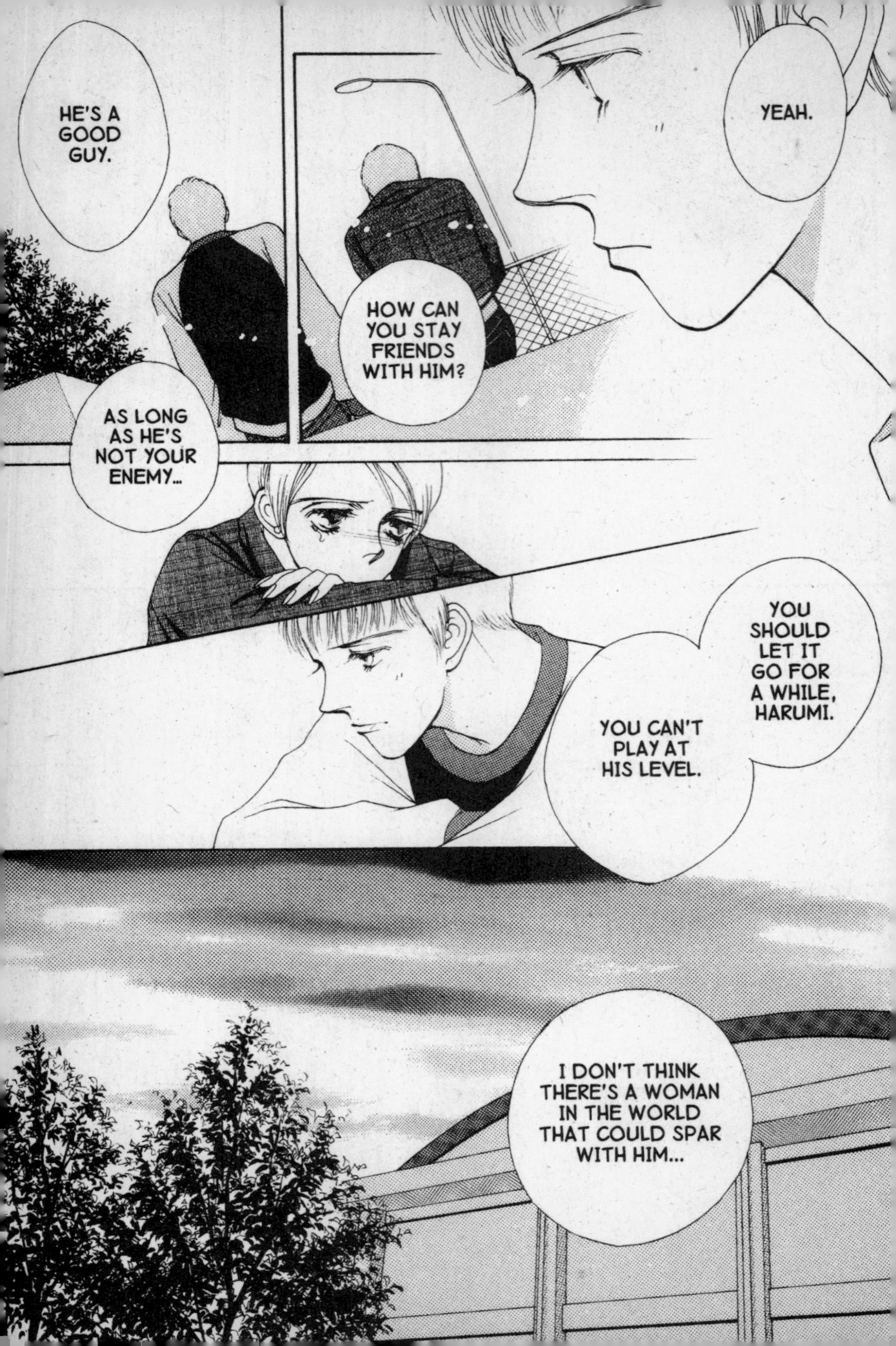
YEAH.
HOW CAN YOU STAY FRIENDS WITH HIM?
HE'S A GOOD GUY.
AS LONG AS HE'S NOT YOUR ENEMY...
YOU SHOULD LET IT GO FOR A WHILE, HARUMI.
YOU CAN'T PLAY AT HIS LEVEL.
I DON'T THINK THERE'S A WOMAN IN THE WORLD THAT COULD SPAR WITH HIM...

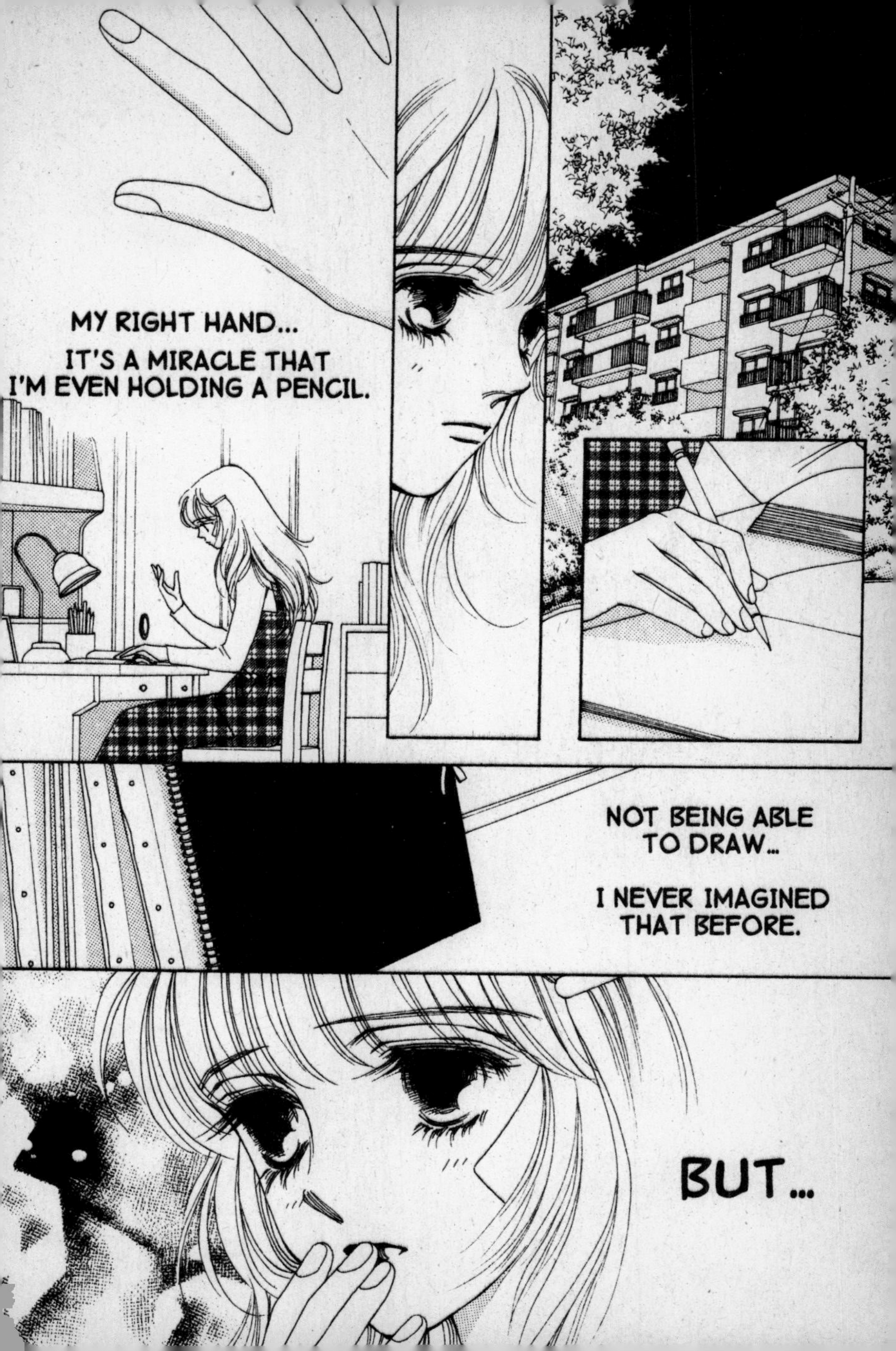
MY RIGHT HAND...
IT'S A MIRACLE THAT I'M EVEN HOLDING A PENCIL.
NOT BEING ABLE TO DRAW...
I NEVER IMAGINED THAT BEFORE.
BUT...

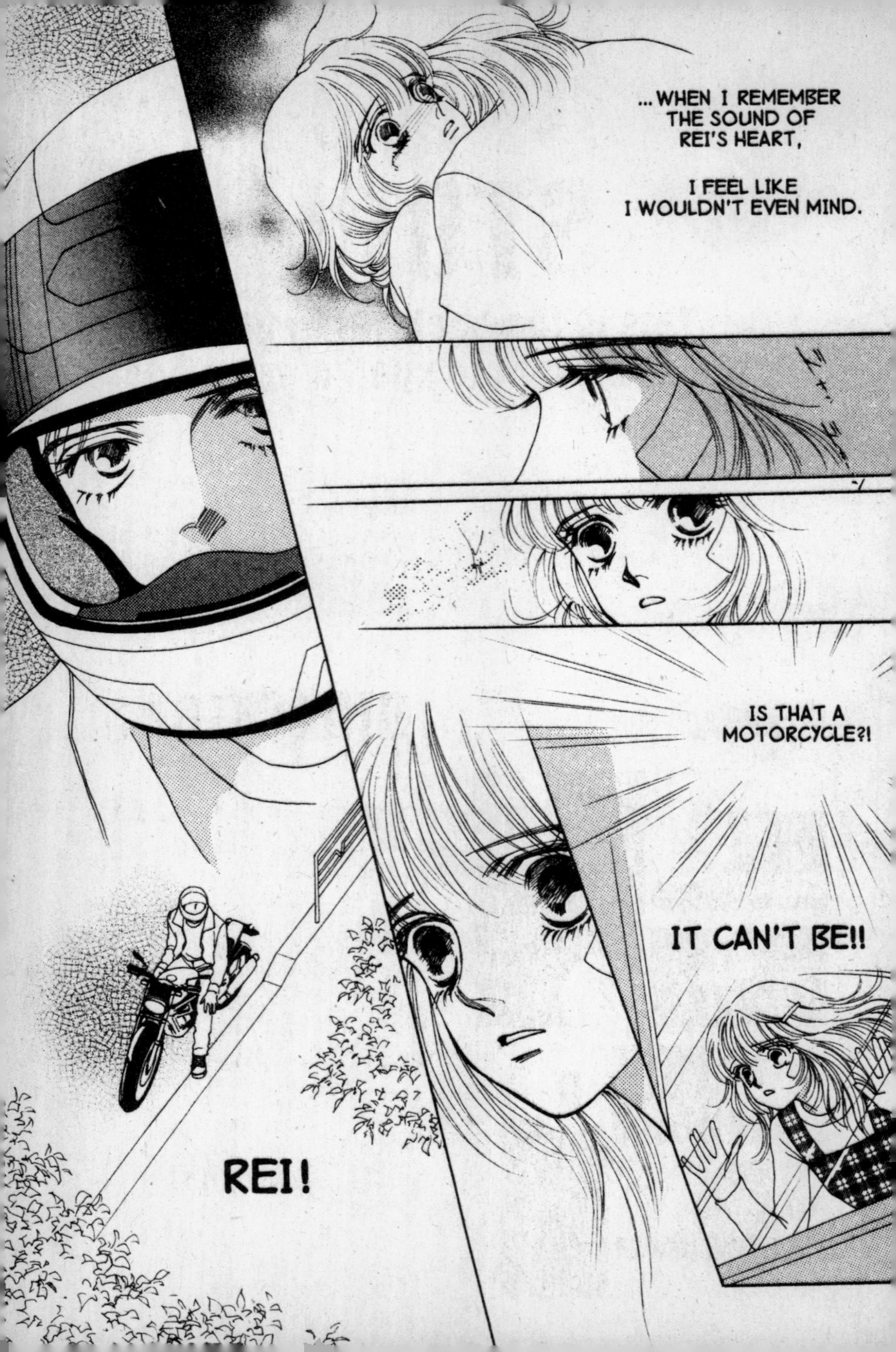
...WHEN I REMEMBER THE SOUND OF REI'S HEART,
I FEEL LIKE I WOULDN'T EVEN MIND.
IS THAT A MOTORCYCLE?!
IT CAN'T BE!!
REI!

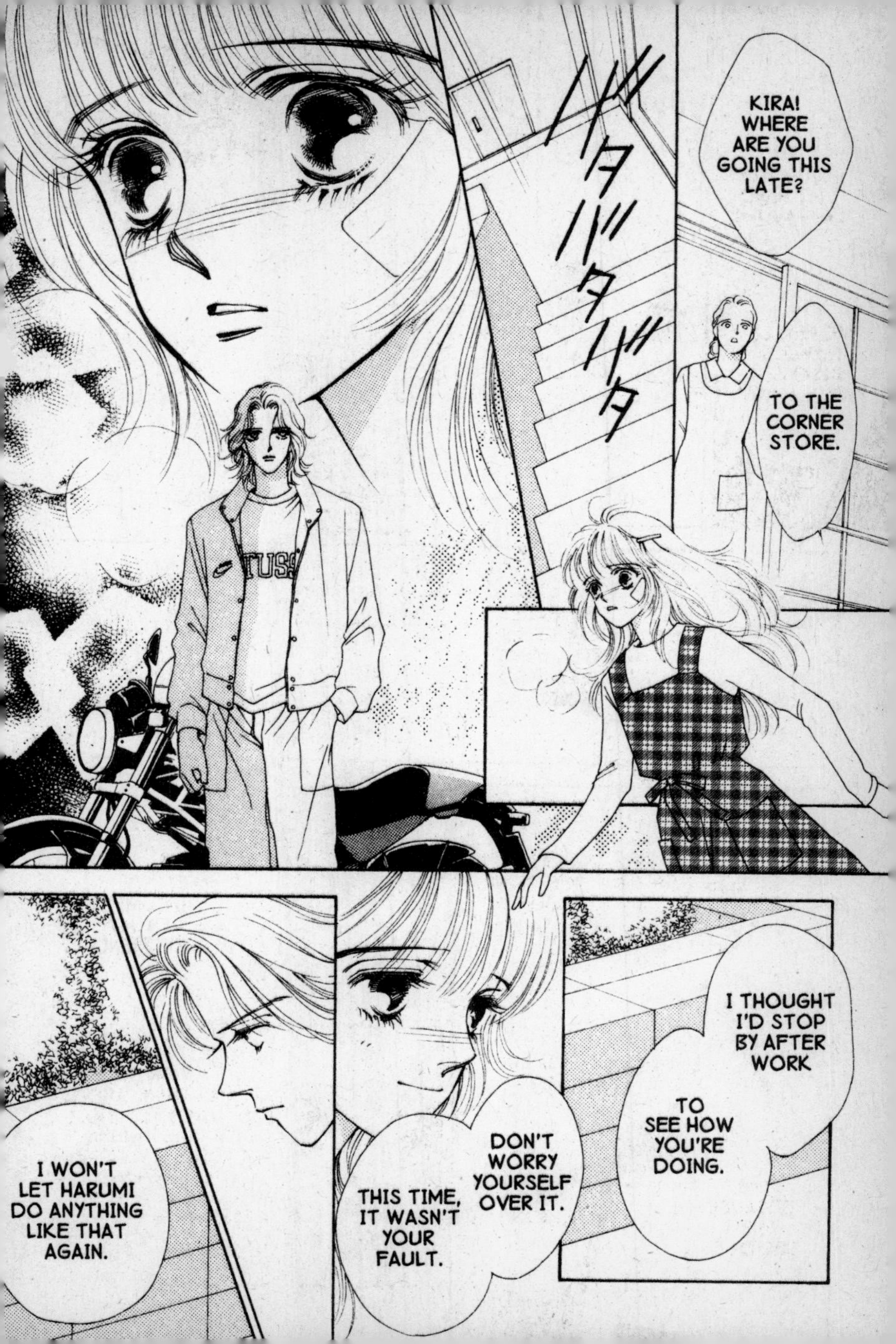
KIRA! WHERE ARE YOU GOING THIS LATE?
TO THE CORNER STORE.
バタバタバタ
I THOUGHT I'D STOP BY AFTER WORK
TO SEE HOW YOU'RE DOING.
DON'T WORRY YOURSELF OVER IT.
THIS TIME, IT WASN'T YOUR FAULT.
I WON'T LET HARUMI DO ANYTHING LIKE THAT AGAIN.

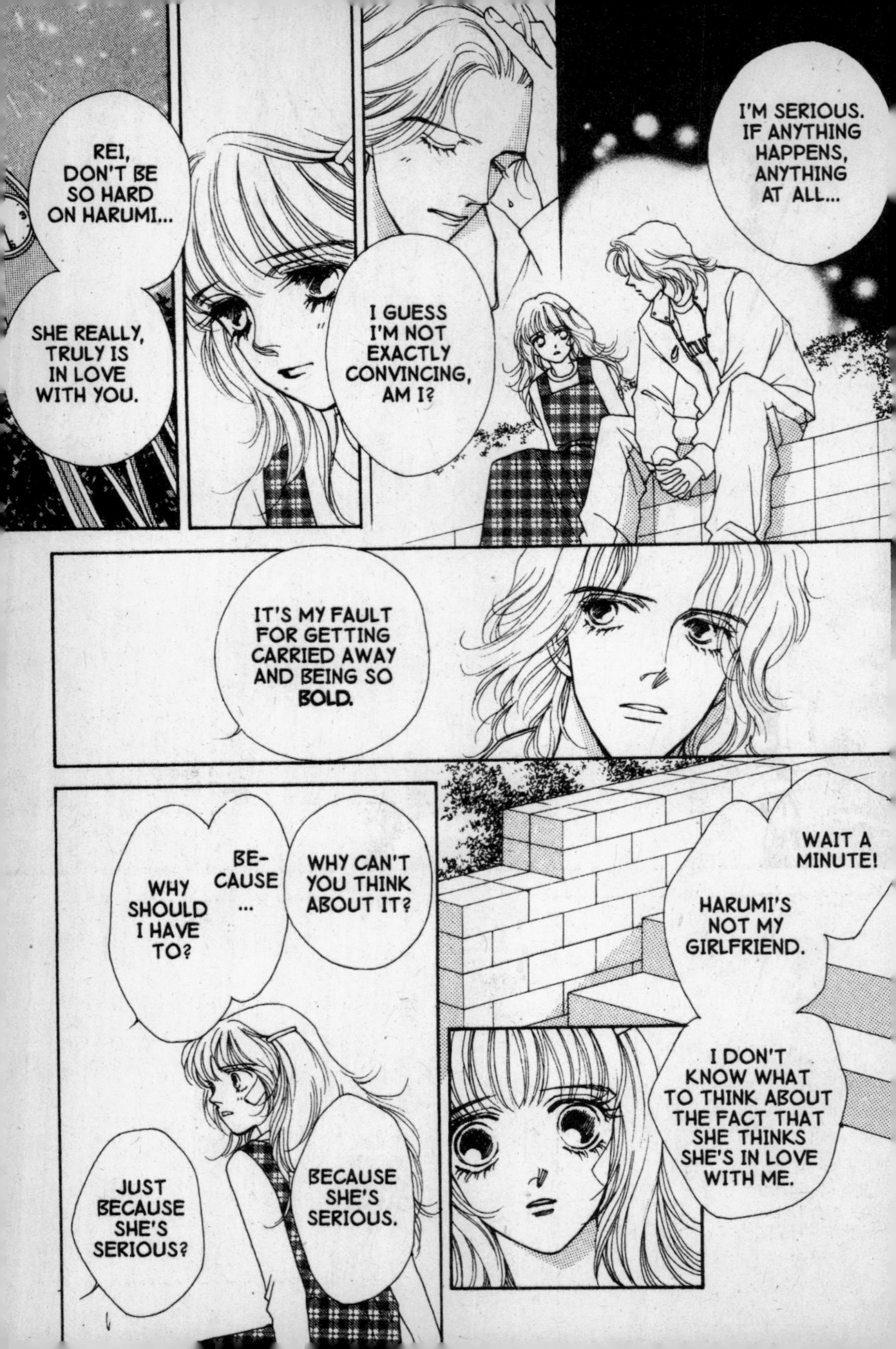
I'M SERIOUS. IF ANYTHING HAPPENS, ANYTHING AT ALL...
I GUESS I'M NOT EXACTLY CONVINCING, AM I?
REI, DON'T BE SO HARD ON HARUMI...
SHE REALLY, TRULY IS IN LOVE WITH YOU.
IT'S MY FAULT FOR GETTING CARRIED AWAY AND BEING SO BOLD.
WAIT A MINUTE!
HARUMI'S NOT MY GIRLFRIEND.
I DON'T KNOW WHAT TO THINK ABOUT THE FACT THAT SHE THINKS SHE'S IN LOVE WITH ME.
WHY CAN'T YOU THINK ABOUT IT?
BE-CAUSE ...
WHY SHOULD I HAVE TO?
BECAUSE SHE'S SERIOUS.
JUST BECAUSE SHE'S SERIOUS?

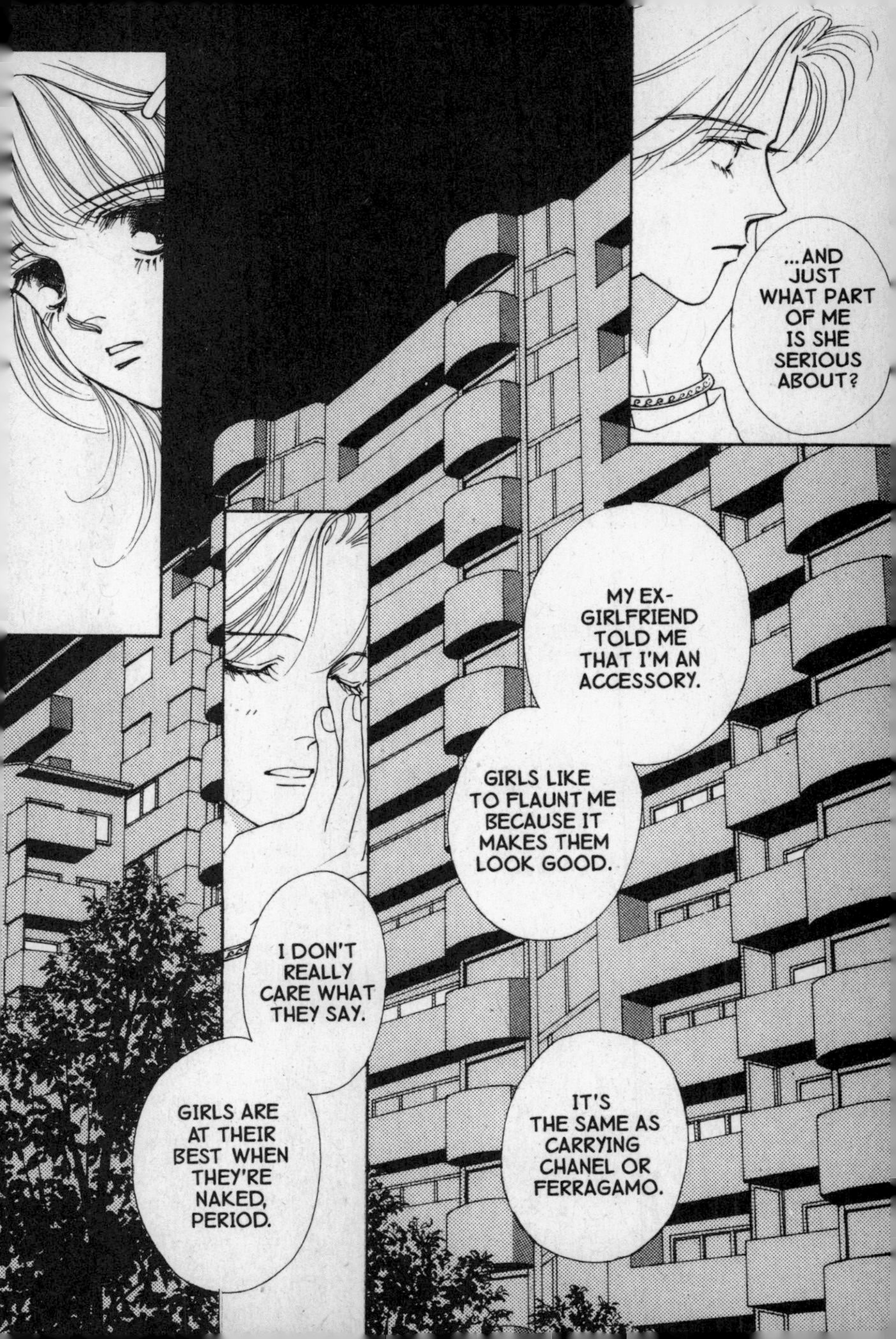
...AND JUST WHAT PART OF ME IS SHE SERIOUS ABOUT?
MY EX-GIRLFRIEND TOLD ME THAT I'M AN ACCESSORY.
GIRLS LIKE TO FLAUNT ME BECAUSE IT MAKES THEM LOOK GOOD.
IT'S THE SAME AS CARRYING CHANEL OR FERRAGAMO.
I DON'T REALLY CARE WHAT THEY SAY.
GIRLS ARE AT THEIR BEST WHEN THEY'RE NAKED, PERIOD.

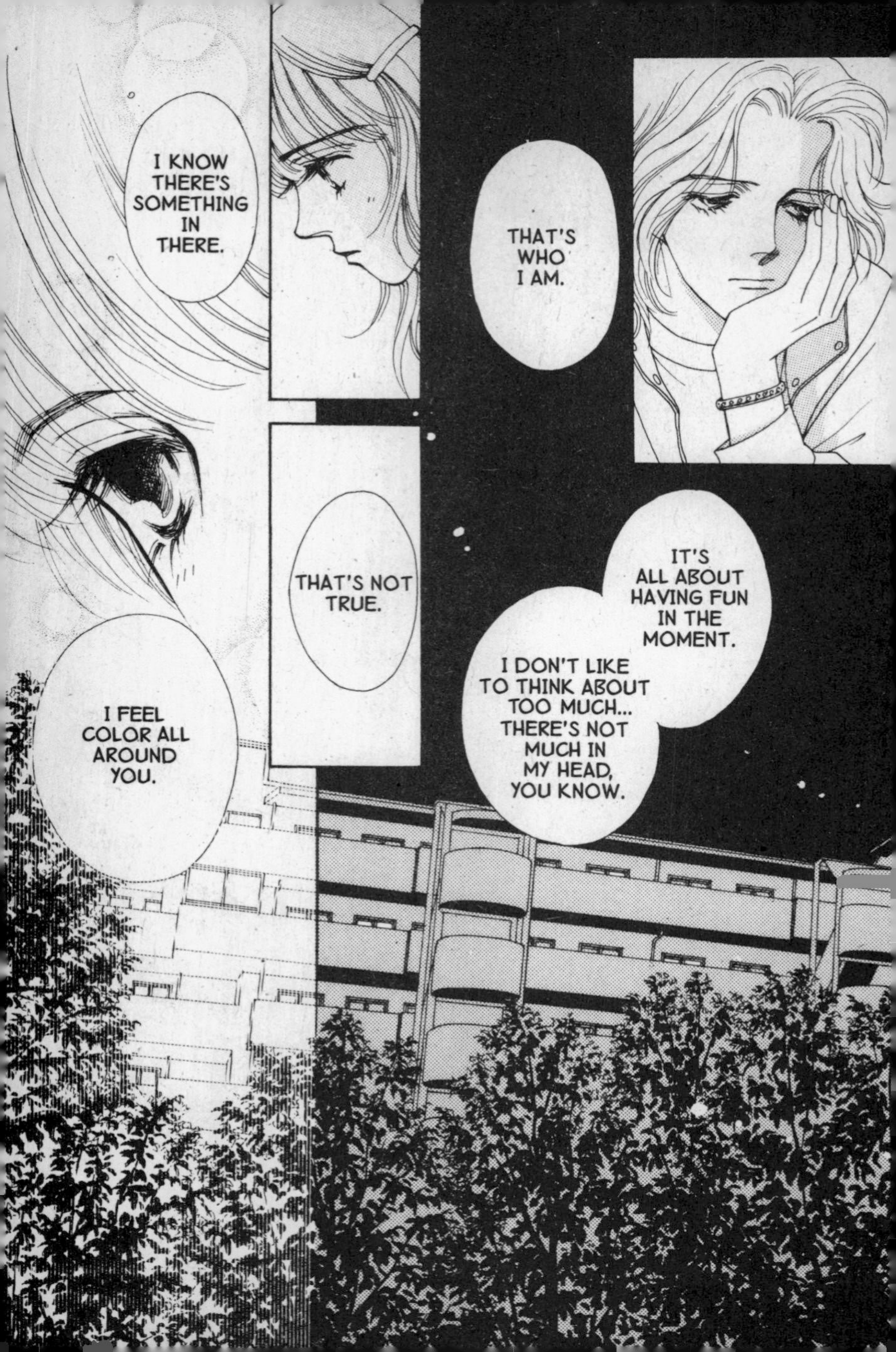
IT'S ALL ABOUT HAVING FUN IN THE MOMENT.
I DON'T LIKE TO THINK ABOUT TOO MUCH... THERE'S NOT MUCH IN MY HEAD, YOU KNOW.
THAT'S WHO I AM.
THAT'S NOT TRUE.
I KNOW THERE'S SOMETHING IN THERE.
I FEEL COLOR ALL AROUND YOU.

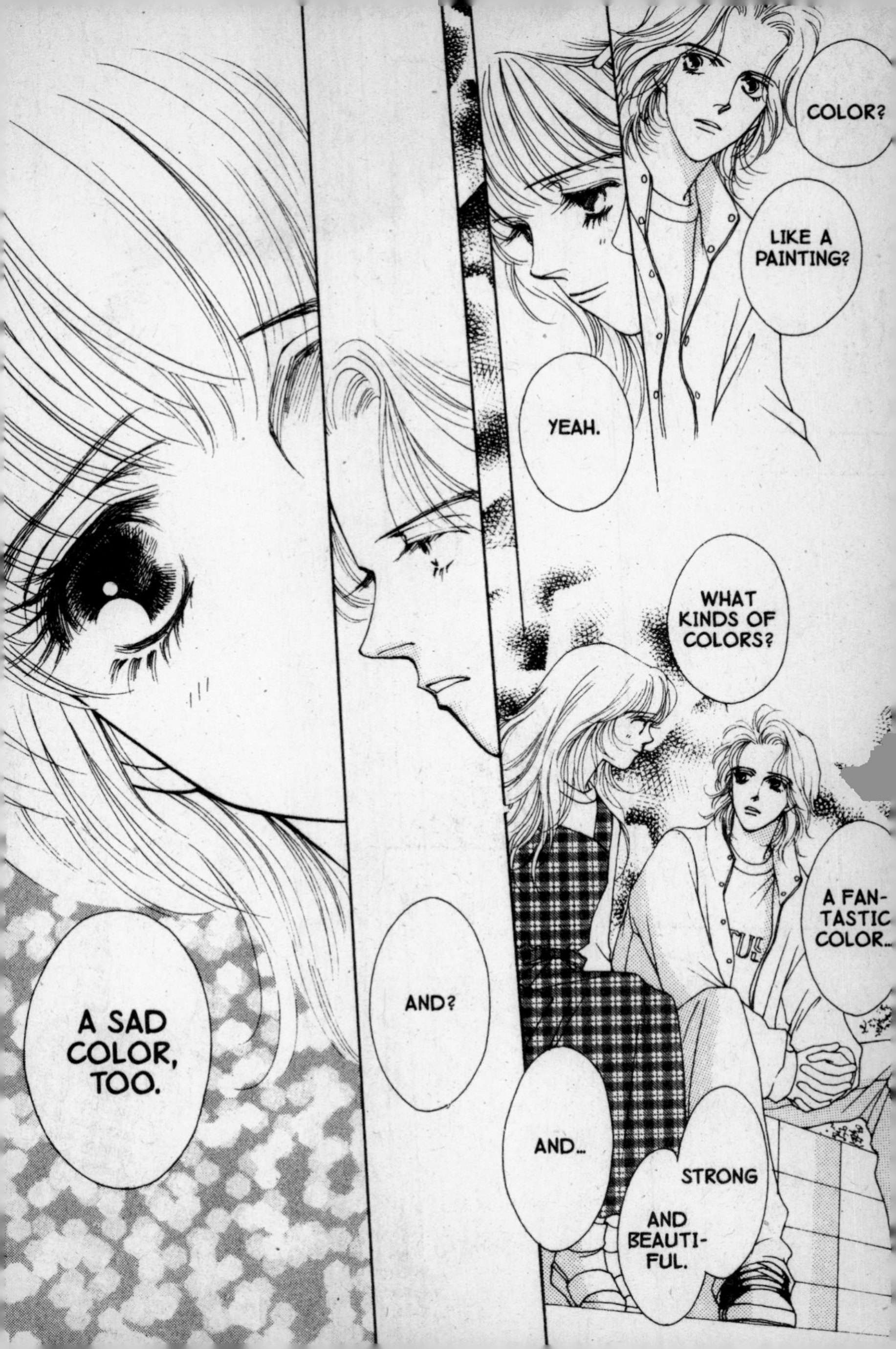

COLOR?
LIKE A PAINTING?
YEAH.
WHAT KINDS OF COLORS?
A FAN-TASTIC COLOR...
AND...
STRONG AND BEAUTI-FUL.
AND?
A SAD COLOR, TOO.

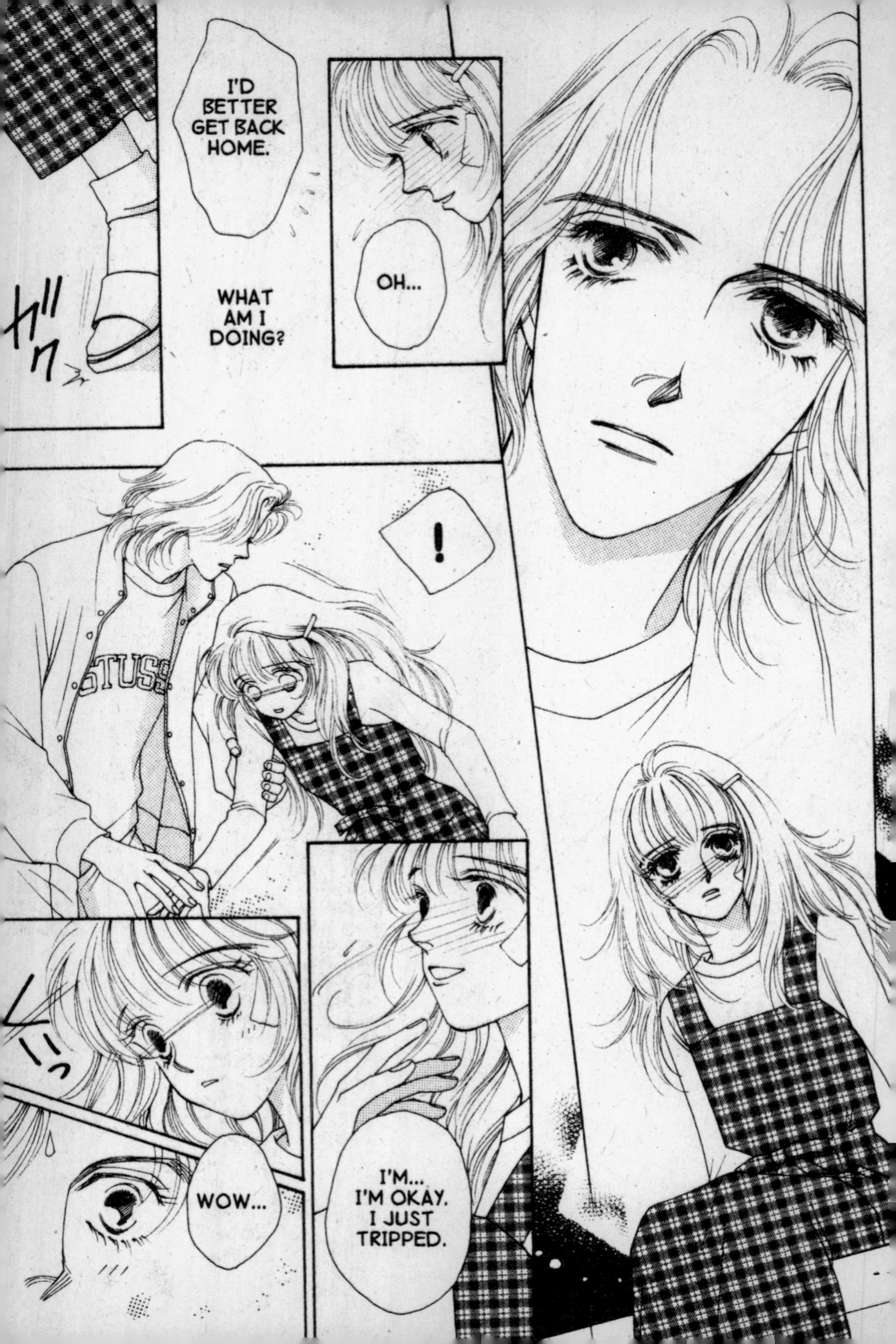
OH...
I'D BETTER GET BACK HOME.
WHAT AM I DOING?
!
I'M... I'M OKAY. I JUST TRIPPED.
WOW...

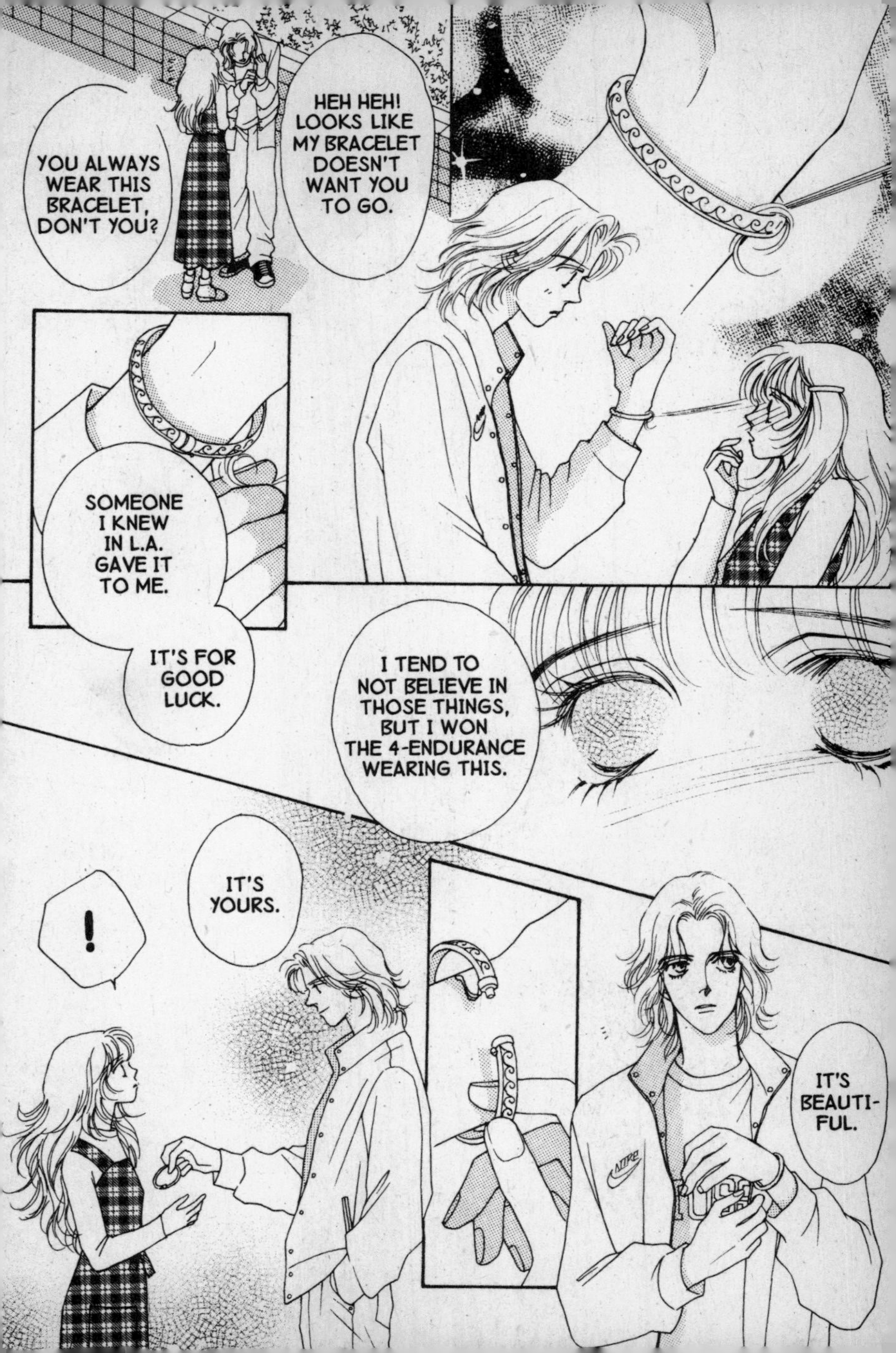
HEH HEH! LOOKS LIKE MY BRACELET DOESN'T WANT YOU TO GO.
YOU ALWAYS WEAR THIS BRACELET, DON'T YOU?
SOMEONE I KNEW IN L.A. GAVE IT TO ME.
IT'S FOR GOOD LUCK.
I TEND TO NOT BELIEVE IN THOSE THINGS, BUT I WON THE 4-ENDURANCE WEARING THIS.
IT'S BEAUTIFUL.
IT'S YOURS.
!

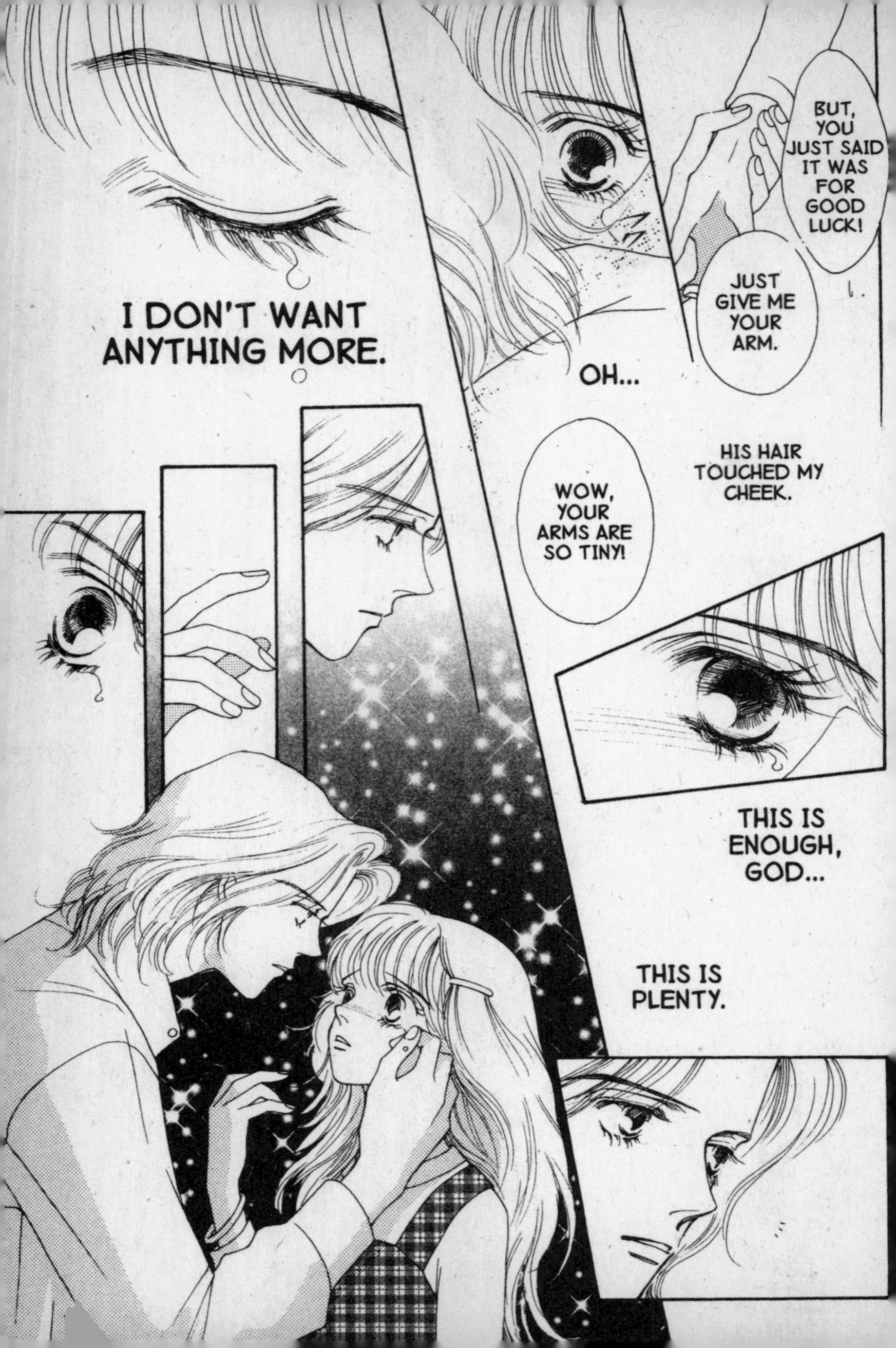
BUT, YOU JUST SAID IT WAS FOR GOOD LUCK!
JUST GIVE ME YOUR ARM.
OH...
HIS HAIR TOUCHED MY CHEEK.
WOW, YOUR ARMS ARE SO TINY!
THIS IS ENOUGH, GOD...
THIS IS PLENTY.
I DON'T WANT ANYTHING MORE.

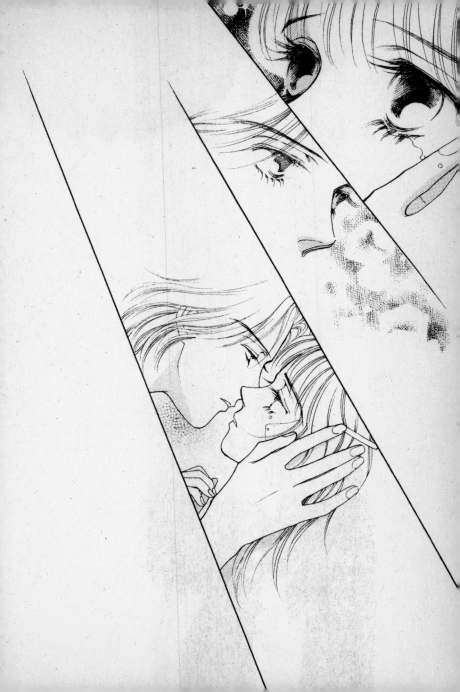

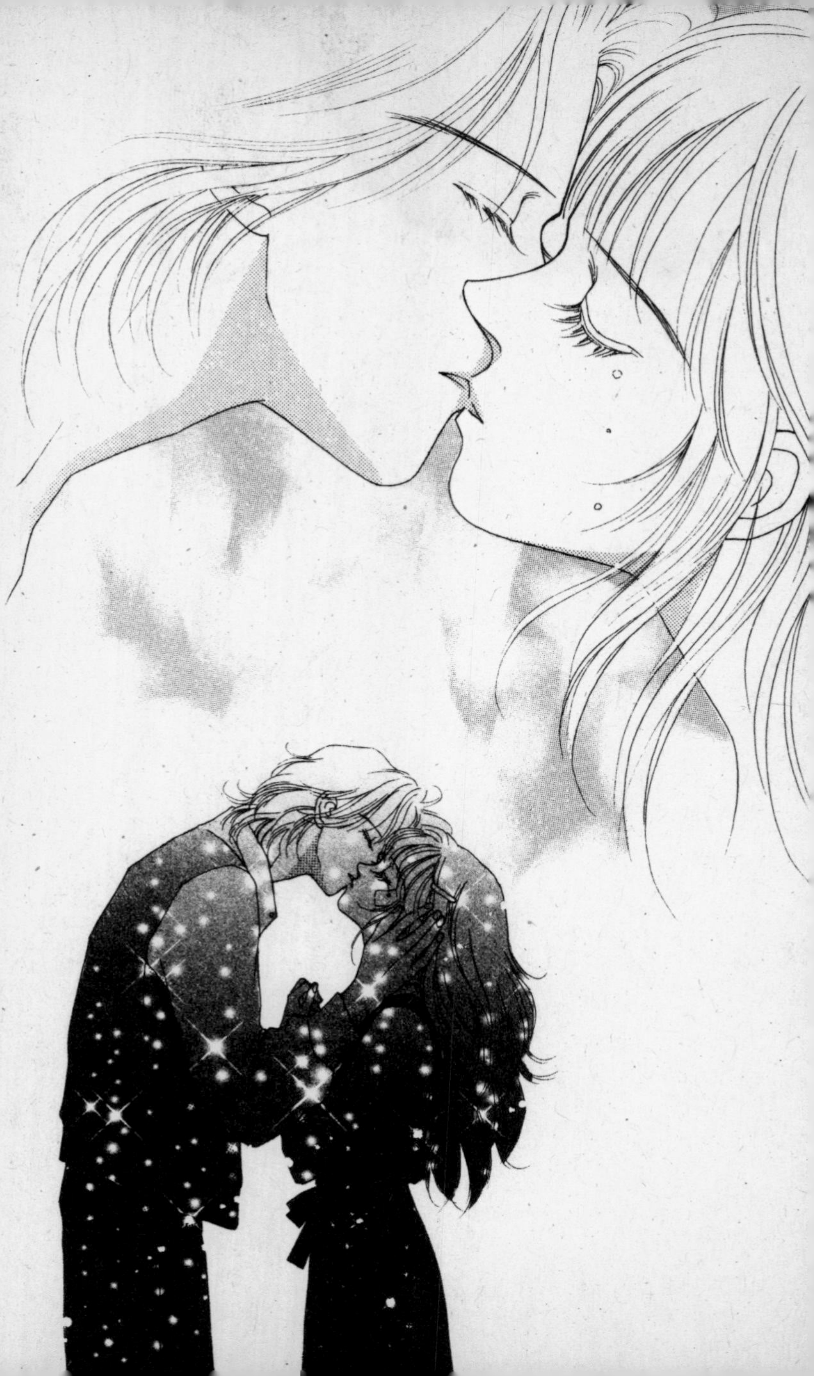

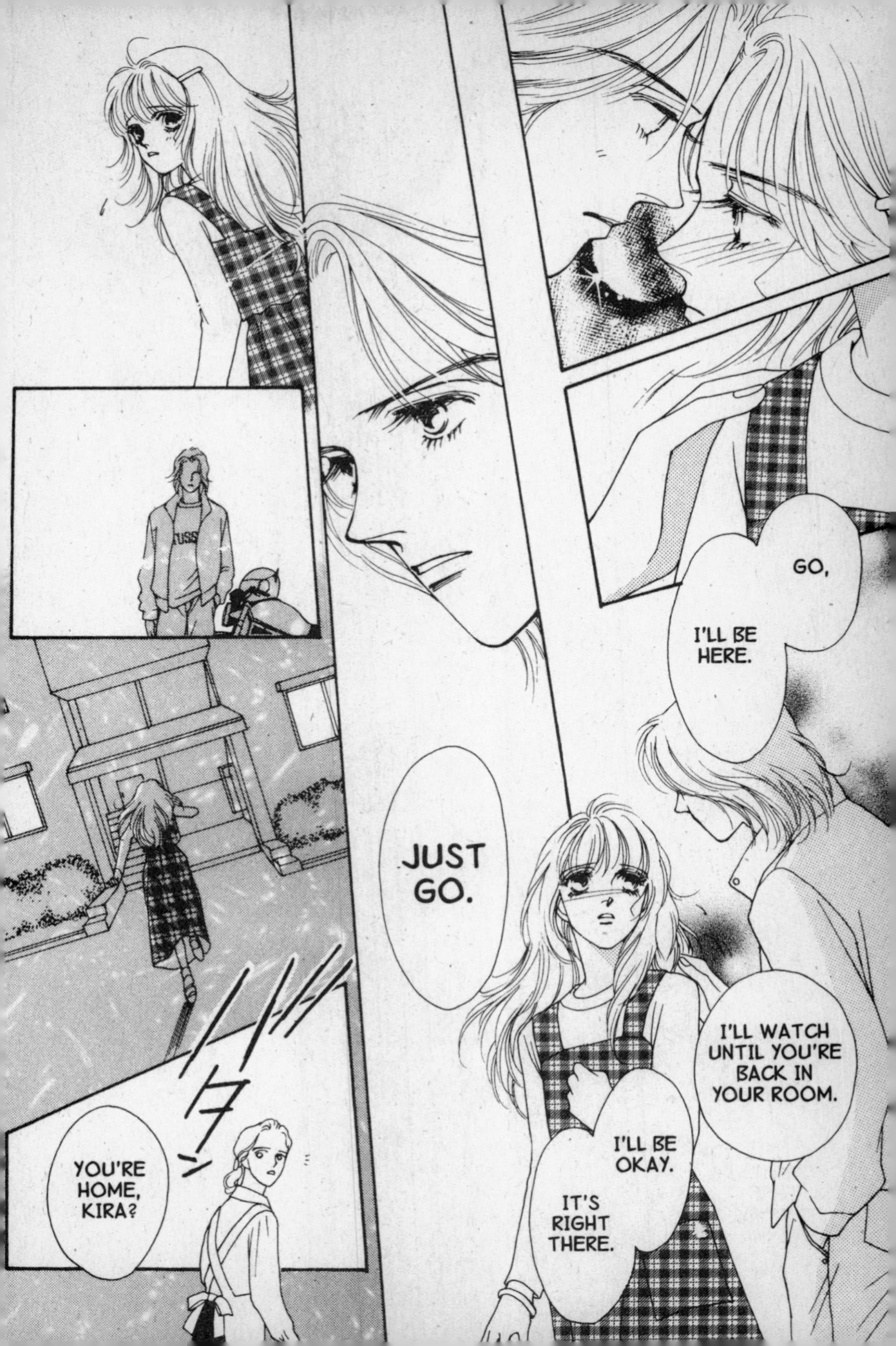
GO,
I'LL BE HERE.
I'LL WATCH UNTIL YOU'RE BACK IN YOUR ROOM.
I'LL BE OKAY.
IT'S RIGHT THERE.
JUST GO.
YOU'RE HOME, KIRA?

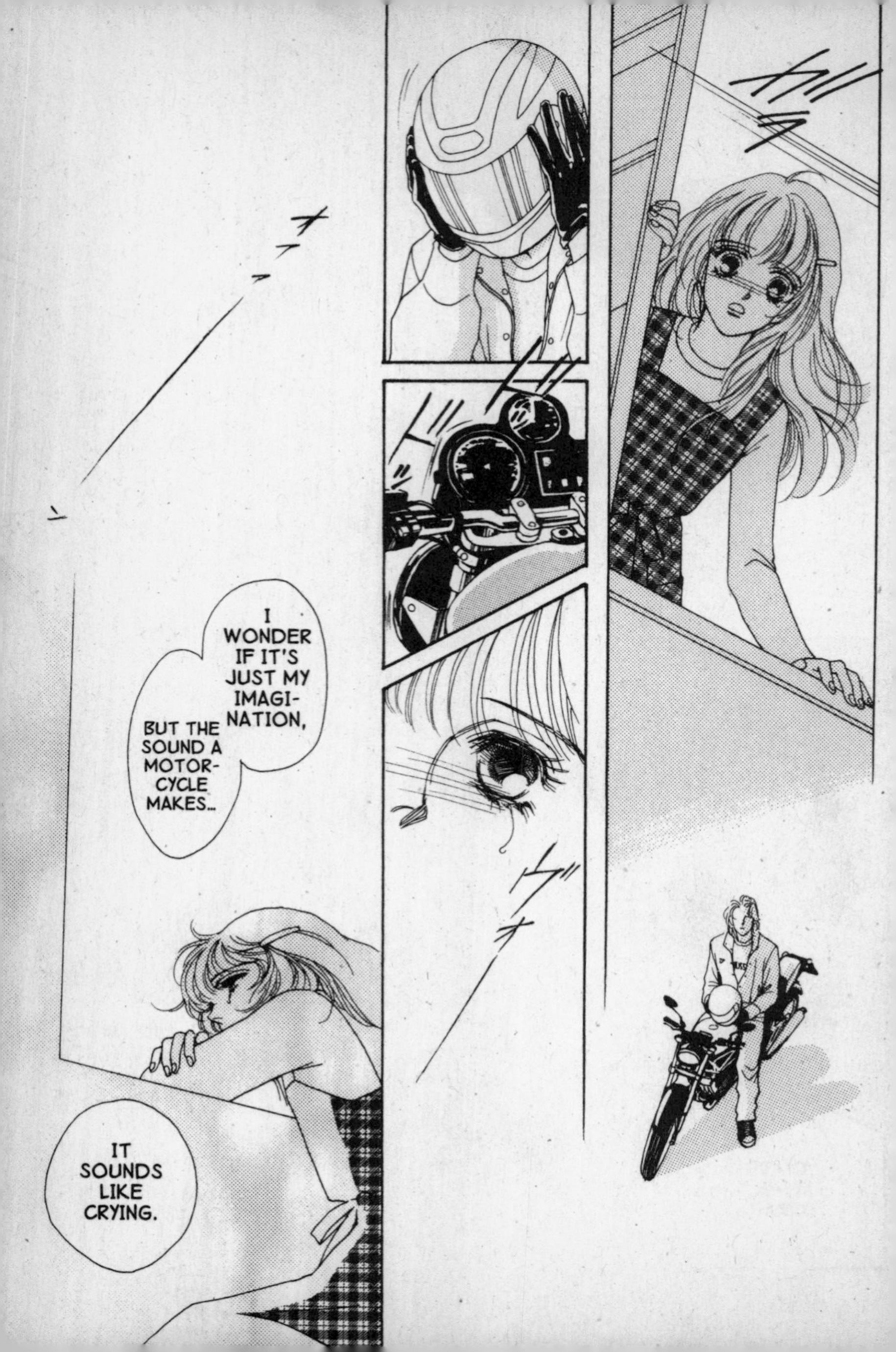

I WONDER IF IT'S JUST MY IMAGINATION,
BUT THE SOUND A MOTORCYCLE MAKES...
IT SOUNDS LIKE CRYING.

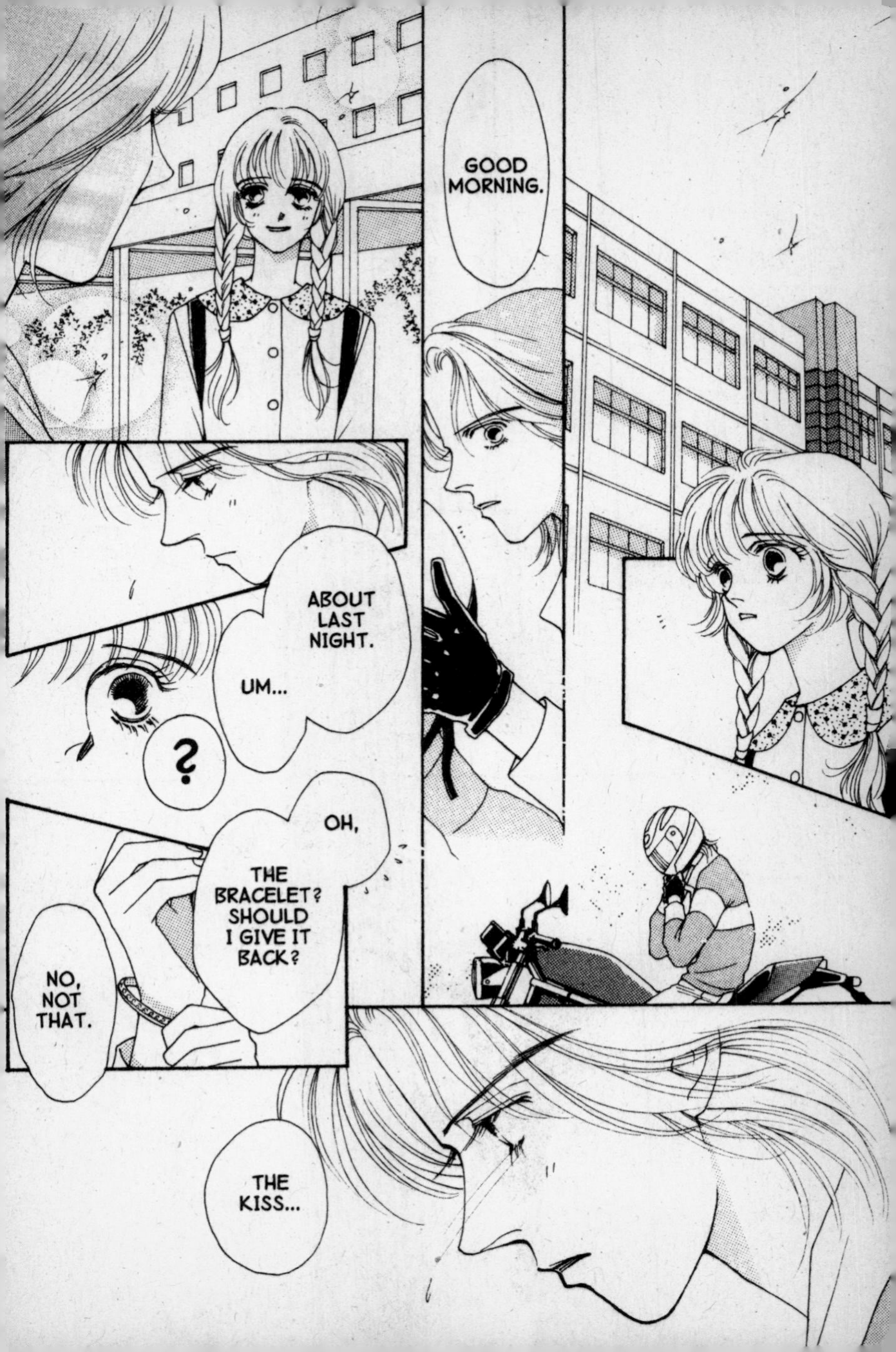
GOOD MORNING.
ABOUT LAST NIGHT.
UM...
?
OH,
THE BRACELET? SHOULD I GIVE IT BACK?
NO, NOT THAT.
THE KISS...

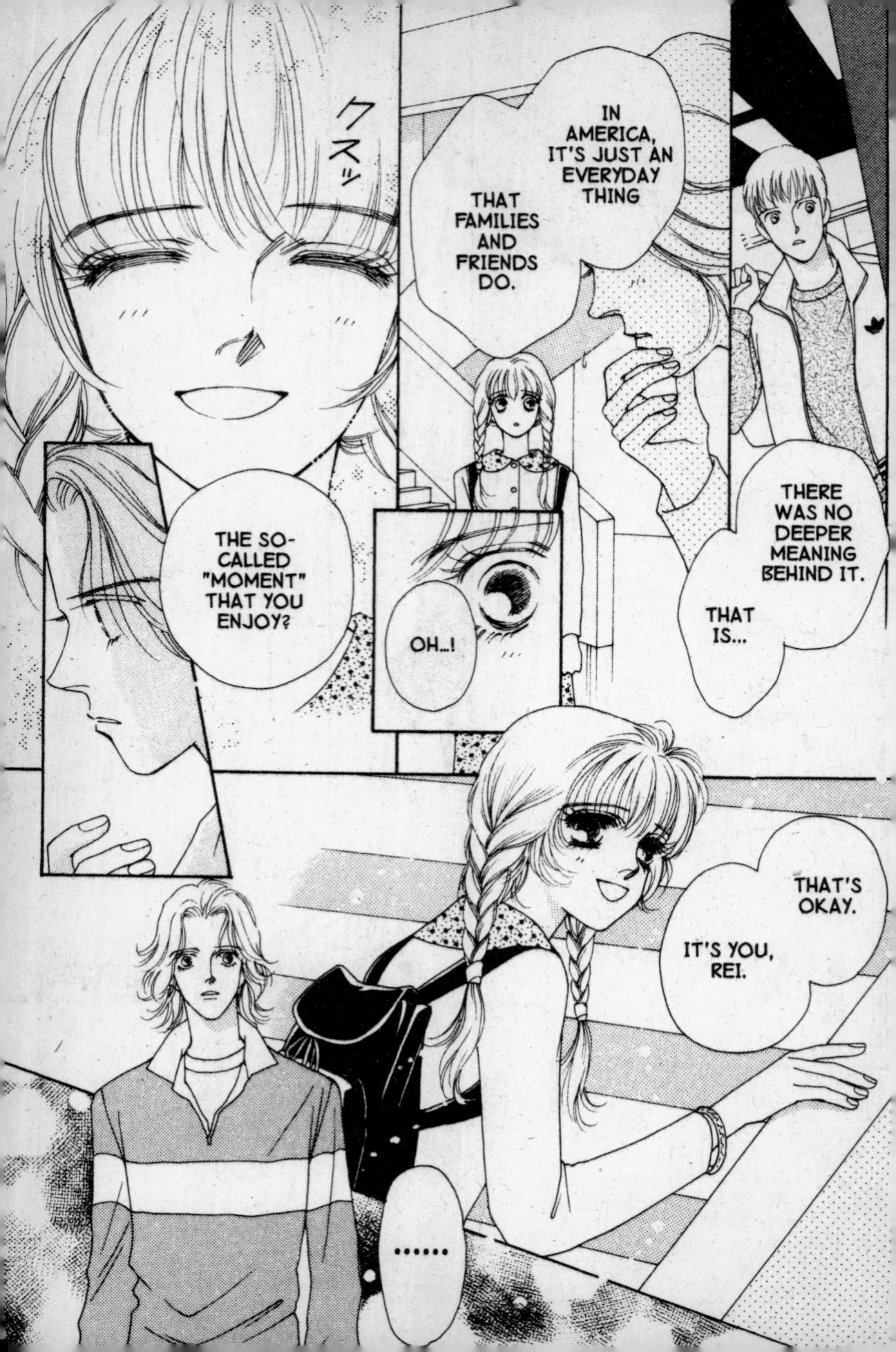
IN AMERICA, IT'S JUST AN EVERYDAY THING
THAT FAMILIES AND FRIENDS DO.
THERE WAS NO DEEPER MEANING BEHIND IT.
THAT IS...
OH...!
クスッ
THE SO-CALLED "MOMENT" THAT YOU ENJOY?
THAT'S OKAY.
IT'S YOU, REI.
......

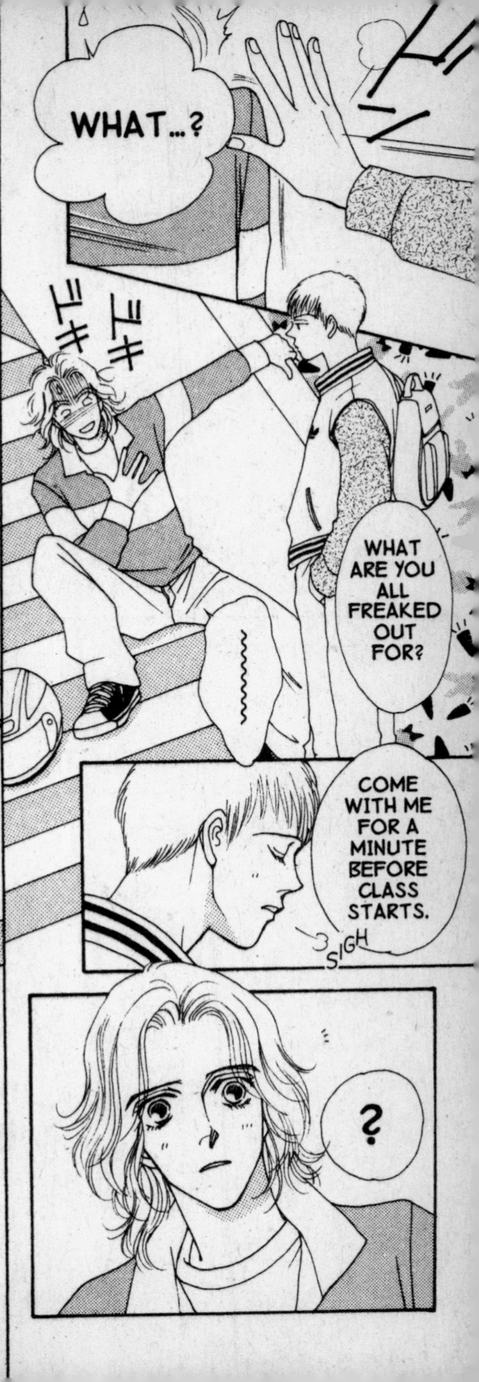
WHAT...?
ドキ ドキ
WHAT ARE YOU ALL FREAKED OUT FOR?
COME WITH ME FOR A MINUTE BEFORE CLASS STARTS.
SIGH
?
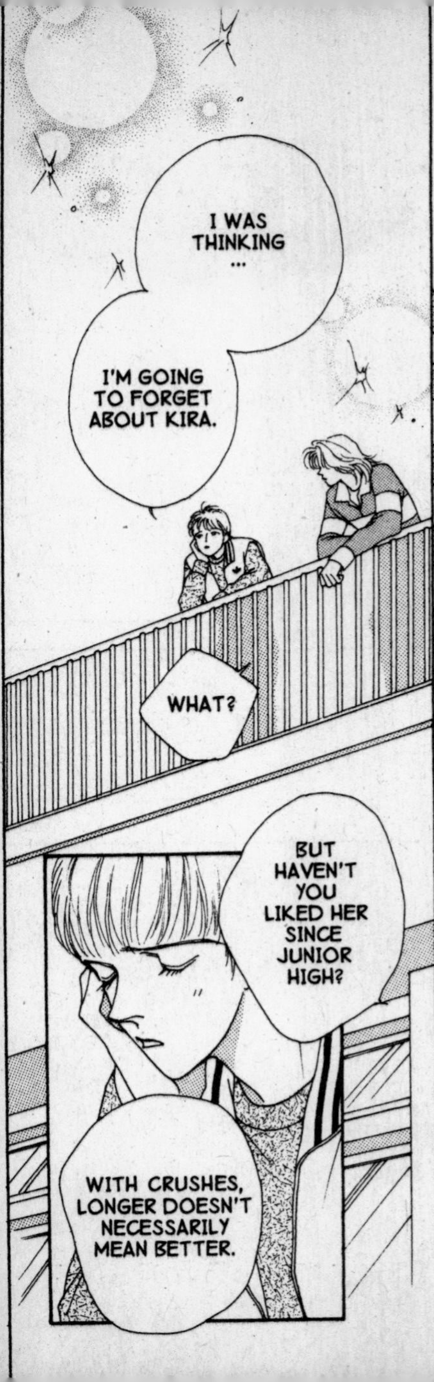
I WAS THINKING ...
I'M GOING TO FORGET ABOUT KIRA.
WHAT?
BUT HAVEN'T YOU LIKED HER SINCE JUNIOR HIGH?
WITH CRUSHES, LONGER DOESN'T NECESSARILY MEAN BETTER.

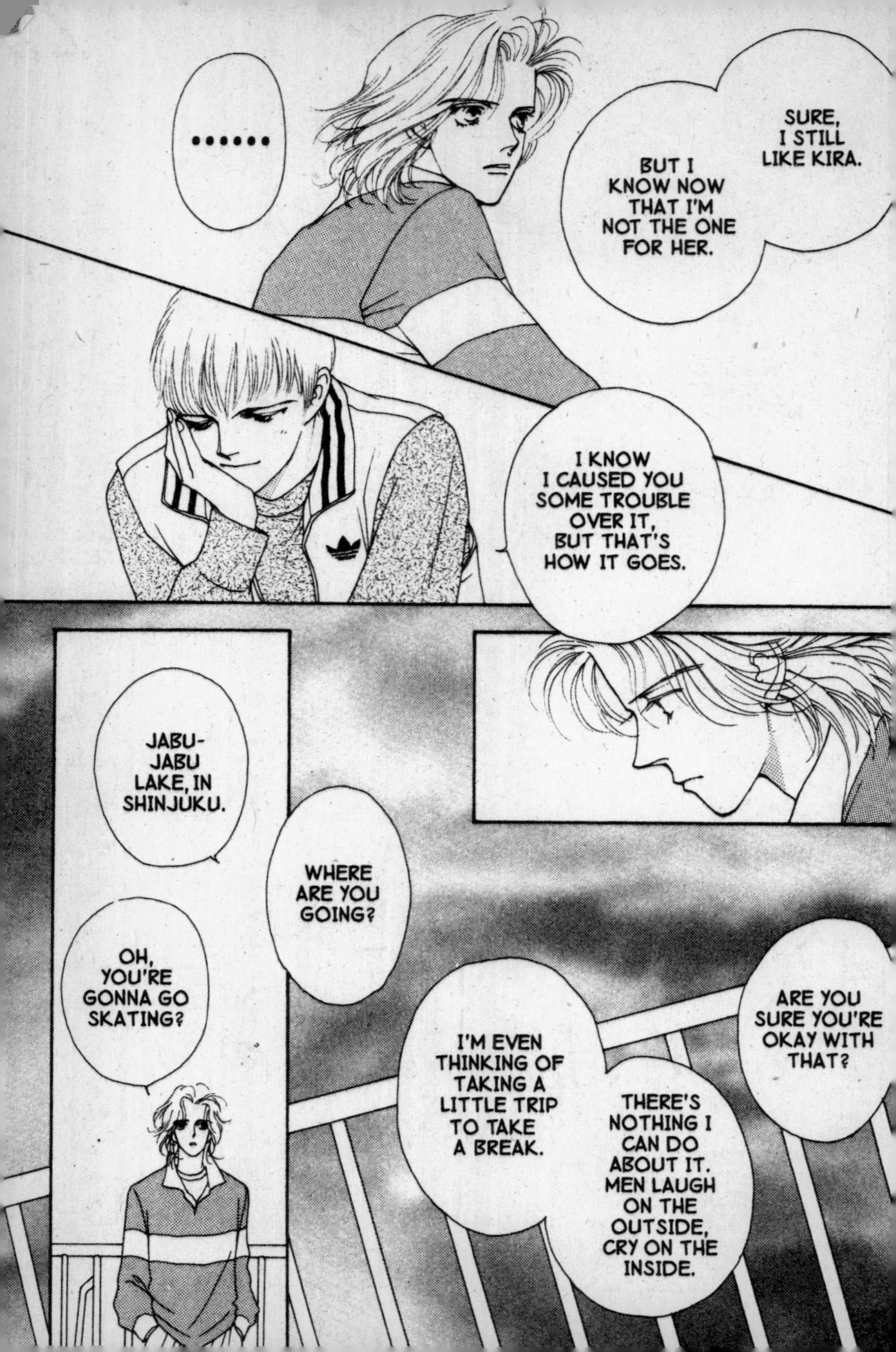
SURE, I STILL LIKE KIRA.
BUT I KNOW NOW THAT I'M NOT THE ONE FOR HER.
......
I KNOW I CAUSED YOU SOME TROUBLE OVER IT, BUT THAT'S HOW IT GOES.
ARE YOU SURE YOU'RE OKAY WITH THAT?
THERE'S NOTHING I CAN DO ABOUT IT. MEN LAUGH ON THE OUTSIDE, CRY ON THE INSIDE.
I'M EVEN THINKING OF TAKING A LITTLE TRIP TO TAKE A BREAK.
WHERE ARE YOU GOING?
JABU-JABU LAKE, IN SHINJUKU.
OH, YOU'RE GONNA GO SKATING?

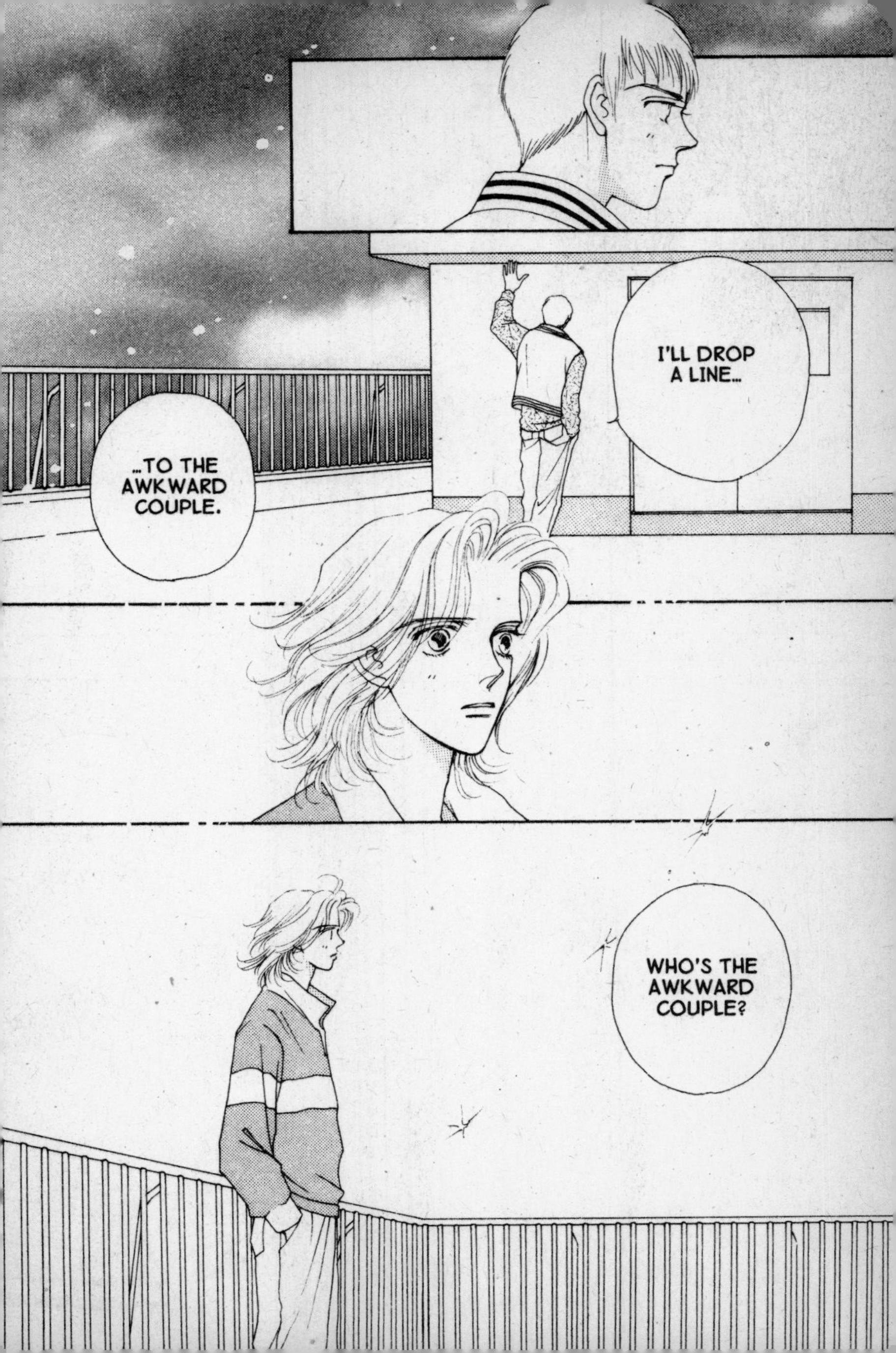
I'LL DROP A LINE...
...TO THE AWKWARD COUPLE.
WHO'S THE AWKWARD COUPLE?

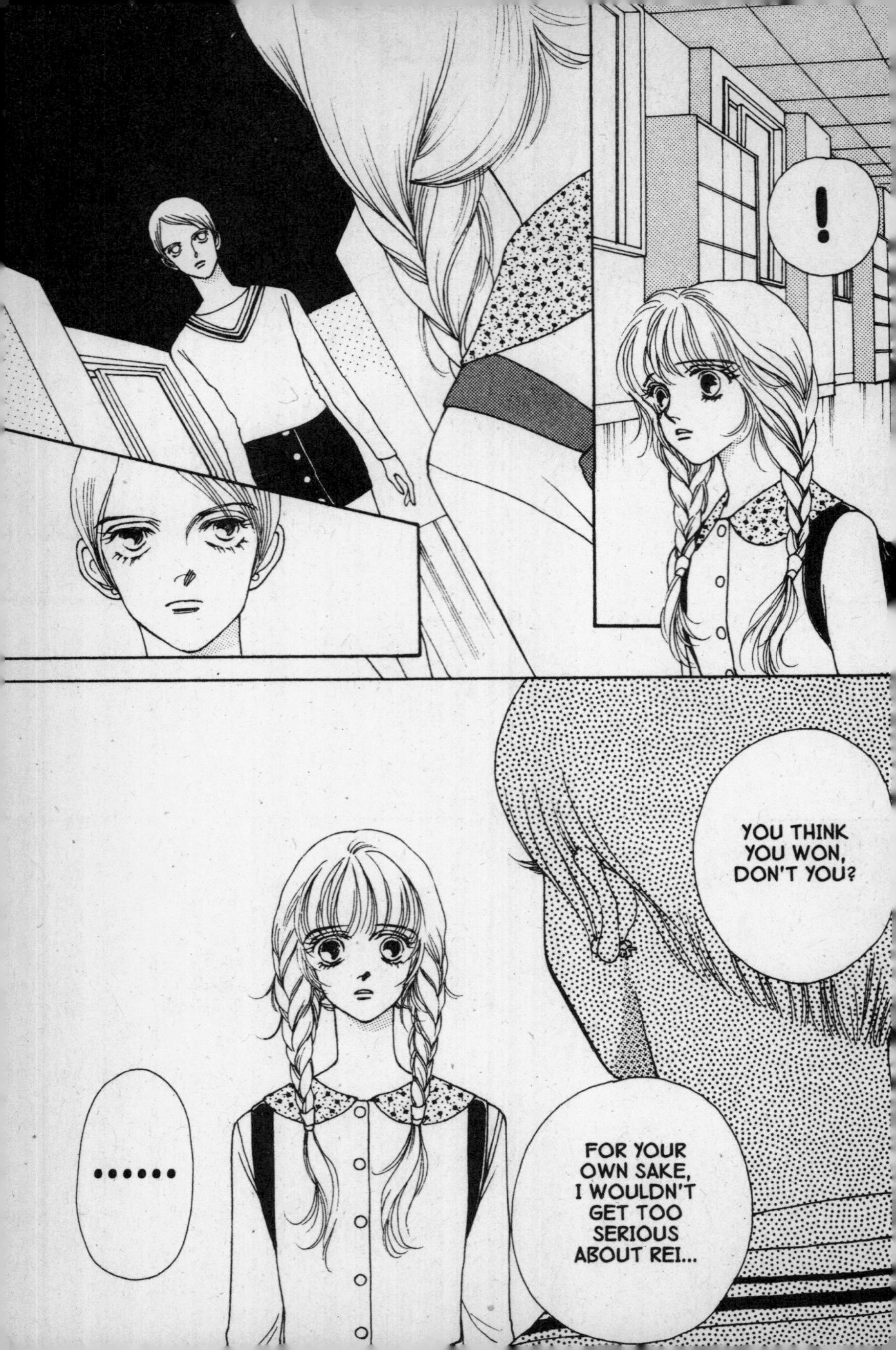
!
YOU THINK YOU WON, DON'T YOU?
FOR YOUR OWN SAKE, I WOULDN'T GET TOO SERIOUS ABOUT REI...
......

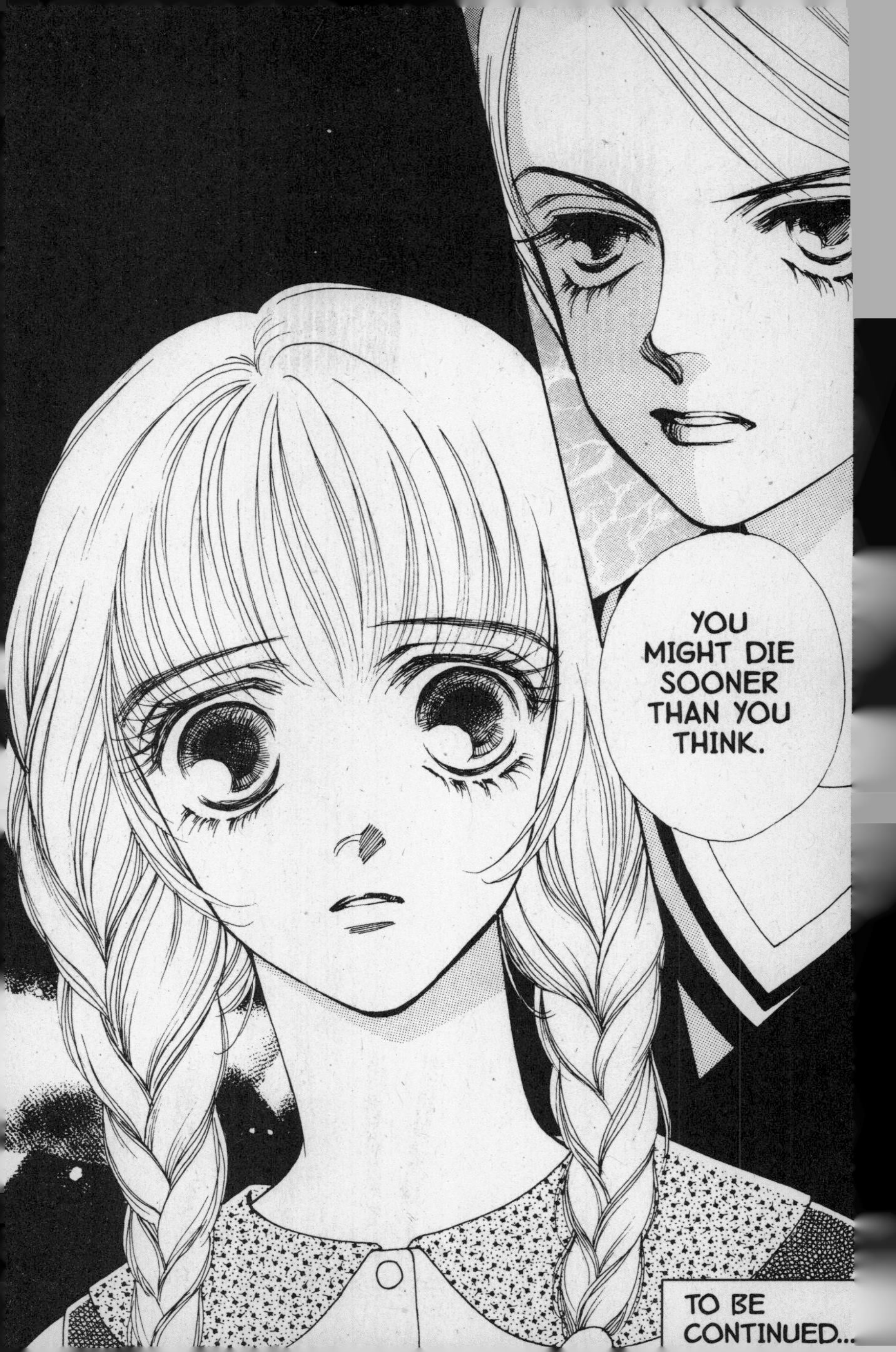
YOU MIGHT DIE SOONER THAN YOU THINK.
TO BE CONTINUED...

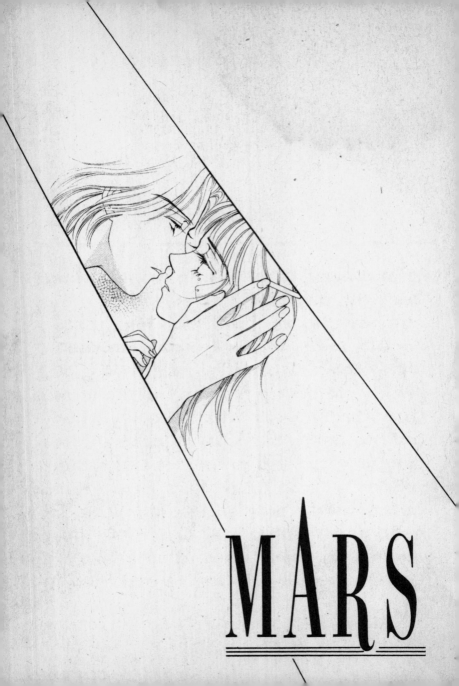

MARS

Available Now...

Volume Two

Rei promised Kira that he would protect her from anything and everything, but he never knew how soon his chance would come. When a conniving class-mate steals Kira's original painting, Rei quickly stands up for her, but his efforts are hardly rewarded. He gets kicked out of school, and now it looks like he might become a permanent dropout. Suddenly, "good girl" Kira finds herself in the middle of a bad situation. She'll need more than a little luck if she ever wants to rescue Rei and salvage her hopes for a future romance.

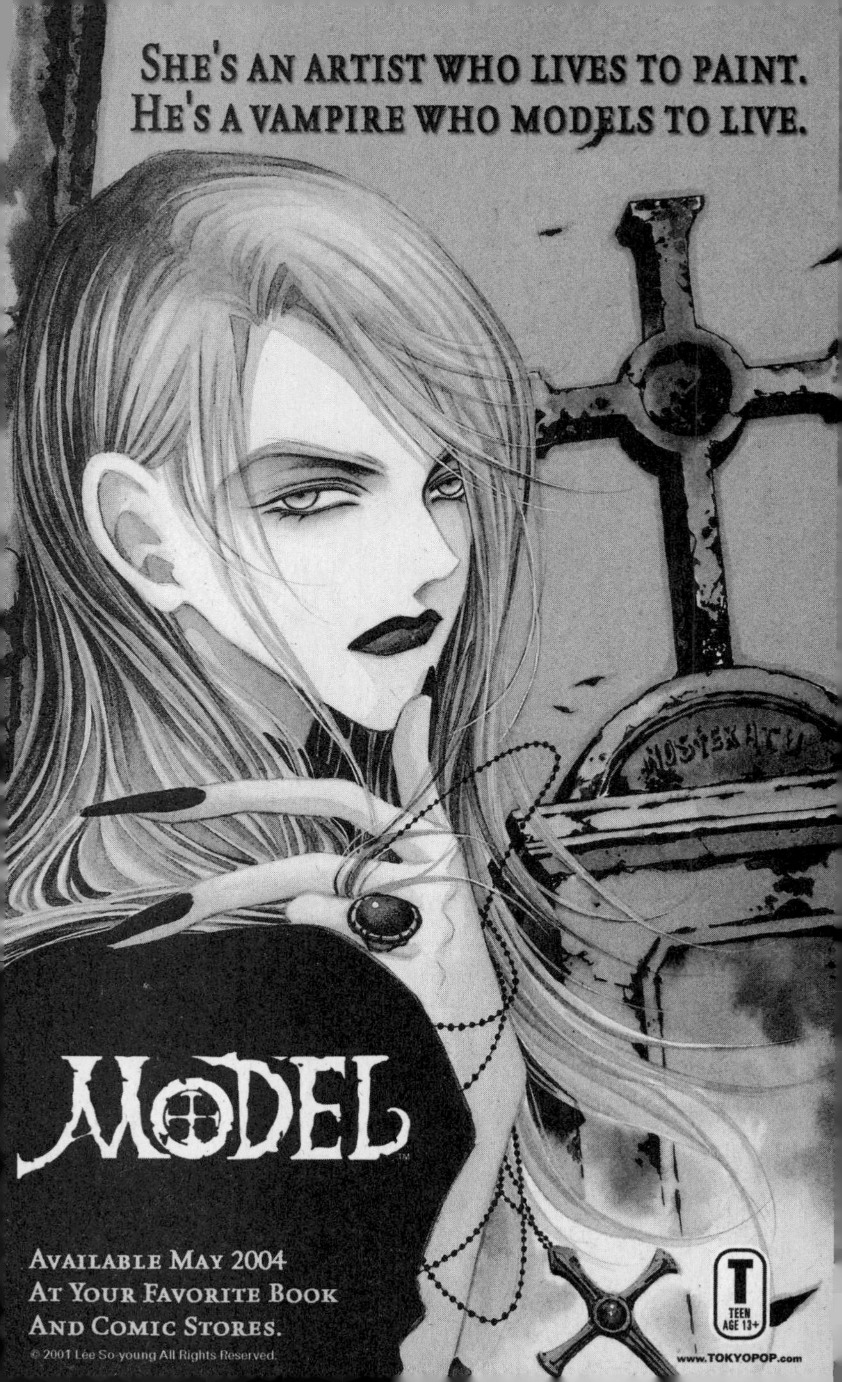
SHE'S AN ARTIST WHO LIVES TO PAINT.
HE'S A VAMPIRE WHO MODELS TO LIVE.
MODEL™
AVAILABLE MAY 2004
AT YOUR FAVORITE BOOK
AND COMIC STORES.
© 2001 Lee So-young All Rights Reserved.
T
TEEN
AGE 13+
www.TOKYOPOP.com

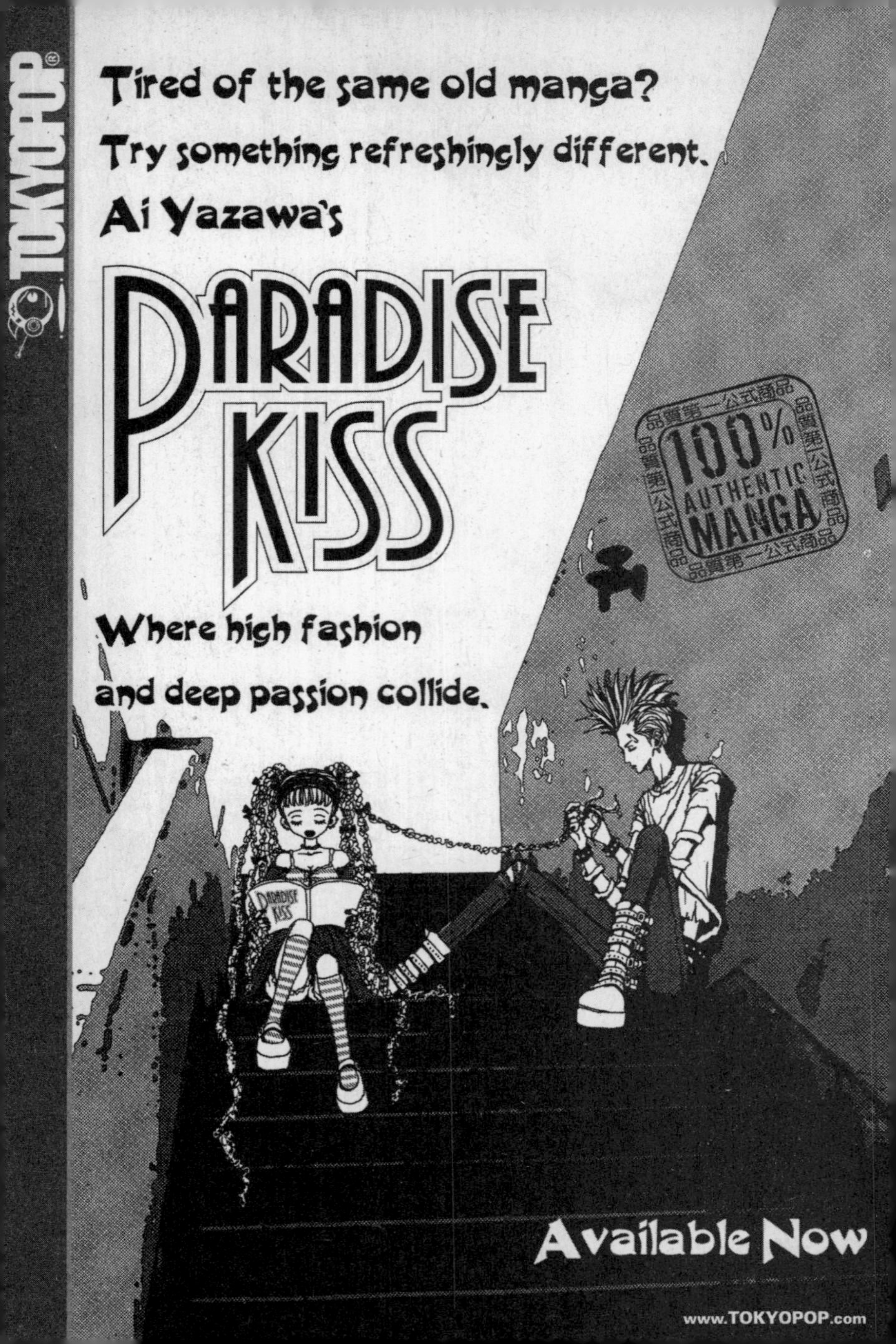
TOKYOPOP®
Tired of the same old manga?
Try something refreshingly different.
Ai Yazawa's
PARADISE KISS
100% AUTHENTIC MANGA
品質第一公式商品
Where high fashion
and deep passion collide.
PARADISE KISS
Available Now
www.TOKYOPOP.com